ILLIBERAL AMERICA

ALSO BY STEVEN HAHN

Forging America: A Continental History of the United States

*A Nation Without Borders: The United States and
Its World in an Age of Civil Wars, 1830–1910*

The Political Worlds of Slavery and Freedom
(Nathan Huggins Lectures, Harvard University)

*Freedom: A Documentary History of Emancipation,
1861–1867: Series 3, Volume 1: Land and Labor, 1865*
(with Steven F. Miller, Susan E. O'Donovan, John
C. Rodrigue, and Leslie S. Rowland)

*A Nation under Our Feet: Black Political Struggles in the
Rural South from Slavery to the Great Migration*

*The Countryside in the Age of Capitalist Transformation: Essays
in the Social History of Rural America* (with Jonathan Prude)

*The Roots of Southern Populism: Yeoman Farmers and the
Transformation of the Georgia Upcountry, 1850–1890*

ILLIBERAL AMERICA

A History

STEVEN HAHN

W. W. NORTON & COMPANY
Independent Publishers Since 1923

For information about permission to reproduce selections from this
book, write to Permissions, W. W. Norton & Company, Inc.,
500 Fifth Avenue, New York, NY 10110

For information about special discounts for bulk purchases, please
contact W. W. Norton Special Sales at specialsales@wwnorton.com or
800-233-4830

Manufacturing by Lakeside Book Company
Book design by Lovedog Studio
Production manager: Julia Druskin

ISBN 978-0-393-63592-8

W. W. Norton & Company, Inc., 500 Fifth Avenue, New York, N.Y. 10110
www.wwnorton.com

W. W. Norton & Company Ltd., 15 Carlisle Street, London W1D 3BS

1 2 3 4 5 6 7 8 9 0

FOR SAOIRSE, DECLAN, AND SUSAN

and

TO THE MEMORY OF IRA BERLIN

CONTENTS

Introduction

1

CHAPTER ONE

THE INVENTION OF THE LIBERAL TRADITION

11

CHAPTER TWO

FEUDAL DREAMS AND COERCIVE POWERS

38

CHAPTER THREE

THE POPE, THE KING, AND THE REPUBLIC

67

CHAPTER FOUR

TOCQUEVILLE, LINCOLN, AND THE

EXPULSIVE 1830s

105

CHAPTER FIVE

THE MEASURES OF BONDAGE

141

CHAPTER SIX

MODERNIZING ILLIBERALISM

174

CHAPTER SEVEN
FASCIST PULSES
210

CHAPTER EIGHT
THE "OTHER" NINETEEN-SIXTIES
247

CHAPTER NINE
NEOLIBERALS AND ILLIBERALISM
282

CHAPTER TEN
SPECTERS OF RACE WAR AND REPLACEMENT
314

Conclusion
349

Acknowledgments
361

Notes
365

Index
417

ILLIBERAL AMERICA

INTRODUCTION

THE TITLE OF THIS BOOK MAY STRIKE MANY READERS as an odd composite if not a contradiction in terms. America has long been associated with liberalism in a variety of senses, certainly in regard to rights and politics. This association has been the basis of American claims to political and historical exceptionalism and to a distinctive historical arc that turned a set of eighteenth-century revolutionary principles into an evolving way of life. Some celebrate the country's long and encompassing liberal dispositions, while others focus on how the promises of liberalism have come up short or been betrayed.[1] Still others regard liberalism as a jumble of ideas and impulses that can, owing to its very conceptual nature, veer just as easily toward racism, sexism, and forms of exclusion as it can toward notions of individualism, equality, and inclusion. And, of course, liberalism has always had those, from the left and the right, who have found it sorely wanting if not at the root of much that has gone wrong. Yet, at all events, critics and defenders alike generally consider liberalism and what is often termed the liberal tradition to be the centerpiece of American society, culture, politics, and history.[2]

As a measure of liberalism's near hegemonic status in the American past and present, the terms "illiberal" and "illiberalism" have rarely been recognized or uttered until quite recently. Almost invariably, these terms are presented as new and unsettling violations and departures from what are called "liberal norms" or "liberal democratic norms." Illiberal ideas, practices, rights-bearing, culture, belonging, and appeals are now associated with regimes and movements showing a number of noxious features: assigned hierarchies, elite rule, restricted popular political influence, militarism, and the marking of internal as well as external enemies. These regimes and movements happily thumb their noses at liberal pretensions and sensibilities, and ridicule liberal notions of social and political practice. They advocate ethnocentric projects of mobilization and governance, religiously inscribed boundaries of belonging, hypermasculinist relations of gender and sexuality, violent means of seizing and securing power, and repressive responses to dissent. The notion of an explicit "illiberal democracy" has already won the admiration of a great many leaders and thinkers on the political right, not least in the United States, where it has emerged as an exemplar of the way forward in a forbidding multicultural world.[3]

This book asks readers to suspend their assumptions about the long and enduring American liberal tradition and instead recognize illiberal currents that flowed across the Atlantic and took hold well before what we would call liberalism ever appeared. In turn, it asks readers to imagine liberalism as one of a number of currents that struggled to define American society, and as a current that was often entangled with illiberalisms from which it could rarely free itself. In so doing, readers will get a better and deeper sense, not of the country's recent departure from long-established and entrenched "norms," but of how our present-day reckoning with the rise of a militant and illiberal set of movements has lengthy and constantly ramifying roots.

To be sure, liberalism has its own complex history and sets of definitions. They include a vision of autonomous individuals who enter into a social/political contract for their own protection, which both Thomas Hobbes and John Locke imagined in their seventeenth-century works. They include a labor-based regime of private property ownership, which Locke explained in his *Second Treatise of Government*.[4] They include a freewheeling marketplace organized around self-interest with limited interference by the state, which classical and neo-classical liberals (and economists) devised in the late-eighteenth and nineteenth centuries. They include a centralized state that administers politics and the economy through an assortment of interest groups, presumably for the public good, which have been the hallmarks of modern liberalism from the New Deal to the Great Society.[5] And they include a minimally regulated—or deregulated—marketplace of global dimensions enabled by policies of the state itself, which neoliberalism has come to represent.[6]

Scholars and political theorists have long argued about liberalism's historical origins, defining features, social flexibility, and rights-bearing capacity. Is liberalism a product of the seventeenth-century Atlantic, the French Revolution, or the development of capitalism? To what extent does the statist or corporate liberalism of the twentieth century resemble the classical liberalism of the nineteenth? How should we understand the political principles and practices of liberalism in relation to the economic? And how widely can liberalism's net be cast in a world of recognized difference organized around class, race, ethnicity, and gender?

The concepts of illiberal and illiberalism are of relatively recent vintage. Ever since at least the French Revolution, liberalism has been set chiefly against conservatism, and, in its twentieth-century political guise, against totalitarianism and authoritarianism of both the right and left. Illiberalism, for its part, has emerged as part of a backlash against modern liberalism, especially against what is perceived as its global and multicultural dimensions. And it has come to embody a collection of ideas that favors fixed hierarchies (notably of gender, race, and nationality) and cultural homogeneity, and that can accept majoritarian methods of wielding power. Illiberalism celebrates the nation and its designated people, Christianity and Western "civilization," the "community" and its defenders, and tightly patrolled territorial boundaries. It stands opposed to cosmopolitan elites and their followers, to a globalized economic system, to supranational political institutions (the U.N, the World Court, the E.U.), to human instead of nation- or community-based rights, and to disrupters of heterosexuality.[7]

Yet, if illiberalism has emerged to describe social relations and political culture in the contemporary world, what sort of window of meaning can it open onto worlds very far from our own in time, even well before liberalism entered the political vocabulary or revealed itself in the ways societies were conceived and organized? Can there even be illiberalism before liberalism or what passes for it? My hope is to demonstrate that as broad concepts, illiberal and illiberalism can encompass a wide range of political and cultural currents of the Euro-Atlantic world from the late sixteenth century on, and, especially, help us explore how those currents flowed on the ground of experience, not as defects of liberalism or as alternatives to it, but rather as coherent ideas and practices regarding social relations, political authority, cultural hierarchies, religious faith, and family formation. Initially tethered to feudal and early modern projects and sensibilities, they would, in changing forms over time, have significant influence on the building of this country: prescribing legitimate types of power, envisioning local and national destinies, confronting the challenges of modernity, and navigating worlds of increasing complexity. In these ways, illiberalism can constitute a formidable framework of historical understanding, and is to be found not at the margins of evolving American society, not as dark threads that occasionally surface, not as paranoic and backward-looking responses to disruptive change, but as central fields of political and cultural force.[8]

One of the dangers in writing a history of "illiberal America" is laying out a story that appears to overemphasize continuities at the expense of changes. And, to be sure, there are features of illiberalism that tend to show up again and again. These features include the overriding will of the community, the suspicion of outsiders and quick resort to expulsion, the recognition of rights and standing chiefly in local or limited arenas, the abiding desire for cultural homogeneity often enforced coercively, the resistance to some forms of authority (often of the state) together with easy submission to those of place and faith, and the embrace of hierarchies of status and power.

But these apparently enduring features gain meaning in the specific historical contexts in which they may play out. At times they can form the basis of "organic" notions of social order in which elite rule and personal domination prevail and are expressed as mutual dependencies, as under systems of enslavement, servitude, or patriarchalism. At times they can form the basis of demands for self-governance organized through quasi-democratic methods, as in nationalist or separatist movements. At times they can form the basis of opposition to the state, as in right-wing populism, and at times they can be packaged as new initiatives of the state itself, as in types of corporatism. At times they are attached to religious fundamentalisms, as in Christian nationalism, and at times they can be utterly irreligious. At times they can fortify social and political repression, as in paramilitarism, and at times they can be adopted by humble folk as means of protection, as in submission to patrons or other figures of traditional authority. Illiberalism should be understood as ever-developing constellations of ideas, relations, and practices that become more complex as it defines itself against or becomes intricately entangled with liberalism.

For the purposes of this book, I recognize both liberalism and illiberalism mainly in political terms: that is to say, in view of their claims about rights, political practice, law, and power. In its most robust portrayals, liberalism imagines a political order based on rights-bearing individuals, wide-ranging civic inclusiveness, highly representative institutions of governance, the rule of law and equal standing before it, the use of democratic (mainly electoral) methods of representation, and the mediation of power by an assortment of civil and political devices (courts, regulations, organizations, and associations). Liberal societies and regimes often deviate from some of these standards but are constructed on the basis of them as a whole. Liberal regimes can be constitutional monarchies if power resides principally on the parliamentary side. They can involve some types of restriction on political participation within a setting of generalized inclusion. And they can include arenas of more directly administered power—sometimes called "states" or "spaces of exception"—especially when it comes to judicial punishment or acute crisis.[9]

Illiberal societies and regimes can be of many types, though they usually share a number of important characteristics. In them, rights-bearing may be defined or limited by specific rulers or be based on communities of race, ethnicity, religion, and gender. Civil and political standing tend to be marked by social and cultural exclusions. Governance can range from democratic to dictatorial and authoritarian, and can involve popular mobilizations or widespread political repression, sometimes a mix of both. Power is often direct, at times personal, at times corporate or collective, commonly displayed and ritualized very publicly; the mediations of the judicial or regulatory variety are less substantial and generally affect only prescribed communities of belonging. Otherwise, power directly links individuals or groups to their rulers (or those who claim to be their rulers) and can literally be inscribed on their bodies. Illiberals and illiberalism acknowledge and encourage the wielding of power in its most naked and aggressive forms, and recognize violence as a legitimate and potentially necessary means of seizing it. At the same time, illiberal societies and regimes show their own deviations and evolutions over time, both shaping and adapting to their particular contexts.

This book is not meant to be an exhaustive history of illiberal America. It is rather episodic, organized not around obscure or generally overlooked sets of events but, instead, around those moments in the past when liberalism and aspects of the liberal tradition are customarily thought to be integral to what was unfolding. In doing this, I hope to complicate and problematize American liberalism, and demonstrate both the ways in which illiberalism represented the dominant impulses or hedged in and compromised liberal objectives and projects. I begin by reminding readers that the "liberal tradition" was a relatively recent creation or invention; that American historical writing and interpretation paid it little attention until the advent of the Cold War. The liberal tradition then managed to endure in the popular consciousness despite a raft of often devastating objections and critiques, for reasons that are important to identify, especially given the current moment. From there, I move back into the seventeenth century and to the designs and process of settler colonialism on the North American continent, the visions of colonizers and colonists, and the types of societies they commenced to establish, calling into question whether liberalism or liberal capitalism was, in any important regard, an early arrival. I then move ahead to the second half of the eighteenth century and to the illiberal currents that swirled through the American Revolution and Constitution-making, informed the perspectives of a great many settler colonists, and left important imprints on Anti-Federalism. Here I place special emphasis on the wide embrace of anti-Catholicism (which remained central to American political culture), the continued appeal of monarchy and hierarchical political authority, and the significance of culturally bounded communities.

The 1830s, the era of Jacksonian democracy and Tocqueville's *Democracy in America*, next come into view, although I focus on the rampant expulsions directed against Native peoples, African Americans, Catholics, Mormons, and political dissidents (especially abolitionists). Expulsion was a phenomenon so widespread and politically corrosive that it worried a young Abraham Lincoln and suggests that the democracy being born was, in its main features, an illiberal and expulsive one. The Civil War and slave emancipation follow, when the "exception clause" of the Thirteenth Amendment opens a lens onto the illiberal threads that wrapped themselves around the liberal impulses of abolitionists and antislavery allies, both while slavery remained legal as well as after it was abolished.

The second half of *Illiberal America* shifts to the twentieth century and the beginnings of the twenty-first. I consider what is commonly called the Progressive era (1900–1920) as a time when illiberalism was being modernized, particularly through the enormous attraction of social engineering—an attraction evident across the Progressive spectrum—and when a top-down view of governance that, together with aggressive racism at home and abroad, in some ways anticipated European fascism. It was followed by reactionary, fascistic, grassroots mobilizations during the 1920s—the Progressive era and the 1920s I see as more interconnected than is customarily acknowledged—that involved expulsive nativism and racism, antiradicalism, and Christian fundamentalism, all of which left their marks on the 1930s and the decades that followed.

Moving further ahead chronologically, I take another look at the 1960s and examine the rebirth of radical right politics in struggles over racial integration, feminism, and anti-communism. These were powerfully captured by the presidential campaigns of George C. Wallace, who honed a rhetoric of grievance and racial hostility that would be enduring. It was a politics and set of ideas that heralded the weakening of modern New Deal and Great Society liberalism at a time when both appeared to have cleared the field of conservative and rightist opponents. I follow with an exploration of the illiberal politics that often accompanied the rise of neoliberal regimes in the United States and abroad, especially in view of the highly punitive, and deeply racist, policies developed to wage the wars on drugs, crime, and welfare, and of the highly exploitive and personal rights–denying character of hi-tech and the internet. *Illiberal America* concludes with a discussion of how "specters" of race war and "replacement" gave rise to the white nationalist and paramilitary right, and soon became mainstream owing to the country's impending demographic transformation, the long-term deindustrialization of Euro-Atlantic economies, and the willingness of the Republican Party to become the institutional vehicle for the radical right's road to empowerment.

In all of this, I offer not an intellectual history so much as a social history of ideas. That is to say, a perspective on how illiberal practices and dispositions took shape at the grassroots, and then influenced how their liberal counterparts would be interpreted and assimilated, how illiberalism would be passed down and then transformed in new social and historical settings.

My intention in this book is not to paint a dark and damning picture of the United States past and present, or to create a scorecard for evaluating the relative strengths of liberalism and illiberalism, or to suggest that liberal principles and achievements are of little importance, perhaps overwhelmed by illiberal pulses and power. Without doubt the principles of universal rights inscribed in the Declaration of Independence, the commitment to republicanism in the Constitution, the crusades against slavery and servitude, the popular struggles over many decades to expand civil and political rights, and the movements to attack poverty and racism stand as important components of the American political tradition, infused as they were with varieties of republicanism, producerism, feminism, and social democracy as well as liberalism. Indeed, they remind us of the range and depth of ideas and visions that contested for power over the course of American history, and that liberalism and illiberalism, even broadly considered, represent only some of them, however significant they may be.

My intention is rather to demonstrate the shaky foundations on which those principles often rested, the enormous obstacles those movements had to overcome, and the ability of some social groups to use those principles to define their own communities while refusing it to others, what one might call political and rights-bearing particularisms. These particularisms have become embedded in many different community contexts, some so deeply that they are difficult to recognize, and have provided members with satisfactions and sources of mutuality that can be very appealing—and hard to reject—until they summon illiberal defenses and mobilizations.

Throughout this book, then, I associate illiberalism with the political right at different points in time. Although I do not mean to equate illiberalism with conservatism, illiberalism has long overlapped and been fortified by traditional or reactionary conservatism, certainly from the late eighteenth century on, as well as with what might be described as anti-liberalism, conscious attacks on and rejections of liberal society and its claims. Of course, it is fair to say that illiberalism is not simply the possession of the right, that the left can also embrace or reflect its forms of rights, rules, and hierarchies. This would especially be the case with leftist, mostly communist, regimes that may have come to power as movements of workers, peasants, and the poor but then lurched toward authoritarianism and restrictive notions of rights connected with party membership and political loyalty. It can also be the case during moments of reckoning when intense battles for inclusion—generally ones of a situational nature—provoke objections to language and views thought to be harmful and exclusionary in themselves, such as can be glimpsed in classrooms and workplaces.[10]

But in the United States, movements of the left, even those organized around the rights and empowerment of specific ethnic or racial groups, have rarely if ever argued for limiting the rights of other groups or individuals. Social justice movements are sometimes accused of reverse racism and bowing to illiberal methods to achieve their ends, of suggesting that their lives and those of their followers matter more than the lives of others, that the attainment of justice for them should come at the expense of those who are either not with them or are against them. In truth, these movements rarely, if ever, make such claims or demands. Rather, in speeches and writings, in demonstrations and electoral mobilizations, they fundamentally insist we acknowledge that over the course of our history the subordinated groups they represent have been treated as if their lives don't matter, as if they are of little value, as if they are readily expendable, as if our conceptions of rights and expectations of justice do not apply to them. And so, their goals have been inclusion because they are refused it, and empowerment because they are deprived of it.

Illiberalism is indeed a political and cultural disposition and ideology of the right, and it has often placed limits on the objectives of those with liberal views and programs. Time and again men and women regarded as liberals, or happily brandishing liberal credentials, make quick resort, when faced with challenges to their ideas of how the world should work, to illiberal solutions simply to maintain order and right their political ships. Their ideals about social and political life often obscure a deeper embrace of cultural hierarchies, and their difficulties in recognizing how power organizes class and politics often obscure how readily they can reach for it when their efforts are disturbed. A history of illiberalism must not only treat the episodes that reveal illiberalism's characteristics and goals from start to finish. It must also treat the episodes when liberal intentions advanced by liberally oriented historical actors end up moving in—sometimes unanticipated—illiberal directions and why. Because a history of illiberal America also shows that the most consistent advocates of universal rights, expansive democracy, and the empowerment of people regardless of their economic, social, or cultural status are—from the colonial settlement of the continent to the founding of the republic to the current day—those who have been denied them.

Chapter One

THE INVENTION
OF THE LIBERAL
TRADITION

T HE ALARMS HAVE BEEN SOUNDING FOR MORE THAN
twenty years, but they have increased dramatically in number and volume during the past decade. "Liberal democracies" and
modes of governance, observers—journalists and social scientists
chief among them—warn, are under attack or have been sidestepped
by political movements and new regimes that express disdain for
democratic ideals, scorn for constitutional limits to their power, and
a proclivity for racist and ethnocentric forms of nationalism. In the
late 1990s, Fareed Zakaria, in a widely cited essay, spoke less of the
threat of authoritarianism than of the rise of what he called "illiberal
democracies": regimes that, while subject to election, rebuff legislative
or judicial oversight and deprive citizens of basic rights and freedoms.
And while his points of reference at the time ranged principally from
Latin America to the Balkans and then to South Asia, he used the
language of contagion, describing illiberal democracy as a "spreading
virus." By 2016, shortly after Donald Trump won the United States
presidency, Zakaria could worry "that we might be watching the rise
of illiberal democracy in the United States." The four years of the
Trump presidency and his violent struggle to stay in power have only
made Zakaria's worries more acute.[1]

Zakaria was hardly alone. The defeats of Arab spring, the rise of
"populist" movements across Western Europe, the hostility to political establishments where liberal democratic governance seemed
stable, and the surprising victories of Brexit in Great Britain, Jair Bolsonaro in Brazil, and, more recently, the Brothers of Italy and the

Sweden Democrats, not only raised mounting concerns but suggested that the "virus" had in fact been spreading, and to areas of the Euro-Atlantic where it previously would have been "unthinkable." For most of the twentieth century, and especially in the second half, conservatives and centrists feared political "contagion" from the left, from socialist and communist movements and parties on what appeared to be a steady march, inspiring revolutionary struggles, regional warfare, and counterinsurgencies, not to mention dividing the globe into rival political economies.

Now the contagion comes mainly from the right—and usually from the far right—and is seen as afflicting bodies politic perhaps more insidiously than the left ever did. It has gained traction where the right had previously been crushed and has challenged political "norms" that are regarded as essential to the bodies' health. "Donald J. Trump's election has raised a question that few Americans ever imagined asking," two Harvard political scientists reflected. "Is our democracy in danger." For many such observers, as well as a growing slice of the public, the answer would now be a resounding and dispiriting "Yes!"[2]

The idea of a reactionary or illiberal challenge to political "norms" has become the conventional wisdom, especially among defenders of liberal democracies, although opinion differs as to when those "norms" first took hold. Some students of European politics point to the fall of the Berlin Wall and the end of the Cold War; many more look to the democratic reconstructions following the Second World War, which commenced in Western Europe and then moved south toward the Mediterranean; and some suggest deeper threads of constitutional liberalism, stretching back to the French Revolution and the first half of the nineteenth century, even if they usually ended up with monarchical garb.[3]

For the United States, however, the "norms" being violated are viewed as fundamental to the country's origin story and the central elements of political culture throughout our history. The ideals of the Declaration of Independence, the checks and balances and Bill of Rights in the Constitution, the early rise and expansion of electoral politics, the celebrations of equality and democracy, and the stability of the political system—with the exception of the Civil War—are widely invoked both to describe the arc of the American political tradition and to distinguish it from other societies around the world. Indeed, these features have long been crucial to the notion of American exceptionalism, answering the questions of why there has been neither socialism nor fascism in the United States.[4]

The identification of American political history and culture with sturdy and expansive liberal democratic norms has been such a component of our civic life and socialization that even critics of American development or contemporary public policies appear to bow to its logic. True, they say, American history has its vile and shameful chapters—slavery, the extermination of Native peoples, Jim Crow racism, nativism, vigilante violence in the name of white supremacy, gender discrimination—but little by little additional chapters have been written so as to make the founding principles more inclusive and robust.

American historians, for their part, have largely embraced some version of a "slavery to freedom" narrative that simultaneously acknowledges the collective sins of the past while laying out what may be seen as a redemption story that privileges the activism of those who embodied the principles, whether they be Black or white. Small wonder that figures like Harriet Tubman and the early Martin Luther King Jr. have won pride of place in the telling of African American freedom struggles, while Martin Delany, Marcus Garvey, Malcolm X, and the Black Panthers (all of whom might help us better understand the current Black Lives Matter movement) have been pushed to the margins. Small wonder that many observers initially regarded the election of Barack Obama to the presidency in 2008 as a sign that the United States had become a "postracial" society. Small wonder, too, that when, in the aftermath of Trump's election, the legal scholar Cass Sunstein assembled a distinguished cast of scholars and intellectuals to address the question "Can it happen here?"—the "it" being authoritarianism or fascism—most thought that, while possible, "it" was unlikely owing in good part to the depth and tenacity of liberal democratic traditions.[5]

"Traditions" are, of course, meant to denote values, practices, rituals, and events that have a lengthy history, are well rooted in the cultures of communities and nations, and are regularly commemorated in some fashion. They are handed down over time and generations. Their power and resilience derive from a shared sense of their inner truths and their significance as part of a collective experience. Yet, some "traditions" that appear to have a deep history are often more recent creations, constructions, or inventions. They are used to express forms of power, legitimate institutions, nurture types of cohesion, and mark new histories forged by older and recognizable actors, lending more recent concerns, conflicts, and ideals the validation of time. "Invented traditions," the historian Eric Hobsbawn wrote, are "set[s] of practices, normally governed by overtly or tacitly accepted rules and of a ritual or symbolic nature, which seek to inculcate certain values and norms of behavior by repetition, which automatically implies continuity with the past."[6]

Some of these invented traditions—the November celebration of Thanksgiving, gift-giving during the Christmas holidays, reciting the Pledge of Allegiance, flying the Confederate flag—are the responses of particular moments that manage to gain traction. Christmas gift-giving began in the 1820s as the market economy grew and brought new patterns of middle- and upper-class consumption to the United States. Thanksgiving was proclaimed a national holiday in 1863 by President Abraham Lincoln to celebrate the survival of the Union during the Civil War (with some revision by President Franklin Roosevelt and Congress in 1941). The Pledge of Allegiance, first penned by minister—and socialist—Francis Bellamy in 1892, was only adopted by Congress in 1942 (and revised to add the words "under God" in 1954). The Confederate stars and bars became part of state flags in the Deep South—and was flown and emblazoned elsewhere—only after the Supreme Court's *Brown* v. *Board of Education* decision (1954) and the surge in Black organizing against Jim Crow. In truth, all cultures have traditions, and most of them, if they endure, are at least in part invented and reinvented.[7]

But the most politically consequential of these traditions attempt to capture the meaning of national origins, the substance of a nation's claims to authenticity and distinctiveness, and the breadth of developments that give national history coherence. In all cases, historical context is crucial to our understanding of how these traditions are made and why they are sustained, even if the traditions are of relatively recent vintage. This is how we may approach America's "liberal tradition" and its "invention."

I

THE STRONGEST AND BEST-KNOWN ARGUMENT for an encompassing liberal tradition in American history comes from Louis Hartz in his eponymous book published in 1955.[8] A political scientist and Harvard professor of government, Hartz argued that what he viewed as the hegemony of liberalism (especially in the Lockean sense of individualism and private property as foundational) in the United States was owed to the decisive break British North American colonizers made with European politics and culture and the consequent absence of an American experience of feudalism. Without a feudal past or tradition, America would also lack the revolutionary or reactionary currents that grow in opposition to or in defense of feudal society, with its prescribed social hierarchies, ascriptive norms and rights, ideas of divine rule, vertical allegiances, and debased peasants. Although he acknowledged divisions of social class in America, Hartz nonetheless insisted that the peasant of Europe became the capitalist farmer while the downtrodden laborer became an incipient entrepreneur. The result was a "democratic hybrid unknown anywhere," so that the impulses toward democracy and capitalism, which could be expected to generate bitter struggle, instead became interconnected, much to the dismay of those Hartz calls the early "Whigs" or upper middle class who had little room to define a particular world view, despite their suspicions of democracy.[9]

Hartz recognized that the American South, with its commitment to slavery and aristocratic pretensions, could be regarded as a potential source of reaction and therefore a rival to a developing liberal tradition. Yet Hartz believed that the slave plantation was a capitalist enterprise (thus slavery was not a form of feudalism or similarly retrograde) and that Jeffersonianism placed liberalism close to the surface, making a "reactionary enlightenment" impossible to construct. Antebellum Whiggery, another potential source of opposition, democratized itself after 1840, and so the economic boom following the Civil War—which Hartz saw as nothing like the French Revolution— defeated elitism and absorbed both the farmer and the worker into the petit-bourgeoisie. Without a serious challenge from the left, Progressive era reformers could then present themselves as pure crusaders and later New Dealers could extend the sphere of the state while retaining the basic principles of Locke and the larger liberal framework. As for the American right, rather than exuding reaction, it came to exemplify the tradition of big propertied liberalism in Europe (the English Whig, the French Girondin) that "hates the *ancien regime* up to a certain point, loves capitalism, and fears democracy."

The power of Hartz's writing flowed from his broad Euro-Atlantic vision and his frustration with the parochialism of American historians who, as he put it, failed to "interpret our history in light of [the] escape from the European past," which alone could reveal—as he believed Alexis de Tocqueville had demonstrated—the American liberal world. The power of Hartz's writing flowed as well from his critical stance toward the very tradition he attempted to uncover. Like Tocqueville, who deeply influenced him, Hartz worried about the unanimity of mind and the absolute moralism that the liberal tradition appeared to promote, all the more so as he contemplated America's new roles in the post–World War II world.

Hartz was by no means the first to suggest a deep historical tradition of liberal values and relations. By the mid-1950s, the idea was widespread among scholars in a number of fields, some of whom, like the historian Daniel Boorstin, exulted in it. But many, like Hartz, both acknowledged the reality and worried about the consequences for the country. "In the United States at this time," the literary critic Lionel Trilling sighed in 1950, "liberalism is not only the dominant but even the sole intellectual tradition." Trilling's colleague at Columbia University, Richard Hofstadter, had already laid out the main lines of argument in his prize-winning biographical collection, *The American Political Tradition and the Men Who Made It*, which appeared in

1948. "The major political traditions have shared a belief in the rights of property, the philosophy of economic individualism, the value of competition," he wrote; "they have accepted the economic virtue of capitalist culture as necessary qualities of man." These, according to Hofstadter, "have been staple tenets of the central faith in American political ideologies" so that they align "men as diverse as Jefferson, Jackson, Lincoln, Cleveland, Bryan, Wilson, and Hoover."[10]

A few years later, in a major critique of Populists and Progressive reformers, Hofstadter simultaneously conceded the power of the liberal tradition while focusing on what he regarded as its "failings" and dangers: its attractions to conspiracy theories, its moral absolutism and crusading spirit, its ambivalence about modernity, its meshing of reform and illiberalism. "My own interest has been drawn to that side of Populism and Progressivism—particularly of Populism," Hofstadter explained, "which seems very strongly to foreshadow some aspects of the cranky pseudo-conservatism of our time . . . illiberal and ill-tempered." By this he meant the Populist movement of the South and West during the 1890s that, according to his reading, traded in nativism and racism even while excoriating the concentrations of economic wealth and power that robbed farmers of their independence. Not surprisingly, Hofstadter would soon be exploring anti-intellectualism and political paranoia in American culture.[11]

The writings of Hartz, Hofstadter, Boorstin, Trilling, and others of the time did not fit seamlessly into prior interpretations of the American past. They in fact represented a sharp break with prevailing historical thinking and historiography. Academic and professional history writing was still relatively new in the 1940s and 1950s. It had taken shape during the last quarter of the nineteenth century—the American Historical Association was founded in 1884—and, like many other fields attempting to establish their bona fides, especially in the social sciences, historians now being trained in formal graduate programs were busy devising approaches and methods that distinguished them from amateurs and dilettantes. To those ends, they focused on the idea of "objectivity" and on research methods that could be regarded as "scientific." The scholarship they produced tended to privilege the history of American institutions and, in an interpretive sense, most wrote of the importance of the British and German (Teutonic) background and thus of continuities between the political cultures of Europe and early America.

Some, writing on the American Revolution, effectively adopted the perspective of the British Empire—they were reckoned as the "imperial school"—and drew into question the salience of colonial grievances. Those interested in the origins of American intellectual and political life found a British-Teutonic "germ theory" of dissemination compelling, which suggested a transatlantic culture and body politic. Those studying the Civil War era leaned toward a sectional reconciliationist view, one emphasizing the absence of fundamental social and political divisions and the importance of a postwar healing process, which was itself taking hold in the country at large. At all events, they considered American history a European creation and Anglo-Saxonism the cultural glue.[12]

The challenge came late in the nineteenth century, very much in the midst of the social and political turbulence produced by the Gilded Age, anti-monopoly radicalism, and early Progressivism. Frederick Jackson Turner, in a still widely recognized and discussed essay, argued both that the "frontier" had been the source of America's democratic impulses and that the "closing" of the frontier by the 1890s (he pointed to the 1890 federal census for evidence) brought an entire era of history to an end while raising questions about what the future might hold. Unlike others in the first generation of professional historians, Turner emphasized discontinuity with Europe and a distinctively American source of political culture. And he became part of an emerging "progressive" school whose ideas would dominate the field of American historical writing for the next five decades. Most closely associated with Charles A. Beard, though also including Vernon Parrington, Carl Becker, John Hicks, Arthur Schlesinger Sr., and C. Vann Woodward, as well as Turner, the Progressives saw social and political conflict as the driving forces in American history. They eschewed the cultural and political inheritances from Europe that historians had once touted and instead emphasized the ongoing struggles of the "people" against the "interests," whether during the American Revolution, the writing of the Constitution, the age of Jackson, the Civil War and Reconstruction, or the Populist-Progressive period. Indeed, in many ways they echoed the political languages of turn-of-the-century radicals and reformers, and, in contrast to their historian predecessors whose sensibilities were conservative, they mostly veered politically left. It was against this formidable field of historical interpretation that the "liberal tradition" was fashioned.[13]

II

THE ENDING OF THE SECOND WORLD WAR, the rapid unfolding of the Cold War, and the developing assessments of "totalitarian regimes" of the right and left inspired a major shift in perspective among historians, social scientists, and other intellectuals in the humanities. Many who were on the political left in the 1930s and may have flirted with communism (or joined the Communist Party) became directly involved in the military battle against fascism— either in combat units or in intelligence agencies like the OSS (Office of Strategic Services)—and emerged from warfare struggling to make sense of an altered political landscape. Although the crucial wartime alliance between the United States and the Soviet Union took some of the sting out of the Nazi-Soviet Non-Aggression Pact of 1939, Soviet moves into Eastern Europe and revelations concerning Stalinist repression raised serious questions about what "peaceful coexistence" in a postwar world would mean.

The failure of Henry Wallace's Progressive Party campaign to offer a viable alternative to the Cold War orientation of Harry Truman and the Democratic Party in 1948 further narrowed the political options for those migrating from the socialist left and reconfigured views of the liberalism that came out of the New Deal. "Since [Roosevelt's inauguration]," Arthur Schlesinger Jr. wrote in 1949, "one has been able to feel that liberal ideas had access to power in the U.S., that liberal purposes . . . were dominating our national policy . . . [and] that the New Deal was filling the vacuum of faith from the cynicism and complacency of the twenties and from the broad lines of the thirties." Convening a symposium on "Our Country and Our Culture" shortly thereafter, the *Partisan Review*, a voice of the anti-Stalinist and liberal left, reflected on "the apparent fact that American intellectuals now regard America and its institutions in a new way." "Until more than a decade ago," the editors acknowledged, "America was thought to be hostile to art and culture. Since then, however, . . . many writers and intellectuals feel closer to their country and its culture. Politically, there is a recognition that the kind of democracy which exists in America has an intrinsic and positive value . . . and more and more writers have ceased to think of themselves as rebels and exiles." Some of the conference participants remarked on how "the Second World War completed the course of spiritual reinstatement," how the "European folly, treachery, and disregard of human rights refuted the claim of superior 'civilization,'" and how "our lumbering American republic, with all its glaring faults, was fundamentally sounder and stronger than its enemies." Lionel Trilling argued that "for the first time in the history of the modern American intellectual, America is not to be conceived of as *a priori* the vulgarest and stupidest nation of the world. . . . There is an unmistakable improvement in the present American cultural situation over that of, say, thirty years ago."[14]

Liberal and left intellectuals did not wish to abandon the federal initiatives and Keynesian policies that the New Deal had advanced during the 1930s and the war; if anything, many feared that without them the country would slip back into the economic depression that had seemed so intractable and enduring only a few short years before. Instead, they were concerned with protecting the freedoms of the individual, of faith, and of the life of the mind that Soviet communism appeared to threaten, and thus they came to cast an increasingly suspicious eye on the "fellow travelers or the fellow travelers of the fellow travelers" whose "sentimentality," in Schlesinger Jr.'s words, "has softened up the progressive for Communist permeation and conquest."[15]

Of particular influence was a growing body of literature produced by social scientists and humanists, many from Europe and some refugees from Hitler's Germany, who began to explore "totalitarianism." This, they came to insist—thinking of Nazism, Italian and Spanish fascism, and Stalinist communism—was not a mere variant of autocratic, authoritarian, or tyrannical rule; it was a distinctive form of political domination and organization new to the twentieth century. Totalitarianism, they argued, fed upon the weakening and collapse of nation-states (thereby creating large groups of stateless and displaced persons) and combined the centralization of power, the destruction of organized opposition, the emergence of cult-like dictatorships, the expansion of state control over private and public life, and the widespread use of state terror with mass bases of support. Indeed, it was both the prevalence of terror and the mobilization of the masses, or the "mob" as some preferred to describe them, that proved especially disturbing and promoted interest in social psychology as well as politics and political economy.[16]

The problem of mass support for totalitarianism became particularly acute as Cold War tensions of the late 1940s and early 1950s made for something of a liberal existential crisis. On the one hand, many liberals looked to shed the taint of communism that had colored the Popular Front of the 1930s and stuck to those who sought to keep the forces of political progressivism and U.S.-Soviet cooperation alive once the Second World War ended. Organizationally, a host of prominent liberal intellectuals, labor leaders, civil rights advocates, and political figures—including the theologian Reinhold Niebuhr, the auto workers' union leader Walter Reuther, the labor lawyer Joseph Rauh, the historian Arthur Schlesinger Jr., Minneapolis mayor Hubert Humphrey, and the former first lady Eleanor Roosevelt— founded Americans for Democratic Action (1947) as an alternative to the Henry Wallace campaign, which they viewed as being duped by the Soviet Union and the Communist Party USA. They soon joined hands with anti-communist counterparts in Europe and Latin America to create the Congress for Cultural Freedom (1950) and its American offshoot the Committee for Cultural Freedom (1951), both of which the CIA was actively encouraging.[17]

With the onset of state-sponsored (on federal and state levels) repression, more than a few liberals accepted or even welcomed the persecution of those who remained on the left as unfortunate but necessary to the security and well-being of the country, regarding the victimized as "agents" of a foreign power and inherent threats to the "life of the mind." Some happily gave names of suspected communists to congressional committees, such as the House Un-American Activities Committee (HUAC), and had little compunction about seeing them fired and blacklisted. The scholars and writers among them—such as Daniel Boorstin, James Burnham, Sidney Hook, James Wechsler, Leslie Fiedler, Irving Kristol, and Granville Hicks—began to identify, and in some cases celebrate, the distinctive features of American politics and culture, whether the two-party system, the pluralist dispositions of the public, the penchant for practicality, the importance of voluntary associations, the widespread ideological consensus, and a fascination with irony and complexity. Arthur Schlesinger Jr.'s *The Vital Center* (1949) tried to capture their perspectives and ambitions. Notable for the moment, Alexis de Tocqueville's *Democracy in America*, long out of print, was reissued in 1945 with a new introduction and reviews in both the *Mississippi Valley Historical Review* (later the *Journal of American History*) and the *American Historical Review*.[18]

And yet, while much of the initiative for these actions came from liberals and the Truman administration, a conservative backlash against the New Deal, the empowered labor movement, civil rights activism, and the spread of communism abroad (most notably the "fall" of China in 1949) pushed the campaign into increasingly intolerant territory and seemed to herald a resurgence on the right. McCarthyism in the nation and the states—demands for conformity, the implementation of loyalty oaths, suspicions of the liberally inclined and irreligious, accusations of communist affiliations, repression of the "disloyal"—served as a backdrop less for conservative concerns about the expanded instruments of state power than for liberal worries about the disposition of the "masses" who, it was assumed, would be the enablers of a potentially tyrannical or illiberal regime.[19]

With the fascist mobilizations of the 1920s and 1930s and the more recent efforts to explain the popular base of authoritarianism in mind, scholars tried to account for the incipient rise of what some called "the new American right." They showed barely concealed contempt—in good part because liberal intellectual guidance seemed to have been rejected—in their writings about the "discontented classes": not working people or the poor but a new middle class

produced by social and geographical mobility; a class feeling themselves "rootless," scrambling for "status and secure identity," anxious
about their place amidst the "heterogeneity" of modern American
life, fearful of being spied upon and betrayed, prone to embracing
conspiracy theories. Like Richard Hofstadter, some of these scholars
looked to the past, to the late nineteenth century and the Populists
in particular, and were struck not by Populist attacks on monopolies
and economic inequality but by their xenophobia, anti-Semitism, and
political paranoia, their tendency to mark out real enemies and blame
the wealthy, especially "Wall Street," for their woes. A few saw direct
links between the Populists of the 1890s and the supporters of Joseph
McCarthy in the 1950s and suggested that anti-communism gave
Catholics, long demonized in American political culture, an opportunity to meld into mainstream America.[20]

The intellectual sensibilities of Cold War liberalism were widely
influential and soon gave shape to the emergence of new fields and to
historical interpretations in developing areas of scholarship. "American studies," whose seeds were planted in the 1930s, came into full
bloom in the 1950s. Hoping to encourage interdisciplinary approaches
to American society—especially to bring students of history and literature together—American studies rode the wave of interest in American distinctiveness and exceptionalism. By the end of the decade,
it succeeded in establishing nearly one hundred programs, some
called "American Civilization," in colleges and universities. Scholars
attracted to American studies wished to explore the country's cultural
and intellectual past that history departments rarely taught, the literary texts that English departments generally ignored, and the lineages
of political culture that politics and political science departments
overlooked. Prominent among the subjects of study during the 1950s
were "myth and symbol" and the making of the "American mind."
Henry Nash Smith's *Virgin Land: The American West as Symbol and Myth*
(1950) explored the American engagement with the trans-Mississippi
West during the nineteenth century, drawing upon popular forms
of expression, like dime novels, as well as more recognized literary
texts. Perry Miller's two-volume *New England Mind* (1939, 1953) portrayed the Puritans both as constructing a serious and unified body of

thought and then as exemplifying the larger American adaptation to a new cultural landscape, with significant legacies for the country as a whole. John William Ward's *Andrew Jackson: Symbol for an Age* (1953) examined the ways in which Jackson and the Jacksonian era took hold in the American imagination. Together, their treatments of iconic figures and ideas set a template for the American studies approach over the next decade and a half.[21]

With the burgeoning civil rights movement as a crucial context, the study of American slavery also showed the interpretive influence of the liberal tradition and the consensus framework. It represented, as well, a dramatic change in interpretive perspective. From the turn of the twentieth century up into the 1950s, the scholarship was dominated by Ulrich B. Phillips and his students, who depicted slavery as a paternalistic institution that elevated backward Africans on the scale of civilization and created a distinctive society in the American South. For slaveowners who, by Phillips's account, maintained the system despite what he argued was its tendency toward unprofitability, slavery was less a business than a life devoted to aristocratic ideals and the supremacy of the superior white race. Although a number of historians—mostly African American—contested this portrait, they were given little attention, and the "Phillips School" prevailed until the mid-1950s and the publication of Kenneth Stampp's *The Peculiar Institution: Slavery in the Antebellum South* (1956).[22]

Stampp was a northerner (Phillips was from Georgia though something of an expatriate; he received his PhD from Columbia University and mostly taught in the North, at the University of Wisconsin, Michigan, and Yale) who had nothing but scorn for the apologetics of the Phillips school and challenged their findings on nearly every front. Whereas Phillips and his students portrayed the slave South as aristocratic and paternalistic, Stampp saw it as thoroughly capitalist and profit oriented. Whereas Phillips and his students suggested that the slave/plantation system slid toward unprofitability, Stampp insisted that it was economically expansive. Whereas Phillips and his students argued that slaveholders treated slaves in a humane way, Stampp emphasized the brutality of the regime. Whereas Phillips and his students saw slaves largely accepting their subordination and the paternalism of their masters, Stampp presented them as resisting their enslavement in a variety of ways. Whereas Phillips and his students assumed that Africans brought their cultural backwardness and heathenism with them to North America, Stampp contended that the Middle Passage broke their cultural ties to Africa and left slaves in a "cultural void" in America. And whereas Phillips and his students saw slaves and other Black people as inferior to whites, Stampp proclaimed that they stood on a plane of equality. "I have assumed," he observed, "that the slaves were merely ordinary human beings, that innately Negroes are, after all, only white men with black skins, nothing more, nothing less."[23]

The Peculiar Institution was clearly a book for the time and it helped inspire a new wave of study. A few years later, Stanley Elkins published his controversial *Slavery: A Problem in American Institutional and Intellectual Life* (1959), in which he both compared American slavery to slave systems in Latin America and argued that, in its American setting, the devastating human impact of enslavement could be likened to German concentration camps, infantilizing the enslaved and accounting for the pervasive and racist "sambo" stereotype long ascribed to African Americans. Needless to say, no paternalism was to be found and, according to Elkins, the special brutality of the American regime was a product of Protestantism and what he called "unopposed capitalism." Elkins's interest in institutional analogy and social psychology (he drew heavily on the work of Bruno Bettelheim) revealed the influence of American studies' interdisciplinarity and how historical comparisons could be used to further ground American exceptionalism. It also showed that the study of slavery would move across disciplinary boundaries, to sociology and, notably, to economics and economic history. The question of profitability was taken up by Harvard economists Alfred H. Conrad and John R. Meyer who, in 1958, joined the attack on Phillips and used new econometric methods to argue that slavery was profitable and had not reached its "natural limits," as some in the Phillips school had claimed.[24]

The slavery studies of Stampp, Elkins, Conrad and Meyer, and others of the time were different in a number of respects, but they shared a framework of understanding and analysis that the ideas surrounding the liberal tradition had reflected and advanced. It was a framework that assumed or argued for the deep and wide historical roots of capitalism and capitalist culture, the nearly universal attachment to private property and competition, the centrality of profit seeking as a basic human motivation, and the expected response of all people to market incentives, where possible. And it presumed that these characteristics could be found across the United States historically, whatever else distinguished different regions of the country. It was, too, a framework that depicted "culture" as relatively brittle, likely to break under the stress of change and then to reconstitute itself in new environments. Adaptation, assimilation, and acculturation became watchwords in history, sociology, and anthropology.

The emergence of immigration studies just at this time also showed the impact of the liberal framework, especially in the work of one of its pioneers, Oscar Handlin. Indeed, although Handlin's most recognized work, *The Uprooted*, appeared in 1951, it anticipated the direction of American historical scholarship in the 1950s. For one thing, like the developing field of American studies, it was interdisciplinary, particularly in its debt to sociology, which focused Handlin's attention on cities and urban life and established a methodological foundation on which later social history would be built. Equally, if not more, important, Handlin—like Hartz and Stampp—envisioned the movement of European peasants (they were represented as the stereotypical immigrants) to the United States as an alienating and disruptive experience that effectively broke their social and cultural ties to the villages of the old rural world and required them to adapt to the modernizing trends in America. "Emigration," Handlin wrote, "took these people out of traditional, accustomed environments and replanted them in strange ground," where they lived, often in a state of "shock," for "many years" before they found ways to adjust and assimilate. Many of the book's chapters were dark; Handlin was committed to conveying the struggles that European immigrants faced. To that extent, it was not unlike John Higham's searing *Strangers in the Land* (1955), which focused less on the immigrants than on patterns of hostility to them (nativism) between the mid-nineteenth century and the Great Depression. But Handlin's larger message was uplift-

ing, as alienation and disorientation became acculturation and incorporation, and Higham's exposure of the illiberal currents it spawned
nonetheless helped implant the more liberal-oriented idea of the postwar period, that the United States was, in the end, a "nation of immigrants" endlessly drawn into its "melting pot."[25]

Even critiques of American foreign policy that began to be
mounted in the late 1950s and early 1960s by William Appleman
Williams and his students at the University of Wisconsin showed the
marks of the liberal tradition mindset. For the most part, American
diplomatic history had been told from the perspective of high-level
policy makers and was configured around the export of liberal values
and the resistance to empire itself. Williams and his students would
have none of that; they wrote of a "non-colonial imperialism" that
emerged at the end of the nineteenth century, made necessary by the
search for new markets overseas, especially in the Pacific, and were
interested in the ways in which popular support was mobilized by
business interests to back these objectives. Written at a time when the
country was flexing its might to ensure what Henry Luce had called
"the American century," the Wisconsin historians sought to make
readers aware of the deep history of American empire and the price it
would continue to exact. But their works did not challenge the idea of
an ideological consensus around capitalist values and dispensations;
rather, they warned that America's liberal democracy both produced
and would eventually be threatened by the need for empire.[26]

Historical conceptions of the liberal tradition at once captured developments in a number of social science fields and, in
turn, lent them traction. In sociology and political science qualitative approaches to society and politics that had prevailed since the
disciplines were established during the early years of the twentieth
century shifted in more quantitative and functionalist directions. In
sociology, structural functionalism, which argued that social systems
tended toward equilibrium and that institutions and social relations
were stable because they served important functions, took off in the
1940s and 1950s, pioneered by Talcott Parsons. In political science, a
focus on political theory and the historical development of political
institutions gave way to a "behavioral revolution" and the blossoming

of "survey research" in the 1950s, as well as to a related orientation to decision-making in which "game theory" and "rational choice" modeling, with interdisciplinary appeal, took hold. Quantitative methods and models became foundational in economics, too, as the analysis of data sets from past and present became the basis for explaining economic dynamics and outcomes. Before too long, the impact was also in evidence in the field of philosophy, especially given its increasingly analytic disposition.[27]

In all of these cases, assumptions about human nature and desires to which the articulation of the long history of liberal consensus lent legitimacy became the basis of examination. The sociologist Daniel Bell in his treatment of "the exhaustion of political ideas in the fifties"—he called this *The End of Ideology*—could therefore write of the United States, echoing Louis Hartz, as "a culture with no feudal tradition, with a pragmatic ethos . . . with boundless optimism for the new . . . [which] have become the norm." The idea of a lengthy liberal tradition, of remarkably recent vintage, was being widely embraced and validated.[28]

III

ONE MIGHT EXPECT THAT the liberal tradition and the related consensus interpretation of American history would, like its progressive predecessor, have an extended reign over historical thinking and writing. But this was not at all the case. By the early 1960s—with the expansion of civil rights protest, the rise of the student left, and American involvement in Vietnam changing the context—the attacks began to come from a number of directions and only grew more wide-ranging and intense over time. The attacks came from historians of slavery and African Americans who forced an encounter with the country's deep involvement with Black enslavement and the struggles of enslaved people to carve out lives and cultures of their own. The attacks came from historians who called into question the importance of capitalism and capitalist values in early America and, in some cases, suggested a long road of capitalist development. The attacks came from historians of the Civil War who insisted that slavery had created two distinctive societies in the United States, one of which rejected the liberal world, that were on an unavoidable collision course. The attacks came from within American studies, interrogating the field's geographical parochialism and its general avoidance of religion, class, race, ethnicity, or gender. The attacks came from new social historians who were not only eager to explore the lives and struggles of ordinary working men and women but who also saw class conflict as a central part of that experience.

The attacks came from immigration historians who demonstrated that cultural ties between Europe and America remained powerful, that the social profile of immigrants was complex, that many of those who moved across the Atlantic subsequently returned to their countries of origin, and that the immigration experience encompassed the Pacific as well as the Atlantic world, which had largely been ignored. The attacks came from feminist historians who bridled at the virtual absence of women and inequalities of gender in the historiography, and began to create a much larger cast of historical actors. The attacks came from historians of Populism and Progressivism who challenged the idea that these movements, especially Populism, were status-anxious and backward-looking; instead, historians came to emphasize Populist economic radicalism, democratic dispositions, and openness to biracial coalitions, and how Progressivism anticipated the New Deal. And the attacks came, even more generally, from historians who rejected, not the entire framework of the liberal tradition, but rather its emphasis on political pluralism and avoidance of the questions of power.[29]

Marxist perspectives on the American past, which had registered almost no impact before, now gained a respected and influential place in historical research and writing. "Class," at most summoned only to be dismissed as an important feature of United States history by liberal and consensus-oriented scholars, was explored in imaginative and consequential ways, especially by students of the slave South and the early working class. Discarding the economic determinism long associated with Marxism, they looked at culture, ideology, and politics along with the relations of production, writing about class as a phenomenon that was "made" by social groups in the process of struggle—and struggle that raised questions about the history and stability of capitalism. So powerful was this new conceptual orientation that even historians who steered clear of Marxist analysis felt compelled to address the significance of class and consider capitalism as more of a contingent than a transhistorical system.[30]

Thus, by the early 1970s, as historians were increasingly interested in recovering lineages of dissent and political radicalism, intent on exposing inequalities, discriminations, and exclusions in our history, aghast at the destructive force of American imperialism, and, in many cases, sympathetic to international liberation movements of the left, the liberal tradition and consensus interpretation seemed to make little sense either of the past or the present. And the many overreaches of the "imperial" presidency and national security state that came into full view owing to the Vietnam War and Watergate seemed to make a mockery of anything like a "liberal democracy."

While quickly and widely criticized by historians—angrily dismissed in many circles—the idea of a liberal tradition retained greater currency in the social sciences, especially in the field of American political development, which focused on institutions, governance, and electoral practices. But whether in sociology or political science, a growing critique was also fashioned, one based on the recognition of race, racial discrimination, class divides, and economic inequality. Some saw the deep structural dislocations in jobs, housing, access to social services, and the prospects for mobility as clear testimony to the liberal tradition's deficiencies or irrelevance. Others emphasized the symbiotic relationships between liberal rights-bearing and racism or the multiple political traditions, including liberal traditions, that could, at any point, be identified. The liberal tradition, once nearly hegemonic a mere decade earlier, appeared to have become nearly moribund in the very fields responsible for inventing it.[31]

IV

YET, IF THIS IS SO, how can we account for the persistent invocation of our liberal tradition? How are we to explain, more than fifty years later, the many journalists and other serious observers who express near incredulity at the vulnerability of our liberal democratic institutions and astonishment at the transgression of liberal democratic "norms"? How can America's liberal tradition survive so tenaciously in our culture and discourses if it had long been abandoned by those best acquainted with our history?

The answer, in part, has to do with the hegemony that mid-twentieth-century liberalism, constructed by the New Deal, had achieved in the two decades after the Second World War. Flushed with victory over fascism, relatively unscarred by wartime destruction, committed to policies that would avert a return to economic depression, positioned to assume leadership of the nonsocialist world, apparently intent on helping to create democratic polities where authoritarianism and fascism had ruled, and presenting itself as the protector of freedom and equality, the American liberal state made itself the standard against which alternative systems were to be measured. The liberal tradition and consensus interpretation of American history, which flourished during this very time, testified to how these liberal sensibilities and objectives had gained influence even among those who could be its most severe critics. And when the challenges to these interpretations came, they kept liberalism and the liberal state front and center, focusing on their contradictions, failings, and hypocrisies. Although critics mostly insisted on conflict rather than consensus and exposed what the liberal tradition concealed and who it left out, they never really offered up an alternative narrative. Indeed, the popularity of social history and its microhistorical—case study—approaches to communities of different sorts, while revealing the diversity and complexity of American history and society, failed to synthesize the new knowledge into an overarching conceptual rival. Some, in fact, came to argue that such a synthesis would simply reproduce many of the exclusions they reviled, that synthesis was itself the problem to be avoided for the sake of a truly inclusive past.[32]

The waning of socialist political struggles across the globe, the transition from military to civilian rule in parts of Latin America, the victories of conservatism in Britain and the United States, and the reform impulses of Mikhail Gorbachev in the Soviet Union during the 1980s were of great importance as well. Together they seemed to diminish interest in Marxism, class, and social conflict and instead encourage a "cultural turn" in historical interpretation and writing. Scholarly attention, particularly in history and literature, shifted to "discourses" and forms of power that liberal regimes deployed and were difficult to contest. Often categorized as "postmodernism," these ideas and sensibilities raised serious questions about "master narratives," truth claims, and Enlightenment notions of rationality, preferring to emphasize contingencies, instabilities, and a much more expansive understanding of what could be regarded as "texts" to be read and interpreted. But while postmodernism can be seen as an implicit critique of the world that liberalism brought into being, the subjects of study—the body, sexuality, gender, race—were themselves produced by bourgeois, liberal societies that scholars were reluctant to problematize as a "system." The critique thereby lacked much of a political edge. In the social sciences, on the other hand, postmodernism had a limited impact; if anything, economics, political science, and sociology became more committed to quantitative modeling, and rational choice theory spread into legal studies.[33]

The rapid collapse of the Soviet Union, the ending of the Cold War, and the emergence of new, ostensibly liberal democratic states in Eastern Europe accentuated these trends while lending the association of capitalism and liberal democracy a credibility it had not had since the 1950s. To many observers it appeared that capitalism had emerged triumphant, that socialism and communism were fatally weakened if not wholly irrelevant, and that liberal democratic regimes had vanquished all rivals. The writer Francis Fukuyama could go so far as declaring an "end of history," by which he meant that humanity's "ideological evolution" had reached something of an "end-point" marked by the "universalization of Western liberal democracy as the final form of human government." By 2006, according to one count, about 60 percent of the world's states could be regarded as democracies and, of these, perhaps two-thirds could qualify as "liberal" democracies: governments chosen by free and fair elections and based on the extension of basic rights and liberties to their citizens. The election of Democrat Bill Clinton in 1992 after more than two decades of Republican control of the presidency, together with Barack Obama's election in 2008, appeared to demonstrate that liberal democracy in the United States remained healthy despite growing popular disenchantment with American politicians and political institutions, the Supreme Court's disconcerting role in making George W. Bush president in 2000, and heightened partisanship in Congress and across the country.[34]

Scholarly interest in capitalism was renewed by the end of the first decade of the 2000s, partly because of the massive global financial crisis of 2007–2008, though there was an ironic twist to historical studies. Rather than looking at a transition to capitalism or capitalism's rise and consolidation or capitalism's transformations, historians began to treat capitalism as a system and phenomenon that has, effectively, always been with us, much as the inventors of the liberal tradition had done, and their attention turned chiefly to the financial instruments that have served to accumulate capital and their long arc of development. Slavery and capitalism have now come to be conjoined to an extent that historians had once debated, and what is called "racial capitalism" seems to be a formation that encapsulates virtually all of American history. Needless to say, capitalism is both implicitly and explicitly subject to withering criticism, but the literature also suggests a mainstream consensus organized around capitalism and white supremacy: a consensus that serves to indict liberal democracy while consecrating its deep roots.[35]

Indeed, America's liberal tradition has been entrenched less by its defenders and beneficiaries than by its critics on the right and left. The long-standing conservative attack that celebrated state rights, racial and social hierarchies, limited democracy, and a small federal government has been overtaken by a radical right attack on the inclusiveness of liberal democracy, the cultural diversity it is meant to embody, and the birthright citizenship that the Constitution prescribes, all in the service of a harsh and often violent white nationalism. Horrified by these illiberal and quasi-fascist dispensations, defenders of liberal democracy are quick to invoke the "norms" of the American political tradition both to isolate and diminish the threat.

Yet critics on the left have played their part as well. Attacking liberalism and liberal democracy for their inattention to economic inequality and the distributions of power and wealth—in fact for contributing directly to the development of a political economy that favors the rich, the well-placed, and the corporation—and for dependence on the vitality of capitalism, the social democratic and socialist lefts thereby concede the depth and formidability of the liberal tradition. And in organizing around the great principles and aspirations that have been articulated historically but have often faltered in practice, they both give the liberal tradition a more substantial history than it in fact has and make it difficult for us to see competing traditions and currents that are anything but liberal.

V

SOME YEARS AGO, a group of scholars, mostly in the field of political science, gathered to reflect on the fate and relevance of Louis Hartz's *The Liberal Tradition in America*, now more than a half century after its publication. Respectful as they were about the book's ambition and influence, its remarkable staying power, they were almost uniformly critical of Hartz's arguments and how they were made. Flat, static, one-dimensional, inattentive to the complexities of American life and the diverse currents of political thought, blind to the disruptions of race, gender, and class: these were the assessments, rather devastating ones, offered up. "*The Liberal Tradition in America* will need to be read to understand the debates and insights it has fueled," one of the critics wrote. "Nevertheless [while] Hartz's classic had a remarkable run, it is time for a different production."[36]

Still, despite the critical barrage, most of the writers not only acknowledged that Hartz needs to be read but also that the idea of a liberal tradition endures and may well be in the process of resuscitation in a number of fields. Although "Hartz's book may now be history," editor Mark Hulliung admitted in conclusion, "the possibility of a liberal tradition in America is still very much in play."[37] Inventions—cultural, intellectual, and political—play their roles and frame our perspectives. They shape our discussions and debates, and over time they can be modified to make sense of a changing world. Indeed, they can be "reinvented" to accommodate special stresses and challenges.

In many ways, we are likely witnessing something of a reinvention of the liberal tradition today, a reinvention that carries less of a critical edge than it did in the 1940s and 1950s. For many who have embraced it, often eagerly, this liberal tradition is meant to suggest that the illiberal and authoritarian tendencies besetting us are themselves the products of a particular moment; that they have sprouted across the political landscape, threatening to suffocate our "norms," while sinking roots so shallow that they may be quickly eradicated.

And yet, the possible reinvention of the liberal tradition also marks the invention and reinvention of other political traditions with which it conflicts and against which it faces enormous challenges in the arenas of politics and political culture. When supporters of Donald Trump channel his slogan "Make America Great Again," they are looking back to a world before a Black man could be elected president, before people of color demanded equal rights, before feminists battled against gender exclusions and inequalities, before sexual identities began to be redefined, before American Protestants had to confront growing spiritual diversity, before immigration from Asia, Africa, and Latin America began to threaten the majority status of white people, and before the federal government served as an enabler of all these developments. The tradition they value is anything but liberal. It emphasizes state rights, community control, patriarchal families, rugged individualism, Christian nationalism, and some form of white supremacy.

To be sure, conflicting traditions such as these are not as neatly edged as they may seem, and people can—and do—embrace portions of both. Indeed, local resistance can turn in very different political directions. But they are not just talking points or matters for celebration and criticism. They are the stuff of political struggle, and they become most consequential when the struggles are most divisive and intense, when fundamentals appear to be at stake. Historical interpretation shapes the political landscape. Whoever owns the past owns the present; whoever's interpretation of how we got to where we

are is most persuasive usually attains power, regardless of the particular form of governance.

Nonetheless, we would do well to recognize the invented qualities
of the "traditions" we claim to value and uphold. Surprisingly enough,
this is something that historians often fail to do. When, in the summer of 2019, Nikole Hannah-Jones of the *New York Times* brought
to publication the "1619 Project," an ambitious effort to suggest an
American origin story that took full account of the foundational roles
that slavery and racism have played in American history, she generated a firestorm of criticism, much of the most condescending from
reputable historians who seemed especially irritated that their work
and wisdom had not been adequately consulted. Insisting upon an
origin story that the liberal tradition played a powerful role in producing, one tied to the universalism of the Declaration of Independence,
the radicalism of the American Revolution, and the misgivings about
enslavement and racial oppression that the Revolution and Constitution embodied, these historians berated Hannah-Jones and her
contributors for their ignorance of the "facts," their efforts to reduce
everything to enslavement and white supremacy, their simplification
of the Founders' views, and their inattention to the efforts of white
people on the part of Black people, whether enslaved or free. They
went so far as to protest the use of the 1619 Project in the schools,
effectively assisting the far right's attempts to whitewash slavery and
race from public school curricula across the country.[38]

Like all historical interpretations, those compiled by the 1619
Project both benefit and suffer from the confluence of histories past
and present. Before the invention of the liberal tradition, historians
regarded the American revolutionaries and Constitution makers as
motivated chiefly by propertied and other economic interests (though
little if any attention was paid to slavery and race) or by exaggerated
critiques of the British empire. Then, in the immediate post–Second
World War period, as the liberal tradition was emerging, attention
shifted to the importance of Lockean liberalism and republicanism,
something of a political and cultural consensus built around individualism, rights-bearing, and capitalist property, before new interpretations came to the fore that recognized the importance of enslavement

among many Founders, challenges offered up by working people and the poor, and a raft of exclusions that readily called universalist pretensions into question. But an origin story resting on American political independence remained, even if impugned.

The increasingly capaciousness and sophistication of historical research and writing, especially on Native peoples and those of African descent, have, in turn, made possible questions about American origins that had not been envisioned before. Looking West across the Atlantic, as we have done until very recently, origins would have to begin, at least, with European settlement. Looking East from the North American continent or Northwest from the African continent, those "origins" may appear very different. And even though origins are very much shrouded in changing myths, these new perspectives raise the prospect of debates that, although edgy politically, deserve to take place. Any way forward that offers some promise of a democratic and multicultural world needs to take serious account of the alternative, and often contested, conceptions of rights, social and family relations, gender and sexuality, race and ethnicity, cultural practice, justice, and governance, from which we must learn however much we may reject or revile them. We would do well to interrogate our assumptions about the nature of the past and the "norms" we have been left, so that it is possible for us to envision something messier, more complex, and less comfortable. That is our history rather than its inventions, which we ignore at our peril.

Chapter Two

FEUDAL DREAMS
AND COERCIVE
POWERS

W HEN ENGLISH ADVENTURERS LOOKED OUT ACROSS
the Atlantic during the latter part of the sixteenth century,
they saw prospects that their rapidly changing world seemed to
inspire. Richard Hakluyt the Elder, the influential geographer and
advisor to Queen Elizabeth I, articulated them when he wrote of the
three "ends" of North American colonization. They were "to plant
the Christian religion," to "trafficke" (that is, to engage in trade), and
"to conquer," though not necessarily in that order. "To plant Christian religion without conquest will bee hard," he admitted, "but Trafficke easily followeth conquest." Hakluyt recognized that Indigenous
peoples, about whom he had learned a bit, might have few needs that
the English could supply. There were, however, other inducements,
as Hakluyt's cousin and namesake, Richard Hakluyt the Younger,
was quick to point out: colonization could be an outlet for the "many
thousands of idle persons . . . within this realm," who, "having no
way to be set on work, be either mutinous and seek alteration in the
state," or resort to "pilfering and thieving."[1]

That the Hakluyts pitched North American colonization as a boon
to central state-building, a means of invigorating trade, a way to solve
the "labor" problem, and a potential source of needful "commodities" has helped reinforce the view of English overseas "expansion"
and colonialism as an important chapter in the history of Atlantic
capitalism. One historian has gone so far as to claim that capitalism
came to North America "in the first ships," but a great many scholars
see the English—and wider European—making of an Atlantic world

in the sixteenth and seventeenth centuries as crucial to the coming of modernity. The notion is hard to resist given what eventually ensued, tending to a close association between capitalist and North American development and, of course, between British North America and the related political cultures.[2]

Yet, looked at from the sixteenth century out instead of from the twentieth or twenty-first century back, the picture appears rather different. The adventurers and investors who signed on, as well as the writers and promoters, like the Hakluyts, who attempted to mobilize support—whether in England or elsewhere on the continent—were not only taken with Christian crusading and the unearthing of commodities, preferably precious metals. They also imagined establishing large landed estates and enriching themselves principally through the extraction of rents and other forms of dues and tribute, not through the cultivation and sale of crops on international markets. Theirs were feudal or neo-feudal dreams that, as the one historian has argued, "might better be seen as the final examples of a late-medieval form of enterprise . . . than as the harbingers of the modern era."[3]

England of the late sixteenth century was neither a feudal nor a static society. What we know of as feudalism—a social system involving decentralized power, ascribed hierarchies, reciprocal obligations, overlapping use rights, and servile (sometimes enserfed) labor—had been unraveling in England and Western Europe since at least the fourteenth century. The dramatic population declines occasioned by the bubonic plague and other pandemics had been reversed almost everywhere. Dues and services owed to lords were, in many cases, being commuted from in-kind to cash. Territorial monarchs were seeking to empower themselves at the expense of nobilities, at times inciting dynastic warfare. The Protestant Reformation had begun to roil the continent and, especially in England, provoked bitter and bloody struggles over the meaning and destiny of the Christian faith. And some noble and gentry landlords, looking to boost crop yields and wool-producing flocks, began to experiment with new agricultural techniques, some of which (especially enclosures) severed the customary ties that peasants and cottagers had to the land and created a growing body of "masterless" men: effectively internal refugees who wandered the countryside or headed to towns and cities and who struck fear into the heart of the established order. No longer subject to the direct authority of their betters, these masterless men were regarded as beggars, thieves, vagabonds, and likely fomenters of unruliness. Over the course of the sixteenth century, the English Parliament enacted new vagrancy codes with severe punishments—whipping, branding, enslavement, banishment, and, for multiple offenses, even hanging—to bring the problem under control. This is what Hakluyt the Younger had in mind when he wrote that colonization could save "greate nombers that for trifles may otherwise be devoured by the gallows."[4]

Yet this was also a world in which subjecthood, vassalage, and servitude remained important and retained their economic and cultural currency amid change. It was a world in which a Christian crusading spirit was reenergized and redirected, setting Protestants against Catholics rather than Christians against Islam, on both sides of the Atlantic, to convulsive and bloody ends. It was a world in which new vertical allegiances were being struck and extra-economic compulsions remained the norm when it came to labor, and in which wealth was generated by familiar commercial devices, control over people and land, and widespread predation. Little wonder that when early English colonizers envisioned their encounters with Native peoples in North America the image that came to mind was of subjects and tributaries to the king—as was true for the Spanish in the Americas—what the historian Nicholas Canny has called "pseudo-feudal ceremonies." With colonization, that is, the social, cultural, and political ties between Europe and North America were by no means broken only to be utterly reconstituted; those ties were redeployed.[5]

The very idea of colonization had a long history in England owing to subjugation by the Roman empire, and it did not immediately conjure overseas conquests and expansions, whether to Asia, Africa, or North America. As late as the 1580s, little attention was devoted to North America despite the urgings of the Hakluyts; for the English, the lands and subject populations at issue were in Scotland and especially Ireland. There, claimants to the English crown were interested in extending their power and authority, and, in the aftermath of the Reformation, bringing "civilization" to those they regarded as savage and heathen. Gaelic Irish, as the English saw them, "live like beastes, voide of lawe and all good order . . . more uncivill, more uncleanly, more barbarous and more brutish in their customs and demeanures than in any other part of the world." Elizabeth I and her minions determined to make the Irish her subjects, reform their "loose and barbarous ways," and suppress those who sought to resist with unbridled brutality. Humphrey Gilbert, best known for reaching Newfoundland before perishing at sea, first served as governor of Ulster and participated in hunting down Irish rebels. "The heads of all those who were killed in the daie," he ordered, "should be cutte off from the bodies and brought to the place where they encamped at night . . . and be laid there" to bring "greate terror to the people when thei sawe the heddes of their deade fathers, brothers, children, kindsfolk and friends."[6]

Conquest was followed by colonization, and the conquerors expected rich rewards. The English crown offered up thousands of acres of land to prospective landlords—especially to those making conquest possible—who then hoped to attract both English migrants and conquered Irish natives to their estates as tenants and laborers. Many more thousands of acres came from the expropriation of lands held by the Gaelic Irish who refused to submit. Recognizing, as Machiavelli had argued not long before, that the expansion of territorial power was better served by wielding it on the ground than from afar, the English looked to establish colonies in Munster and Ulster, moving well beyond the "pale" of previous occupation. The colonies were described as "plantations," not in the sense of large commercially oriented estates, but rather in the sense of settlements that embodied English civil, political, and spiritual life, including the hierarchies and aristocratic flavors that the conquerors valued or to which they aspired. Before the 1640s, the colonization of Ireland brought about 100,000 migrants from England, Scotland, and Wales, outpacing the streams crossing the Atlantic and making for an important early experience of colonialism.[7]

I

DURING THE NEARLY TWO CENTURIES of English colonization that preceded the American Revolution, roughly 800,000 men,
women, and children migrated across the Atlantic or from the Caribbean to North America. Of these, about 600,000, or 75 percent, came
in some condition of unfreedom. Perhaps as many as 350,000 were
of African descent and had been enslaved in West and West Central
Africa and endured the horrific Middle Passage or had been reex-
ported as slaves from parts of the West Indies. As many as 250,000
were Europeans, mostly English and Irish, who had entered into
indentured servitude either before they departed the British Isles or
when they arrived in North America. Both servants and the enslaved
arrived in all of the English colonies, and in so doing, gave important shape to the political economies and legal regimes that developed
there even if their numbers varied from placed to place. Which is to
say that the peopling of British North America was fed by the transport of coerced laborers and that the societies built from Massachusetts to Georgia were framed, to a greater or lesser extent, around
their presence and the work they did.[8]

The development of servitude and slavery in British North America followed an arc that had already been defined by the Portuguese
in Brazil, and then by the Spanish, English, French, and Dutch in
the Caribbean. Once a marketable crop had been found—sugar in
most areas of the Western Hemisphere, tobacco and rice in North
America—European colonizers first attempted to coerce or enslave
Native peoples to cultivate it. When that failed, as it mostly did outside of colonial Mexico and Peru, they turned to a familiar source:
servants of European descent whose terms generally depended on the
colonies in which they arrived.[9]

The English may have abandoned slavery, serfdom, and vil-
leinage (feudal tenancy) in their homeland much before, but servitude had a long and still significant history, with labor at many sites
being performed under the supervision and personal domination of
an employer or "master." Apprentices learned the skills of a trade.

Household servants tended to kitchens and children. Farm tenants on customary leases cultivated crops and raised livestock. Orphans and paupers were ordinarily "bound out" to keep them under control. At all events, they bowed to the personal power and direction of the master and could be subject to harsh discipline, including corporal punishment, for disobedience and insubordination. Many for all intents and purposes belonged to their masters during the terms of their service. Modern notions of "free labor" were neither current nor enforced by the courts. Landowners and other employers in England simply assumed that the only way to get someone to work, and keep them at it, was by means of force and extra-economic coercion. And there were few grounds for disputation.

If anything, the indentured servitude that emerged in the North American colonies was harsher and less predictable than in England, especially though not exclusively in the Chesapeake colonies of Virginia and Maryland. The largest number of servants arrived in the Chesapeake between 1630 and 1690, when they made up 80 percent of the 79,100 European migrants and somewhere between 20 and 30 percent of the entire labor force. For the most part, they were laborers from humble backgrounds, young, likely unmarried, overwhelmingly male, with little or no personal property, who had signed contracts for terms of service ranging from four to seven years. During their terms, the servants were the property of their masters, subject to the masters' authority, and expected to perform the work that masters demanded of them. They could be, and were, bought and sold. Refusal to obey their masters or running away from them—a particularly common form of resistance—would result (if caught) in whippings, brandings, or longer terms of service, or all of these if they were repeat offenders. Should they complete their terms, indentured servants were entitled to "freedom dues," which included a new suit of clothes, several bushels of corn, farming tools, and possibly access to land. But, certainly during the first half of the seventeenth century, the mortality rate from disease, overwork, and Indigenous raiding was such that few could expect the dues that "freedom" might offer. Like other Europeans in the population, they died in droves.

The high mortality rate made servants an economically sensible investment compared to the other coerced labor option becoming available: enslaved Africans. The first of these appear to have arrived in English North America some time in 1619, along the Virginia coast and under the auspices of Dutch and Portuguese traders (and they cost twice what servants did). August 1619 has long been identified as the moment when "20 and odd negars" were initially sold to English colonists, though there is evidence that enslaved Africans were in Virginia since at least the previous spring. Either way, little is known about them except that, for the next three decades, enslaved Africans were few in number, lived principally within the laws of servitude, and probably worked alongside European servants in the fields; some even managed to gain manumission. Indeed, during the first half of the seventeenth century in English North America, there may have been more people of African descent outside of the Chesapeake than inside it despite the development of the tobacco economy.[10]

The rise of a staple-growing economy in the Chesapeake, founded on the coerced labor of servants and slaves, framed the English settlement process there and the forms of political power that would come to dominate the colonies for decades. In 1618, as tobacco production began to take hold, the Virginia Company, chartered by the Crown in 1606, adopted a "headright" system to encourage the migration of planters and laborers. English household heads could receive land grants for themselves along with additional acreage for family members and indentured servants. And although most of the Chesapeake farming units during the seventeenth century were relatively small in size and worked principally by household labor with, perhaps, a few servants or slaves, the makings of a social system based on large landed estates and large numbers of coerced laborers soon became evident.[11]

The Crown appointed the most important colonial officials, and the governors of Virginia illustrated how the worlds of politics and estate-building were mutually reinforcing. Francis Wyatt and William Berkeley, two of the early governors, came from noble and landed gentry backgrounds respectively, had aristocratic ambitions for the colony, and took care to construct their own versions of lordly life replete with land, servants, and slaves. Berkeley, who served as governor for nearly three decades over two different terms (1641–52, 1660–77), rewarded his allies with land and licenses to trade with Native peoples, appointed wealthy landholders to office, and had nothing but contempt for the smallholders and servants who could not participate in Virginia's governance yet were burdened with taxes to support Berkeley's regime. "I thank God there are no free schools nor printing," Berkeley scoffed, "and I hope we shall not have these for a hundred years; for learning has brought disobedience and heresy into the world." As the *Southern Literary Messenger* reflected nearly two centuries later, "we find power of every sort—legislative, executive, judicial, and military—uniting in the hands of a class of men who, as descendants of the ancient nobility of England . . . and as proprietors of large estates, masters of indented servants, and lords of slaves, controlled the Social destinies of the colony."[12]

The headright system, devised in colonial Virginia, was embraced by the proprietors of the prospective colony of South Carolina, with the hope of luring planters from the increasingly crowded island of Barbados, where sugar production had taken off on the backs of enslaved laborers at mid-century. Their vision was decidedly manorial, as the Fundamental Constitutions of Carolina, drafted in 1669, made clear. The proprietors wished to divide the Carolina colony into counties, each composed of signiories, baronies, precincts, and manors, with vast estates (up to 12,000 acres) over which proprietors and chosen grantees would preside. To "avoid erecting a numerous democracy," a proprietary council would govern the colony as a whole and a hereditary nobility would be established. A number of courts under the supervision of proprietors, signiories, and baronies but also involving councilors and jurors who were property-holding freemen, would have the powers of trial and punishment. And, acknowledging the social basis of the society, "every freeman of Carolina" was given "absolute power and authority over his negro slaves, of whatever opinion or religion soever."[13]

Remarkably, the Fundamental Constitutions was written in large part by John Locke who, in 1669, may already have drafted parts of his *Two Treatises of Government*, regarded by many as one of liberalism's founding texts. There, Locke attacked Robert Filmer's notions of patriarchy and divine rule, depicted an atomized state of nature and the contractual basis of government and civil society, presented individual labor as the foundation of private property claims, and imagined the self-ownership that all people possessed as "inalienable." Slavery, Locke described as "so vile and miserable an Estate of Man," but, at least in the abstract, he understood legitimate forms of enslavement as the consequence of captivity in "just wars."

In this, Locke was echoing long-held views on the European continent, not to mention practices in regular use among societies in Africa and the Western Hemisphere where, in effect, captives traded their lives for service to their captors. Less abstractly, Locke had investments in the newly established Royal African Company that marked England's direct entry into the Atlantic slave trade as well as in Bahamian landed estates. The point here is not the hypocrisy of John Locke, who linked illegitimate (and heritable) slavery to the system of absolute monarchical power; it is rather that from the earliest articulations of what would come to be called "liberal universalism," exclusionary impulses were at play that would always threaten to teeter into and fortify illiberal projects and sensibilities.[14]

Locke's investments suggest some important changes in the development of enslavement in English North America. By the time the settlement of South Carolina took shape, after 1670, the colonies of Barbados and Virginia had begun shifting away from the use of white indentured servants, importing more enslaved Africans, and compiling codes of law that were distinctive to a regime of slavery that was African-descended. These codes not only included an assortment of provisions and prohibitions meant to hedge in the worlds of enslaved laborers and enhance the power and prerogatives of their enslavers; they also included laws to define slavery's permanence and heritability (matrilineal), equate Blackness with enslavement, delimit the role that Christianization might play in the status of the enslaved, and distinguish the subordination of the enslaved from that of indentured servants.[15]

This shift owed to a confluence of developments that, in one way or another, touched the mainland and Caribbean alike. The supply of white indentured servants began to dry up as economic conditions in England improved and the servants already in the colonies proved increasingly difficult to control. Colonial officials, particularly in the Chesapeake, resorted to extending terms of service, enacting more severe punishments for insubordination, and limiting what few civil and political rights freed servants could claim. Governor Berkeley refused to call elections to the colonial assembly (the House of Burgesses) for years after 1660, and in 1670 the long-sitting assembly disfranchised landless white freemen because they had "little interest in the country" and "doe oftener make tumults at the election to the disturbance of his majesties peace." It all blew up in their faces. Small-scale rebellions erupted in 1661 and 1663, and, in 1676, freemen, servants, and some of the enslaved rose up in what has come to be known as Bacon's Rebellion, the largest in the history of colonial North America. The rebels torched the Virginia seat of government (Jamestown), forced royal Governor Berkeley to flee, and nearly toppled the colonial regime.[16]

At the same time, the English Crown had coordinated with London merchants to organize the Royal African Company (1660), which put English slave traders on the ground along the African coast and enabled them to transport the enslaved from Africa directly to English colonies in North America and the Caribbean. English enslavers consequently had greater access to enslaved laborers than was the case when they had to deal with the Portuguese, Spanish, or Dutch. Larger numbers of enslaved laborers became available as well. Not surprisingly, the Crown, newly restored to power after two decades of civil warfare in England, was keen to promote the development of slavery and slave regimes not only in South Carolina and the Chesapeake but also in the Mid-Atlantic and New England colonies, where the enslaved could already be found in small numbers. In the Mid-Atlantic and New England, a similar political and legal trajectory unfurled—new laws and codes focused on enslavement were enacted—even as enslaved people were, for the most part, absorbed into economic activities constructed mainly around household production and forms of mercantile activity.

For the next century, slavery became increasingly important to the North American colonial economies up and down the Atlantic coast.

The Narragansett country in Rhode Island looked something like the Chesapeake, boasting large landed estates and enslaved laborers supplied by Newport merchants, Quakers prominent among them, who were some of the most active slave traders in the Atlantic. In the hinterlands of southeastern Pennsylvania, in the Jerseys, on Long Island, and in the Hudson and Delaware Valleys, enslaved men and women worked in diversified agricultural economies, while in the port cities of Boston, New York, and Philadelphia they were numerous as laborers and domestic servants. Perhaps as many as half of the white households in these ports, often headed by artisans and merchants, included enslaved workers. Farther to the south, the slave-based staple economies expanded rapidly, and in South Carolina a Black majority could be found as early as 1710.[17]

The emergence of African-descended enslavement as a social system in British North America and, owing to their numbers and economic centrality, as the basis of social order in Virginia, Maryland, Delaware, the Carolinas, and Georgia may have allowed most white Europeans, especially those of humble station, to avoid the kind of direct exploitation they had suffered as indentured servants and to have some hope of becoming independent landowners during the course of their lives. In this way, rather than continuing as a repressed laboring class who looked upon their masters and landlords as their exploiters, they could begin to view the world more from the perspective of the exploiters themselves, holding power over dependent members of their households and perhaps hoping to join the ranks of enslavers.[18]

Yet we must be careful about making too much of this logic. By the end of the seventeenth century most of the readily accessible land in the Chesapeake had been engrossed by large landholders and speculators; many former servants were left with the choice of tenancy within the bounds of the colonies or the search for land in territories claimed by Native peoples. In Maryland during the 1690s, three-quarters of free household heads had very little or no property and could expect a life of rude subsistence. Those who managed to obtain small tracts of land struggled to raise sufficient food and market crops, often found themselves in debt, and depended on the services of large landowners for supplies and the marketing of what tobacco they may have grown. It would, according to one careful historian, stretch the meaning of the term to call them "yeomen." The backcountries of the Middle Atlantic, the Chesapeake, and the Carolinas thereby filled up with armed and, in many cases, desperate white men who looked to take matters into their own hands, sparking brutal warfare with Native peoples and inviting the scorn of the wealthy elites. There would be reckonings of different sorts in later decades.[19]

Thus, the notion that the institutionalization of African-descended enslavement and the decline of white indentured servitude produced a binary of Black slavery and white freedom in British North America is, to say the least, misconstrued. The social relations that marked the turn of the eighteenth century, and continued for long thereafter, can far better be understood as a spectrum of dependencies along which "free labor," in a form familiar to us, was at the far end. Most European inhabitants in the countryside were tenants, laborers, and servants or they lived in states of dependency (wives and children) in the households of property owners. As for those who began to work for wages, whether in rural or urban areas, their legal status remained in the category of "master and servant," which lent employers enormous power, even if the relation was initiated by contractual agreement, and left workers with an assortment of burdens, including penalties for a contract's breach. William Blackstone confirmed this in his *Commentaries* of 1765, widely referenced in American jurisprudence, and it endured until late in the nineteenth century. Labor's coercions in their starkest forms of enslavement and servitude gave North American colonialism its main economic dynamics. Along a wider spectrum, they fueled the economic growth and early industrialization of what became the United States.[20]

II

AMONG THE PASSENGERS on the famed *Arabella,* which sailed from the coast of England to Salem, Massachusetts, in the spring of 1630, were eight servants, "names unknown" according to records of the voyage, who tended to the needs of John Winthrop. Puritan though he was, Winthrop was also to the manor born—Groton Manor in Suffolk, to be precise, where Winthrop did become "lord of the manor"—and was undoubtedly accustomed to collections of servants as he looked after affairs of the estate and his law practice. But there were incentives other than household maintenance and creature comforts to bring the servants along. Like that of Virginia, the charter for the new plantation of Massachusetts Bay rewarded stockholding "adventurers" with grants of 200 acres and an additional 50 for each worker they carried in. These servants would be crucial to turning Winthrop's 600-acre tract along what the English called the Mystic River into "Ten Hills Farm," which would include among its denizens both enslaved Natives and enslaved Africans.

Perhaps because servitude was so familiar to him, Winthrop did not seem troubled by the enslavement of Native or Black people. His eldest son, Henry, was involved in the colonial founding of Barbados in the late 1620s, and Winthrop himself noted without comment the arrival in Massachusetts from the West Indies in 1638 of the first enslaved Africans. They apparently had been traded for seventeen enslaved Native Americans as well as for supplies of cotton and tobacco. Later on, Winthrop's youngest son, Samuel, emerged as a wealthy enslaving planter on the island of Antigua, residing on an estate he named "Groton Hall," commemorating his English birthplace. Meantime, when the Massachusetts General Court (the colonial assembly) crafted a *Body of Liberties* in 1641, long hailed as an early antecedent of the constitutional Bill of Rights, "bond slaverie villinage, or Captivitie among us" was prohibited "unles it be lawful Captives taken in just warres, and such strangers as willingly belie themselves or are sold to us," not exempting those judged to be in servitude "by Authoritie."[21]

Those who recall Winthrop and his famed text (some call it a sermon) "A Modell of Christian Charitie" for its seemingly utopian idea of establishing a "citty upon a hill," might usefully remember too how Winthrop began the text. He exhorted his followers that "God Almighty . . . hath soe disposed of the condition of mankind, as in all times some must be rich, some poore, some high and eminent in power and dignitie, some mean and in submission." In this, Winthrop expressed a Puritan view of social relations organized in hierarchies of high and low, superiors and inferiors who could "delight in eache other" and "knitt" themselves together, "as one man," into something of an organic whole. And it was a view that gave shape to the "plantations" that Puritans established during the seventeenth century in Massachusetts, Connecticut, and much of what John Smith had already dubbed "New England" for its physical likeness to the countryside he knew in Old England.[22]

The "plantations" set down in Plymouth, Salem, Massachusetts Bay, and other parts of eastern New England have been reckoned, since at least the 1950s, as seed beds of a later American republic and liberal political dispositions more generally. This is because formal agreements—the *Mayflower Compact*, the *Body of Liberties*—were made among the migrants and settlers to organize a "Civil Body Politic" or a "little commonwealth," to enact "just and equal laws," and lend an assortment of rights to the inhabitants (especially the male inhabitants). The plantations also established town meetings and elective institutions that encouraged wide participation in community affairs and seemed to reflect a parliamentary orientation while anticipating an eighteenth-century republicanism. Yet Winthrop's text should caution us against making over-direct connections and, instead, suggest that the context and political dynamics were far more complex and, perhaps, far less liberal or republican than they might appear. What "knitt" the plantations together were not rights, representation, local democracy, and economic independence; they were faith, conversion, interventions, deference, interdependence, exclusions, and coercions.[23]

This is not to say that New England plantations were "traditional" peasant villages transplanted on North American soil. Those who made up what historians have called the "great migration" of the 1620s and 1630s were more likely artisans, shopkeepers, merchants, ministers, and lawyers than farmers. And they came mainly from the south and southeast of England, from rural places in close proximity to towns and cities, where economies and local governments had been undergoing a variety of reforms, organizationally and spiritually. These reforms were then reflected in the "towns" that plantation authorities created.[24]

In Massachusetts Bay, the General Court would grant tracts of land to aspiring townships (that doubled as congregations), which would, in turn, distribute lots and parcels to families for dwelling, cultivation, and forage. The parcels would be held in "freehold" rather than "leasehold," and they were considerably larger than what rural folk in England could expect to farm. But, as the making of Winthrop's Ten Hills Farm demonstrated, the plantation proprietors, persons of status (religious or political), and those with larger families and servants would be privileged and come away with more sizeable landholdings. "Proportionable to his estate," as it might be put. They would, as well, serve disproportionately as members of the General Court and as town "selectmen," as those who fashioned the governance of the plantation and the towns. Which is to say that plantations and townships envisioned unequal and overlapping property claims; that freeholds were made by townships and could not be separated from the powers and claims that townships and their proprietors possessed. "A New England town," the historian Allan Greer writes, was "an active creator of new landed property" much in the manner of the feudally inspired and chronologically coincidental Canadian seigneurie.[25]

In this empowered capacity, townships ordinarily held back a substantial amount of land ("undivided commons") for future distributions: for the children, and later the grandchildren, of town inhabitants so that they could continue to reside in the township and have a landed/freehold basis for their own families, subsistence, and trade. By extension, what is striking over the course of the seventeenth century and, in many cases, well into the eighteenth, are the roles that town governing institutions, whether of church or state, played in marking the rules and boundaries of economic life. These involved the surveilling of households, the instruction and punishment of children, the organization of labor, the availability of land, and admission to the township itself.

Indentured servants did not migrate to New England in the large number characteristic of colonies to the south and, especially, to the Chesapeake. During the seventeenth century, roughly 86,000 Europeans came as servants to the Chesapeake (about 80 percent of all migrants) while only 4,000 came to New England (about 17 percent of all migrants). And it appears that New England laborers were paid relatively high wages compared with other English plantations in North America. But the political economy of New England towns also revealed various forms of servitude, particularly for the young, accompanied by efforts to enforce discipline, fasten the subordination of laborers, and construct a culture of severe punishment for those who refused to submit. Servitude could involve apprenticeship, the "binding out" of children to other families, long-term dependency in patriarchal households, or, quite simply, work for someone else. As the historian Edmund S. Morgan argued, anyone so employed was, by definition, a "servant" in township eyes. Debtors and those convicted of offenses against the town could also be subject to servitude.[26]

John Winthrop's *Journal*—the most remarkable source we have for the early history of Massachusetts Bay—devoted more attention to punishments for misbehavior than to sermons emphasizing proper conduct, and the whipping post was in regular use to discipline servants or children for sloth or disobedience: usually with crowds in attendance. The *Massachusetts Body of Liberties* prescribed a "40-stripe" maximum, harking to *Deuteronomy* 25:1–3, while most of the New England colonies responded to insubordinate behavior in the 1630s and 1640s by extending the terms of guilty servants, much as was done in the Chesapeake. Young men and women who lived alone, or not under some sort of "domestic government," were eyed with great suspicion and subject to harassment or banishment. "Both servants and children," historian Barry Levy writes, "faced years of subordination, menial work, and physical correction at a time of youthful energy and lust."[27]

The means by which townships policed the social relations and behaviors of their inhabitants—policed their interior spaces—were matched by their patrolling of township boundaries. These were two sides of the same coin of social order and political stability. Township authorities controlled admission and access to its lands, could require bonds from those seeking to engage in trade, expelled those who transgressed community norms or proved to be too much of a burden on town resources, and "warned off" outsiders who threatened the labor pool or were regarded as "transients." Roger Williams's and Anne Hutchinson's expulsions as heretics are best known, but theirs were only the most glaring examples of what we might call cultural "cleansings" that proved crucial to the organization and defense of plantations and townships. As the founders of Dedham, Massachusetts, put it, "We shall by all means labour to keepe off from us all such, as are contrary minded. And receive only such unto us as be such as may be probably of one harte, with us as that we either knowe or may well and truly by informed to walk in peaceable conversation . . . for the edification of each other in the knowledge and faith of the Lord Jesus." One historian has described these sensibilities and the repressive actions they provoked as "local xenophobia."[28]

The Puritan faith, even in its contested forms, gave enormous reinforcement to these social and political imperatives. Indeed, they were mutually constitutive. It is true, of course, that Puritanism, like Protestantism more generally, broke with many of the hierarchical aspects of Catholicism and advanced ideas that could be associated with liberal modernity. Protestants rejected the power of the pope and the priesthood, the centralization of sacred authority, the rituals and ceremonies of the church, the Latin Bible and Mass. They embraced a relationship with God that was personal and direct rather than mediated by priests and other clerics. They disdained icons and saints, priestly wardrobes and the sacrament. They wished, instead, to construct a simpler and purer church of Jesus Christ. For Protestants and, especially, for Puritans, the congregation was the basic unit of their church (they were also known as "Congregationalists"), and they insisted that congregations choose and, if necessary, dismiss their own ministers, that the Bible be read, studied, and discussed (and so it had to be translated into English from the Latin), and that congregants behave in godly ways. From the outset, Puritans referred to themselves as "the godly"; the term "Puritan" originated in the mid-sixteenth century as one of insult and derision.

At the center of Puritan theology and thought was the notion, shaped by Luther and Calvin, of a "covenant of grace." This meant that God's offer of salvation was premised on faith rather than obedience and works, and was determined even before birth ("predestination"). Puritan congregants shared the experience of "justification" (salvation) in an intense emotional and spiritual conversion, enacted before the entire congregation, which would consecrate each and all of them as "visible saints," who could then become church members. Good behavior could never be a means to the end of salvation; it was merely a sign of salvation. "Sanctification flowes from Justification," as the Puritans had it.[29]

Yet, so much of what bounded Puritan godliness and lived experience was a rigid and even authoritarian understanding of the deployment of God's power. Puritan faith was based on the idea of human depravity and sinfulness for which neither submission nor the good offices of the devout nor any form of human agency could atone. God's dispensation of grace to the saintly few had no logic that humans could divine—God was, in effect, unfathomable—but his word and teachings, according to Puritans, were clearly and unerringly recorded in the Bible. The world, they believed, was neatly divided between "visible saints" who had been rewarded with God's grace and the mass of sinners who could not be forgiven and implicitly threatened the Devil's lures and destruction. Even those whose personal relationship with God enabled their justification were themselves the field of God's sovereignty rather than their own. And even the justified, the regenerated, person faced the ongoing temptations of sin though now fortified with the means to resist it. Piety in all of life's domains was regarded only as the sign of salvation, as the visible indicator. "The chief value of a Puritan's actions in his own eyes was symbolical," the historian Perry Miller tells us; "they were emblems of his election rather than ethically commendable deeds." Although salvation was believed to be an "ascertainable experience" that also could be recognized with "outward evidences"—as in the narrative of personal conversion—Puritans were nonetheless plagued by doubts that could easily slide into despair.[30]

Thus, while the Puritan faith ostensibly created a community of God's graced, it also produced searing emotional and existential struggles that help account for the heavy hands of authority coming down continuously in public and private life. No real distinction between the public and private could, in fact, exist, for as John Winthrop intoned, "a family is a little common wealth, and a common wealth is a greate family." There was no room for different interpretations of scripture, no leeway for violations of God's commands, no place for the unregenerate, no flaunting of township rules and expectations. Any of this suggested that the saved could be sinners after all. Church and state had discrete spheres of activity but were also inextricably linked. While ministers could not hold political office, only church members—visible saints—could vote for and become officeholders themselves. And while townships and plantations adumbrated, often at considerable length, the rights that could be claimed, those rights were available only to members of the church and the town in which they resided. In effect, the very idea of "rights," not to mention "obligations," were relevant in a specific community context. There was nothing of the universalism that we have come to associate with liberal modernity or that was being articulated by radical Levellers back in England. The rights and obligations, enforced by what could be brutal and summary community justice, "knitted" the saints together against the anti-Christ, whether in Catholic or Protestant guise.[31]

As might be expected, the social and cultural order that Puritan plantations devised during the first half of the seventeenth century proved difficult to maintain. Population pressures owing to births and immigration pushed at the boundaries of townships and eventually led to partitions or out-migration and the creation of new townships to the west or north. The shrinking of the "undivided commons" made it more difficult for parents to provide for their children, provoking generational tensions or the relaxing of patriarchal power. And although the children of visible saints automatically became church members, fewer of them experienced conversion and thereby raised serious questions about the meaning of church membership and the town community. The "halfway covenant," which offered partial church membership to the grandchildren of visible saints (1662), was one accommodation to change.

Especially startling, and revealing, were examples of rebelliousness from those among the most exploited and subordinated: children and servants. Many had suffered corporal punishment; some had suffered expulsion and subsequent transiency. But others could find ways, within the parameters of township life and Puritan faith, to inflict their own forms of justice and potentially lethal punishment on adults. The notorious and deadly episode of witchcraft in Salem, Massachusetts, one of the oldest of the townships that was rent by many of the stresses of growth and conflict, erupted, after all, among female children and servants. And while their initial accusations targeted older women who defied Puritan norms, including an enslaved woman of Native descent, the accusations quickly moved up the social ladder and threatened to upend the Salem elite before religious and political authorities stepped in. This would be the last of more than ninety witchcraft crises that roiled New England over the course of the seventeenth century. But the dynamics at play would find different expressive outlets, and it was no accident that the Salem witch trials occurred at a time of warfare with Native peoples to the north that strained the resources and wherewithal of the town.[32]

III

FOR THE MANY THOUSANDS of Indigenous peoples who lived in villages large and small along the Atlantic coast, some part of wide-ranging constellations of social and political power, the arrival of European settlers would not have raised many eyebrows. Since the late fifteenth century if not before, European explorers, traders, and fishermen had made contact with them and began to exchange goods that were quickly absorbed into Indigenous societies and eventually entered their own networks of trade, reaching as far west as the Great Lakes region and as far south as the Gulf Coast. What moved across Native North America even more rapidly were pathogens that in some cases sickened and claimed the lives of villagers well before they laid eyes on Europeans. The impact would be catastrophic and indelibly mark the balances of power on the ground and the larger arc of colonialism. At the beginning of the sixteenth century, according to some estimates, between five and ten million Native peoples were to be found on the North American continent; by the end of the eighteenth century there were probably no more than 600,000.[33]

Historians and other scholars who developed the idea of an American liberal tradition had even less to say about Native peoples in North America than about enslaved Black people and the larger system of enslavement. If anything, they seem to have accepted the perspectives of seventeenth-century European settlers who regarded Natives as primitive sorts who engaged in hunting and gathering rather than sedentary agriculture for their subsistence and had little or no sense of private property (John Locke gave expression to this view in his *Second Treatise*), or as savages and heathens. At all events, Native peoples appeared to evaporate in the face of the liberal juggernaut, though not before contributing to various "myths" about the colonial settlement of North America and to cultural visions of the trans-Mississippi West.

Now we know much better. Thanks to remarkable studies over the past half century, we have come to recognize the complex worlds that Native peoples constructed and reconstructed well before contact with Europeans, the many linguistic groups that emerged among them, the range of political economies and trading networks they fashioned, and the political and diplomatic relations that held them together and made for alliances and warfare. We have also come to see how Europeans and Natives transformed each other through contact, conflict, and accommodation: making new cultural and political worlds however much they were marred by contrasting objectives and misapprehensions.[34]

English settlers in the Chesapeake and New England encountered rather different Native societies. In Virginia, a powerful Powhatan leader (Wahunsonacock, their *mamanatowick* or paramount chief) had organized an Algonquian-speaking confederation of as many as thirty tribes that together engaged in horticulture and fishing as well as hunting. In New England, smaller bands, each with their own sachems or chiefs, were connected with Wampanoags, Mohegans, Pequots, Patuxets, Narragansetts, Massachusetts, Pennacocks, and Nipmucks, who also combined farming and fishing with hunting and gathering. What they all shared was an idea of power based on trade, tribute, gifting, submission, and the use of space.[35]

In some important respects, the English were not all that different in their ideas of power. Their plantations were made possible by royal charters. They imagined trade and tribute as central features of their relations with Native peoples. Their landholdings even in freehold were distributed by townships or companies and carried obligations to families, churches, and the town or plantation. Their commons were controlled by the towns and the proprietors. Thus, when the English and Natives met, each expected to incorporate the other into their own vertical systems of hierarchy as allies, tribute payers, and—for the English—possibly as coerced laborers, something in the manner of what was envisioned for Ireland. Very early on, Virginia colonists brought the Powhatan chief gifts from England's King James I and asked him to come to Jamestown, receive a crown, and swear allegiance to their king. Wahunsonacock would have none of it. He had already captured, ritually adopted, and released the colonists' leader John Smith, and, so far as he was concerned, the English had effectively submitted to him. "If your king have sent me presents, I also am a king, and this is my land," Wahunsonacock admonished. "Your father is to come to me, not I to him, nor yet to your fort." It was going to be a struggle for domination, with tensions mounting and sparks flying, all the more so when Virginia colonists found a staple crop in tobacco. In 1622, Wahunsonacock's successor launched a massive attack on the English, killing a quarter of the colony's population and, in turn, provoking a decade's worth of devastating retaliations.[36]

The issue of land claims and the use rights that accompanied them have been, as this suggests, of great importance in accounting for the deepening conflicts between English settlers and Native peoples up and down the Atlantic coast. And they have often been presented as involving fundamental differences in the ways in which land claims were understood and misunderstood: the English embracing private and salable property, cloaked with exclusivity; Native peoples viewing land more communally, with various use rights recognized. Even before he sailed to Massachusetts, John Winthrop sought to explain what "warrant" the plantation settlers had "to take that land, which is and hath been of long time possessed of others." "They inclose noe Land neither have they any settled habitation, nor any tame Cattle to improve the Land by," Winthrop noted, "and soe have no other but a

Naturall Right to those countries. Soe if we leave them sufficient for their own use, we may lawfully take the rest." He and others saw in the ways Native peoples plied their subsistence, and their gender division of labor in which women tended to the crops while men hunted and fished, the evidence of backwardness and savagery. But, for the most part, they also believed that Native lands had to be purchased and the purchases documented by deed. Native leaders and negotiators, on the other hand, viewed the "sales" as agreements to "share" in the use of the land rather than permit the settlers outright possession.[37]

Yet, too great a distinction may be misleading. Natives understood the diverse needs that English settlers would have, whether space for dwellings and fields or access to forests, streams, and shorelines for hunting, fishing, and the collection of wood fuel, although these use rights—which could accommodate notions of landed property—were mostly imagined in connection to alliances and tributary relations between the parties. Settlers not only regarded land acquisition and use as a form of transactional possession; they could also regard it as a product of personal relations or moral obligations. Roger Williams, who was a defender of Native (in this case Narragansett) land rights while maintaining a strong commitment to the project of coloniza-tion ("subduing this barbarous Countrey"), thought of the English settlers as seeking "an entrance," an acknowledgment and acceptance of their presence, together with "a Sufficiency," so that they could sustain their settlements with food and forage. At the same time, the English rejected exclusivity as to their farmsteads, for they claimed use rights—hunting, fishing, and foraging—both on unenclosed pri-vate landholdings as well as in the forests and meadows that had not been parceled out among them—and could well have been territory claimed by Native groups. By the mid-seventeenth century, colonial law ratified the arrangement, requiring settlers to fence in their crops instead of their livestock, a practice that would prevail in much of rural North America until late in the nineteenth century.[38]

As it happened, some of the most explosive settler-Native con-flicts derived not from the expansion of the settlers' private landed property but rather from the settlers' use of unenclosed land to raise their pigs and cattle, which they did insist were exclusively theirs.

Native peoples, who relied on game instead of livestock for their meat supply, did not enclose the fields where they cultivated maize, squashes, and pumpkins, and thus stood to have their food crops trampled by the settlers' foraging animals while provoking the settlers' animosity if they either took up or killed the marauding beasts. Colonial encounters in seventeenth century North America, that is to say, were not characterized by two discrete systems of land use, one of which involved modern ideas of absolute private property and one of which was an obverse communalism. The encounters instead revealed complex understandings of use rights, ownership, and obligation that were more appropriate to a world still in the orbit of medievalism rather than on the threshold of modernity.[39]

Unlike their Spanish and French counterparts, English colonizers had little interest in missionizing and converting Native peoples to Christianity. Massachusetts Puritans, under some pressure after they massacred and enslaved around 1,500 Pequots in a brutal 1636–37 war, selling some to the West Indies, did construct a number of "praying towns" in the 1640s. There, with effective confinement and close surveillance, they looked to evangelize and tutor the Native inhabitants in the English ways of speech, dress, and work. Not surprisingly, only a few hundred, most of whom belonged to small and vulnerable bands, submitted to such a regimen, confirmation, if it were necessary, that most were irredeemable heathens. Whether in New England or the Chesapeake, English settlers formed alliances with Natives for the sake of trade and security, while doing their best to force Native groups into the status of tributaries: that is, until the opportunity to extirpate them from the landscape arose. To such an end, the 1670s proved to be an especially explosive and consequential decade, coinciding as it did with the restoration of royal authority in old England and with the great enlargement of the English and great decline of the Native populations in Atlantic North America.[40]

In Virginia, years of Native-settler skirmishing on the western frontier, often over problems of foraging livestock, was intensified as Governor Berkeley saw the Restoration as an opening to advance his neo-feudal vision of landed estates. He recruited younger sons of the English aristocracy and gentry, whose prospects in England were dimming but who could bring resources and servants with them, to stake new aristocratic claims. The recruits had names like Byrd, Jefferson, Bland, and Culpepper, and they would soon be purchasing enslaved Africans. Needless to say, there was scant room for the freed servants and smallholders who, as Berkeley acknowledged, were "Poore, Endebted, Discontented, and Armed." And when their complaints about the neighboring Susquehannocks went unheeded by the Berkeley regime—which wanted to keep trading relations intact and conflict at a minimum—they took matters into their own hands. With John Washington, George's great-grandfather, in the lead, they marched on the Susquehannocks and murdered five of their chiefs. Now Berkeley got the warfare he tried to avoid, and soon, in 1676, a massive rebellion of smallholders, servants, and some of the enslaved as well. When the smoke finally cleared, the rebellion had been crushed—twenty-three of the rebels were hanged—but the Natives saw the writing on the wall. The remnants of the Powhatan chiefdom agreed to accept the "King of England" as their "Soveraigne" and the ultimate holder of their lands in return for protection from aggressive English settlers. Left to their own devices, the Susquehannocks moved northward and disturbed local balances of power as they went.[41]

An equally convulsive episode roiled New England at nearly the same time. Under pressure to surrender both their lands and their weapons, and vexed by the livestock inundating their fields, Native peoples—the Wampanoags in particular—sought to establish a diplomatic equilibrium with Puritan settlers. The Wampanoag sachem Metacom and his brother in fact went before the Massachusetts General Court asking to be granted English names in recognition of their political parity, "subject to the Kinge of England." Metacom thereby became "King" Philip. But there was no parity to be had, only submission, and when the murder of a christianized Native led to the seizure and execution of three of Metacom's advisors by colonial officials in 1675, Metacom launched an all-out war. The Wampanoags would not be alone; they were joined by most Algonquian-speaking people in the region, leaving few, including the decimated Pequots, to support the English side. The Wampanoags and their allies not only inflicted massive damage on English settlements; they also attempted to destroy as much of the English cultural imprint as possible, burning and desecrating dwellings and churches, fields and fences. For months it appeared that New England plantations might be entirely leveled and the settlers driven into the sea.

It was not to be. Fired by their own sense of spiritual conquest and aided by an alliance with Mohawks to the west who were bitter enemies of the Algonquian peoples, the English settlers turned the tide with a brutality that surpassed Metacom's warriors. Before it was over, Metacom himself was shot down, mutilated, and decapitated, his skull set atop a Plymouth tower for all to see. Roger Williams now exulted in the "quenching [of] the Phillipian fire": "God has prospered *us* so that wee had driven the Wampanoogs with Philip out of his Countrie and the Nahigonsiks out of their Countrie and had destroyed multitudes of them in Fighting and Flying, in Hunger and Cold . . . and that God would help us Consume them." The English suffered major losses, but for the Wampanoags and other Native peoples of New England what has become known as "King Philip's War" was a complete disaster. Two thousand were killed or executed. Another three thousand perished from the consequences of hunger, disease, and dislocation. One thousand, including Metacom's young son and wife, were enslaved and shipped off to the West Indies. Perhaps two thousand became refugees, many driven north to settle among the Abenaki. In all, roughly half the population was lost. Those who survived and remained in place learned the new order of things. They would either be remanded to one of four praying towns or forced into servitude for the settlers. So it was that the Puritan plantations, in further rounds of cleansing, began to erase the Native presence from the New England landscape.[42]

IV

THE "MIDDLE COLONIES" of English North American colonialism have come to exemplify many of the features associated with a liberal tradition of social organization, politics, and values. Compared with New England to the north and the Chesapeake to the south, they appeared to be ethnically diverse, religiously tolerant, favorable to the prospects of family farmers, at relative peace with Native peoples among them, and quickly prosperous. "The best poore man's country in the world," as early Pennsylvania was described.[43]

But here again it is best to look outward from the seventeenth century than backward from our own time, for in many respects the "neo-feudal" dreams that shaped colonizing projects beginning in the late sixteenth century and gained support from the Restoration were still very much in evidence. William Penn had converted to Quakerism and imagined a colony that could serve as a refuge for fellow Quakers, a site of religious liberty, and an example of fairness toward the Natives. But Penn and his family already had estates in England and Ireland, and the charter he received in 1681 for 45,000 square miles of land west of the Delaware River was suffused by manorialism. Penn was made the "true and absolute" proprietor of the "Province and Seigniorie" of "Pensilvania," free "to erect any parcels of Land . . . into Mannors." To that end, he quickly sold off half a million acres, much of it in 5,000- to 10,000-acre tracts, and often extended powers to the purchasers to fashion a "barony" with the right to "hold court baron, view of ffrank pledge, and court leet by himself or stewards." Rather than scattered farms, Penn hoped to see manor-centered "agricultural villages" taking hold and initially planned for a bicameral assembly with a house of "lords" and one of "renters." Like the Puritans, he thought "Subordination and Dependency" quite natural and inevitable, and counseled "obedience to superiors, love to equals, and help and countenance to inferiors." As might be expected, servants were part of the mix from the outset (about one-third of the early arrivals), encouraged in much the same way as in Virginia and Massachusetts. Enslaved Africans were soon at work too and, although relatively few, their numbers would grow over the course of the eighteenth century both in the countryside and in the city of Philadelphia.[44]

The Jerseys, like Carolina and to a lesser extent Pennsylvania, were to be organized around aristocratic landholders and rent-paying tenants, and East Jersey was quickly controlled by Scottish investors who imagined large estates and their own version of lordships and made themselves into a board of proprietors with extensive powers over lands and leases. To the north, the Hudson Valley, initially a channel for the Dutch-Native fur trade, saw the emergence of immense manors owned by patroons and staffed by lease-holding tenants, that made easy transitions once the English took charge of Nieu Netherland and the growing port of Nieu Amsterdam. There would be reckonings, as early as the eighteenth century in the Jerseys when smallholders began to struggle over land claims. The manorial world of the Hudson Valley would endure for another century still, to be challenged when patroon paternalism finally broke down.[45]

The culturally polyglot nature of the Mid-Atlantic was surely of significance. Even Carolina and the Jerseys provided havens of religious (Protestant) freedom, and were populated by Swedes, Norwegians, Finns, Netherlanders, Scots-Irish, Irish, Welsh, Germans, French, Flemings, and Walloons, together with a multiplicity of West African ethnic groups and the English: "a crazy patchwork of overlapping linguistic, cultural, and religious zones . . . perhaps the most racially, ethnically, and religiously mixed place in the world," as the historian Peter Silver observes. But if this suggested an early multiculturalism, the reality was far different on the ground. These ethnic and religious groups, when possible—save for the Africans—constructed their own communities and, like the Puritans of New England, both policed themselves, sometimes with struggle, and eyed outsiders with suspicion. Like the Puritans, too, they often celebrated the opportunity to gather and worship as the product of divinely ordained destinies, thereby digging trenches between themselves and others who were not so fortunate and could be regarded as rivals if not as enemies. "*Pennsylvania* is a complete *Babel*," some Moravians scornfully complained. "There are so many different religions here in the countryside," a German settler sighed, "that many times I have not known what I should think about it." Benjamin Franklin seemed to have reached a conclusion. Noting with alarm that the Germans "will soon . . . outnumber us," he called those who descended on the polls during one election, "the Palatine Boors herding together."[46]

As much as the estates that loomed over many acres from Carolina up through New York and Rhode Island, these communities were not just in the process of moving toward something more open, more tolerant, and more liberally inclined. They were very much part of a world constructed by neo-feudal dreams, regimes of coerced labor, social hierarchies, and strong cultural and religious allegiances. With their own insularities, pretensions, and potentially fearful postures, especially toward Native peoples, they left powerful and often disturbing legacies for the future.

Chapter Three

THE POPE, THE KING, AND THE REPUBLIC

O N THE MORNING OF 14 AUGUST 1765, BOSTONIANS woke to a startling sight. An effigy, marked as British secretary Andrew Oliver, was hanging from a tree known as the Great Elm at Deacon Eliot's Corner on the South End of town. Strung up alongside it was a boot (for Britain's Earl of Bute) with the likeness of a devil, pitchfork in hand, crawling out. Boston's sheriff and his officers soon attempted to remove the effigies, but discovered that they could not do so "without imminent danger of their lives." Small wonder. "Almost the whole town," according to one observer, was streaming to Eliot's Corner to watch and participate in a street theater that lasted for hours. When darkness fell, the effigy was taken down and, in a large procession—some derisively called it a "mob" but others described a "great concourse of people" including "gentlemen"—carried it past Boston's Council Chamber where "three Huzzas" were given "by way of defiance." The procession went on to Andrew Oliver's dock where a new building had been erected and, in a matter of minutes, "pulled it down." Then it was on to Oliver's house where the effigy was "beheaded" and "all the Windows next the Street" broken.

From there the crowd carried the effigy to nearby Fort Hill where they burnt it in a "Bonfire made from the Timber they had pulled down from the Building," and then returned to Oliver's house, which they occupied after he and his family had fled. When, around 11:00 p.m., Massachusetts lieutenant governor Thomas Hutchinson and the sheriff showed up and tried to "perswade" them to "disperse," the "ringleader's" greeting was alarming: "The Governor and the Sheriff! To your Arms, my boys!" A "volley of Stones followed," which the two officials "narrowly escaped." Massachusetts governor Francis Bernard tried to call out the militia but learned that many of its members were "probably . . . in the mob," so "nothing more could be done." The crowd finally dispersed around midnight, "at their own Time," but gathered again twelve days later, now targeting custom house and admiralty officers and then laying waste to the home of Lieutenant Governor Hutchinson. "Such ruins were never seen in America," Hutchinson said of the destruction.[1]

The provocation for these crowd actions and what were deemed "riots" was the Stamp Act: a parliamentary tax on newspapers, documents both legal and commercial, and a raft of other printed materials (including playing cards) meant to raise revenue for a British treasury badly depleted by the Seven Years' War—or the "French and Indian War" as it was known in North America. Protests erupted throughout the colonies, especially in port towns where these "papers" were most consequential to everyday life, and they came in a variety of forms. Resolutions were passed, objections penned, meetings held, mostly organized by merchants and members of provincial assemblies who began to rail against the injustice of a tax imposed by a distant parliament without the participation of those burdened by it. Or "no taxation without representation," an eminently republican notion. Patrick Henry steered the radical Virginia Resolutions through the colony's House of Burgesses. Yet the protests also opened a window onto the popular political culture of the era as artisans, laborers, and maritime workers took to the streets and engaged in their own ritualized expressions of grievance and retribution. And although Boston's was especially noteworthy, popular protests occurred in many coastal towns, from Portsmouth, New Hampshire, to Newport, Rhode Island, to Annapolis, Maryland, and to Charleston, South Carolina.[2]

For Bostonians, the choreography was easy to decipher. Andrew Oliver, a prosperous and well-connected city merchant, had been commissioned as the stamp distributor; the Earl of Bute had been British prime minister when Parliament determined to extract revenue from the North American colonies and leave an army there. During the day of the fourteenth, the protest organizers had Oliver's effigy "stamp" the goods farmers and tradesmen brought to market.

Oliver's building on the dock was declared to be the "stamp office" before it was "pulled down to the Ground" and the timber "stamped." Oliver's house was then subject to "assaulting and defacing" while his effigy was subject to a rite of execution before being set ablaze. The custom house and admiralty officials supervised colonial trade, directly affected by the tax, and Hutchinson, whose house was "completely plunderd and sackd," had been in public office for years, accumulating substantial wealth and power. He had also initially called out the sheriff and later accompanied him to Oliver's house in an effort to quell the riot. Not incidentally, Andrew Oliver was Hutchinson's brother-in-law, and, while Hutchinson thought the stamp tax ill-advised, the crowd viewed him as an enabler. "Such is the resentment of the people against the stamp duty," he reflected, "that there can be no dependence on the general court to take any steps to enforce or rather advise the payment of it." Bowing to the public wrath, Oliver quickly resigned his post, as did officials tasked with collecting the tax in other colonies, and before long Parliament itself yielded and repealed the hated act.[3]

One of the "ringleaders" of the Stamp Act "mob" was Ebenezer Mackintosh, a shoemaker, best known until this point for his role as captain of the "South End gang" during the annual, and extremely raucous, Pope's Day celebrations. Commemorating the failed Catholic "gunpowder plot" to blow up Parliament in 1605, Pope's Day (known as Guy Fawkes's Day in Britain) was a largely plebeian and youthful male affair replete with effigies of the pope, the devil, and often the Stuart (Catholic) pretender to the English throne, who were paraded through towns on wheeled platforms, inviting derision and scorn, before they were immolated in a bonfire. In Boston, rival South End and North End gangs each built their own horse-drawn stages with larger-than-life popes dressed in finery and the devil (sometimes the devil's "imps" too) usually coated with tar and feathers. The gangs would advance toward each other, brawl, and try to capture the other gang's effigies. In the end, the winners set the wagons and effigies aflame. No small amount of violence and destruction accompanied the annual rite.[4]

Historians' chief interest in Pope's Day has been in relation to the radicalization of British Americans, especially those of humble station, in the run-up to the American Revolution. They note how cultural forms and rituals like Pope's Day were readily adapted to more overtly political purposes and forms of expression. And we can see good examples of this in the effigies and bonfires that were centrally a part of the Stamp Act protests, and would continue, in a number of different ways, to mobilize public sentiment and punish the mighty British for violations of what were regarded as the colonists' rights. For his part, Ebenezer Macintosh, already a veteran of the French and Indian War, was probably involved in the Boston Tea Party some years later and then certainly fought for a time in the Continental Army during the Revolution. "A Scotch shoemaker was the leader of all our mobs during the time of the Stamp Act," one Bostonian wrote, "and has ever since continued a leading man among us." Yet, what has often been neglected or minimized in historical assessments is the powerfully illiberal strain of anti-Catholicism that coursed through all of this.[5]

I

ANTI-CATHOLICISM IN BRITISH NORTH AMERICA grew out of the Protestant Reformation, Henry VIII's break with the Church of Rome, and the imperial rivalries that set England against Catholic Spain and France. Even more important, Catholicism and "popery" became, by the eighteenth century, the shorthand for tyranny and oppression and thus the enemy of republicanism and what there was of an English identity. However else they differed, John Winthrop and Roger Williams alike fled the "popish relics" in old England and sought to ward off the "anti-Christ" in New England. The deepening rift between Parliament and King Charles I from the 1620s clearly reflected competing views of sovereignty and prerogative as well as the ambitions of sections of the gentry and urban merchants. But it was inflamed by Puritan energies among the Parliamentarians and their hatred of Charles and his Bishop William Laud for their efforts to accommodate Catholics. The bloody English Civil War of the 1640s would allow radical political sensibilities to surface and, in some cases, flourish, but, as the Levellers would reveal in their famed Putney Debates (1647) over the political way forward, they were encased in an English (and anti-Catholic) nativism. Oliver Cromwell's visceral hostility to Catholics and their "heathenism customs and pagan rites," played out in England and Ireland, while the Glorious Revolution of 1688 secured the monarchy against the Catholic menace, with implications on both sides of the Atlantic.[6]

Republican thought of the seventeenth century took hold in this climate of parliamentary struggle, political revolution, and "antipopery." Indeed, what made the work of republican theorists like Algernon Sidney, James Harrington, John Locke, and John Milton possible were the rumblings of the Puritans and Presbyterians in the House of Commons, the Levellers and Independents in the New Model Army, and the even more radical Quakers, Diggers, and Ranters who called into question not only private property and the prevailing social relations of the realm but also the spiritual hierarchies that were so central to Catholicism and the ideas of divine rule. Together they imagined a state of nature in which all were equal and a political society founded on popular consent, representative governing institutions, and a notion of the "public good" that would express the "virtue" necessary to the task. Popular consent was simultaneously a powerful and vague concept and one around which there was a good deal of disagreement. Who were the "people" entitled to offer their consent and be represented? Most of those on the ground as well as among the better-known thinkers believed that property ownership—especially landed property—had to be the basis of political participation, and that an independent and arms-bearing citizenry offered a republic its best protection against internal and external enemies. The radicals among them rejected property qualifications as an unacceptable species of hierarchy and oppression, although only the most radical of all could conceive of servants, paupers, women, or other dependents as part of a body politic. But there seemed to be an abiding sense that a republic, even the sort of democratic republic that few "republicans" could embrace, required a cultural glue that Protestantism either implicitly or explicitly provided.[7]

Anti-Catholicism was not driven by large or growing Catholic populations. Mid-seventeenth-century England counted roughly 120,000 Catholics, perhaps 6 percent of the whole (of course there were likely more given the overall repressive atmosphere), and, outside of Quebec, British North America counted less than 1 percent, with Catholic footholds chiefly in New York, Pennsylvania, and Maryland. Instead, anti-Catholicism was driven by social and political tensions, by fears of conspiracy, subversive power, and corruption, all of which Pope's Day embodied. Over the course of the eighteenth century, and especially after mid-century, the North American coastal economies produced increasing social stratification, especially as the British government attempted to clamp down on trading relations that transgressed the boundaries of the imperial order. Boston, New York, and Philadelphia built their first poorhouses and the share of wealth controlled by the colonial elite grew. Stamp Act protesters may have focused on the potential consequences of parliamentary taxation, ritually punishing those officials who appeared ready to enforce it, but the pillaging of Oliver's and Hutchinson's homes, the breaking of glass windows (which only the prosperous could afford), the destruction of fine furniture, and the raiding of their wine cellars smacked of class resentments. The iconography of Pope's Day, with the effigy of the pope dazzlingly costumed, suggested how anti-Catholic and anti-aristocratic sensibilities could feed off one another.[8]

The question of corruption and its easy association with popery proved particularly appealing as colonial leaders and protesters tried to articulate their mounting opposition to British rule. Corruption, in the republican lexicon, meant pursuing self-interest rather than the public good, accumulating power at popular expense, manipulating the people for private gain. That is to say, power unchecked. It was the very image of the pope and the world of Catholicism that he thrived upon. The pope had unbridled power, denied freedom, and demanded submission. William Blackstone was not alone in believing that Catholicism and freedom were antithetical and that the "popish clergy" were guilty of "frauds and abuses." No proper society, he warned, could possibly be run by Catholics. Sometime after the Stamp Act protests, the Boston radical Samuel Adams insisted "that much more is to be dreaded from the growth of popery in America than from Stamp Acts or *any other acts* destructive of men's *civil* rights," and he worried that Catholics might come to compose an "imperium in imperio," or a nation within a nation.[9]

A few years later, members of the Continental Congress reacted to the Quebec Act (1774), which permitted the practice of Catholicism, allowed the return of Jesuit missionaries, and dramatically expanded the territory of the province into the Great Lakes region and Ohio Country, by fretting about King George III's intention "to establish the Romish Religion and IDOLOTRY" across North America. "Last night," the *New York Journal* reported that very year, "a Gallows with the figures of 3 Men suspended by the Neck, said to represent Lord North, Governor Hutchinson, and Solicitor Wedderburn, with another Figure representing the Devil, were carried through the principal streets of the City, attended by several Thousand People, and at last burnt before the Coffee-House Door." So it was that Pope's Day provided the script—an illiberally inflected one at that—for the popular critique of British imperial governance.[10]

II

THE ICONOGRAPHY OF ANTI-POPERY was readily adaptable to anti-monarchy. The effigy of the pope, bedecked in gorgeous attire and sparkling jewels, could easily have been switched out for a king sitting upon the platformed throne under the watchful eyes and influence of the devil, the great "deceiver." Stamp Act protests in Boston and elsewhere used versions of the Pope's Day ritual to capture the tenor and extent of popular hostility to the tax, as would other politically conscious colonists who bridled at the assortment of impositions the British government heaped upon them. Yet, before 1776, the king was rarely if ever the object of grievance and anger; the targets, instead, were British officials (like Oliver and Hutchinson), ministers, and military officers. When, for example, outraged New Yorkers mounted a Pope's Day–inspired protest against the British Intolerable Acts of 1774, the effigies hanging from contrived gallows were of royal governors, military commanders, and the prime minister, not King George III. If anything, the king was still regarded as the colonists' protector not only against a corrupt Parliament and ministry but also against the ever-present threat of popery.[11]

Loyalty to the English king was widespread and deep in colonial North America, especially after the Glorious Revolution. Search as we might for early indications of the anti-monarchism that erupted during the American Revolution and appeared to frame both the Articles of Confederation and the Constitution, the political culture of the British colonies for the first seven and a half decades of the eighteenth century was organized around the celebration of and submission to royal authority. The political calendar across the colonies, in hinterland villages as well as in seaport towns, was suffused with royal commemorations, whether of the king's (or queen's) birthday, the anniversary of his/her coronation, or of the larger imperial order. The arrival of royal governors, even those who were native-born, occasioned large turnouts, elaborate processions, the firing of cannon, and the marching of militia units. Puritan New Englanders who otherwise scorned public ritual nonetheless cast their objections aside to welcome the embodiments of royalism. Newly appointed Massachusetts governor Jonathan Belcher found all of Boston "preparing for his . . . Reception" in 1730. "Turrets and Balcony's [*sic*] were hung with Carpets, and almost every Vessel was blazon'd with a rich Variety of Colours. . . . The vast Multitude of Spectators express'd, in their united Shouts, an unusual Joy [while the] Regiments discharged their duty in triple Vollies [and the] Evening concluded with a Bonfire and Illuminations." Pope's Day itself, mobilizing popular anti-Catholicism, simultaneously reified Britain's Protestant empire, "the Wonderful deliverance," as one diarist put it in 1758, "the Protestants met with on Nov. 5th."[12]

Although monarchism and republicanism are generally regarded as oppositions, as forms of governance fundamentally different and antagonistic, this is more of a view created by founding narratives than one recognized through much of the eighteenth century. In the midst of the English Civil War, Thomas Hobbes explained how an absolute ruler—the "leviathan"—could represent the popular will, while John Locke, who imagined popular consent producing a parliamentary form of governance, nonetheless later insisted that a well-regulated society required an executive with discretionary authority and that such power was not at odds with the liberty of his subjects. Locke welcomed the Glorious Revolution and thought England's "ancient constitution," with a mixed monarchy, symbolized history's best form of government. North American colonists may have jealously guarded the prerogatives of their elective colonial assemblies, but as tensions mounted in the empire during the 1760s and 1770s more and more of their leaders decried the overreach of Parliament and emphasized the sovereignty of the king. Indeed, what political scientist Eric Nelson calls "dominion theory" gained increasing traction among those laying out patriot grievances: the notion that Parliament's power and jurisdiction ended at the British coastline, that Parliament had no authority to legislate for the North American colonies, and that only the king connected the colonies and the metropolis.[13]

A Massachusetts loyalist thus explained, with sarcasm, that "when the stamp-act was made, the authority of parliament to impose internal taxes was denied but their right to impose external taxes . . . was admitted." Eventually, however, after other duties were set, "it was only taking one step more to extricate ourselves entirely . . . and flatly den[y] that parliament had a right to make any laws whatsoever, that should be binding upon the colonies." Rather, as Pennsylvania's James Wilson, soon to sign the Declaration of Independence and later serve in the Constitutional Convention, put it: "To the King is entrusted the direction of management of the great machine of government. He is therefore the fittest to adjust the different wheels, and to regulate their motions. . . . The connection and harmony between Great Britain and us . . . will be better preserved by the operation of the legal prerogatives of the Crown, than by the exertion of an unlimited authority by Parliament." Thus, the demand was not that Parliament recalibrate and pursue reform—believed impossible because of how corrupt the institution had become—but that the king recover the powers Parliament and its ministers had grabbed. North America, patriot writers argued, was effectively "outside the realm." Parliament was the enemy and the king the ally in the struggle.[14]

The embrace of monarchical power and representative institutions was hardly contradictory in the world of the eighteenth century. This was the English settlement that the revolutionary seventeenth century had devised, and it was quite compatible with the social and political relations in North America. However much "sovereignty of the people" was deemed the basic principle of political organization, representative bodies on both sides of the Atlantic were dominated by relatively small elites, often by interconnected families. Power was understood and displayed in tangible and personal ways, and patronage was both the vehicle of authority and the means by which poorer and middling sorts obtained security and perhaps some measure of mobility. Vertical allegiances and ideas of reciprocity served as the structures and connecting tissues of urban and rural societies alike, and notions of "liberty" and "equality" were recognized not as abstract, universal concepts but rather as the ability to oversee or participate in this patron-client system. The glorification of the yeomanry, Jefferson's "cultivators of the earth" who were the most "valuable citizens" and most "wedded to liberty," was not a call for a producers' republic or democracy. It was an expression of the solidarity that could be forged in the countryside between large and small landowners: a solidarity based on property ownership, patriarchy, and command of labor (household or otherwise) that, in turn, undergirded the deference that the landed elite expected. This was a deference reinforced, among ostensibly "independent" men, through participation in the militia when military titles were conferred on the well-to-do, "treating" (providing alcohol) at the polls on election day, the organization of pews at church, and services the wealthy offered in economic life.[15]

The strength of monarchism and deferential culture encouraged a form of what one scholar has called "naïve monarchism" in the face of developing conflicts in the British imperial system. When rights were trampled upon, reciprocities rejected, or understandings violated, the king could be appealed to as something of a lord "protector" whose wishes were not being carried out or were being wholly transgressed.

There was a strong and complex logic at work. Common to many societies based on monarchy or lordship, the effort to invest the ruler with benevolent intentions both enhanced the ruler's authority and challenged the pretensions of elites on the ground, serving as a form of empowerment for those who had little of it. Enslaved people proved especially adept at constructing alternative structures of power to find allies in their brutal battles. During the 1770s, an enslaved preacher in South Carolina gave his followers a relevant history of royal succession. King George II, he told them, had "rec[eive]d a Book from our Lord by which he was to Alter the World" and free the slaves, but failed to do so and had "gone to Hell." But now, the "Young King [George III]" would carry out the Godly injunction and "set the Negroes Free." The preacher was not alone. Across the eighteenth century and into the nineteenth, slave rebellions—in the British colonies and elsewhere—were often accompanied by rumors that the king had determined to emancipate the enslaved only to have his will thwarted by their enslavers. It was a view that gained some legitimacy when, during the early phases of the Revolutionary War, Virginia's royal governor, the Earl of Dunmore, offered freedom to slaves who left their masters and joined the British side. Enslaved people, much like their owners and the larger free population in North America, had become familiar with imperial culture and politics and sought to use that knowledge to their advantage.[16]

The final collapse of royal authority and the writing of the Declaration of Independence came, significantly, when George III refused the appeal of the Second Continental Congress to take charge of events and put the empire back on its proper course. It was July 1775, months after the first battles had taken place at Lexington, Concord, Bunker Hill, and Breed's Hill, and yet the Congress addressed him as "your majesty's faithful subjects" and spoke of a "just and mild government" and the "remarkably important . . . benefits" that the "union between the Mother country and these colonies" had produced. They blamed "your Majesty's ministers" for the "delusive pretences, fruitless terrors, and unavailing severities" that "have been dealt out," and "with the utmost deference . . . beseech[ed] Your Majesty that your royal authority and influence may be graciously interposed to procure us relief." This is known as the "Olive Branch Petition." But George III refused to play the role that the Congress and patriot leaders had written for him. He rejected the petition and instead declared the colonies "in open and avowed rebellion" and "levying war against us."[17]

This, together with Thomas Paine's widely read and explicitly anti-monarchical pamphlet *Common Sense*—itself a testament to a political and popular culture of monarchism—proved to be the final straws. Battle lines that had been forming since the 1760s were now tightly drawn. Not only British officials but also "Loyalists" and "Tories," those who chose to support the British empire, suffered harassment and ritualistic punishments. They could be fined for refusing Patriot oaths, prevented from teaching, preaching, or practicing law, or driven out of the communities in which they lived. Subjected to rites of popular justice, they could be tarred and feathered, ridden on rails, whipped, or, in a gesture toward Pope's Day, carted around the town or village for shaming and derision. Some were killed in what became civil warfare marked by persecutions, sexual violations, and outright atrocities. In Virginia, Patriot magistrate Colonel Charles Lynch was so quick to hang suspected Loyalists that he lent his name to a horrific category of extralegal execution. John Adams, one of Boston's Patriot leaders, who acknowledged that the majority of colonists supported the British or remained neutral, nonetheless insisted that he would *hang his own brother* if he sided with the Loyalists (his brother didn't).[18]

Yet, a scene in New York City had special political meaning. On the evening of 9 July 1776, after the new Declaration of Independence had been read to a gathering of soldiers serving under the command of George Washington as well as to many men, women, and children in attendance, a crowd, led by the self-designated "Sons of Freedom," marched toward Bowling Green, at the southern tip of Manhattan, where an imposing lead statue of George III on horseback had been standing since 1770—well after the Stamp Act protests. In a symbolic act of regicide, crowd members lashed ropes around the statue, pulled it down, and apparently cut off the head and impaled it on a spike, a punishment fit for a traitor. The rest of the statue was then shipped to Litchfield, Connecticut, where, apparently, the lead was melted down and recast into more than 40,000 musket balls. Like Andrew Oliver, King George III was now declared dead. But it remained to be seen whether some manner of kingly authority would persist in a vision of governance.[19]

III

IN EARLY 1764, a company of about 250 men, most of Ulster and Presbyterian descent, who farmed in the hill country of Lancaster and Cumberland counties, Pennsylvania, marched, arms in hand, toward Philadelphia. Called the Paxton Boys (from one of their towns named Paxtang), they were angered at the Quaker-dominated provincial government for its failure to adequately protect them and their families, its callous disregard of their dangerous predicament, and the representational inequality on which Quaker proprietor power rested. So determined and threatening did they appear that the generally pacifist Quakers mobilized in self-defense, and the new governor, John Penn, called upon Benjamin Franklin, not a Quaker himself, to organize a militia and try to negotiate with the armed men. Halting in nearby Germantown, the Paxton Boys instead drafted "A Declaration and Remonstrance" laying out their grievances and demanding redress. Their sympathizers at the time, along with historical interpreters for long thereafter, portrayed them as the embodiments of what the American Revolution and the American republic would be about: landholding citizens of modest means struggling against oligarchic rule.

The sympathizers and interpreters may have been right for the wrong reasons. Like other settlers along the Pennsylvania frontier, the Paxton Boys had come under fierce Native attack during the recent French and Indian War. And although a formal peace treaty had already been signed between the British and French, a Native confederation including Delawares, Shawnees, Wyandots, Senecas, and Cayugas continued the fight in what is known as Pontiac's War. Their raids, stretching from Pennsylvania south into Virginia and North Carolina, left hundreds of settlers dead and thousands fleeing to safer locales.

The Paxton Boys complained not only of the provincial government's refusal to come to their defense but also of the support and protection the government had offered to their "savage Enemies." Determined no longer "to suffer any Indians of what Tribe soever, to live within the inhabited Parts of this Province," they had already slaughtered twenty Conestogas (descendants of the once-powerful Susquehannocks) residing peacefully on a provincially created tract known as Indiantown, and were headed toward Province Island, in the Delaware River off Philadelphia, to kill the Indians residing there. They professed themselves "loyal Subjects to the best of Kings, our rightful Sovereign GEORGE the THIRD, firmly attached to his Royal Person, Interests, and Government" and "equally opposite to the Enemies of his throne and dignity." "GOD Save the KING," they proclaimed.[20]

The Paxton episode was one of many in the British North American hinterlands, or "backcountry," that had been erupting since the 1740s and would continue to do so at least until the end of the eighteenth century. From the Carolinas to the Maine district of Massachusetts, they generally involved white settlers who tried to secure their land titles, bridled at the apparent collusion between land speculators and provincial and later state governments, and condemned the imbalances of political power that left them vulnerable to expropriation or attack. They often railed against the rich and their supporters in the government, mobilized against officials who tried to evict them or foreclose upon them for unpaid debts, articulated a theory of property based on labor and possession, and presented themselves as defending the survival and integrity of their "communities" against the forces that might destroy them. Like the Paxton Boys, they also regarded Native peoples as savages who had no right to occupy any territory within the bounds of their societies and were therefore to be removed or exterminated. That the provincial and imperial governments might intercede on the Natives' behalf, either to sustain trade or avoid warfare, or, in rare cases, might acknowledge Natives as British subjects, only fueled the settlers' anger, as the Paxton Boys' horrific actions and explanations demonstrated.[21]

The contradictory currents of eighteenth-century backcountry rebellions are important to recognize as context for the early democratic discourses that could emerge in their midst. And they help us see the political and cultural baggage that would be passed down. There can be no doubt that settler resistance to the neo-feudal dreams of many proprietors or the speculative schemes of landed elites shaped the economic landscape and political sensibilities of British North America and the early American republic. Ideas about the nature of property, the legitimacy of representative government, and the very notion of "popular sovereignty" developed in these violence-laden conflicts as they had done in the midst of the English Civil War. Yet in their construction of the savage threat as well as in the autonomy of what they regarded as their communities, they left debilitating and illiberal legacies for many decades to come.

Historians have, for the most part, treated backcountry unrest and rebellion as manifestations of geographical sectionalism (the coast against the interior) and developing social cleavages (the elite coast against the yeoman backcountry). There is a good deal of truth to this. But it obscures as much as it reveals. Colonial settlement of the British North American interior proceeded very rapidly during the eighteenth century and continued apace after the American Revolution. According to one estimate, migration to the frontier between 1760 and 1800 shifted most of the population increase of the time to districts where there had been few if any settlers of European descent in 1760, a demographic phenomenon that was and remains unprecedented in American history. Socially liminal zones such as these drew settlers searching for land who were often linked together by ethnicity and faith, and confronted them with an assortment of challenges that could breed discontent and eventually encourage rebellion. In some cases backcountry rebels were aspiring slaveholders (South Carolina) and in some cases manor tenants on long-term leases (New York). In some cases they called themselves "Regulators" and in others they were known as "Liberty Men" (Maine), "Green Mountain Boys" (Vermont), or "Wild Yankees" (Pennsylvania). Almost everywhere, they drew upon traditions of community justice to intimidate and punish their enemies, and almost everywhere they were landowners, would-be landowners, or cultivators on what they believed were secure tenures.[22]

The major confrontations that took place did indeed involve back-country settlers of relatively modest means against elites either to the east (who controlled the provincial/state government) or in their midst. The rebels' complaints reflected the insecurity of or difficulty in establishing their land titles, the cost of credit, the burdens of rents, the imposition of taxes, the power of speculators, and the corruption of local officials. They organized to prevent sheriff's sales and dis-possessions, halt court proceedings that threatened their property, and inflict damage to the dwellings of judges and tax collectors or to the buildings that symbolized the power they held. In the process, they articulated ideas about just and unjust practices. They exalted those who worked the soil and insisted they had the right (perhaps God-given) to claim land improved by their labor. They condemned the speculative amassing of land and other forms of wealth, espe-cially when it came at the expense of smallholders. They raged against "moneyed men" and landlords as well as the legal and political insti-tutions that gave them power. And they protested forms of oligarchic rule—itself illiberal—and their lack of adequate representation in legislatures or assemblies. Some called for limits on the accumulation of wealth and land, and some suggested redistributionist measures. They seemed to be republicans in the making, and, on occasion, democratically inclined republicans at that: heirs of the seventeenth-century Levellers and possible progenitors of a new type of politics.[23]

Yet conflicts internal to the backcountry not only set yeoman farm-ers against landlords and proprietors; they also set yeoman farmers against local denizens who engaged in hunting and fishing for their subsistence, squatted on land without bringing it under cultivation, and were often accused of stealing horses and livestock. From South and North Carolina to Virginia and Pennsylvania, backcountry set-tlers complained of "strolling" hunters who seemed "little more than white Indians," who had more children than they could care for, were "idle and disorderly" with "no settled habitation, nor visible Method of Supporting themselves by Industry or Honest Calling," "ranging the Country without Home or Habitation." Pennsylvania's Benjamin Rush, who signed the Declaration of Independence, looked back on an eighteenth-century frontier filled with "settlers nearly related to the Indian," building "rough cabins" and feeding their families on "Indian corn, game, and fish." They would fight, in Rush's view, a "species of war" with the farmer, the "Conqueror," whose "weapons are the implements of husbandry."[24]

Thus, Regulators and similar associations across the backcountries of the Southeast and Middle Atlantic called for the establishment of local courts where there were none, ferries, roads, and currency as well as the securing of land titles, the adjustment of taxes, and the end of speculative corruption. In the meantime, they might punish the "roguish and troublesome" among them as they did the unfortunate John Harvey on the South Carolina frontier in 1769, by chaining him to a tree and inflicting five hundred lashes while beating drums and playing fiddles. The "war" that Benjamin Rush described involved both the exploited against exploiters and the settled agriculturalists against hunters and others who rejected the ways of sedentary producers. It was a battle to make the backcountry safe for small property and, in some cases, slaveholders. And it was a battle at times being waged by "loyal subjects of His Majesty King George" who, they were certain, would recognize they were "wronged or oppressed, or else they would never rebell against [his] laws."[25]

Regulators vilified hunters too because, however much they were likened to "Indians," their gaming in the woodlands and other subsistence practices threatened to provoke Native raids against farming settlements. Indeed, much like the Paxton Boys, Regulators and their allies sought to exclude Native peoples from the boundaries of the communities they were establishing either through episodic violence or by instilling fear. Although provincial officials often acknowledged Native peoples as part of political society and wished to avoid outbreaks of warfare, this was not a view that backcountry settlers were willing to embrace. For them, Natives had no place, even as subordinates, in their social order. There was no culture of exchange and cooperation to be constructed, no trading or diplomatic relations to be protected. There was just removal, by force if necessary, from the perimeters of their settlements and from the lands to the west that they prized. Even western Pennsylvania's "Black Boys," who blackened their faces and dressed in Native garb as they attacked provincial officials trading with or supplying Native peoples and did not have murderous intent, nonetheless imagined the territory as populated by white people alone.[26]

Backcountry rebellions and resistance movements had significant influence on the American Revolution and the political struggles that attended and followed it. Escalating conflicts, land riots, and the harassment of imperial officials created a crisis of order in many of the colonies that threatened the gentry and eventually pushed many of the reluctant among them to embrace independence, if only to regain control of their social and political worlds. For the farmers and small planters who became Regulators, the mobilizations for revolution, especially from 1774 on, created opportunities to reorganize governments that oppressed them and empower themselves against enemies in their midst. The foot dragging among members of the gentry, including those like Thomas Jefferson who would emerge in the Revolution's leadership, was undermined both by British efforts to win the support of the enslaved and by the interest of angry yeomen in a more favorably balanced political system, very much energized by Tom Paine's *Common Sense*.[27]

And yet, the vision adopted by Patriot-supporting backcountry farmers was decidedly localistic. As historian Michael McDonnell writes, they "consistently demonstrated their commitment to their farms, families, and neighborhoods and put the protection of them ahead of provincial and Continental concerns." South Carolina's Regulators, Pennsylvania's Paxton Boys, Vermont's Green Mountain Boys, and Maine's Liberty Men aligned with the Patriot side but did so chiefly to gain the upper hand in their own struggles whether for land and security or against speculators, provincial elites, imperial corruption, and the imbalances of power in governance. The "defense of community" proved a compelling motivating force to join either side or remain neutral. More than a few of the North Carolina Regulators moved farther west or into what would become east Tennessee, where they hoped to establish a state of Franklin. Many more backcountry farming folk fought against the British in their militias rather than the Continental Army, and often returned home after a limited service. "Winter soldiers and springtime farmers," one historian calls them. Within a short period of time, the military might of the American Revolution was carried principally by the poor, the landless, and the transient; those who had no community to defend.[28]

Moving toward the frontier, defense of community became indistinguishable from lethal hostility toward Native peoples, only in part because most of them, like most hunters and "troublesome" backcountry inhabitants, supported the British. In the western districts of the colonies, especially in the Ohio Country, where thousands of white settlers had migrated despite the Proclamation Line of 1763, the Revolution was, effectively, an Indian war, a continuation of the brutal fighting that had erupted during the Seven Years' War and never died down: a "twenty years' war," as Colin Calloway puts it. In 1778 the Second Continental Congress determined that Senecas, Cayugas, Wyandots, and Onondagas, as well as some Ottawas, Chippewas, Shawnees, and Delawares, were arrayed against them, and Native militants, their "renegade" warriors, set on recouping previous losses. Carrying the war into Indian country, Patriot soldiers did whatever they could to prevent that from occurring. The troops severed Native trade routes to cut off the supply of goods, destroyed Native villages, and burned their crops so there could be no return. George Washington, as commander of the Continental Army, ordered a scorched earth policy against the Iroquois, especially the Senecas and Cayugas among them. Even so, there was no military rout or significant change in the lands under Native control west of the Appalachians; Natives more than held their own and won some victories. It was, rather, the peace between the Americans and the British that would be catastrophic, clearing North America of a powerful ally and unleashing a rush of farmers, planters, and speculators who were intent on pushing Native peoples out and taking hold of their lands.[29]

IV

THE DESTRUCTION AND RITUALIZED DECAPITATION of George III in lower New York in 1776 was indicative of a sea change in the political mood of colonists who supported the Patriot side. As Tom Paine had urged, they appeared to be wholly rejecting monarchy and, owing to their long experience with elective colonial assemblies, embracing the republic as their form of governance. With remarkable speed given the circumstances of revolutionary warfare, the colonies-turned-states drafted new constitutions that put legislatures, based on direct or indirect representation, at the center of their independent governments and generally restricted the powers of the governors (or "presidents," as three of the states called their chief magistrates) who were, themselves, selected by their legislatures and often limited in the terms they could serve. Most of the legislatures were bicameral, chosen by popular vote (usually on an annual basis), and expanded in size to increase the number of representatives, bringing them closer to their constituents and accommodating grievances that backcountry rebellions wanted addressed.

Republican experimentation could go further still. Three of the states had unicameral, elective legislatures, and one of them, Pennsylvania, where the old elite was effectively overthrown, dispensed with a governor, limited representatives to serving only four years in seven, and crafted a particularly robust "Declaration of Rights," which were deemed "natural, inherent, and inalienable." Although all of the states had property qualifications for voting and officeholding, Pennsylvania only required a year of residency and the payment of "public taxes" for "freemen" to exercise the franchise. As a testament to what had been done, not only conservatives in the state but more than a few revolutionary leaders expressed shock at what one called this "mob government." John Adams, who continued to regard the British constitution as "the most stupendous fabric of human invention," sneered at Pennsylvania's unicameralism because the common people were "as unjust, tyrannical, brutal, barbarous, and cruel, as any king or senate [when] possessed of uncontrollable power."[30]

That the governments devised by these constitutions in this most republican of moments varied in their structures, franchise requirements, bases of representation, and executive forms suggests that republicanism in action fit no specific molds. Although many of the constitutions began with a bill or declaration of rights, announcing as

Virginia's did "that all men are by nature equally free and independent, and have certain inherent rights" which could not be deprived
or divested, only Vermont's limited the reach of slavery and servitude,
and even there not definitively.[31]

And while access to the franchise and to officeholding were generally enlarged, electors were expected to demonstrate a "permanent
common interest" in their communities and officeholders a far more
substantial material stake to indicate their virtue and wisdom as well
as independence from any "foreign prince, person, prelate, state, or
potentate," such as the Catholic pope. Overall, the political community imagined across the new states was to be composed of propertied
or taxpaying men of European descent who shared the Christian, and
in most cases Protestant, faith, and whose sovereignty was displayed
by representation in their governance. New Jersey's constitution provided that "there shall be no establishment of any one religious sect
in this Province," but immediately went on to declare that "no Protestant inhabitant of this Colony shall be denied the enjoyment of
any civil right" and "all persons professing belief in the faith of any
Protestant sect . . . shall be capable of being elected to any office of
profit or trust . . . or being a member of any branch of the legislature."
Catholics would be deprived of holding office in the state for nearly
another century.[32]

The first state constitutions assume great importance because they
established ideas of belonging and exclusion, governance and participation, rights that inhered and could be exercised that were enduring.
They were important, too, because they took their place within a confederation that was "a league of friendship" and therefore effectively
a treaty among individually sovereign states designed chiefly to win
the War of Independence. The Articles of Confederation, drawn up
by the Second Continental Congress in 1777 and not fully ratified by
the states until 1781, provided for a Congress that would represent
each of the states and could conduct foreign affairs, declare war, raise
an army, adjudicate conflicts between the states, and requisition funds
necessary for its expenditures. But Congress had no power of taxation; that was left entirely to the states, as was the oversight or police
power of all affairs, with the possible exception of those involving

Native peoples, within their borders or among their citizens and their citizens' dependents, meaning slaves, servants, and family members.

Viewed from the present, the sort of confederation that the Articles provided seems something of a placeholder until a more rational, elaborated system could be devised. The weaknesses of the Articles seem readily apparent, at least if the end product was to be a central state and unified country. Yet viewed from the early 1780s, this was not necessarily the case. The rebellion against British rule built on growing suspicions of consolidated and distant power, and the political horizons of much of the leadership did not stretch beyond their states and localities. That was where meaningful power relations were constructed, deployed, and contested; where webs of patronage were spun; where the boundaries of rights were defined. We must also remember that successful rebellions in the Western Hemisphere against Spanish imperial rule—in Bolivia, Chile, Venezuela, and Mexico among them—made for a collection of republics rather than for a large one, and that the centrifugal forces in North America would remain formidable and politically consequential.

The post-Revolutionary period was to be challenging and complex under any circumstances. Foreign alliances had to be built among competing empires and global war-makers. Military defense had to be maintained to protect a newly independent group of states. Boundary lines and navigation rights, as on the Mississippi River, had to be secured to facilitate commerce. Potential conflicts between sovereign states had to be settled. And a financial apparatus had to be developed to enable the repayment of war-related debts and provide the Confederation with resources to conduct its affairs. Tall orders. But had the problems of the half decade following independence revolved principally around matters of diplomacy, the adjustment of relations among the states, or the managing of finances, the Articles could well have prevailed for a time, perhaps with amendments. Instead, what the Articles called "the United States of America" experienced a confluence of troubles and plunged into a crisis that recalled some of the darkest days of the 1760s and 1770s. The resulting economic depression may have been the country's deepest before the 1930s, with explosive and threatening consequences.

The crisis had something of a domino effect, linking the political, economic, and social, and reigniting some of the backcountry revolts of the pre-Revolutionary era. Independence may have liberated the states from the confines of the British imperial system, but it initially led to the suspension of what had been a robust trade and deprived the states of access to the very lucrative markets of the British West Indies. Then, once the Treaty of Paris was signed, Britain flooded American ports with manufactured goods, draining the states of hard currency while disabling the flow of cash that the West Indian trade had previously brought in. The crunch hit merchants, artisans, and laborers in American port cities very hard (wage levels dropped by more than 25 percent), and it quickly spread into the countryside where credit-starved farmers and planters saw demand in urban and export markets shrink and the prices they could get for their produce and staple crops drop.[33]

With levels of indebtedness rising, foreclosures on land and live-stock became regular occurrences. Virginia's St. George Tucker, a prominent lawyer, revolutionary officer, and judge, estimated that not "one Tidewater planter in twenty" could settle his debts. Cultivators on a smaller scale were even more vulnerable. Yet the crisis worsened immeasurably because of the obligations that the Confederation and the states had incurred to carry on their War for Independence. Their creditors ranged from foreign lenders to American speculators and to revolutionary war veterans. And, since the Confederation Congress lacked the power to impose taxes, it had to make requisitions on the individual states. The states, which had their own war debts to repay, turned to highly regressive taxes on individuals (known as poll, or head, taxes) and land. By the mid-1780s, the tax burdens across the states far exceeded what the British government had demanded in the years before independence was declared, and those taxes had to be paid in very scarce gold or silver currency, known as specie. The many farmers whose dealings with commercial markets were limited at best, and whose indebtedness was normally local and payable in kind or labor, could not themselves escape the demands and conse-quences of state taxation.[34]

The expansion of representative legislatures that many of the new state constitutions prescribed opened one possible avenue of redress. Legislatures could, of course, have refused the Confederation's requisitions, invoked their sovereignty, eased their financial burdens, and very clearly defined the limits of the union, if not crippled it entirely. This did not happen, save in two cases, because merchants and creditors were well represented and believed that the viability of the Confederation and of their state governments, not to mention their own wealth and social standing, might be at stake. But legislatures were also more susceptible to popular pressure, especially from the rural counties and backcountry districts, where debtors began to demand that courts be closed, foreclosures suspended, taxes adjusted, and the debt revalued—often organizing protests and attacking government officials. Some questioned whether the very meaning of the Revolution had been abandoned, as speculators and other financial interests bought up bonds and promissory notes at much reduced values but expected to have the interest on them paid in full. In Cumberland and Franklin counties, Pennsylvania, angry farmers in 1786 developed "the Plan," which called for scaling down the value of public and private debts, taxing unproductive or unoccupied land, and restricting the size of speculative landholdings. Others insisted that state taxes be accepted in paper currency or in kind. "The security of American liberty," a New York farmer declared, "requires a more equal distribution of property than at present."[35]

With annual elections the norm, state legislatures could see dramatic turnovers in their representatives, and bills to address the debt crisis quickly enacted. More than half of the states issued paper currency, often in large amounts, that would be accepted as legal tender for taxes and market transactions. Elsewhere, different forms of debtor relief either passed or were blocked by the elite state senates. Popular pressure steadily mounted, and legislatures saw the need to respond adequately or face turmoil on the ground. Yeomen and planters, as distressed property holders, could join forces, even though yeomen were most likely to lead resistance to tax collections, court warrants, and sheriff's sales.[36]

The consequences of legislative inaction became most apparent in

Massachusetts. There Boston mercantile interests continued to dominate the legislature and not only kept highly regressive taxes in place but raised them in 1786 to meet another round of requisitions from the Confederation Congress. Petitions for debt relief were haughtily ignored, and in the summer of 1786, protest escalated when farmers in central Massachusetts mobilized to shut the courts down and halt the seizure of tax-delinquent property. With a bow to their predecessors, they called themselves "Regulators," and their rebellion soon spread to the west. "We are in a state of Anarchy and Confusion bordering on Civil War," one of John Adams's correspondents fretted to him at the time. The state's governor looked to crack down but had trouble finding military support until wealthy merchants funded a private militia. When the Regulators, now led by revolutionary veteran and indebted farmer Daniel Shays, marched toward an armory in Springfield late the following January 1787, a violent clash seemed inevitable.

It proved a mismatch. Confronted by an armed force of more than 3,000 men under the command of a revolutionary war general, the rebellion collapsed and many of its leaders, including Shays, fled. Now more than a few of the elite, including Adams, called for their version of bloody vengeance. Martial law was declared, several hundred of the rebels were indicted, eighteen were convicted and sentenced to death, and two were eventually executed for their deeds. Cooler heads then prevailed. Of those captured or accused, 4,000 received amnesty in return for signed confessions, while the legislature mended its ways and acted to ease the plight of the state's debtors. As for Shays, whose name would forever be attached to the episode, he was pardoned a year later, only to be marked as an anarchist and traitor after he returned to the state. Worn down by the hostility, Shays moved on to a small town in western New York State where he lived impoverished until his death in 1825.[37]

Shays's Rebellion has become the symbol of the tumultuous 1780s, though its impact would have been far less significant had it not exploded amid popular resistance and rebellion throughout the new United States. Almost everywhere debtors pushed back against sheriffs, deputies, and tax collectors, sometimes keeping them "off by force of arms" or by "throw[ing] every difficulty" at them. In Washington County, Pennsylvania, in 1786, a tax collector was seized and in a rite of shaming had "one half of his hair [cut off], cued the other half on one side of his Head, cut the Cock of his Hat, and made him wear it in a form to render his Cue the most Conspicuous." In Virginia several courthouses were set aflame, and in western Greenbrier County the justices were prevented from sitting. When the New Jersey legislature refused to endorse paper money, courthouses there were nailed shut; outside one of them, a crowd of farmers impaled an effigy of the governor, who was also an opponent of paper currency. About two hundred protesters in New Hampshire went so far as to surround the state legislature and demand "an emission of paper money," giving the legislators "1/2 an hour" to respond. The response was the show of a cannon. "The temper of the ... people is not confined to one state or to one part of a state, but pervades the whole," George Washington learned to his dismay. Indeed, as Alexander Hamilton observed, the effects of Shays's Rebellion "spread like wild fire."[38]

The widening unrest, the protests against extortionate speculators and legislators, the resistance to tax collection and sheriff sales, and the attacks on government officials and symbols of their authority frightened the political as well as economic elite. They worried less about the specter of another Shays's Rebellion than about the capitulation of state legislators to demands that, they believed, indulged the excesses of debtors and jeopardized financial stability. Republicanism had apparently nurtured democratic spirits, and democracy had run rampant. It needed to be reined in, perhaps with more coercive political institutions. Gentry critics and their allies in the public sphere questioned whether the people had sufficient virtue to maintain a republic, if a "different form of government" would be necessary, if, in fact, a "military government would be better than no government." None other than James Madison, Alexander Hamilton, John Jay, and George Washington wondered privately if a king would better protect those of wealth and property in the event that a "republican remedy" could not be found. Stunningly, Nathaniel Gorham of Massachusetts, then president of the Confederation Congress, indirectly approached Prince Henry of Prussia about becoming king of the United States.[39]

V

BY THE MID-1780s, members of the Confederation Congress recognized some of the shortcomings of the Articles and looked, unsuccessfully, in the direction of reform. With Congress unable to find a
way forward, however, increasingly shaken elites began to think that
some sort of extraparliamentary convention would be necessary if
only to amend the Articles and bolster the union of states. After a
preliminary meeting in Annapolis, Maryland, to set the groundwork,
that convention met in Philadelphia in the spring of 1787.

So much attention has been devoted to the plans, compromises,
and divisions that went into the making of the U.S. Constitution that
it is easy to overlook the impulses that got the delegates to Philadelphia in the first place. Twelve of the thirteen states were represented; only Rhode Island failed to attend. Most of the delegates had
been connected with the Continental Army during the Revolution,
were members of the Confederation Congress, or both. Most were
also wealthy, well-educated, and congregants in the elite Episcopal
Church. The delegates had, that is, crucial experience in creating and
maintaining a unity necessary to achieve and defend independence.
And most shared an interest not only in providing for a stronger and
more effective union but also in limiting the damage state legislatures
could inflict on property holders, creditors, and well-to-do investors.
They saw in the "insurrections" erupting around them the bitter
fruits of a republic gone awry, and viewed their challenge as shifting
power, especially over finances, from the states to the central government, taming democratic excesses at the grassroots, and enabling the
central government to suppress domestic insurgencies as well as foreign threats. Few shared Thomas Jefferson's take on Shays (Jefferson
was in Paris at the time), "that a little rebellion now and then is a good
thing," least of all James Madison, to whom Jefferson was writing.[40]

Sometimes lost in considerations of the battles between the small
and large states, or the slaveholding and non-slaveholding states, or
those more and less concerned with democracy and the powers residing in branches of the government, were the broad areas of agreement

on the type of republic that the Constitution should authorize. Delegates agreed that a bicameral Congress would be the representative body, representative districts would be large in size to put the lid on popular influence and, in the case of the upper house, be appointed by state legislatures for lengthy terms, and Congress would have the power to impose taxes. In response to the recent upheavals, they prohibited states from coining money, emitting "Bills of Credit," or "impairing the Obligation of Contracts." Delegates agreed that there should be a chief magistrate who could wield considerable powers over foreign and domestic affairs, would not be subject to direct popular election (thus the "electoral college"), and could exercise what was known as a "qualified negative," that is to say veto power over acts of the Congress. And they agreed that members of the federal judiciary would be appointed "during good Behaviour," or for unrestricted terms. More than a few of the delegates, led by Alexander Hamilton, argued for a president with a life term; supporters of this initiative in the convention included four state delegations (New Jersey, Delaware, Pennsylvania, and Virginia) together with Madison and Washington. John Adams, who was not at the convention, nonetheless backed Hamilton's idea and went so far as to suggest that the United States would eventually evolve into a "hereditary Monarchy" as an "Asylum against Discord, Seditions and Civil War." In the end, the president would have a four-year term but with the possibility of indefinite "re-eligibility." "I know of no first magistrate in any republican government," Adams could then acknowledge, "excepting England and Neuchatel [a Swiss canton] who possesses a constitutional dignity, authority, and power comparable to his."[41]

Worries about the ability of the federal government to contain the irresponsible actions of the states or the rebelliousness that might arise at times of stress and hardship were flagged in a number of places. The Constitution's Preamble listed to "insure domestic Tranquility" as one of the goals of a "more perfect Union," and Congress was invested with the power (Article I, Section 8) to call "forth the Militia to . . . suppress insurrections" as well as to "execute the Laws of the Union" and "repel Invasions." Madison, who wanted a Union "clearly paramount" to the states, hoped Congress would have the power to veto objectionable state laws as a way to derail the potential tyranny of a majority there. Needless to say, the "insurrections" many of the delegates feared were not only those of enraged "freemen." At a time of slave unrest and rebellion in the Caribbean and on the mainland, including the flight of thousands of slaves to the British during the Revolutionary War, they also feared "insurrections" of enslaved people of African descent. The recognition the slave system received throughout the Constitution, the commitment of the federal government to the protection of chattel property (such as the Fugitive Slave Clause), and the political rewards that enslavers won (such as the Federal Ratio, better known as the Three-Fifths Clause, and the postponement of any reckoning with the Atlantic slave trade) demonstrated whose interests the new federal republic was meant to serve.[42]

Small wonder that the delegates at the Philadelphia convention quickly placed a veil of secrecy over their proceedings and that much of what we understand about the tenor of the Constitution comes both from the text and from representation by its formidable advocates, collectively calling themselves "Publius," in the *Federalist Papers*. In a series of remarkable essays, John Jay and, especially, James Madison and Alexander Hamilton laid out the case for the Constitution's ratification, emphasizing its strengths (certainly compared with the Articles) and taking on some of the critics who quickly emerged, including the sixteen delegates who refused to sign the document at the convention's end. The Constitution, they insisted, framed a republic that could protect the United States from foreign intrigues, diminish the likelihood of serious conflicts between the states, provide direct and indirect representation for the country's inhabitants, enable those of wisdom and virtue to serve, and empower the central government to assume the responsibilities of securing financial stability and domestic order without encroaching upon the sovereign powers of the states. Madison explained quite brilliantly how a large territory with diverse "interests" was best suited to the maintenance of a republic, and even Hamilton, who had favored a life term for the president and called attention to the repressive authority that a republic needed to wield, nonetheless took pains to write of the "total dissimilitude between [the president] and the king of Great Britain" and instead likened the president's powers to those of "a governor of New York."[43]

Supporters of the Constitution, which had to be ratified by nine of the thirteen states, had a number of important advantages in the contest. Known as Federalists, they could count most people of wealth, especially in coastal cities, on their side. They mobilized major resources and networks of communication to advance their arguments and strategies across the states. And they controlled most of the newspapers. All of which translated into seats at ratification conventions and expeditious procedures there. Opponents of ratification, derisively called Anti-Federalists by the Federalists, had a steep hill to climb. They were scattered across the states, had bases of strength in the countryside and smaller towns where few newspapers were published or circulated, and had difficulty rallying voters to take part in a ratification process that unfolded very quickly. They also faced some heavy-handed tactics and outright bullying on the part of Federalists. "*Bad* measures in a *good* cause," one Federalist conceded. Even so, the Anti-Federalists made an impressive run and the arguments they mounted help us understand the ideological currents on both sides, as well as some of the illiberal tendencies that went into the making of the American republic.[44]

The American origin story is so tightly bound to the writing and ratification of the Constitution that we often ignore both the extent and substance of opposition to it. Instead, we focus on how to interpret the meaning of the Constitution, what the "Founders" intended, and how later amendments fundamentally reshaped it. At best, we acknowledge the role of the Anti-Federalists in demanding the inclusion of a "bill of rights," which was not part of the original text, and which they succeeded in doing, effectively tying them to the Constitution and making them little more than a loyal opposition. And, indeed, the absence of a bill of rights, something that many state constitutions contained, did raise the hackles of many who penned essays calling either for the Constitution's rejection or its modification.

Because only a handful of newspapers aligned with the Anti-Federalists, it is difficult to grasp the full range of their views or the political and social geographies they represented. But what we

do have offers up important perspectives. Anti-Federalism was concentrated in rural and village districts of northern and western New
England, New York's Hudson Valley, and western Pennsylvania, Virginia, and the Carolinas. It could flare, as well, in plantation districts
closer to the Atlantic coast. These were areas that had been rapidly
settled, were engaging in extended warfare with Native peoples, and
commonly resisted the policies and corruption of colonial and state
governments. They were also areas that had been touched by the
Christian evangelism of the First Great Awakening (chiefly the 1730s
and 1740s) and the related rise of the Baptists and Methodists. To
a much lesser extent they were domains of slaveholders jealous of
their prerogatives. More often than not they were adversely affected
by the economic tribulations of the 1780s and sought to protect themselves by disabling the arms of creditors and the courts and demanding redress from the state governments. Although they were ready to
submit to local leaders (or were themselves local leaders), they were
wary of outside elites and the predations those elites might commit.
They were prideful of their community ways and disciplines, and easily threatened by those they did not know or who were unlike them.
Many, especially in the backcountry, retained deep hostility to Catholics and the hierarchies of power they ascribed to Catholicism. They
wished, as one settler in the Maine district put it, "to Cut down all the
poopery [Popery] and kill the Devil and give the world of mankind
some piece by stopping the progress of Rogues and Deceivers and
helping every man to his rights and privilidges and libertys."[45]

The Anti-Federalist arguments therefore reveal the political objectives of the framers and the political sensibilities of those who became
the framers' opponents. Although Anti-Federalists' thought cannot
be neatly categorized, and varied depending on the social class and
geographical locations of the writers, most shared an interpretation
of what the Constitution and its structure of governance threatened.
Anti-Federalists warned of the consolidation of power the Constitution brought about at the expense of the states. They warned of the
great distance of the new government from most of its constituents.
They warned of the limited representation it offered owing to the size
of the congressional districts and the method of selecting senators.

They warned of the elite and aristocratic tendencies the Constitution encouraged by failing to provide for annual elections and rotation in office. They warned of the congressional authority to impose taxes, and the prospects for judicial tyranny and threats to jury trials. And they warned of the potential power of the president, especially owing to his codependence with the elitist senate. "The general government will consist of a new species of *executive*, a small senate, and a very small house *of representation*," the Federal Farmer wrote. "As many citizens will be more than three hundred miles from the seat of government as will be nearer to it, its judges and officers cannot be very numerous without making our government very expensive . . . [and] as to powers the general government will possess all the essential ones . . . and those of the states a mere shadow of power."[46]

Anti-Federalist writers may have placed special emphasis on one or a few of these matters in their discrete essays, or may have built a case for rejecting the Constitution over the course of several essays. But together they identified what most of the framers in fact sought to do as well as the dynamics of power that the Constitution's republic could unleash. And although Federalists attempted to dispel many of the Anti-Federalists' fears, they could not stanch their belief that the Constitution constructed a new republic and a new central state that bore little relation to the political worlds that Anti-Federalists wished to defend. Their fear that the United States under the Constitution would likely end up as a monarchy or demagoguery became especially clear when Anti-Federalists challenged James Madison's argument that a republic was best secured in a large rather than small territory.

The Revolution's leadership and the Constitution-makers who set to work in 1787 were students of the classical world, and of the Greek and Roman republics in particular. They were also acquainted with John Locke and the English commonwealthmen who together developed notions of natural rights, civil and political society, and republicanism. Many would avidly read Baron de Montesquieu's *The Spirit of the Laws*, published in France in 1748, which reflected on the character of different forms of governance. Most pertinent was Montesquieu's notion that it would be "natural for a republic to have only a small territory; otherwise it could not long subsist." "In an extensive republic," Montesquieu warned, "the public good is sacrificed to a thousand private views; it is subordinate to exceptions, and depends on accidents." This James Madison took on in *Federalist 10*, effectively inverting Montesquieu's logic to suggest that the many interests in a large republic would prevent any one of them from dominating while at the same time enabling the worthiest candidates for office to be selected.[47]

Anti-Federalists widely accepted Montesquieu's argument not only for its logic but also for its compatibility with the record of the past. "History furnishes no example of a free republic anything like the extent of the United States," New York's Brutus admonished. Others wondered whether a government "in so extended a territory would be practicable, consistent with freedom" or whether "large and consolidated empires" could be anything but "full of misery." Yet the Anti-Federalist critique of a large republic reflected more than an understanding of what may have succeeded or failed in Greece or Rome, or, perhaps more recently, in the Netherlands and the Swiss cantons. It often reflected a profound localism of the sort that backcountry yeomen and enslaving planters had expressed in their battles with colonial and state governments. "In large states," Agrippa of Massachusetts predicted, "the same principles of legislation will not apply to all the parts," and so to "promote the happiness of the people it is necessary that there should be local laws . . . and that those laws should be made by representatives who are immediately subject to the want of them." Brutus insisted that "in a republic, the manners, sentiments, and interests of the people should be similar." Pennsylvania's Centinel went further, arguing that "a republic . . . can only exist where the body of the people are virtuous and where property is pretty equally divided," where, in sum, the "people are sovereign" and capable of fending off "aristocracy, monarchy, or despotism."[48]

Anti-Federalism therefore had special appeal to those who recognized power in personal and familial terms, saw themselves as members of communities bounded by ethnicity, culture, and faith, were wary of outsiders and distant legal and political institutions, and imagined proper government as closely aligned with them and protective of their "manners, sentiments, and interests." If they demanded a bill of rights in the Constitution, it was less to specify the natural or civil rights they had as free people and Americans than it was to rebuff potential invasions by the central government and secure local rights and authority as they understood them. Those rights and obligations often involved patriarchy, faith, moral consensus, economic reciprocities, and ideas of community justice. They could also nurture ambivalence about or hostility to the relations and values of the marketplace, particularly more distant markets over which they had little control, translating, by contrast, republican virtue into an image of organic community life, with its own hierarchies and coercions. In these ways, enslavers and members of the landed gentry could share with yeomen and even some tenants a sense of the importance of local power and patronage that might be under threat.[49]

For the most part, Anti-Federalists relied on tracts, newspapers, and ratification convention debates to express their opposition to the Constitution. But things could turn violent, particularly when they discovered that the Constitution had been ratified with a speed that did not allow them to participate adequately. Thus, in the late winter of 1787, a celebration of the Constitution in the town of Carlisle, Pennsylvania, was disrupted by a large crowd of Anti-Federalists who fashioned effigies of two of the elite Federalists in the state, Thomas Kean and James Wilson. Led by a militia captain "who declared he was inspired from Heaven," they marched through the streets "with shouts and most dreadful execrations" and burned the effigies in front of the courthouse. Elsewhere in western Pennsylvania, farmers closed down roads leading into their villages and communities, walling themselves off from the new structures of political power that undermined the authority of local justices. It would not be long before the new central government's determination to pay off the war debt held by speculators provoked a massive, armed protest there and in backcountry districts of Maryland, Virginia, and Kentucky, much in accord with sympathizers in Carlisle. With echoes of Shays's Rebellion, this uprising in 1794 shook the foundations of the administration of George Washington and raised questions about the power that the federal government was ready to wield against its own people. The president answered by mobilizing nearly 13,000 militiamen from Pennsylvania and adjacent states to suppress the insurgency. He then rode out at their head to meet those we would come to call the "whiskey rebels."[50]

VI

THE DECLARATION OF INDEPENDENCE, with its invocation of natural and inalienable rights, and the Constitution, with its foundational idea of popular sovereignty, bookend the American origin story and have long been recognized as the moments when political traditions of liberalism and republicanism were enduringly set in place: forerunners of what eventually would be termed "liberal democracy." Many scholars and writers emphasize a direct line between "Lockean liberalism," "commonwealth republicanism," and the revolution that created the United States, and see the Constitution as the wise settlement that a liberal republic would require. To be sure, some argued about the significance of grassroots mobilizations in making the embrace of independence possible, of backcountry rebellions in expanding the notion of what a republic should mean and who it should serve, and of struggles between elites and the people as driving the dynamics of change. But whether they are advocates or critics, few doubt that liberal republicanism was the end product of America's revolutionary moment.

It is worth pointing out that "liberal" was not yet a political term in the eighteenth century; in its use, liberal rather meant a disposition to generosity or cosmopolitanism. *Liberal* and *liberalism*, as additions to the political lexicon, may in fact have been more a result of the French Revolution than of the American or the English. What's more, the markers of American origin must be understood and interpreted in their own context, and here the picture is more complex and unsettling. By the middle of the eighteenth century, ideas of natural equality and inalienable rights were already embedded in the world views of those in the Euro-Atlantic who regarded themselves as enlightened. As Jefferson later acknowledged, he did not put forth "new principles, or new arguments, never before thought of" in the

Declaration but instead articulated "the common sense of the subject." Jefferson also made a case less for some idea of abstract universalism than for placing Americans on an equal political footing with the British to validate their strike for independence. After all, only a few years later Jefferson would be documenting the inferiority of Black people, and explaining why Black inferiority made it impossible for them to live together with whites under conditions of freedom.[51]

For its part, popular sovereignty has a genealogy that could, perhaps, be stretched back to the Magna Carta, though certainly to the parliamentary struggles of the seventeenth century. As such, historically, it replaced the divine right of kings as the organizing principle of governance, and as central to the legitimacy of either direct or virtual representation. Yet, as Edmund Morgan has shown, popular sovereignty, like the divine right of kings, is itself a construct and set of fictions that enable structures of power and, generally speaking, the rule of an elite, whether imagined as "natural," wealth-based, or meritocratic. Thomas Jefferson, who prided himself on helping to eradicate important features of aristocratic society—primogeniture, entail, and noble titles—nonetheless assumed that a republic would depend on the elevation of a natural aristocracy that might gain accretions from the few "geniuses" who could be "raked from the rubbish." The ratification of the Constitution, considering the fears of democracy that encouraged its writing, gave rise in the 1790s to what has been called a "monarchical republic," one in which some of the scaffolding of monarchy remained or was redeployed. Although George Washington expressed his resistance to kingly authority, many advising him or serving in his administration hoped he would bring the appropriate dignity and majesty to the office of president, modeled of course on what was familiar to European courts. Some simply assumed he would serve as president for the remainder of his life. Philadelphia's Benjamin Rush could depict the new American government as one "which unites with the vigor of monarchy and the stability of aristocracy all the freedom of a simple republic."[52]

The prospect of some sort of monarchy emerging in the United States, likely a mixed monarchy of the type that Rush suggested, was not only accepted in elite circles; it had a much wider provenance than we might assume. "There is," Benjamin Franklin told the Constitutional Convention, "a natural inclination in Mankind to Kingly Government." Backcountry rebels who assailed aristocratic corruption and demanded the democratization of colonial legislatures rarely called the legitimacy of the king into question. If anything, a protective monarch fit comfortably into their own ideas of community life based on paternal power, access to propertied independence, cultural homogeneity, and patronage as a mediator of inequalities. Such a monarchical figure fit, as well, with their determination to exclude or destroy threatening outsiders, whether Native peoples or "white Indians." Rebels and Regulators could mount a formidable critique of speculative wealth, lordly pretensions, and elite exploitation. They could also call for greater representation, policies more favorable to small producers, and security from government invasions. In many ways, they prepared the road to independence, constructed new models of popular governance, and set limits to the conservative reaction of the late 1780s. But, more often than not, the worlds they struggled to defend were those in which "rights" were delimited by gender, age, faith, and race and were meant to be locally prescribed and enforced. To these communities, and the states of which they were a part, were left the supervision of households, labor, and the conduct of politics. The social and political consequences going forward would be significant.[53]

Where the universalist possibilities of the Declaration of Independence were most unmistakably recognized was among the most subordinated, exploited, and repressed people in the independent United States. In early 1777, a petition arrived at the Massachusetts General Court from eight enslaved men of African descent. They wrote in the name of "A Great Number of Blackes detained in a State of slavery in the Bowels of a free & Christian Country" to show that "thay have in Common with all other men a Natural and Unaliable Right to that freedom which the Grat Parent of the Unavers hath Bestowed equalley on all menkind and which they have Never forfeited by any Compact or agreement whatever." In their telling, they had been "Unjustly Dragged by the hand of a cruel Power from their Derest friends and sum of them Even torn from the Embraces of their tender Parents [and] . . . Brough hear Either to Be sold like Beast of Burthen & Like them Condemned to Slavery for Life." They had already sent "petition after petition . . . to the Legislative Body of this state" and could only "express their Astonishment" that the petitions had "Never Bin Consirdered" even though "Every Principle form which Amarica has Acted in the Cours of their unhappy Dificultes with Great Briton Pleads Stronger than A thousand arguments in favowrs of your petioners." They therefore asked "your honours to give this petion its due weight & consideration & cause an act of the Legislatur to be past Wherby they may be Restored to the Enjoyments of that which is the Naturel Right of all men—and their Children who wer Born in this Land of Liberty." Three of the eight petitioners signed with their "mark."[54]

As best as we know, this petition was no more successful than their previous petitions had been, ignored or cast aside by the legislators they addressed. But this time the political ground was shifting in a way they could hasten. Four years later, an enslaved man of African descent named Quok Walker sued in Worcester County court for his freedom. Walker had been born in Massachusetts in 1753 to parents who had been enslaved somewhere on the Slave or Gold Coasts of West Africa and brought on the dreadful Middle Passage to that North American colony, joining nearly 5,000 enslaved men, women, and children already there. For reasons that are unclear, one of Walker's owners had promised to manumit him when he turned twenty-one, but the promise was reneged after that owner died. Walker then fled his enslavement, only to be recaptured and badly beaten.

In his pleas before the court, Walker argued that slavery was not only contrary to the Bible, but contrary as well to the recently written and ratified constitution of the state of Massachusetts whose first article declared that "All men are born free and equal, and have certain natural, essential, and inalienable rights [including] the right of enjoying their lives and liberties." The jury accepted the logic and morality of Walker's claims and granted him freedom along with 50 pounds in damages. In so doing, they set slavery in Massachusetts on a lengthy road to extinction. It would not be the last time that enslaved people took some of the high principles articulated at America's founding well beyond what the founders intended.[55]

Chapter Four

TOCQUEVILLE, LINCOLN, AND THE EXPULSIVE 1830s

I N 1835, ALEXIS DE TOCQUEVILLE PUBLISHED THE first of his two-volume work, *Democracy in America*. He had come to the United States from France in 1831 with his friend and compatriot Gustave de Beaumont, and, while their main purpose was to study American prisons and penitentiaries, they traveled widely and observed closely the nature and elements of this newly independent republic to offer perspective on what was happening in France and Europe more generally. Although neither man was alive during the revolutionary decade of the 1790s, both bore witness to the revolution of 1830 and the July monarchy that emerged in its wake and sponsored their journey. As Tocqueville recognized, the old feudal and aristocratic order was unraveling and a new one, based on different principles and relations, was steadily taking its place, with the "noble [having] gone down in the social scale, and the commoner gone up." It was, he believed, something of a "double revolution" unfolding irresistibly, and so, from the first, Tocqueville intended to cast his net well beyond the penitentiaries and produce a far more capacious account.[1]

Tocqueville made a wise choice. *Democracy in America* has come to be regarded as one of the seminal texts in American political and cultural history and, to this day, is central in framing popular and academic understandings of American political culture and distinctiveness. Tocqueville marveled at the "equality of conditions" he found across the land, the robust democratic practices he observed, especially at the local and associational levels, the fluidity of social life, and the strength of republican institutions despite the scale of the republic itself. A second volume, which appeared in 1840, was more sobering in its assessments but little different in the overall picture it portrayed. Indeed, in many ways, Tocqueville's *Democracy in America* would serve to validate what has often been represented as "Lincoln's America" or the "Lincoln ideal," a society organized by the energies of small producers—artisans, yeoman farmers, and small manufacturers—by the prospects of economic independence and social mobility, and by a political democracy based on white adult male suffrage (by nineteenth-century standards, universal suffrage). It was a society that informed ideas of American exceptionalism and one that thousands of men would fight, at great cost, to preserve under the leadership of Lincoln himself.

Abraham Lincoln had a very different view of the United States at the time. In January 1838, just three years after *Democracy in America*'s first volume was published, a twenty-eight-year-old Abraham Lincoln, already an Illinois state legislator, spoke before the Young Men's Lyceum of Springfield (there is no indication that Lincoln read or was familiar with Tocqueville's new work). Lincoln's topic was "The Perpetuation of Our Political Institutions," and in it he issued a startling and somber warning. After expressing gratitude to "our fathers" for the political gifts they handed down, he nonetheless spoke of the dangers that the country and its institutions faced. Those dangers did not come from abroad, from foreign powers and armies, as many of his forebears had imagined, but rather "must spring up amongst us." "There is," Lincoln observed, "something of an ill-omen among us." What he meant was "the increasing disregard for the law which pervades the country; the growing disposition to substitute the wild and furious passions, in lieu of the sober judgments of the Courts; and the worse than savage mobs, for the executive ministers of justice." "This disposition is awfully fearful in any community," Lincoln continued, "and that it exists in ours, though grating to our feelings to admit, it would be a violation of the truth, and an insult to our intelligence, to deny. Accounts of outrages committed by mobs, form the everyday news of our time. They have pervaded the country from New England to Louisiana—they are neither peculiar to the eternal snows of the former nor the burning suns of the latter . . . neither are they confined to the slaveholding or the non-slaveholding states. Alike, they spring up among the pleasure hunting masters of southern slaves, and the order loving citizens of steady habits." These passions, Lincoln worried, could lay the path for tyranny unless a new "political religion" based on "reverence for the laws" and "cold, calculating, unimpassioned reason" took hold.[2]

Lincoln's thoughts are especially striking not only because they appear as counterpoints to Tocqueville's but also because they seem to defy conventional understandings of what was afoot in the United States during the 1830s. This was the era, as many understand it, of Jacksonian democracy and the market revolution, the time when the elective franchise was broadened and deepened, economic opportunities were beckoning, social and geographical mobility were widely experienced, legal institutions were protecting property and promoting development, social reform became the order of the day, and abolitionism reared its head. The 1830s were foundational to liberal individualism, the sanctity of private property, and the practice of democracy, the moment when elements of American exceptionalism and the liberal democratic ideal solidified. How was it, then, that Lincoln could see American institutions in such jeopardy, the rule of law at such risk, the legacies of the founders in such potentially dark repose? And how could the perspectives of Lincoln and Tocqueville, who seemed to provide many of the materials for the popular view of the 1830s, be so much at odds? What did Lincoln see that Tocqueville apparently didn't? Did they understand the unfolding of the country's history in different ways? Or could it be a matter of timing: Tocqueville traveled the United States in 1831–32 and Lincoln spoke in 1838?

It turns out that there is less of a riddle than first meets the mind. A close reading of Tocqueville reveals many of the concerns that Lincoln later voiced. The difference was more of register than of substance, of example than content. Taken together, Tocqueville and Lincoln help shed light on a decade when liberal values, sensibilities, and behaviors were shaky at best and illiberal currents coursed mightily, perpetually threatening to overwhelm them. None of these currents proved more odious than an expulsionism on wide display.

I

WHEN ABRAHAM LINCOLN CAME before Springfield's Young Men's Lyceum to warn of the fate of American political institutions, he was not speaking in abstractions or of information gleaned only from the newspapers. He was responding to especially brutal events that occurred nearby. In 1836 a free Black man named Francis McIntosh, who worked aboard a Mississippi River steamer, was accused of murder while ashore in St. Louis and burned alive by a large and enraged white mob. Among the locals to condemn the McIntosh lynching was Elijah Lovejoy, a minister, abolitionist, and editor of a St. Louis newspaper. Before long, Lovejoy's press was destroyed by proslavery sympathizers, and Lovejoy fled across the Mississippi River to Alton, Illinois, setting up his newspaper where there might be more safety. But although Alton was in a state where slavery had been deemed illegal, the political temper of the town was hostile to abolitionism, and in November 1837 Lovejoy's press was again targeted for destruction. In the violent encounter that ensued Lovejoy himself was murdered.[3]

The immediacy of these defilements of the rule of law and constitutional protections notwithstanding, Lincoln was well aware of the larger context in which they occurred. Lovejoy was one of many abolitionists subjected to mob brutality over the course of the 1830s, and McIntosh was one of many African Americans victimized by white terrorism. Whether in rural or urban areas, in small towns or large cities, in the South, Northeast, or Midwest, thousands of Americans quite simply went to the torch, the knife, the noose, or the gun to ward off what they saw as threats to their power, privileges, and community prerogatives. Matters of politics and faith often provoked these violent eruptions even though the ballot box and denominational diversity have long been heralded as vital elements of American democracy and culture. But more than anything else, it was slavery and race that was proving volcanic.

Abolitionism had been growing in the United States since the time of the Revolution, owing chiefly to the arguments and actions of African Americans, both enslaved and free. They had been petitioning for freedom, pushing legislatures in states like Massachusetts to enact emancipation laws, and decrying the cowardice of colonizationists who wished to join emancipation to the expulsion of the freed Black population and who, through the 1820s, neared the limits of white antislavery sentiment. But in the 1830s, the abolitionism that African Americans had constructed upon the principles of the Declaration of Independence and Christian morality took off on a grassroots basis, drawing sympathetic white men and women into its orbit. In 1831, William Lloyd Garrison began publishing *The Liberator* and organized the New England Anti-Slavery Society; very quickly abolitionist societies sprouted, first in the larger cities, and then into the countryside where the population loomed much larger. By the time Lincoln spoke before the Lyceum Society, there may have been 1,000 antislavery societies with more than 100,000 members across the Northeast, Middle Atlantic, and Midwest.[4]

Abolitionism gained enormous energy from the spiritual transformations that had been convulsing Protestantism since the middle of the eighteenth century and, especially, since the revivals of the Second Great Awakening during the early decades of the nineteenth. Building upon ideas of benevolence and the worth of all human beings regardless of their worldly stations, revivalists depicted individuals not as inveterate sinners (in the way of Calvinists) but as moral free agents who could choose good over evil, achieve salvation, and help eradicate sin by joining legions of evangelicals intent on convincing others to do the same. Most of the leading white abolitionists, women as well as men, either were converted during the Second Great Awakening or were Quakers who had long been guided by an inner light and a commitment to nonviolence. Abolitionists thereby came to regard slavery as more than a moral or political wrong; they regarded it as a sin and slaveholders as sinners. Yet religious injunctions were only part of the threat that abolitionism seemed to embody. Abolitionists went door-to-door to try to persuade their neighbors to embrace their cause, and thereby pioneered new forms of political mobilization. They launched massive petition campaigns, often led by women, to force state legislatures and the federal Congress to confront the evils of enslavement. They boycotted slave-made products to limit the markets that slaveholders might supply. And they implicitly called into question other forms of hierarchy and power—of gender, class, and race—that had been foundational to notions of social stability.[5]

The morally and theologically grounded arguments of abolitionism also proved central to the construction of what might be called the "liberal self": a notion of self-possession or self-ownership that Hobbes and Locke imagined in their states of nature and that served as the basis of political consent, claims to private property, and the formation of civil and political society. To be sure, Hobbes and Locke explained how self-ownership and consent could go into the making of an all-powerful sovereign or the unequal distribution of property or even enslavement. And political thinkers since Machiavelli had insisted that a republic—the best form of governance—would only survive if a collective sense of the public good was nurtured, a sense that most agreed rested on property (and especially landed property) ownership. The "liberty" so prized in a republic required economic independence to achieve and sustain; and what it meant to be free and an active participant in political life was inextricably tied to the ability to provide for oneself, to avoid depending on others for one's livelihood.

Abolitionism, with the moral ballast of Christian Arminianism—the notion that salvation can be achieved through personal will—disrupted the republican formula, made self-ownership the fundamental basis of freedom and independence, and turned the public good into the dictates of conscience (and potentially the pursuit of self-interest). Abolitionists expressed their faith less in the wisdom and integrity of communities—though they fed off their own communities of conscience and faith—than in the moral capacities of individuals. Instead of a spectrum of dependencies or a web of obligations, at least outside of the family, abolitionists saw a binary of slavery and freedom. They took Locke to one of his logical conclusions.[6]

From the first, abolitionism depended on the financial support and heavy lifting of African Americans. They composed the majority of subscribers to abolitionist newspapers and did the main work of protecting vulnerable Black settlements in the North and fugitives from slavery in the South. There was no other way forward since only a handful of whites were drawn to the abolitionist banner. The main narrative, then, has been how abolitionism increased its white following and eventually energized a broader antislavery movement that could take national power.

But there is another, generally overlooked, story of oppositional forces that helps us understand what abolitionism was up against and what the opposition's discomforting historical meaning might be. Indeed, although we tend to highlight the road that the states of the Northeast and Middle West traveled away from slavery, sympathy for slaveholders and support for the institution of slavery were widespread there well into the nineteenth century. Some of the most influential early proslavery tracts were written by members of the New England clergy (and would continue to be written by native New Englanders) soon to be fortified by Federalist-inspired conservatism. They came to reject the notion of universal equality, the rights claims of the poor and subordinate, and the principles associated with Jefferson for the conservative wisdom of Edmund Burke. Congregationalism was strongly disposed against any form of abolitionism, and Yale and Princeton trained generations of clergymen and theologians in the conservative ways. Authority, order, and obedience were the pillars to be resurrected.[7]

Although colonization is generally regarded as a moderate form of antislavery, it is better seen as a manifestation of the illiberal tendencies cascading across much of the country in the early years of the nineteenth century. Like Jefferson himself, colonizationists had little more than a rhetorical interest in the abolition of slavery; at best they imagined a day in the very distant future when slavery might be gone and the African-descended population gone along with it. They equated abolitionism with social disorder, the inversion of timeless hierarchies, threats to private property, and racial "amalgamation" (or mixing). They hoped to chart a path that gestured to the evils of enslavement while securing the economic and political benefits—and the elite rule—that slavery made possible, a path involving a very long transition not from slavery to freedom (because there would be no freedom in the United States for the enslaved) but rather from a society resting on an enslaved Black labor force to a white republic: an expulsionism being pursued simultaneously in relation to Native peoples and to those seen as religious heretics.[8]

The character and political dispositions of colonizationists were perhaps best revealed by their involvement in the increasingly violent anti-abolitionism of the 1830s. Reacting to the formation of abolitionist societies and especially abolitionist denunciations of colonization as morally bankrupt, they began by calling public meetings and, through resolutions, handbills, and the press, warning abolitionists of what they would face if they did not cease their "operations": harassment, arrest, banishment, or subjection to the "law of Judge Lynch." Colonizationists and other anti-abolitionist allies proclaimed that they would not permit the gathering of "incendiary individuals" within "corporate bounds" putting their prosperity at risk and their social order in jeopardy. Abolitionists, they thundered, were intent on "inflam[ing] the passions of the multitudes, including women and children, and boarding school misses and factory girls," having women "turn their sewing parties into abolition clubs," and promoting race mixing and the "mongrelizing" of the Anglo-American population with the blood of Black inferiors.[9]

But it was the anti-abolitionists, not their abolitionist enemies, who inflamed the public passions. Once abolitionist societies and newspapers were established in a city or town, anti-abolitionists attempted to break up their meetings, shout down their speakers, destroy their presses, ransack the homes of their leaders, and, on occasion, drive them off. Full-scale anti-abolition "riots" and "mobs" erupted during the middle years of the decade—well over one hundred in all—not only in large cities like New York, Boston, Philadelphia, and Cincinnati but also in smaller urban centers like Newark, New Jersey, Concord, New Hampshire, and Utica, New York, and even in villages like Canterbury, Connecticut, and Berlin, Ohio. Although fatalities were few in number, the destruction and terror were widespread and consequential. Garrison was dragged through the streets of Boston, and the newly built Pennsylvania Hall in Philadelphia, a meeting site for abolitionists and other reformers, was burned to the ground. Recognized as abolitionist allies, none suffered more from terrorism and devastation than the small Black enclaves in their midst or on their perimeters; Black people, not white people, were most vulnerable to lethal violence.[10]

The choreography of anti-abolitionist violence is particularly significant because it suggests that the idea of "mobs" and "riots" obscures what was really the persistence of older forms of political expression. Although some of the rioters came from the lower reaches of the social order, looking to vent their hostilities and dissatisfactions, the leadership came chiefly from the ranks of merchants, bankers, lawyers, and public officials whose families were of older stock and conservative Protestant denominations. Many were Episcopalians. By and large they were closely identified with the seaboard mercantile economies of the eighteenth and early nineteenth centuries, not the emerging manufacturing economies, as well as with the local political establishments. They were, that is, considered to be the old elite, the "aristocracy of the North," "prominent and respectable gentlemen," "gentlemen of property and standing." They likely had been Federalist in their politics and colonizationists on the slavery question. Not incidentally, their actions were often accompanied by cacophonies of shouts, tin horns, clanging pots, and whistles evoking the rituals of rough justice that communities had long inflicted on those accused of transgressing their norms. Abolitionists could be pelted with rocks and rotten eggs, tarred and feathered, and otherwise publicly shamed, symbolizing both rejection and retribution. "Anti-abolitionists," writes historian Leonard Richards, "saw their opponents as the vanguard of a challenge to their basic prerogatives, defy[ing] the right of settlers and residents to impose their own patterns of behavior . . . threaten[ing] the authority of fathers and husbands . . . bypass[ing] the authority of city fathers, and challeng[ing] the dominion of local elites." It was the political dynamic of the "crowd," either led or condoned by the elite, in action.[11]

The eruption of violent anti-abolitionism not only reminds us of what the abolitionists confronted; it also demonstrates that abolitionism was as much about the nature of a post-emancipation world as it was about emancipating the enslaved and ridding the country of the system of slavery. During the 1830s, Black people still burdened by the status of enslavement could be found in the Northeast, Middle Atlantic, and the Midwest in relatively small numbers. They were either fugitives from states in which slavery remained legal or were still left in thrall by a gradual emancipation process that had begun in the late eighteenth century and had not fully played out. But by that time all the states north of the Ohio River or Mason-Dixon line had committed themselves to seeing slavery's demise, even if that would require more than one legislative action. Abolitionism developed in a world confronting the ending and aftermath of slavery; the struggle was over what a postemancipation society would look like and what sort of relations and hierarchies would frame the lives and prospects of newly liberated slaves. What would freedom mean and to what extent would the liberal self be generalized?[12]

The picture is a discouraging one, and it had powerful implications for what lay ahead. The obstacles to abolition were twofold: slaves were private property and their owners expected some type of compensation upon their emancipation; but since slaves themselves were viewed as propertyless and degraded, bereft of resources, their emancipation would enlarge a dependent population likely to stir disorder and become charges on local governments, if not become criminals. With few exceptions, white Americans of the period thought of Black people—enslaved or not—as occupying the lowest rungs of the social and culture ladder, unable to climb higher. Many, like Jefferson, believed that people of African descent were simply inferior to whites and incapable of taking on the responsibilities that freedom required. But even abolitionists worried about whether the violence, exploitation, and forced submissions of enslavement so ill-prepared slaves for freedom that they would have to be closely managed and tutored before being fully accepted as equals. For the writer and Garrisonian Lydia Maria Child, slavery promoted "treachery, fraud and violence" and left the slave to "his wretched wanderings." "They are treated like brutes," she warned, "and all the influences around them conspire to make them brutes." Small wonder that colonization proved so appealing.[13]

Short of federally organized expulsion, states and localities resorted to a variety of punitive measures to confine the formerly enslaved, hedge their mobility, deprive them of education and political power, and leave them in a nether world of coercions. Many women and men who managed to depart bondage found themselves ensnared in short- or long-term servitude, which courts in many cases permitted. Freedmen were generally denied voting rights or disfranchised if they had once enjoyed them, and they faced significant restrictions on their ability to sue or testify in courts of law, not to mention serve on juries. Municipalities often excluded them from or segregated them in the use of public facilities, including new public schools. Midwestern states like Ohio, Indiana, and Illinois, where slavery had been outlawed from the advent of statehood, nonetheless enacted "Black Laws" requiring African Americans to register, post bond, limit their stays, and find white patrons to vouch for them. White Californians included an antislavery provision in their first constitution but also attempted to exclude all Black people from the state. Whites in the Oregon Territory not only excluded all Blacks from coming within territorial borders but prescribed "not less than twenty nor more than thirty-nine stripes" and potential re-enslavement for those determined to remain. The specter of Jim Crow first came to life in the antebellum North rather than in the postbellum South.[14]

This was the context in which new ideas about race and white supremacy were constructed, drawing from intellectual currents moving across the Atlantic and mainly through the Northeast and Mid-Atlantic. Ideas about difference and hierarchy organized around culture and religion were turned into notions of racial inferiority as Euro-American thinkers attempted to square Enlightenment ideals of human equality and rationality with apparent otherness in their midst. In this way, an emerging liberal world view effectively tripped over its own social inventions and helped nurture racist theories. Southern proslavery ideologues, beginning in the 1830s, were then happy to yoke them to an argument that had more to do with explicitly rejecting Enlightenment principles along with the radical possibilities of evangelical Christianity.[15]

Yet there is more to the story. The "Black Laws" proliferating across the states that had moved against slavery were not simply manifestations of a new racism; they built upon much older settlement and poor laws that came within the recognized "police powers" of localities and were designed to secure them against threats to their safety, health, and well-being: threats coming from those deemed paupers, vagrants, vagabonds, and criminals; transients and dependents who would burden communities economically, likely spread disease, and violate the rules sustaining social order. "Regardless of what they believed about the nature of race itself," writes historian Kate Masur, "[the] justification for race-based laws became part of the deep currents in political and legal thought which heightened their power. From the colonial period to the Civil War, white northerners regularly characterized free African Americans, as a group, as dependents, vagrants, or criminals who lowered the moral standing of the community." The role of government, white Americans widely believed, was the protection less of individual rights than of the integrity of communities, with the hierarchies, social norms, notions of justice, and resorts to expulsion that they had devised: the protection of the illiberal worlds that were proliferating across the country.[16]

II

ON THE EVENING OF 11 AUGUST 1834, only a day after a mob of several hundred young white men, many of them Irish, destroyed a Black settlement in Moyamensing, Pennsylvania, just outside of Philadelphia, a large number of Protestants marched toward the Ursuline convent in Charlestown, Massachusetts, well in view of famed Bunker Hill. The convent had been moved there in 1828 and was devoted to educating young girls, some poor Catholics but many Protestant (mostly Unitarians) from well-to-do families who could pay the tuition. For the most part, relations between the convent and its Protestant neighbors had been amicable despite the intensifying anti-Catholicism in Boston and New England at large. But in the summer of 1834 rumors began to circulate of a young woman, a Sister Mary John, being held against her will. The crowd gathered at the convent around 8:00 p.m. shouting "no popery" and "down with the cross," and demanding Sister John's release. They were refused and told to disperse by the mother superior, with a warning about "twenty thousand Irishmen" who would be unleashed if they stood their ground. Incensed, the crowd, estimated as a couple of hundred, soon broke into the convent, desecrated its contents, and set the building ablaze. A fire company arriving on the scene joined as many as two thousand spectators in watching the convent turn into a smoldering ruin. All the nuns managed to escape.[17]

It was no accident that a scathing memoir of a woman's time at the convent, emphasizing near-imprisonment and spiritual coercion, had become public in the weeks before the conflagration or that the fiery evangelist Lyman Beecher had been in Boston just a day earlier railing against Catholics, Catholicism, and the proliferation of their schools. Nor was it an accident that a number of volumes and newspaper stories had been published in recent years that depicted convents as dens of sexual transgressions and infanticide, and convent schools as the means of converting Protestants and advancing Catholic dominion. Since the 1790s, as the Catholic, and especially the Irish Catholic, population of the Northeast grew, the revivals of the Second Great Awakening had been scorching city and countryside alike, offering up a shared cultural experience to Protestants while hardening their views of those regarded as the anti-Christ in their midst. Boston had already witnessed attacks on Irish enclaves that had been stirred by the exhortations of revivalists.[18]

We generally associate the evangelism of the period with a disposition toward personal relationships with God, salvation, self-improvement, and the planting of an inner drive toward good works and reform. That is true. But there was, as well, a powerful orientation—sometimes parallel, sometimes interconnected, sometimes oppositional—to order, social hierarchy, and Christian trusteeship, which could have enormous appeal to Christians fearful of a rapidly changing world around them, as well as to enslavers who bridled at being called sinners. The self-designated prophet Robert Matthias won a devoted following in New York, including the Black woman we would come to know as Sojourner Truth, by preaching a message of rigid patriarchy and the subordination of women and children, and by attempting to build a theocratic kingdom. Among the strongest defenders of slavery in the South were evangelical ministers and slaveholders who wished to convert, not emancipate, their slaves, and worried about the corrosive effects of revivalism elsewhere.[19]

The convent burning tapped into fears of a world in disarray, a market economy posing new perils, and power relations that appeared to be shifting. Nuns, after all, were single women who rejected family and household and chose to live under the authority of priests whose vows of celibacy were easily doubted. They were foundational to the Catholic Church—itself an extension of a foreign, anti-republican conspiracy as many imagined—and, as teachers, the means by which Catholic power in the United States would grow. They also embodied a more general process by which women were increasingly engaged in public life, in reform and politics, even if they lacked the franchise, including the disorder that could occur along with it. As in anti-abolitionism, anti-Catholicism now turned in expulsive directions.

In 1835, the prophet Matthias, who was fleeing a host of legal troubles in New York, found his way to the town of Kirtland in northeastern Ohio, where he met up with another self-anointed prophet named Joseph Smith. Born in rural Vermont shortly after the turn of the nineteenth century, Smith moved with his family to western New York during the 1810s, where the evangelicalism of the period proved especially intense. The "burned-over district" it came to be called. Here Smith not only experienced a spiritual awakening but claimed to have had a vision in which an angel named Maroni directed him to two buried golden plates that predated the Bible. By 1830 Smith had translated and published the writings on the plates as the *Book of Mormon*, begun to attract a coterie of followers, and organized the Church of Christ (later the Church of Jesus Christ of Latter-Day Saints or LDS). According to the prophecies of the golden plates, the Zion or New Jerusalem was to be in North America and Native peoples were descendants of one of Israel's Lost Tribes.[20]

Like other prophets of the time and Puritans before them, Smith sought to restore an earlier, purified Christian church. The *Book of Mormon* depicted a God who had emerged from manhood, Jesus as God's literal son, a millennial vision of God's kingdom on earth, a personal relationship with God, a patriarchal order, and a notion of priestly authority. Not surprisingly, Smith's early adherents and converts tended to be New Englanders who had migrated west, and unlike many other spiritual seekers—Campbellites, Shakers, Millerites—Smith's church, quickly known as Mormons, attracted many followers. In 1831 Smith moved to Kirtland in Ohio's Western Reserve while sending some of his disciples to Missouri, where they hoped to establish the true Zion. Already a site of religious enthusiasm, Kirtland almost immediately embraced Smith's project and within a short time, hundreds more arrived to join. Out in Missouri, Smith intended to make Jackson County and its town of Independence the center of the Mormon world, and when they subsequently moved from there to Nauvoo, on the Mississippi River in Illinois, the population—supplemented by two thousand transatlantic migrants—soon exceeded twelve thousand, surpassing Chicago in size.[21]

Yet, much as this appeared a success story, signs of trouble were evident even before Smith and his Mormon flock made it to Kirtland. Smith's New York neighbors eyed his church and newly baptized converts with suspicion, and threats of violence against them were soon in the air. At this point, Smith only suffered arrest and charges as a "disorderly person" before being acquitted. But he could see the handwriting on the wall and left for Ohio. There things took a turn for the worse. Fearful of Smith and his growing number of followers, an angry crowd of about fifty locals descended on Smith's house in early 1832, dragged him out, and gave him a dose of tar and feathers, the customary punishment for those who violated community norms and were marked for expulsion. Missouri was the next stop and a deadly one. In no time, Jackson County Mormon settlements came under attack. Homes and farms were torched, printing presses destroyed, and twelve hundred Mormons run off across the Missouri River to nearby Clay County and its environs. There, full-out warfare erupted in 1838, during which a group of Mormons was massacred, Smith was apprehended and jailed, and Mormons were ordered by the governor to leave the state or face summary punishment. Relatively isolated Nauvoo appeared to offer more safety; to it Smith fled in

hopes of avoiding prosecution or lynching in Missouri and of recon-
stituting a community of the faithful. The problem was that as Mormon power grew, the hostility of non-Mormons grew along with it.[22]

It may be imagined that the Mormon embrace of polygamy sparked
hostilities, threatening as it did the familial ideals that Protestants had
long recognized as a bedrock of social order. But although rumors
about plural marriage percolated as early as 1830, there was little substance to them before Smith began to construct a relevant theology in
Nauvoo after 1840. Indeed, by the time polygamy took hold (sparking internal controversy too), Mormons had made themselves anath-
ema for many other reasons. Mormonism was regarded by many as a
"fake" and fanatical religion that rejected the Protestant faith. Mormons missionized among Native peoples, without much success, and
were thereby accused of inciting aggression among them. Mormons
had an ambiguous position on the slavery question, seemed open to
converting free people of color, and attracted followers mainly from
the Northeast and Middle Atlantic where slavery was being undermined, especially worrisome to whites in Missouri. And Mormons
became formidable in number, consequential politically, and ready to
defend themselves militarily. Suspicious observers saw Mormons as a
people apart and, in submitting to priestly figures like Joseph Smith,
as subverting American republicanism, however illiberal its nature or
its maintenance demanded. Some compared Mormonism to Catholicism and Islam and thereby to the prospect of foreign interventions
and conspiracies.[23]

The bloody Mormon "war" of 1838 in Missouri was provoked
by an election-day fray that August when non-Mormons attempted
to prevent Mormons from voting. "A Mormon has no more right to
vote than a negro," one angry Missourian exclaimed. Pitched battles
followed over the next few months, including the slaughter of seventeen Mormon men, women, and children at the Haun's Mill encamp-
ment. One of the assailants who murdered a ten-year-old boy crowed
that "nits will make lice, and if he had lived he would have become
a Mormon." Smith and other leaders were arrested and charged with
arson, murder, and treason, and the governor issued an expulsion
and extermination decree. "The Mormons must be treated as ene-

mies," he proclaimed, "and must be exterminated or driven from the state if necessary for the public peace. Their outrages are beyond all description."[24]

Smith managed to escape prosecution and, like Elijah Lovejoy before him, fled Missouri for Illinois, where he and his followers initially received a solid welcome, including from Stephen Douglas and Abraham Lincoln. There they secured 700 acres and a charter from the state legislature for their new town of Nauvoo (the name has Hebrew origins). Mindful of their previous experiences, Smith and the other Mormon leaders sought political autonomy, and were pleased to be granted control over their local government and courts as well as the right to organize a militia. The charter, they insisted, represented their "Magna Carta." Yet, like Elijah Lovejoy too, Illinois soon turned into a cauldron of hostility for the Mormons. Although Nauvoo sought relative isolation, word spread about the power that Smith had accrued, his efforts to build a priestly kingdom, poten- tial "alliances" with Native peoples nearby, the apparent openness of Mormons to racial mixing, and the spread of plural marriage among them: all owing to the words of disgruntled Mormons who had bro- ken with Smith. But especially explosive was Nauvoo's tendency to play Democrats and Whigs off against each other and become a swing voting bloc. Smith went so far as to declare his candidacy for the United States presidency in 1844 and then impose martial law in Nauvoo in the face of legal harassment from outside. Arrested and charged with treason and rioting, Smith and his brother were jailed in the town of Warsaw in June to await trial. But the quickly orga- nized Warsaw Committee of Safety saw to it that justice would be a community affair. They broke into the jail and murdered the Smith brothers. Several months later, the Illinois legislature repealed Nau- voo's charter and effectively forced the Mormons out. The governor of Missouri had threatened Mormons with expulsion or extermina- tion; there and in Illinois Mormons were treated to both. Smith's suc- cessor, Brigham Young, thus looked west to territory still claimed by Mexico and headed to the Great Basin, likely to "be coveted by no other people." But by the time Young and his beleaguered followers came through the Wasatch Mountains and began settling the Great

Salt Lake Valley, the U.S.-Mexican War had ended and the region was controlled by the United States. More struggles lay ahead.[25]

III

THE USE OF THE TERMS "mobs" and "riots" to describe episodes of racial and cultural violence is meant to distinguish them from the politics and political practices of the time. And, on the face of it, there seems to be good reason for doing so. Although local elections appear to have drawn impressive levels of voter participation in many places during the early republic, the 1820s and 1830s are widely regarded as the era of political democratization in the United States, when the foundations of what is commonly called a liberal democratic system came into being. Most states either eliminated or modified property-owning requirements for voting and officeholding. Many more public offices on the state and local levels became elective rather than appointive. Mass political parties emerged for the first time, with the Democrats and Whigs replacing the Republicans and the Federalists. And most of the states made the popular vote, not the state legislature, the determinant of electors in presidential contests, which remains the case to this day. With the exception of Rhode Island, the most urbanized and industrialized of the states, all of this occurred peacefully, through legislative acts that had a great deal of support. By 1840, most adult white men were fully enfranchised, and turnout in elections, especially national elections, soared to near 80 percent of those eligible, a level at which it would remain for the rest of the century. A new electoral arena had been constructed and it appeared to be vibrant and more inclusive.[26]

Yet the arenas of formal electoral politics and of intimidation and expulsion were more interconnected than we might imagine, so that traditional means of political expression and practice were often reinforced rather than undermined by the democratization process. In cities and the larger towns, election campaigns drew heavily upon the symbols and cadences that had long characterized street demonstrations and commemorations. Torches, banners, raucous shouting, men

and boys in regalia, fifes and drumbeats all marked parades and processions as new political parties sought to demonstrate their strength
and popular support. Their practices clearly fed off the rituals of legit-
imation and sanction that were familiar to local denizens and had
already been displayed in the emerging political culture of the early
republic. Indeed, the campaigns often depicted politics as a form of
warfare between opposing sides in which urban space was being contested and the harnessing of local power would serve to vanquish
political foes.[27]

Not surprisingly, the scenes at polling places on election day ampli-
fied the tenor of struggle as representatives of competing parties and
candidates jostled with one another, screaming insults and epithets,
lubricated by the alcohol fundamental to successful electioneering,
as they tried to round up their supporters and strike fear into their
enemies. "Each one talking loud and fast," a participant in an 1838
St. Louis municipal election observed, "bringing forward the voters
telling them who to vote for, challenging the votes of everyone with
who they have the faintest shadow of a chance; handing out tickets,
crossing out names, with many arguments pro and con . . . some imi-
tat[ing] the Barking of Dogs and some the Roaring of Bulls, all making as much noise as they could." Scuffling and fighting often broke
out, with local toughs brought in to enforce party discipline and drive
the opposition off. "Cursing, drinking, sometimes fighting, getting
black eyes and bloody noses . . . coming home with coat torn off and
sometimes minus a hat," seemed standard fare for election day. And
when ethnic or religious antagonisms were added to the mix, as they
often were by the 1830s, the political faithful might inflict physical
punishments of varying severity on the other side. On occasion, a
prospective voter might be killed: shot, knifed, or battered to death.
According to one estimate, election "riots" during this period may
have claimed nearly ninety lives and left many more with serious injuries. Elections, in the words of the editor of the New Orleans *Bulletin*,
were "a hell's holiday of drunkenness and perjury and bludgeons."[28]

The act of voting itself could be ensnared in a coercive shroud.
The Constitution left it to the states to determine both the method
of voting and the qualifications of voters, and, as might be expected,

an assortment of practices was to be found. But everywhere, voting was a wholly public event. Printed ballots were in general use by the 1830s, and they would be handed out at the polls by party loyalists; *viva voce* (by voice) voting, widespread during the colonial period, still took place in five states. Either way, employers, merchants, and master craftsmen could look on as their employees and clerks walked up and deposited their ballots or announced their choices. Harassment, shaming, and related reckonings, as in so much else, were part of the political stew.[29]

In the countryside and in rural villages, democratization often served to strengthen rather than undermine patron-client politics and the martial demeanor that might surround it. New political parties, on their way to organizing mass constituencies around sets of ideas and policies, often tapped into rival clan and kinship networks, as gentry families continued their quests for power and authority in different garb. If anything, the expansion of elective offices, especially at the local level, gave members of the elite even more opportunity to enlarge the scope of their patronage by sponsoring humbler men as candidates for positions—sheriffs, tax collectors, surveyors, magistrates—that brought salaries or fees, not to mention the prospect of useful services. Large landowners might have the polls located on their property, host party barbecues and meetings, and supply alcohol to their enfranchised clients on election day. In Sugar Creek, Illinois, John Drennan's Prairie, on his large spread of land, served as the polling place, muster ground, and stage stop, and, by one account, voters converged there to hear the last of the candidates' speeches and then "commenced the drinking of liquor." "Long before night a large portion of the voters would be drunk and staggering about, cursing, swearing, hallooing, yelling, huzzaing for their favorite candidates," then "throwing their arms up and around, threatening to fight, and fighting." Men like Drennan, a Democrat in this instance, could offer prospective candidates the benefits of their influence, help defray the costs of electioneering, and act as sureties if their clients won an election and had to post what were substantial officer bonds. This, after all, was just another dimension to the world of vertical allegiances and reciprocal obligations—protection, work, credit, loans, and assistance in times of trouble in return for loyalty, votes, skills, and the readiness to intimidate foes—that had long suffused rural life and would continue to do so until new social relations fractured it.[30]

Nowhere were these dynamics more fully in play, or more militarized, than in the states and districts in which large numbers of enslaved people were held captive. Although historians have customarily treated politics there as if the electoral arena could be imagined separately from the arenas of enslavement, and have frequently described a robust *herrenvolk* democracy, or a democracy among members of the dominant race, no such distinction can so neatly be drawn. The central imperative of politics, at all levels of governance, was maintaining control over enslaved laborers and policing the plantations, farms, and vast stretches of the countryside enslaved people might seek to traverse.[31]

Militia companies and slave patrols, often interconnected, were thereby the instruments for deploying the slaveholders' power and herding the energies of white inhabitants, whether or not they owned slaves, who were required to serve and, by the 1830s, able to vote and hold office. Militia musters were political as well as civic and social events, given over to more than drilling, parading, and firing muskets. They were usually the largest community gatherings that took place yearly, often at times of ritual celebration and commemoration, bringing out men, women, and enslaved people to witness what William Faulkner called the "more or less" citizen-soldiers enacting both the military basis of social order and the social hierarchies that composed it. At the musters, members of prominent local families effectively assembled their supporters, whose uniforms they likely supplied, and thereby demonstrated the extent of their following together with their power and influence. There, in sponsoring the large barbecues that often culminated the musters, they showed their wealth, generosity, and patronage. And there they also vied for election or appointment as militia officers, and either laid the groundwork for their own campaigns or provided space and occasion for the stump speeches of favored candidates. In many areas, new political parties never fully disentangled themselves from the family and kinship allegiances that long formed the foundation of political identity, or from the notion that political differences were to be regarded as personal insults and aspersions demanding vengeance. Fittingly, the smallest units of electoral politics were known as militia districts.[32]

A political culture that thrived on sidearms, street gangs, truncheons, and fists as well as rallies, conventions, and grassroots mobilizations was not confined to the fields of local politics. It suffused the halls of legislative power too. The infamous episode in which South Carolina congressman Preston Brooks strode into the United States Senate chamber and nearly beat Massachusetts senator Charles Sumner to death with his cane in 1856 has been regarded chiefly as a symbol of the intensifying conflict over slavery and thus something of an exception in the world of formal political institutions. But this was hardly the case. State legislatures were often rife with physical threats and fisticuffs that could easily move in more lethal directions. In 1837, the speaker of the Arkansas House of Representatives responded to what he considered a slight from another representative by drawing his bowie knife and stabbing to death his verbal assailant who, it appears, had drawn his own weapon a bit too slowly. The U.S. Congress, and especially the House of Representatives, was not much better even before the slavery question so deeply divided the political dispositions of its members. At its bloodiest, Maine congressman Jonathan Cilley was killed in a duel by Maryland congressman William Graves over a bribery accusation that involved party more than person, but members routinely carried weapons onto the floor. The body had its known enforcers or "bullies," generally southerners rather than Yankees. As Representative Galusha A. Grow of Pennsylvania later put it, "Crowd some hundreds of men together on an afternoon or night; fill them with the partisan ardor, perplex them with doubt as to the personal gain or loss that may follow their vote on the question at issue, and instill them with envy of, or ill-will toward, their fellows, and you have abundant material for a row. All that is needed is an excuse, and that too often is found." Congress did manage to outlaw dueling in the District of Columbia in 1839, to limited effect, and quite remarkably Preston Brooks proposed that members of Congress check their firearms, though not their knives, in the cloakroom before stepping onto the floor. A real man, as Brooks seemed to believe, could do honor's business without them.[33]

Politics was, to say the least, a rough, rowdy, and very much of a male theater of public power; indeed, a fierce celebration of the gender exclusions that kept women and other dependents on the outside. The selection of polling places in town and country (saloons, livery stables, courthouses, and militia grounds), the routine consumption of alcohol, the commonplace drunkenness, the swearing and physical violence were not only designed to reward loyalists and intimidate foes who, in principle, could participate. They were meant to create sites of political belonging and nonbelonging, warning off, and, if necessary, expelling those not welcome to tread there. Over the course of the nineteenth century, various campaigns to reform political practices, including those demanding the enfranchisement of women, explicitly acknowledged the coercions, harassments, intimidations, and frauds that appeared firmly embedded in electoral politics.

Popular ideas of conspiratorial threats to the republic and of expelling or otherwise suppressing the offenders became an important component of political party formation, especially early on. One of the targets was Freemasonry, which first took hold in British North America—by way of Britain—in the 1730s and by the Revolutionary era had spread among officers in the Continental Army. George Washington and Benjamin Franklin could be counted among its members. Accordingly, two Masonic symbols, the pyramid and the eye, would be included in the Great Seal of the United States and, to this day, on dollar currency. Masons saw themselves as embodiments of the Enlightenment, advocates of reason, science, and ethics, and cosmopolitan figures in a rapidly changing world. Freemasonry thus tended to appeal to men of the middle and upper classes, with an urban or metropolitan bent, who looked for a social environment that would aid their cultural and professional ambitions. As might be expected, Freemasony attracted a large share of Episcopalians, Unitarians, and Universalists but, while Christianity was a significant inspiration, the organization did not exclude non-Christians and was generally ecumenical.[34]

The problem was not only the Masons' exclusivity by gender as well as class, enforced by the dues required and the ease with which a prospective member could be blackballed. It was also the secret rituals and oaths that bound the Masons together and raised the suspicions of those who looked in from the outside. The tipping point came in 1826, when a disgruntled member in western New York State threatened to reveal the Masons' secrets and quite suddenly disappeared, presumed to be murdered. At the very least, he was never seen again. The reaction was immediate and stormy. "Antimasons," as they called themselves, disrupted the Masonic meetings and vandalized their property. The Masons initially returned the favor. Before long, the Antimasons moved in a political direction, hoping to purge local and state offices of Masonic influence (many offices were in fact held by Masons) as a means of ridding the country of the organization. Utilizing a language of expulsion and excommunication, they established a political party to facilitate that end, mobilizing impressively in New England and the Mid-Atlantic. Their intent was to use the instruments of the state to advance their goals, demanding in particular the repeal of Masonic lodge charters and the outlawing of Masonic oaths.[35]

Antimasons are generally regarded as the country's first "third party," and they do have the distinction, in 1831, of holding the first national political convention. Ironically, given the number of Masons among the Revolutionary leadership, Antimasons portrayed them as anti-republican and infused with the spirits of hierarchy and aristocracy: as something of a closed international conspiracy intent on gaining control over American life and defiling both local democracy and evangelical Christianity, somewhat in the manner of Catholics, to whom they were, on occasion, compared. Although Antimasonic constituencies could bleed into one another, they were most robust in rural and small-town districts of the Northeast that were feeling the effects of the market intensifications of the period, especially through which the revivals of the Second Great Awakening had swept. Indeed, the attachment to localism, the experience of evangelicalism, and the encounter with the new dynamics of the marketplace seemed characteristic of Antimasonry's supporters, many of whom believed that

Masons corrupted Christianity. They made their presence felt. By the early 1830s, Antimasons were the largest political party in Vermont and nearly so in Pennsylvania, the second largest in Massachusetts, and of consequence in Rhode Island and New York.[36]

The Antimasons, like many future third parties, proved short-lived, and on that account we may wish to dismiss their significance. But their subsequent political trajectories suggest otherwise. By the later 1830s the Antimasons had left the scene after achieving great success. They had driven Freemasonry into an astonishing retreat from which it would not recover until after the Civil War. But Antimasons did not then simply retire from the political arena. For many of them, the next stop was the Whig Party and then the new Republican Party, perhaps an indication, as historians often find, of the reform energies and commitment to antislavery Antimasonry may have fostered. That may be. Yet the trajectory also reminds us of the baggage of nativism, anti-Catholicism, and anti-Mormonism that the legatees of Antimasonry brought with them, especially those who moved to Republicanism by way of the nativist Know Nothings, as was common in the Northeast. When, therefore, the Republican Party made its first run for national office in 1856, it crafted a platform that called upon Congress to exercise its "imperative" and constitutional duty "to prohibit in the Territories those twin relics of barbarism—Polygamy and Slavery."[37]

IV

IN THE SPRING OF 1832, a twenty-three-year-old Abraham Lincoln volunteered for the Illinois militia, called up by the state governor to join federal troops in combating a group of Sauks, Meskwakis, and Kickapoos, also known as the "British Band." Perhaps two thousand in number, about three-quarters of whom were women and children, the band had reoccupied homelands from which they had been expelled owing to an earlier, contested treaty and the pressure of white settler colonialism. Their leader was Black Hawk, a Sauk warrior, and when a militia unit opened fire on them, they retaliated.

Fighting then spread across northern Illinois and what is now southern Wisconsin for nearly four months. Although they managed to
inflict damage on some of the militia companies, who also suffered
from a cholera outbreak, and encourage neighboring Ho-Chunks
and Potowatomis to raid forts and settlements left undefended, Black
Hawk's band suffered a crushing defeat that August at the Battle of
Bad Axe and was pushed back across the Mississippi. Black Hawk
himself initially managed to escape capture only to be taken into custody a bit later and jailed for a time in St. Louis. Thereafter, he lived
out his few remaining years, in utter defeat, on tribal lands west of the
Mississippi.[38]

Lincoln did not see action in what is known as the Black Hawk
War, though he did bear witness to the casualties that Black Hawk's
band inflicted on some of those soldiers who did. Instead, Lincoln
was delighted to have been elected captain of his New Salem militia
company and to use his militia service for political purposes, mostly
in jesting about the boasts of rival Democrats as to their own military
exploits. When he came before the Springfield Lyceum six years later
to warn about the epidemic of mob violence and the flouting of the
rule of law that he believed threatened the country, Lincoln made no
mention of the use of state and federal law to carry out the largest
mass expulsion in American history. For the Black Hawk War erupted
in the context of the Jackson administration's determination to extirpate the land claims of Native peoples residing east of the Mississippi River and force them onto lands roughly between the Platte and
Red rivers west of the Mississippi and the new states of Arkansas and
Missouri. The lands to which Native peoples were expelled would be
known as "Indian" or "Western" territory, to be supervised by a commissioner of Indian affairs and the commandants of military bases.[39]

The expulsion, or "removal," as it is customarily known, represented continuity and change. From earliest settlement, many American colonists doubted whether they could live in peace with the
Natives around them, hungry as they were for access to more land.
Although trading relations were also robust and consequential from
the first, an expulsionist impulse was always in evidence, especially in
the backcountry, even if mitigated by traders or the colonial govern-

ments. The bloody warfare that the American Revolution unleashed in what was still regarded as "Indian country" bore testimony to that impulse, which was only exacerbated by American independence and the flooding of the trans-Appalachian west with white settlers. The Constitution offered limited clarity, though it acknowledged the Native presence. It excluded "Indians not taxed" from being counted for the purposes of congressional apportionment, and gave the federal government the authority, in the "commerce clause," to regulate trade with them as well as "with foreign nations, and among the several states."[40]

During the early republic and into the 1820s federal officials recognized Native territorial claims and, like the British before them, saw treaties and formal exchanges as the mechanisms through which to adjust them. Yet there was little agreement as to how the interests and ways of white settlers and Native peoples might mesh. Their very different ideas about property, subsistence, and gender relations not only made for conflict but also led many settlers to view Native societies as backward and barbaric, as obstacles in the path of civilization's advance. But there still seemed to be flexibility at the federal level. Henry Knox, who served as secretary of war in George Washington's cabinet, was not alone among policy makers in hoping that Natives could, in fact, be "civilized": encouraged to abandon hunting and raiding, take up farming, become literate, live in nuclear families, convert to Christianity, and adopt Euro-American styles of dress. It was, of course, an old idea, harking back to Puritan "praying towns," refurbished so that Natives might more readily sell off their "surplus" lands and find an unobtrusive place on the American landscape. Protestant missionaries looked to lend a hand.[41]

The Cherokees made cultural accommodation a major, if divisive, goal. Led mainly by tribal members who had intermarried with Euro-Americans, they took up sedentary agriculture, the enslavement of African Americans, production for the market, the patrilineal family, and the Christian religion. They also established a government with a bicameral legislature, elective representation, and a court system, while adopting a written language and constitution together with a newspaper, the Cherokee *Phoenix*, published in their now-capital of

New Echota in north Georgia. Over time, social differentiation made for a society with a small elite of planters and enslavers at the top and a much larger peasant and hunter-gatherer class at the bottom. By the 1820s, Cherokee society, stretching across north Georgia and western North Carolina, had come to look very much like the white American society surrounding it.[42]

The Cherokees were not alone in pursuing an accommodationist path. Creeks and Chickasaws became enslavers. Shawnees residing along the Ohio River Valley adjusted their economic practices and availed themselves of schooling and missionizing, as they were encouraged to do. It made no difference. Little changed in the language of inevitable decline and destruction that even sympathetic white Americans used to describe the Native future, an ineffable law of nature that would see the triumph of white civilization and the doom of those who tried to resist. Nor did the new cultural dispositions prevent the state governments of Georgia and Alabama from ignoring tribal sovereignties and extending their jurisdiction over Native lands, even when the U.S. Supreme Court ruled otherwise. The only things left to sustain Native homelands east of the Mississippi were favorably disposed ears in Congress and especially in the White House, who might then respond.[43]

But the 1830s were a time when expulsionism proved to be a popular solution to the social "problems" presented by African Americans, Catholics, Mormons, Masons, and Native peoples, indeed by any group capable of defying the hegemony of a white Christian republic. And by then a president had been elected who empowered the white settlers of the trans-Appalachian West and South, and who had been honing his expulsive skills for decades: Andrew Jackson. Jackson may have won early fame for his part in defeating the British at the Battle of New Orleans (1815), but he gained, and continued to gain, special notoriety for his exterminist attacks on Native peoples and their Black allies. The attacks began with his massacre of Seminoles and fugitives from enslavement at Negro Fort in Florida and of Creeks at the Battle of Horseshoe Bend (1814), which also forced the Creeks to surrender twenty-three million acres of their lands in Georgia and Alabama. Although he would use the language of civilization and humanism to defend it, President Jackson pressed vigorously for Congress to expel all Native peoples from United States territory east of the Mississippi. Called the Indian Removal Act of 1830—in full, "An act to provide an exchange of lands with the Indians residing in any of the states or territories, and for their removal west of the river Mississippi"—the enabling legislation drew significant opposition from the Northeast and Middle Atlantic, including a large petition campaign organized by female activists on their way to becoming abolitionists. Still, it passed that spring after tight votes in the Senate and House.[44]

Ostensibly, the Jackson administration would negotiate with Native tribes, have them exchange homelands for land in Indian Territory, pay them for any improvements they had made, allocate funds for relocation, provide annuities for tribal leaders, and offer support for a year after Natives arrived at their western destination. In truth, the process was coercive and the resources provided were utterly inadequate. Indian Territory was uncharted and already home to Native peoples on the Plains, and the issue of removal was a source of deep conflict within each of the affected tribes. Black Hawk himself represented but a minority of the Sauk in attempting to regain lands from which they had been driven; most of the Sauk remained on the western side of the Mississippi under the leadership of Keokuk. In Florida, Seminoles, led by the Black fugitives among them, dug in their heels and fought U.S. troops for six years (the Second Seminole War, the longest American war until Vietnam) before being subdued in 1842.[45]

The tribal divisions and suspicions sown by the federally directed expulsions followed the refugees who managed to survive the ordeal, the "Trail of Tears," when they finally arrived in Indian Territory, and shaped their social and political lives for years to come. A great many did not survive, young and old, women and men, adults and children—perhaps a quarter of them in all. They perished along the way, from exposure, disease, and starvation. But what *was* the destination, in the larger geopolitics of the country, for those who endured expulsion and arrived at the western lands designated for them? *What* were the lands? In theory, the United States promised "forever" to "secure and guaranty" these lands to the expelled Natives and protect them in their occupancy even though the lands were not conveyed in fee simple or freehold ownership. Yet the destiny of this territory over time was entirely unclear. While other territories created by Congress since the Northwest Ordinance of 1787 were regarded as states in the making, there was no such political arc imagined for the new Indian Territory. For all intents and purposes, it was an internal protectorate marked by impermanent boundaries, conflicting jurisdictions, and obscure lines of governance, a status wholly distinct in the United States, set apart and within simultaneously. It was, at once, a liminal space and a harbinger of the country's imperial future.[46]

Abraham Lincoln would face the challenge of Native status and belonging in unexpected ways. As president and commander-in-chief, determined to suppress the Confederate rebellion of 1860–61, he had to decide what to make of Indian Territory. After all, following Fort Sumter Lincoln called upon all the states for volunteers, thereby hastening the stalled secession process in the Upper South, while the Confederates made an alliance with slaveholding Cherokees, Creeks, Chickasaws, Choctaws, and Seminoles that recognized Indian sovereignty and brought them Indian troops. Lincoln did nothing of the sort. Not unlike his early rejection of African American enlistment, he rebuffed the idea of recruiting Native soldiers and instead halted annuity payments to the tribes and withdrew all federal troops from the area. He would later think better of this, but soon had a bigger problem on his hands. At the very time Lincoln was drafting his Preliminary Emancipation Proclamation in August 1862, the Santee Sioux in Minnesota launched a rebellion aimed at reclaiming lands they had surrendered under duress.[47]

Strapped for manpower and reeling from major defeats at the hands of Confederates in the eastern and central theaters, Lincoln nonetheless sent General John Pope to Minnesota to put the rebellion down. Vowing "to utterly exterminate the Sioux if I have the power to do so" and treat them "as maniacs and wild beast," Pope spent the next ten months at the task, in the process killing and scalping Sioux leader Little Crow and rounding up nearly two thousand Sioux prisoners, who were tried by a five-man military commission "for being connected in the late horrible outrages." The commission sentenced 303 of the prisoners to be hanged, and sent their verdict to Lincoln for his approval. Lincoln was shocked not only by the scale and severity of the punishment but also by the thinness of the evidence used to convict and the bitter temper of the commissioners. Nonetheless, he eventually agreed to the execution of thirty-eight Native men. On 26 December 1862, days before the Emancipation Proclamation would be signed, they were hanged at Mankato, Minnesota, the largest official mass execution in American history. Only one Confederate rebel, the commandant of the prisoner-of-war camp at Andersonville, Georgia, not any member of the political and military leadership of the Confederacy, would suffer such a fate. As for the remaining Sioux and perhaps two thousand Ho-Chunk suspected of participating in the uprising, Congress moved to void all their treaties, expel them from their reservations and the state of Minnesota, terminate annuity payments, and effectively force them out onto the open plains.[48]

Lincoln was not simply an expulsionist. He could lend a sympathetic ear to reformers like the Episcopal bishop of Minnesota, Henry B. Whipple, who wished to root out corrupt practices among Indian agents and effectively make Native peoples wards of the federal government, bringing them within civilization's embrace. "If we get through the war and I live," Lincoln told Whipple during a White House meeting, "this Indian system shall be reformed." Yet Lincoln also viewed Native peoples as "savages" and could scarcely imagine them as part of the "people of the United States." Thus, when the president invited a delegation of tribal leaders from the Plains to meet with him in March 1863, hoping to discourage them from offering support to the Confederacy, Lincoln spoke of the "great difference between the pale-faced people and their red brethren both as to numbers and the way in which they lived." "The pale-faced people are numerous and prosperous," Lincoln lectured, "because they cultivate the earth, produce bread, and depend upon the products of the earth rather than wild game for subsistence."[49]

There was an unnerving ring to this. Seven months earlier, Lincoln had met with a group of African American leaders as to their future prospects and began by insisting that "you and we are different races. We have between us a broader difference than exists between almost any two races." "Whether it is right or wrong," he continued, "this physical difference is a great disadvantage to us both . . . we suffer on each side . . . [and] it affords a reason at least why we should be separated." While acknowledging the mistreatments and humiliations that they endured, Lincoln blamed "the colored race" as well as the "institution of slavery" for the war convulsing the country and explained his support for having them colonized outside the United States, perhaps in Liberia or in "Central America [which] is nearer to us." "Colonization," a form of exile and expulsion, Lincoln believed, was the proper solution to the dilemmas of Black and white. So, too, would something like it be the appropriate solution to the troubles besetting the "pale-faced" and their "red brethren": "the plan of concentrating Indians and confining them to reservations," removing and expelling them from the "steady expansion of the population . . . over the new and unoccupied portions of our country." It would provide a "proper government of the Indians" and render the West "secure for the advancing settler." With a new and very much of an illiberal twist on the concept of a "house divided," Lincoln told the Congress in 1862 that "a nation may be said to consist of its territory, its people, and its laws," and "that portion of the earth's surface which is owned and inhabited by the people of the United States, is well adapted to be the home of one national family; and it is not well adapted for two, or more. Its vast extent, and its variety of climate and productions, are of advantage, in this age, for one people, whatever they might have been in former ages."[50]

V

ALEXIS DE TOCQUEVILLE CONFINED his discussion of America's Native peoples and enslaved Blacks chiefly to one of the seventy-five chapters that compose *Democracy in America*. But it is easily the lengthiest and most troubling about the country's future. "These topics are like tangents to my subject, being American and not democratic, and my main business has been to describe democracy," he wrote. "So at first I had to leave them on one side, but now at the end [of volume one] I must return to them." Tocqueville saw Natives as "savage" and "uncivilized," and largely uninterested in becoming civilized even though he knew of the Cherokees who clearly showed the capacity for civilization. Like many white Americans, Tocqueville thought that "the Indian race was doomed to perish," while acknowledging the "forced migrations" to which Native peoples were subjected and the "tyranny of government" that was added to the mix of greedy settlers. The "tyrannous measures" adopted by legislatures, especially of the southern states, convinced him that "the complete expulsion of the Indians is the final objective to which all their simultaneous endeavors are directed."[51]

Yet, while the presence of Native peoples revealed the expulsive designs of white Americans, for Tocqueville slavery and "the presence of the blacks on their soil" posed the "most formidable evil threatening the future of the United States." The enslavement of other human beings was surely an "evil"; Tocqueville would soon become a founder in France of the *Société française pour l'abolition de l'esclavage*. But, as was true for Thomas Jefferson, Tocqueville viewed the "evil" deriving, as well, from the impact of slavery on the master— "penetrating [his] soul"—and the "presence of blacks on their soil," making it "almost impossible to abolish." Although he spent very little time in the South, Tocqueville insisted that "almost all the marked differences in character between northerners and southerners have their roots in slavery" and, especially, that "the prejudice rejecting the Negroes seems to increase in proportion to their emancipation, and inequality cuts deep into mores as it is effaced from the laws." "Race prejudice," Tocqueville observed, "seems stronger in those states that have abolished slavery than in those where it still exists, and nowhere is it more intolerant than in those states where slavery was never known."[52]

Although Tocqueville deployed the language of colonization and was certainly aware of the American Colonization Society, he did not think it feasible to send even the natural increase of the enslaved population to Liberia. That population was simply growing too fast. The destiny of the country and slavery, therefore, would remain inextricably entwined, and, in asking "what are the chances that the American Union will last?," he did not seem especially optimistic. While some Americans complained of the "centralizing tendency" of the federal government, Tocqueville thought it was "getting visibly weaker." Every time the states and the federal government had "gone into the ring" of conflict, he claimed, the federal government was forced to retreat, even when constitutional interpretation was at issue. And the future of slavery seemed intractable. "Amid the democratic liberty and enlightenment of the age," the institution of slavery could not last, but "great misfortunes" would attend its demise. "Either the slave or the master will put an end to it. . . . If freedom is refused to the Negroes in the South, in the end they will seize it themselves; if it is granted to them, they will not be slow to abuse it."[53]

In important respects, the picture that Tocqueville painted of the United States in the early 1830s was one that the Anti-Federalists had imagined: a robust popular sovereignty that empowered the will of the community while fending off the encroachments of the federal government. But under his broad-brush strokes an unsettling montage could be exposed. For many readers, Tocqueville's was a celebration of the equality of condition, the democratic impulses, the political energies, the associational dispositions, and the thriving localism to be found in the United States. Some political theorists of the present day in fact see in Tocqueville the materials of a communitarianism and the prospects for reviving a collective public life. Yet the issues surrounding slavery and Native peoples should alert us to a dark underbelly that Tocqueville was not reluctant to expose. There was the "tyranny" or "omnipotence of the majority" to which a democracy like the United States was especially susceptible and which could easily revive the sort of despotism that absolute monarchs had once wielded. "What I find most repulsive in America is not the extreme freedom reigning there," he averred, "but the shortage of guarantees against tyranny. When a man or party suffers an injustice in the United States to whom can he turn? To public opinion? That is what forms the majority. To the legislative body? It represents the majority and obeys it blindly."[54]

Although Tocqueville depicted the "local community" as the foundation of democracy and republicanism, it was also there that public opinion and majority tyranny could be most directly experienced and destructive. He spoke of county inhabitants "spontaneously forming committees . . . when a serious crime has been committed . . . with the object of catching the criminal and handing him over to the courts," and of "citizens . . . in the new states of the southwest . . . almost always taking justice into their own hands." He worried that while an aristocracy could not be established anew in this world, "associations of plain citizens can compose very rich, influential, and powerful bodies, in other words, aristocratic bodies." And he noted that "from birth . . . the American of the South is invested with a sort of domestic dictatorship . . . the first habit he contracts is that of effortless domination." Tocqueville could think of no country in which "there is less independence of mind and true freedom of discussion than in America." Should Americans ever give up republican government, Tocqueville predicted, "they will pass rapidly on to despotism without any very long interval of limited monarchy." Indeed, he thought it quite possible that "at some future date," Americans might "restrict the sphere of political rights, taking some of them away in order to entrust them to a single man." Such a new despotism would "degrade men" rather than "torment them," have them "quit their state of dependence just long enough to choose their masters, and then fall back into it."[55]

Tocqueville did not stay in the United States long enough to witness the sort of mob violence that Lincoln warned of at Springfield. But there is no reason to believe that he would have been surprised by it. Reading *Democracy in America,* one senses Tocqueville's curiosity and wonderment, his fascination with the constant movement, argument, and civic activity he saw around him, his identification of almost endless connections and contradictions, and his worries about "this irresistible revolution [toward equality] advancing century by century over every obstacle and even now going forward amid the ruins it has itself created." Tocqueville's America—with a raucous indiscipline masking a troubling uniformity of mind and spirit, with democratic impulses wrapped around brutalities and expulsions, with what political theorist Sheldon Wolin calls "fierce provincial loyalties" tied to a sprawling union, a "strong sense of local citizenship [and] dispersed power" linked to a "weak central authority," a "decentered corporativism" and "feudalization"—seems more like a ticking time bomb than an example of secure political destiny. In Tocqueville's skillful hands, that is, we have the outlines, not of a liberal democratic exceptionalism, but forms of illiberal democracy.[56]

Chapter Five

THE MEASURES
OF BONDAGE

T HE GALLERIES OF THE HOUSE OF REPRESENTATIVES
were filled and the spectators aching with anticipation. It
was the late afternoon of 31 January 1865, and, when all discussion
"ceased," the Speaker broke the "profound silence" and declared that
a vote would be taken "upon the pending proposition." That proposition was the Thirteenth Amendment to the United States Constitution. Only months before, the amendment had been rejected by
this very body, but now, after the elections of 1864 strengthened the
hands of Republicans, the outcome would be different. Needing two-
thirds of those present, "the resolution . . . was agreed to by yeas 119
and nays 56," just more than enough, and when the "presiding officer" announced the results, "the enthusiasm of all present knew no
bounds." "For several moments," according to a correspondent from
the *New York Times*, "the scene was grand and impressive beyond
description . . . everyone feeling that the occasion justified the full-
est expression of approbation and joy." Before the year was out, the
amendment would be ratified by the requisite number of states and
inscribed into the republic's founding document.[1]

The Thirteenth Amendment's language was spare and concise, a
departure from the various statutes and proclamations marking the
emancipation process that unfolded during a war still to be won.
Although alternatives had been proposed, including one that harked
back to the French Revolution of the 1790s and linked emancipation
with citizenship for the enslaved, the members of the Senate Judiciary
Committee, where the amendment was crafted, chose to employ the
words of Article VI of the Northwest Ordinance of 1787. So, too, had

a number of states carved from the Northwest Territory that outlawed slavery within their boundaries from the outset, as had David Wilmot in his famed "proviso" of 1846. "Neither slavery nor involuntary servitude, except as a punishment for crime whereof the party shall have been duly convicted, shall exist within the United States or any place subject to their jurisdiction." An enabling clause then gave Congress the power to "enforce" the amendment by "appropriate legislation."[2]

This was, in many ways, the great liberal hour. Slavery was abolished, in one fell swoop, in the thirteen states where it remained legal, unencumbered by compensation for the enslavers or the threat of colonization or a protracted emancipation—as in the states of the Northeast and Middle Atlantic and floated not long before by President Abraham Lincoln—for the enslaved. Congress followed, over the next two years, by establishing birthright citizenship and prohibiting debt peonage in the United States. A new nation-state was being constructed on the liberal foundations of self-ownership, free labor, legal equality, and civil belonging not apparently compromised by race or ethnicity.

Yet the Amendment's inclusion of "involuntary servitude" as well as the "exception clause," long overlooked by scholars and political interpreters though now being revisited owing to mass incarceration, raise serious questions about the coercive relations and practices that could and could not remain in place. Thomas Jefferson had included the words "involuntary servitude" and the exception clause in the Ordinance of 1784 that he drafted for the organization of the Northwest Territory (the Confederation Congress removed it from the final version), interested as he already was in penal reform. Nathaniel Dane of Massachusetts added it to what became the Northwest Ordinance's Article VI, though it is not entirely clear why he did. Perhaps it was his familiarity with the judicial language of the *Quok Walker* case that put enslavement on the road to abolition in his state. Some scholars argue that the exception clause was effectively "boilerplate." Others suggest that the influx of British indentured servants who had been convicted felons and suffered transportation to the colonies as punishment for their offenses made the exception clause necessary to the functioning of the labor system and the migration of settlers to the

Northwest Territory. As for the Thirteenth Amendment, although Charles Sumner would regret allowing the exception clause to be included, there was scarce mention of it in the congressional debate over the amendment's passage.[3]

There is good reason for viewing the Thirteenth Amendment's exception clause as permitting the subsequent criminalization and repression of the formerly enslaved Black population of the southern states. The explosion of criminal offenses on the statute books of states and municipalities that clearly targeted Black men and women and made them vulnerable to various penalties and forms of incarceration has long been recognized by historians. The leasing of Black convicts to private interests—especially railroad and mining companies—was widespread and particularly notorious, but it coexisted with other forms of criminal punishment that pressed thousands of Black people into debt and near-servitude. Since courts often invoked the exception clause in rejecting claims that some of these devices violated the Thirteenth Amendment, the path from one to the other may seem more direct than crooked.[4]

Still, there is a larger context to consider. For the most part, the central "problems" of the late eighteenth and nineteenth centuries are regarded to be those of "slavery" and "freedom." How was it that slavery, which suffused human history for millennia and had thrived in North America since the seventeenth century, came to be understood as morally and politically objectionable? In turn, what would the freedom that followed slavery mean for those who paved the road of abolition and fought to secure it by force of arms? In this respect, historians and other scholars effectively adopt the conceptual binary of slavery and freedom that liberal thought has long imagined. Slavery and freedom are inextricably linked; they are both oppositions and mutually constitutive. They frame what many see as liberal modernity.[5]

But if we take a closer look at the idea of "involuntary servitude" together with the Thirteenth Amendment's exception clause, if we can see how the pieces of the Thirteenth Amendment might have come together in the minds of framers who were exploring a wide universe of social relations, then we may recognize that the binary of slavery and freedom is somewhat contrived, that it obscures a deeper problem: the problem of "coercion," the forms of coercion that would be legitimate and illegitimate in an age of emancipation and in a modernizing world. We may recognize, that is, the illiberal chords chiming in the liberal hour.

I

ALEXIS DE TOCQUEVILLE came to the United States with Gustave de Beaumont in the early 1830s to take the measure of the new penitentiaries being built. They hoped to find models that might address the deficiencies of the French system of criminal punishment, and they marveled at the *"monomonie"* of penal reform that "estimable men" and those "for whom philanthropy has become a matter of necessity" seemed to have "caught" in America. As Tocqueville and Beaumont understood it, these estimable men "find in the penitentiary system a nourishment for this generous passion" and a "remedy for all the evils of society." Reflecting on what they learned about the penitentiaries in Philadelphia, Auburn and Sing-Sing, New York, and Baltimore, they expressed reservations about the severity and "despotism" to be found inside the prisons' walls, but were positively inclined as to the logic and goals of penitential confinement. Unlike in France, where convicts mixed with one another and appeared more corrupt and degraded by the time they were released than when they entered, the American system seemed bent on offering convicts the possibility of rehabilitation and self-improvement.

Tocqueville and Beaumont wrote approvingly of the individual isolation that inmates were subjected to, whatever the other differences in regulations between the institutions, and were especially impressed with the labor that most were required to perform. Although they questioned the general practice of denying inmates remuneration for their work, they nonetheless saw this as a strike against the idleness that likely led to crime in the first place and as a way to teach each of the inmates "a business which may support him when he leaves the prison." In these respects, Tocqueville and Beaumont saw the American prisons as making "all moral contagion among the imprisoned . . . impossible," "completely" curing the corruption that afflicted French prisons and permitting the inmates to "contract habits of obedience and industry, which render them useful citizens."[6]

Tocqueville and Beaumont's translator, Francis Lieber, had their report dedicated to Roberts Vaux, an acknowledgment of the transatlantic nature of penal reform. A Philadelphian from a prominent Quaker family, Vaux was a leader in the Philadelphia Prison Society and a strong advocate of the penitentiary as a form of punishment; he had devoted a great deal of energy to the construction of the Eastern State Penitentiary, which opened in 1829 and served as an example for reformers in Europe as well as the United States. In this, Vaux followed in the footsteps of Benjamin Rush, a Philadelphia physician, Enlightenment-inspired thinker, and signatory of the Declaration of Independence, who saw in the penitentiary a humane alternative to the corporal and public forms of justice that predominated. In 1787, Rush founded the Philadelphia Society for Alleviating the Miseries of Public Prisons and published *An Enquiry into the Effects of Public Punishments upon Criminals and upon Society.*

Influenced by the writings of Montesquieu, Britain's John Howard, and especially the Italian Cesare Beccaria, Rush regarded the practices of corporal punishment and public executions—the norm on both sides of the Atlantic—as symbols of monarchical despotism and tyranny, misbegotten efforts to inscribe the personal power of the ruler on the bodies of convicts and remind those in attendance of the terrors that could await them. Rush thought little better of the public penal labor that the Pennsylvania Assembly established in 1786 as an alternative to the whipping post and pillory, for it invited chaos on the streets where convicts generally worked and potentially nasty examples for those who viewed them. Instead, he began to argue that criminals should be removed from the community and placed in "a large house . . . erected in a convenient part of the state" for the purposes of repentance and self-reformation, shielding them from both the eyes and influences of the larger public. Indeed, Rush advised that this house ought "by no means be called a prison or by any name that is associated with what is infamous in the opinion of mankind" and be run by "persons of established character for probity, discretion, and humanity."

Yet it was not only the substitution of private for public punishment that distinguished Rush's vision. He also called for the division of these "houses" into cells for the solitary confinement of inmates and the "carrying on [of] such manufactures as can be conducted with the least instruction, or previous knowledge." Recommending that punishments "be accommodated to the constitutions and tempers of the criminals, and the peculiar nature of their crimes," Rush insisted that they "consist of bodily pain, labour, watchfulness, solitude, and silence," and that the "labour . . . be so regulated and directed, as to be profitable to the state." Which is to say that the regimen should combine isolation with useful labor, sparing the community of contamination and providing the inmate something other than idleness.[7]

Rush's ideas had enormous influence not only in Pennsylvania but across the Northeast, Middle Atlantic, and Midwest. In 1790, a penitentiary was constructed to adjoin the Walnut Street jail in Philadelphia—the first of its kind in the Euro-Atlantic world—and by the early nineteenth century penitentiaries could be found in eight northern states along with Maryland and Virginia. Organizationally they fell into one of two variants, both showing the marks of Rush's prescriptions: the first, known as the "Pennsylvania system," put inmates in solitary confinement day and night; the other, known as the "Auburn system," allowed inmates to congregate silently during the day with a return to solitary confinement at night. In either case, the inmates' daylight hours were devoted to labor, and in neither case were inmates to communicate with one another.[8]

The Auburn system became the principal model, perhaps because Walnut Street inmates rioted in 1820 but more likely because of how penitentiaries of this type deployed the work of the inmates. Virtually everywhere, their labor was contracted to private employers and manufacturers who paid the penitentiaries a fee. In some cases, the inmates worked at the establishments of the employers, though more commonly the employers brought all the equipment and materials into the penitentiaries where the inmates would work under the close supervision of the keepers. For the penal institutions, the arrangement became crucial to their financial well-being; for the inmates, it amounted to what historian Rebecca McLennan calls "contractual penal servitude." Charles Dickens, who traveled the United States in 1842 and visited penitentiaries, could compare the Auburn-type prisons to textile factories in their allocation of space and the intensity of the work; at Eastern State penitentiary in Philadelphia, where solitude prevailed day and night, he found an experience of "torture and agony" but nonetheless commented on the labor: "Occasionally, there is a drowsy sound from some lone weaver's shuttle, or shoemaker's last, but it is stifled by the thick walls."[9]

By the time Dickens toured the country, the great majority of penitentiaries operated according to this contract labor system despite protests from a number of quarters. Some critics called for a return to the regime of public punishment or public labor, insisting that criminality and discipline remain a community issue. Others questioned the prospects of convict reformation, especially when they regarded criminal behavior as a manifestation of inherent sin. But the most sustained resistance came from the fledgling labor movement of the 1820s and 1830s, the city trades councils and workingmen's political parties, that bridled at the competition convict labor offered up and condemned it for degrading the work of mechanics. In the minds of many journeymen and artisans who were already feeling the pressures of the era's market intensifications and dilution of trade skills, convict labor was little better than a species of servitude and slavery, dishonoring both free labor and free laborers.[10]

Advocates of penitentiaries acknowledged that confinement, solitude, and enforced labor amounted to involuntary servitude though they would not have likened it to enslavement. Indeed, a great many counted themselves among the critics of slavery and were active members of antislavery societies. For them, public and corporal punishment and enslavement were of a piece, signs of tyranny and despotism of the *ancien regime* that had to be replaced by an enlightened and humanitarian order. Roberts Vaux, to whom Tocqueville and Beaumont had dedicated their volume, was not only an admired penal reformer; like many Quakers of the time he spoke out against slavery and was a member of the Pennsylvania Abolition Society.

He was not alone. Almost everywhere in the Northeast and Middle Atlantic of early-nineteenth-century America, as well as across the Atlantic, penal reformers had their feet in organized antislavery. Tocqueville himself helped found the *Société pour l'Abolition de l'Esclavage*, in 1835, the very year that the first volume of *Democracy in America* was published.[11]

Attacking slavery while embracing the penitentiary may seem a remarkable contradiction in moral and intellectual terms, but it captured the nature of elite reformism of the late eighteenth and early nineteenth century. Imagining themselves as enlightened humanitarians who relished progress and civility, reformers of the Euro-Atlantic world objected to the forms of personal power, the physical cruelty, and the despotic sway that both enslavement and traditional types of punishment typified. The whip and the gallows symbolized these practices as well as the barbarism of the old order more generally. Not surprisingly, there were a good many Quakers among the reformers, especially in the United States, who recognized the violence that was central to these arenas of discipline and that contaminated those who wielded it just as surely as those who suffered it.[12]

And yet, the intermixing of antislavery and the penitentiary demonstrated that the reformers, Quakers and others, worried deeply about the disorder that slave emancipation could present. Unlike Jefferson, most rejected the idea that people of African descent were innately inferior to white Europeans. But they did believe that the experience of enslavement left a deep scar on Black morals, character, and dispositions, debasing them and encouraging idleness, dependence, and criminality. Some sort of gradualism seemed essential to the emancipation process as nearly all reformers understood it, and many came to think favorably of colonization as a way to expel the potential problems of a growing emancipated Black population and perhaps benefit the formerly enslaved as well. Still, whether they supported colonization or not, they insisted that emancipation required an array of social and cultural supports—educational, economic, and spiritual—and the devising of new legal codes and practices. In the manner of colonization, penal reform and the penitentiary represented a reckoning, not with slavery but with its remnants in a post-emancipation world.[13]

It is, therefore, no accident that the timeline of emancipation statutes and the construction of new legal codes and penitentiaries in the Northeast overlapped: the ending of slavery would render codes designed to support the slave system moot and weaken the personal disciplinary power of enslavers. But it was a lengthy roll-out. Responding to the ideologies of the Revolution and Enlightenment as well as to the petitions of enslaved Blacks and free people of color, Pennsylvania passed the first abolition law in 1780, joining Vermont and Massachusetts where constitution-writing and judicial decisions paved the way in 1777 and 1780 respectively. Connecticut and Rhode Island followed in 1784, New Hampshire in 1785, New York in 1799, and New Jersey in 1804. In virtually all cases, a process of gradual emancipation was initiated, most often with the children of enslaved people becoming free when they turned twenty-one or twenty-five or twenty-eight, depending on their gender and the state in which they found themselves. Even when slavery was declared unlawful by state constitutions or the courts, few of the enslaved quickly gained their freedom. Instead, they often entered a netherworld of coercions, in which enslavement was effectively exchanged for long- or short-term servitude. For them, and for most of the enslaved people of the Northeast, emancipation was a long gray tunnel to traverse without a clear destination in view.[14]

The closest connection between abolitionism and penal reform came in New York. With the largest enslaved population north of the Chesapeake—over 20,000 in 1790—lawmakers in the state had been dodging emancipation since the mid-1780s, when the New York Manumission Society was established. But their hesitancy and worries seem to have been allayed after they authorized a revised criminal code and the construction of a new penitentiary in 1796. Three years later, the legislators passed An Act for the Gradual Abolition of Slavery, modeled on the law in Pennsylvania, releasing from bondage the children of the enslaved born after July 4 of that year (1799). Elsewhere, the relation between penal reform and abolition was less

direct though unmistakably associated in an atmosphere of enlightened reformism. Massachusetts began to use Castle Island, in Boston Harbor, to house convicted criminals from all over the state in
1785. Local facilities enabling solitary confinement began to sprout
up in the 1790s, and in 1805 the state opened Charlestown prison,
which could house three hundred inmates. Vermont's first penitentiary opened in 1807, New Hampshire's in 1812, and New Jersey's in
1798, much like New York in anticipating the state's emancipation
statute of 1804.[15]

The point is not that the abolition of slavery produced the penitentiary or vice versa. The point is that abolitionism and penal reform
fed off the same cultural and intellectual currents that, on the one
hand, sought to break the heavy chains of enslavement and corporal punishment long weighing on the bodies of those afflicted and
instead cultivate their souls, while on the other hand stirring fears of
disorder and unruliness that required instruments of coercion. Involuntary servitude, like enslavement, was being drawn into question on
moral and political grounds, but not if those regarded as threats to
the community could be expelled and subjected to hard and draining
lessons in the ways of civilized society, none more important than
steady productive labor.

Involuntary penal labor became the standard in the North and
West before the Civil War, well in advance of the convict labor system that emerged in the postbellum South. In a sadly ironic, though
eminently illiberal, twist, once the war broke out some prison manufacturers received lucrative contracts from the federal government,
and the labor of inmates was turned to supplying war materials and
soldiers' kits, not unlike the Confederacy, where slaves and some convicts did related work. "Just as the Civil War proved a massive force
for industrialization more generally in the North," Rebecca McLennan writes, "war mobilization had the long-term effect of committing prisons—and prisoners—ever more deeply to productive labor
and profit-seeking enterprise." Little wonder that the Senate Judiciary Committee followed precedent in excepting inmates from the
Thirteenth Amendment's prohibition on slavery or involuntary servitude; penal labor had become an accepted practice in the "free labor"

North and was contributing to the defeat of the Confederate rebellion and the triumph of free labor across the United States.[16]

Yet, although the rise of the penitentiary and the eager embrace of penal labor were chiefly phenomena of the northern states, there was, as antislavery thinkers probably expected, a racial edge to incarceration. Whether in Massachusetts or New York, Pennsylvania or Ohio, men and women of African descent, some still enslaved, were disproportionately represented in the prison populations: somewhere between one-quarter and one-half in states with very few Black people in total. They joined other poor and racialized inmates, more and more of them Irish, who were struggling their way through an expanding, though increasingly stratified, market economy. The penitentiary thereby marked a new process of class formation with which an emerging industrial society would become familiar. But in the simultaneous attack on the barbaric practices of an older regime and the suspicious eyes reformers cast upon the destinies of formerly enslaved Black people, one can see the idea of Black criminality taking shape.[17]

II

When President Abraham Lincoln and his administration determined to suppress the Confederate rebellion to the South, they had not made a decision about slavery's fate there. If anything, Lincoln hoped to keep slavery and slaves out of the conflict, ordering his military commanders to forcibly repress rebellious slaves if they seized the opportunity to rise.

Lincoln did win the presidency at the head of a party committed to keeping slavery and enslavers out of federal territories west of the Mississippi River, and so firm was his adherence to the idea that he refused to modify or give it up in exchange for a peaceful settlement of the secession crisis. But like most members of his—the new Republican—party, he believed that emancipation was in the hands of the states, would take place gradually, and was best secured by wedding it to the colonization of the freed population. Lincoln continually sought to assure Confederates and other white southerners that he did not intend to interfere with "domestic institutions"; the Constitution, he conceded, did not give the federal government such power. And had the war ended quickly or with an armistice, enslavement would have endured a long death and the constitutional amendments we associate with the war and Reconstruction—the Thirteenth, Fourteenth, and Fifteenth—would not have been enacted. Whether some semblance of the antebellum union would have been preserved is unclear, but given slavery's importance to the political and economic life of the country and the repressive apparatus necessary to sustain it (southern Democrats vied for the presidency in 1860 on a platform demanding a federal slave code to enforce the *Dred Scott* decision of 1857), the aftermath would have been extremely ugly for Black, and perhaps for all laboring, people.[18]

What made the emancipationist moment of the Thirteenth Amendment possible was the political resolve of the enslaved and the ability of the U.S. military, with armed slaves in the ranks, to achieve an unconditional victory. Over the course of the war, the enslaved staged their own rebellion: imagining allies and enemies in the fight, defying orders of various kinds to stay put, taking flight from plantations and farms and heading to Union lines, forcing the Lincoln administration to confront the slavery question, joining the army's struggle against Confederate rebels, and demanding civil and political rights together with freedom. Little by little, the edifice of enslavement was weakened and destroyed. Slaves in flight were accepted into U.S. Army lines and eventually declared free if their owners were aligned with the Confederacy. Congress abolished enslavement in all federal territories ("except as a punishment for crime") and in the federal capital, with compensation for enslavers. Lincoln proclaimed emancipation, without compensation for slaveowners in all areas under Confederate control and encouraged the other states in which slavery was legal to abolish it (with mixed success) within their borders. And the U.S. Army recruited enslaved men and soon sent them to the battlefront, enabling them to earn freedom for their families as well as for themselves. Black troops were among those who marched into Richmond, the putative capital of the Confederacy, on 2 April 1865.[19]

The problem was that the emancipation process unfolding since 1861 involved congressional statutes and proclamations deemed acts of war, so that their long-term survival and constitutionality were in question. Republicans and their Black allies worried that if nothing else were done, hostile Democrats could overturn emancipationist legislation or the Supreme Court could rule that emancipation proclamations lacked force once the war had ended. More and more Republicans came to believe that the best way to secure the abolition of slavery was through a constitutional amendment—none had been ratified since 1804 and none had ever been repealed—and their hands were strengthened by a massive petition campaign launched by abolitionist women.[20]

Still, it was not an easy task. How should emancipation be framed? What would be the new status of the enslaved? Should emancipation bring citizenship with it or other rights that white Americans already enjoyed? Should emancipation bring land and other resources to the enslaved since economic independence was thought by many to be the foundation of genuine freedom? How much power should the federal government have to enforce emancipation, given that enslavers had fought for decades to keep Black people subject to their absolute authority? The discussion and debate, the hostility of many northern Democrats, and the need to gain the support of three-quarters of the states suggested that a strong but narrow purview was most likely to succeed. And since the language of the Northwest Ordinance was well known and already deployed at the state and federal levels—and since it would not compromise forms of servitude and coercion that underwrote the penitentiary system and contributed to the war effort—it seemed easiest to embrace. After all, Jefferson could be invoked to validate the measure. The amendment offered no rewards to the enslavers, heaped no penalties upon the enslaved, and gave the federal government the right to enforce it through "appropriate legislation," which Radical Republicans believed would require the extension of civil and, possibly, political rights to the freedpeople.[21]

The testing ground for emancipation and the Thirteenth Amendment for, as Republican senator Jacob Howard of Michigan put it, making Black people "the opposite of the slave . . . a freeman" came in the southern states where enslavement had been legal and the basis of the social and political order. Here, the notion that slavery and freedom were simply "opposites" quickly came undone, and the emancipationists themselves generally led in the undoing. Throughout the Euro-Atlantic world, antislavery activists—even radical abolitionists who helped construct the slavery/freedom binary—believed that the formerly enslaved would have to be tutored in freedom before they could become productive and law-abiding members of a free society. This belief helped lay the groundwork for gradual emancipation in the northeastern United States and for the abolition of slavery in the British empire, which had provided for a multiyear "apprenticeship" prior to a full emancipation. Advocates of abolition in Europe and the United States worried that the enslaved had been too debased by violence and repression to stand up on their own, lacked proper understandings of private property and family life, had vulgar notions of sexuality and few ideas of personal responsibility, and would not respond to the incentives of the marketplace. Much in the way that they viewed the poor, the "paupers and vagabonds" in their midst, many abolitionists feared that, when emancipated, enslaved people would become idle, thriftless, and burdens on society.[22]

In truth, it was the former enslavers not the formerly enslaved who needed the tutoring. Years of dominating, coercing, harassing, and punishing the enslaved had taught enslavers that Black labor had to be "commanded." Blacks, they believed, were ignorant and lazy and, left to themselves, would be profligate and unreliable. With any semblance of free Black labor allowed, the fields would go to weed and the economy to ruin. Accordingly, once Andrew Johnson's generous Reconstruction policies enabled former enslavers to regain political power, they acted promptly to create a legal regime that would return Black people to a condition of near-abject submission. That legal regime was associated with what were called "Black Codes." Although the codes varied from state to state, they generally hedged in the mobility of Black people, limited their ability to purchase landed property or practice a skilled trade, forced them into signing labor contracts, prescribed the use of corporal punishment for insubordination, circumscribed their rights in court, remanded

Black children deemed orphans into servitude (called "apprentice-ship"), and criminalized a raft of activities that could be crucial to Black self-subsistence.[23]

Recognizing this effort for what it was, a concerted attempt at near re-enslavement, the federal government voided many of these laws and, through the vehicle of the Freedmen's Bureau, ostensibly sought to make contract rather than coercion the basis of post-emancipation labor relations. Mostly staffed by U.S. Army officers, the Freedmen's Bureau oversaw the transition out of enslavement, requiring white employers to submit contracts for approval and Black employees to adhere to contract demands, so long as compensation was thought adequate and corporal punishment proscribed. This was exceptionally difficult to enact. White landowners resorted to an array of what Bureau officials termed "outrages"—personal and vigilante violence—to tame any independent dispositions that Blacks may have shown. For their part, Blacks feared returning to work for their previous enslavers, knowing full well what was likely in store, and sought instead to crawl out from under their thumbs, preferably by gaining access to land though more immediately by enlisting the support of the Freedmen's Bureau to rein in the whites. The results were mixed at best.

Land reform would have been a major step in the direction of an expansive and economically based Black freedom. The Republican-dominated federal government had gestured in this direction by taking almost one million acres of southern land under its control during the war, allowing General William T. Sherman to reserve 400,000 acres of prime plantation land along the coast of South Carolina, Georgia, and Florida for exclusive Black settlement, and tasking the newly established Freedmen's Bureau with supervising potential land redistribution. But such a radical fulfillment of emancipation quickly foundered, threatening as it did both the general security of private property and the viability of an economy long fueled by plantation agriculture. The granting of citizenship, basic civil rights, and the elective franchise to Black men—no small steps given the world of *Dred Scott* that had previously suffused the country—was as far as radicalism would go.[24]

Black political empowerment, owing to the Reconstruction Acts of 1867, lent the post-emancipation South a distinctiveness compared to any of its counterparts in the hemisphere, save for Haiti. Especially in the Deep South, Blacks could run for and attain local and state office (and in some places congressional office) and organize their communities politically. They could serve on juries and as magistrates and sheriffs, fighting off some of the injustices and repression that otherwise would have been inflicted. By all accounts, they had a commitment to democracy and democratic practice that had never before been seen in the South, and their tenacity and political acumen enabled them, despite all manner of white subversion, to participate in electoral politics and wield meaningful power in some places into the 1890s.[25]

Yet even before Reconstruction ended, coercive measures were put, or remained, in place that strengthened the hand of white landowners and employers, undermined the maneuvering room of Black laborers, and made Black men and women vulnerable to incarceration. Vagrancy laws required Black people to have "gainful employment" by a certain date or risk arrest. Enticement laws prohibited employers from luring laborers away with the promise of higher wages and better working conditions. Fence and game laws extinguished common rights to hunt, fish, and forage livestock. And planters' associations were formed to solve the "labor question": that is, the question of disciplining Black labor. "A great deal of severe legislation will be required to compel negroes to labor as much as they should do," Virginia's proslavery theorist George Fitzhugh had already concluded.[26]

The vagrancy and enticement laws were designed to coerce freed Black workers into accepting the labor contracts that landowners and other employers offered and prevent competition over their hiring. Both these measures had deep histories in the United States and British North America, and, in the states where enslavement remained lawful until the Civil War, vagrancy ordinances had been deployed against poorer whites and, especially, free people of color. Indeed, the criminalization of vagrancy can be traced at least to the Statute of Artificers, enacted in mid-fourteenth-century England, to discipline the growing body of "masterless men" there. And it is clear that vagrancy was regarded as a "problem" to be solved by the police power of states and localities across the country from well before the founding of the Republic. But, as was true elsewhere too, the law of vagrancy in the post-emancipation South provided for the arrest, fining, jailing, and, in many cases, the hiring-out of convicts to private employers, where they joined Black prisoners convicted of other petty offenses who were unable to pay their fines and court costs and compelled to work them off. In some cases, local sheriffs organized the public "sale" of convicts to the highest private bidders; at all events, Black men and women were being cast into involuntary servitude.[27]

The hiring-out of vagrants and other convicts set the basis for what came to be known as the "convict lease system," one of the most horrific features of post-emancipation Black life in the South, though one that had its start chiefly under the auspices of Republican-controlled Reconstruction governments. Strapped for revenue, focused on rebuilding and expanding the southern transportation infrastructure, and well aware of the private use of convict labor in the northern states, Republican governors and legislatures enabled counties and then their states to lease out not individuals convicted of petty crimes but entire prison populations. Among the main beneficiaries were railroad companies, some of which had previously relied upon enslaved labor, and mining enterprises looking to profit from coal, phosphates, and other minerals that could be extracted; large-scale cotton plantations as well as turpentine and lumber camps also found laborers this way.[28]

Some of the southern Republican governments looked to reform the system, but once their regimes were toppled, post-Reconstruction Democrats continued and expanded the convict lease, gaining the financial rewards that permitted them to drastically reduce tax rates from their Reconstruction-era levels. In many of the southern states, the revenues from these leases paid for the lion's share of their annual expenditures. Yet this should not be regarded as a mere throwback to the political economy of slavery. The convict leases provided labor to the more advanced and modernizing sectors of the southern economy, demonstrating quite vividly how involuntary servitude and economic development could go hand-in-glove. Railroad construction increasingly linked the southern states to the Midwest and Northeast, as well as to southern ports and rising commercial centers like Atlanta, while the mines and labor camps helped fuel a rapidly industrializing nation and the transportation networks that sustained it. As might be expected, new labor organizations and political insurgents—the Knights of Labor, the Greenback-Labor party, the Farmers' Alliance, and eventually the Populists—demanded that convict labor and the convict lease be abolished.[29]

What made convict lease particularly infamous—and increasingly noteworthy outside of the South—was the massive expansion of Black incarceration it promoted and the dreadful conditions to which convict laborers were subjected. Between 1865 and the turn of the twentieth century, Black prison populations from the Carolinas to Texas increased more than tenfold—with the greatest jumps following Reconstruction—and some of the major extractive and industrial establishments, like the Tennessee Coal and Iron Company, whose mines were located outside of Birmingham, came to rely heavily upon convict labor. The lessees were, in turn, responsible for working, clothing, housing, feeding, and tending to the convicts (state prison officials abandoned any oversight or regulation) and, given the almost continuous flow of convict labor that counties and states made available, there was every incentive to drive the convicts as hard as possible and brutally punish those who might resist. Although mortality rates are difficult to determine, some scholars suggest that they may have run as high as 25 percent annually, far exceeding averages on the Middle Passage of the Atlantic slave trade. In 1880s Mississippi, evidence shows that a ten-year sentence was not survivable. Those who managed to survive shorter terms or to escape (which occurred frequently) were usually broken in body and spirit.[30]

Shortly after the ratification of the Thirteenth Amendment, former Confederate general John T. Morgan recognized the potential loophole that had been provided to southern whites who were intent upon reducing Blacks to a familiar status of abject submission. "As the Constitution of the United States [gives] the power to inflict involuntary servitude as a punishment for crime, a suitable law should be framed by the state jurists [to] enable them to sell into bondage once more those Negroes found guilty of certain crimes." Although they said little about the exception clause during the congressional debates, this is just what some Republicans feared, especially when they saw direct evidence in the Black Codes being passed by many of the former rebellious states. "The negro refusing to work for wages is seized as a vagrant, [and] sold to service for the best wages that can be procured for three months," Minnesota senator Ignatius Donnelly warned, "if he runs off he shall work another month with balls and chain for nothing." And it does appear that many of the Thirteenth Amendment's Republican framers imagined the exception as a "punishment for crime" in an extremely limited way, only applicable when a convict was specifically sentenced to "hard labor" rather than for an assortment of minor violations.[31]

There is, however, no evidence of a legal challenge ever being brought against convict leasing as a violation of the Thirteenth Amendment's prohibition of "slavery or involuntary servitude." Indeed, it was not until the early twentieth century that peonage cases were successfully adjudicated in federal courts as violations of both the Thirteenth Amendment and the Anti-Peonage Act of 1867. The social and political power of those who profited from the involuntary labor of convicts and peons was simply too great; the illiberal practices of their use and exploitation too well established and well recognized in politics and law, however much they departed from the liberal-oriented ideals. The consequences continue to haunt us.[32]

III

THE HEAVY-HANDED AND RACIALLY repressive character of the post-emancipation, and especially post-Reconstruction, legal and labor regimes in the South have long suggested a regional exception to the nationalization of "free labor" that the Civil War and the Thirteenth Amendment appeared to herald. After all, from its founding in the early 1850s, the Republican Party proclaimed its devotion to the liberal ideals of "free soil, free labor, free men" and their achievement against the tyrannical designs of the "slave power." But the history of gradual emancipation and involuntary penal labor in the Northeast should give us pause about imagining clear regional distinctions, and particularly about thinking of slavery and free labor as neat oppositions in any part of the country. Concerns about the legal apparatus a free labor society required for social stability as wage labor became increasingly common pushed many states and municipalities outside the South to adopt a variety of coercive measures. And some of the strongest advocates were one-time antislavery reformers who showed little patience for any "able-bodied" men without gainful employment.[33]

As in the post-emancipation South, the main instruments deployed were vagrancy laws and incarceration. In May 1866, while congressional Republicans were contesting the southern Black Codes and the coercive devices brought against newly emancipated Black people, the Republican-dominated Massachusetts legislature passed "An Act Concerning Vagrants and Vagabonds." The act made "all idle persons who, not having visible means of support, live without lawful employment" subject to arrest by local police and confinement in the county house of correction or workhouse for up to six months if convicted by a trial justice or police court. Although relatively few arrests and convictions occurred during the first year of the law's operation, the Massachusetts Board of Charities observed that it "has been put in force with some stringency in Lowell, Lawrence, and other cities," and "that country towns also need to enforce it strictly." "When this shall be done throughout the State," the Board assured, "we shall be measurably relieved of a very troublesome class of persons." Board members included its secretary, Franklin B. Sanborn, and Samuel Gridley Howe, both abolitionists and "secret six" supporters of John Brown.[34]

Massachusetts was hardly alone. During the 1870s, many of the states of the Northeast and Midwest set their sights on beggars and others deemed "vagrants," who were to be rounded up, brought before the local authorities, and, if convicted (very little evidence was required), sentenced to terms of forced labor, often to the benefit of private interests. Indeed, in the aftermath of the Panic of 1873 and the severe depression it brought on, the number of harsh vagrancy statutes multiplied from New England to New York and from Pennsylvania to Illinois. This occurred despite the thousands who had been thrown out of work or suffered from the chronic effects of underemployment, who appeared idle and transient, or were left to begging for their survival, owing to no fault of their own. And, as in Massachusetts, charity reformers, many of whom were veterans of the antislavery campaign, emerged as the architects.[35]

While the economic depression of the 1870s exacerbated the effects, it was the growing importance of wage labor more generally that created a crisis for many of the reformers. Understanding free labor in close association with individual rights and responsibility as well as the opportunity for self-improvement—as the moral alternative to the dehumanization of enslavement—reformers and many other liberal-minded observers had not reckoned with the dependencies and vulnerabilities that wage labor of the mid-to-late nineteenth century inherently entailed. No longer a step on the ladder toward economic independence, as Lincoln had once crowed, wage labor was rather a status of increasing permanency and one heavily occupied by men and women who were immigrants or first-generation Americans with limited mechanical skills and little property, and Catholic or non-evangelical Protestant in faith.[36]

The backlash was already apparent in the 1840s and 1850s as thousands of Irish-Catholic immigrants arrived in the United States and took up berths at the lower end of the social scale, as laborers, canal diggers, domestics, and urban construction workers. Nativist rioting erupted in a number of cities—Philadelphia, Boston, and New York in particular—and by the early 1850s a nativist political movement was taking hold across the Northeast. Calling themselves the "American" or "Know Nothing" party, they fed off the country's deeply laid anti-Catholicism as well as its evangelical-inspired social reformism to view Irish Catholics as beholden to "demon rum," subject to the distant pope, subservient to political bosses, and mired in poverty and idleness. Instead of demanding immigration restriction (save for paupers) or expulsion, however, nativists sought to undermine their potential political power—and that of the Democratic Party, which cultivated their support—by lengthening the naturalization period from five to twenty-one years and denying the foreign-born both voting and officeholding rights. Availing themselves of the disintegration of the Whig Party over the slavery question, nativists mounted impressive political campaigns from New England to the Middle Atlantic and to parts of the Midwest and Far West, especially in northern California and Oregon, where hostility focused chiefly on Chinese (regarded as heathens) and Hispanics (Catholics). In Massachusetts, Rhode Island, Connecticut, and New Hampshire, nativists rode a tsunami of popular support and took control of the state governments. For a time, in fact, it appeared that the American Party would replace the Whigs as one of the two mass political parties in the United States. When the party then faltered over the slavery issue most of its constituents moved to the Republican Party, which melded Protestant reformism, anti-Mormonism, and anti-Catholicism with free-soil antislavery and colonization.[37]

The mix of antislavery and anti-Catholicism was not only a phenomenon of American political culture. Class and political economy were very much in play as well. The democratization of the elective franchise during the 1820s and 1830s took place at a point in time when the white population of the United States was overwhelmingly Protestant and wage labor had yet to assume great importance, even as the market economy expanded into the hinterlands; the problem of extending full political rights to poor and economically dependent men therefore remained of limited concern. The expectation was, as Lincoln had suggested, that those who began their lives with few resources and at work for wages would acquire productive property (land, skills, and tools) and the independence that went along with it.

Organized nativism signaled an important transformation: the emergence of a juridically free though propertyless and culturally threatening section of the American working class. The growing division of labor in manufacturing, the decline of artisan shops, the development of transportation networks, together with changes in the flow of Atlantic migration all marked a shift from an economy based on household production to one built around capitalist social relations, wage labor chief among them. The response was significant. Many white Protestants sought to exclude the foreign-born, and especially foreign-born Catholics, from the political arena or dramatically raise the bar for their entry. Drawing upon a tradition of denying paupers, convicts, and transients political rights, they began portraying Catholic immigrants as exemplifying the traits of poverty, thriftlessness, drunkenness, rootlessness, and criminality: for all intents and purposes, racializing them. From the outset, that is, the American working class was not only racially, ethnically, and culturally hybrid; it was racialized to its core and, save for a brief window in the mid-twentieth century, would remain so to this day.

The political offensive against many wage workers did not end with the decline of nativism and the Know Nothing Party or with the Civil War and emancipation. If anything, it was reignited once the war ended, even as civil and political rights were being granted to formerly enslaved men. As a new industrial economy took shape—propelled in part by wartime policies—with as many as two-thirds of the gainfully employed working for wages and demands for labor reform being loudly voiced, political elites, many of whom were Republicans and one-time foes of enslavement, began to question the wisdom of universal manhood suffrage. They feared the political process was being corrupted by ignorance, vice, fraud, and radicalism, destroying what had once been a sound and stable republic. "A New England village of olden time, that is to say some forty years ago," the historian Francis Parkman argued in 1878, "would have been safely and well governed by the votes of every man in it. [B]ut now that the village has grown into a populous city with its . . . thousands of restless workingmen, foreigners for the most part, to whom liberty means license and politics means plunder, to whom the public good is nothing . . . universal suffrage becomes a questionable blessing." Charles Francis Adams, the son of President John Quincy Adams and an antebellum free-soiler, saw the problem in continental perspective. "Universal suffrage can only mean in plain English the government of ignorance and vice," he scoffed as early as 1869, "it means a European, and especially a Celtic, proletariat on the Atlantic coast; an African proletariat on the shores of the gulf, and a Chinese proletariat on the Pacific."[38]

The Fifteenth Amendment, the last of Reconstruction's constitutional triumvirate, which established that the "right to vote" could not be denied on the "grounds of race, color, or previous condition of servitude," was ratified in 1870. But the ink was barely dry before northern states and municipalities began to conjure restrictions to the franchise and the political power of working-class communities in their midst. They had an assortment of ideas, all of which side-stepped the amendment's proscriptions. They talked of separating out elections having to do with budgets and taxation, and limiting the electorate for them to property owners (stakeholders as they saw it); establishing literacy and toughened residency requirements for prospective voters; providing for at-large, as opposed to ward- and district-based, elections; holding fewer elections and making more local offices appointive rather than elective; and advancing civil service reform with a scornful eye on the spoils that were doled out to the party faithful. They looked with special contempt at urban political machines, the very embodiments of what political democracy seemed to have become with the influx of immigrant voters, and vowed to dismantle them through the courts and reform legislation. Before the 1880s, when independent labor parties mounted successful campaigns in many cities and states, they mostly failed to achieve their goals, blocked by the interests and constituencies still wedded to an expansive (manhood) political democracy. But they laid a foundation for voter suppression and franchise limitation that would be enlivened in the post-Reconstruction South and the late Gilded Age North and West.[39]

One of the states that refused to ratify the Fifteenth Amendment was California. Admitted to the Union in 1850 with a constitution that prohibited enslavement, it was nonetheless governed during the 1850s by southern sympathizers. State legislators narrowly rejected secession, limited the civil rights of Black people, and subjected both Indians and the Chinese to highly coercive labor relations. By 1870, discriminatory laws concerning Black testimony in court had been repealed and the system of apprenticeship that reduced hundreds of Indians, mostly women and children, to servitude in the households of whites had been outlawed owing to Republican legislative efforts. Yet, even in the eyes of Republicans, Indians were now free *to* work not *from* work; harsh vagrancy laws would remand them to forced labor for several months while a regime of compulsory, generally agricultural, labor and circumscribed mobility was put in place on federally supervised reservations. "The hoe and the broadaxe would sooner civilize and Christianize than the spelling book and the Bible," one of the government's Republican Indian agents predicted, noting that the children in particular should work until "humanized by systematic labor." The logic of penal reform and of the free labor market coalesced in the turn to coercion.[40]

It was not the potential enfranchisement of Native peoples who had been denied birthright citizenship under the Fourteenth Amendment, or of African Americans, who were few in number, that rankled many white Californians. It was the potential enfranchisement of the Chinese, who had come to compose more than 10 percent of the labor force in the state and were to be found in town and countryside, in mines, in fields, and on railroad construction crews. Indeed, the challenges to enslavement and involuntary servitude of the period's emancipationism fueled not a drive to peel away the burdens that encased Chinese workers but an expulsionism reminiscent of the 1830s and the colonizationist impulses long threaded through antislavery thinking. Marking the Chinese as "coolies" and coolies as slaves, California Democrats disingenuously used antislavery principles to exclude Chinese men and women from being brought into the state: they passed enabling legislation called "An Act to Prevent the Importation of Chinese Criminals and to Prevent the Establishment of Coolie Slavery," only weeks after the Fifteenth Amendment won ratification in February 1870. While some Republicans protested at the time, more and more of them came to see Chinese exclusion as yet another antislavery measure; their votes in Congress underwrote the highly illiberal Chinese Exclusion Act of 1882.[41]

Post–Civil War vagrancy ordinances not only took a tougher and more punitive stance against those who were idle and appeared to resist participation in the labor market. They also homed in on newer human products of the industrializing order: migrant laborers, increasingly called "tramps" and eventually "hoboes," who moved between city and countryside, often following the harvest and reflecting the seasonal nature of capitalist employment itself. Especially in the upper Plains and Far West, where large-scale and highly mecha-nized (sometimes called "bonanza") farms came into being, streams of migrants flowed through their fields and then on to lumber and mining camps, railroad construction sites, and urban places where work might be had.[42]

Beginning in the mid-1870s, therefore, most of the states in the North and West adopted laws that strengthened the power of land-owners to coerce migrants into accepting the wages they offered and then targeted those who "tramped" by foot, river, or rail, and could be spotted at railroad depots, steamship landings, taverns, and gam-bling houses, as well as on the streets. In some places special consta-bles were created to arrest them; in some, the local police were tasked with enforcement; and in some, ordinary citizens could haul tramps in. But everywhere the tramps were subject to incarceration and usu-ally coerced labor on county farms, roads, and workhouses, in mines and quarries, and in manufactories. Known as "winter tourists," migrants who came to Los Angeles made up nearly 10 percent of the population and a very large portion of those to be found in the city's jails. Although Mexicans and Indians had once predominated among them (the state's 1855 vagrancy law was known as the "Greaser Act"), by the end of the nineteenth century the tramps and inmates were overwhelmingly white, though racialized as "degenerate," "irreclaim-able," and "depraved."[43]

IV

WHEN THE THIRTEENTH AMENDMENT won congressional approval in 1865, Radical Republicans imagined more than the death of slavery throughout the United States. They also imagined the tri-umph of "free labor," an ideal they had celebrated and struggled to nationalize for at least two decades. As Senator Henry Wilson, the "cobbler" from Natick, Massachusetts, insisted, "free labor" signified personal autonomy and empowerment as opposed to the dependence and degradation of enslavement, an institution which oppressed poor whites in the South just as surely as it did enslaved Blacks. Free labor, the "right to the fruits of his labor," as Wilson repeatedly defined it, would serve to elevate the poor and dignify the work that all free men did. Not just the absence of slavery or servitude, free labor was a positive symbol, fortified by equal standing and respectability. It was the foundation of a civilized and democratic republic.[44]

Yet, given the coercive measures that surrounded the African American transition out of slavery and into "freedom" as well as the coercive instruments that accompanied the great expansion of wage labor in the North and West, what was "free labor" in practice? Where was the voluntarism that free labor was meant to inscribe and the power that participants were to bring into the relation? The truth is that whatever Radical Republicans such as Wilson imagined, free labor and the wage relation had not experienced anything like the transformation that abolition brought to the regime of enslavement. If anything, they were still weighed down by the dictates of the English common law and contested meanings of "involuntary servitude." Rather than products of liberal ideals, free labor and the wage relation remained relics of a "belated feudalism," both in the coercive powers still in place and in the jurisdictional authority of the courts.[45]

What did this mean? The English common law, adopted by all the states following the Revolution, depicted wage labor as a species of servitude ("serves for wages"); its regulation fell under the rules and understandings of master-servant jurisprudence. In this, the laborer was "free" in the sense that he/she was not legally subordinate and could enter into an employment contract voluntarily. At the same time, the employer was recognized as having a property interest in the employee's labor and great power in the relationship so long as the contract lasted. Employees were subject to breach-of-contract penalties if they left before the contract expired or had been lured away by another employer (who could also be penalized for "enticement"). And while those penalties were generally criminal through much of the eighteenth century, by the nineteenth they were mostly pecuniary—in effect, the forfeiture of wages under the contract law of "entirety"—unless a person of color committed the offense. Then the penalties could be criminal.[46]

Most vulnerable were agricultural laborers who usually entered into yearly contracts, from planting through harvest, and were not paid until the crops had been brought in. Should they quit work beforehand, even in response to harsh or abusive treatment, they sacrificed all their wages unless they could demonstrate that the contract had been wrongfully terminated: a course of action that laborers would find difficult if not prohibitive to pursue. For their part, employers had enormous leeway in establishing the conditions of work and firing laborers even if near the end of the contract. It was not uncommon for an agricultural employer to wait until late in the season before dismissing an employee and gaining what amounted to unpaid labor for the portion of the contract that had been fulfilled. Although mechanization steadily reduced the number of year-long employees in northern and western agriculture—seasonal harvest labor increasingly sufficed—in the South, freed Black men and women were particularly at risk. They had managed to resist, at least in the cotton- and tobacco-producing areas, the reimposition of gang labor and instead struggled their way to sharecropping, when plantations and farms were divided into plots worked by the croppers and their families. A small measure of independence, it appeared. By the 1870s, however, southern courts had determined that sharecroppers were legally wage laborers; that they had no control over their growing crops and received a share of the crop in lieu of cash wages once debts for provisions had been deducted. With limited literacy and little education, sharecroppers were easy prey for unscrupulous landowners who could not only swindle them out of their shares but turn them off before the shares were even distributed. And once Reconstruction governments had been driven from power, Black croppers and other laborers had no real avenues for their grievances to be addressed.[47]

Domestic servants and journeymen as well as many skilled workers may also have agreed to lengthy (mostly annual) contracts, even if the contracts were not in writing, and they too faced the loss of wages if they quit. Semiskilled and specialized operatives, who became more and more important in the staffing of mechanized factories, had a related problem on their hands. They were subject to the near-absolute authority of the foreman, overseer, or contractor.

The "foreman's empire" it was called, and by all accounts foremen lorded over hiring and firing as well as the rhythms and remunerations of work, rewarding those who pleased them and doling out penalties—including fines—to those who crossed them. Coming out of the ranks of skilled mechanics, the foremen nonetheless answered to the bosses, not the workers, and were often likened to drivers on slave plantations. The notion of "wage slavery," which was central to the developing critique of Gilded Age capitalism, encompassed such subordination in the workplace together with the economic dependence and long hours that came along with it.[48]

Both master-servant jurisprudence and the foreman's empire raise fundamental questions about the meaning of involuntary servitude that the Thirteenth Amendment prohibited. Up through the eighteenth century and well into the nineteenth, legal culture recognized a distinction between voluntary and involuntary servitude—the former being initiated by means of contract—and while state legislatures in the Northeast enacted emancipation statutes between 1780 and 1804, and the Northwest Ordinance appeared to govern the social organization of the Midwest, there was no corresponding attack on indentured servitude. Indeed, the emancipation process itself in New England and the Middle Atlantic often saw court-approved transitions from enslavement to indentures of varying terms. The Northwest Ordinance was also evaded in this way. Little by little, lawsuits brought by employees for the recovery of wages forced state courts to wrangle with the issue and begin to move in a different direction. By mid-century, the growing opinion was that no distinction could be drawn between voluntary and involuntary servitude; they were one and the same, and, therefore, servitude in any form represented an unacceptable violation of free labor standing.[49]

Still, the boundaries of coercion remained on shaky ground. Although courts in Massachusetts and Indiana had ruled that voluntary labor was defined by the legal right to quit, to withdraw one's labor without penalty, the courts in Illinois and the New Mexico Territory ruled that so long as a labor agreement had been entered into voluntarily, neither the length of the contract term nor the requirements for leaving with pay were relevant to the matter of servitude. Recognizing the dual structures of contract and servitude that these rulings established, Congress attempted to legislate the Massachusetts and Indiana view but failed to do so despite the 1867 Anti-Peonage statute. The ambiguities remained, particularly when the cases related to establishments outside the South. Not until the early twentieth century would the Supreme Court begin to take up the matter and decide along lines that the Massachusetts and Indiana courts had laid out.[50]

As these divergent rulings suggest, the courts played a central role in defining the nature and power balances of the employment relation. While they had been moving away from common law precedent and toward a set of doctrines based on freedom of contract when it came to manufacturing and commerce, they mostly held fast to the common law when it came to labor, regularly deploying a language based on masters and servants. There seemed, in fact, to be two separate bodies of law emerging, and the social profiles of the judiciary, at all levels, demonstrates why this may have been the case. The post–Civil War Supreme Court was dominated by Republican justices from the Northeast and Midwest who were generally aligned with the moderate and conservative wings of the party. Their major opinions in the 1870s and 1880s not only narrowed the reach of the Thirteenth and Fourteenth amendments and the Civil Rights Acts of 1866 and 1875, but in so doing also strengthened the hands of employers of Black labor in the southern states who expected to use coercive methods of exploitation and resort to paramilitarism to defeat strikes and other Black political mobilizations. Other federal judicial appointees were overwhelmingly Republican and bourgeois in background: their perspectives had been shaped by a world of commerce, manufacturing, or finance, and their educations would have acquainted them with social Darwinism, the common law, and the economic instrumentalism of the antebellum courts.[51]

At the state level, matters could have been different because judges might be elected rather than appointed and both Democrats and Republicans filled these posts. But, in reality, once we move away from magistrate and other local courts, the social backgrounds and legal dispositions of the judges were more alike than different. They came from privileged families or were sponsored by them; were eager to expand their jurisdictional authority; rallied around contractual freedom; and generally held workers responsible for pushing back against their employers' demands. As a consequence, the struggle for "free labor" and labor rights as working people understood them took place in two very different and unequally empowered arenas. One was the legislative—municipal and state—in which working-class wards and districts populated by rural and urban producers could elect sympathetic representatives who might enact reforms related to hours, wages, and working conditions. The eight-hour workday was the great issue of the time (the norm was ten hours or more), the source of massive mobilizations, and it achieved some breakthroughs as a result. But the other arena was that of the courts, where the logics of master-servant and contract freedom prevailed, and working people were dealt stinging defeats when employers contested reform legislation. Here, in the ultimate power of judicial review, "belated feudalism" was in evidence.[52]

The courts had long hobbled journeymen and skilled workers who attempted, during the early decades of the nineteenth century, to organize in defense of their trades and the new forms of exploitation they were facing. In the post–Civil War era, the courts were quick to issue injunctions against strikers and their unions and permit the use of federal troops, state militias, or new national guard units to suppress labor disputes in the interest of employers. Eugene V. Debs, the president of the American Railway Union, who was arrested and incarcerated for defying such an injunction during the Pullman strike of 1894, saw quite clearly how the power of the courts worked. "As soon as the employees found that we were arrested and taken from the scene of action," Debs testified before a federal strike commission, "they became demoralized and ended the strike. It was not the soldiers that ended the strike. It was not the brotherhoods that ended the strike. It was simply the United States courts that ended the strike." In effect, the courts simultaneously represented the interests of employers and lent them the police power—the hiring of gunmen, vigilantes, and private armies—necessary to defeat striking workers and enforce the coercive boundaries of the employment relation. Before long, employers in a corporate form would gain the protection of substantive due process under the Fourteenth Amendment, constituting themselves as petit kingdoms—sometimes in league with one another—with pliant courts to carry out their plans when municipal councils and state legislatures attempted to rein them in.[53]

V

SOME SCHOLARS AND POLITICAL OBSERVERS have been quick to resolve the contradictory social developments of the nineteenth century by homogenizing them: by insisting that enslavement persisted in the South in other forms; that convict lease and related carceral repression represented some of those forms; that the Thirteenth Amendment was a weak reed and with its "exception clause" an inadequate protection against re-enslavement; that convict laborers could be regarded as "slaves of the state"; and that Jim Crow followed fast upon Reconstruction and added legal ballast to the re-enslavement of Black people by casting them out of the formal civil and political life of the South much as enslaved people had been. There is, needless to say, evidence to support this view, as well as Black people who could describe some of the structures of power in the post-emancipation South, convict lease chief among them, as "worse than slavery."

Yet, by flattening this complex history we avoid reckoning with the spectrum of coercions that engulfed the Euro-Atlantic world and how movements against the most egregious forms of them—enslavement and involuntary servitude in this case—ended up lending moral sanction to others. The historical actors who should compel our attention are not the enslavers and their legatees who never really gave up on the idea that enslavement was the appropriate and God-mandated status for people of African descent or even for poor people of European and Asian descent. They long insisted that inequality and difference defined the human condition and coercions of many sorts were necessary to the order and prosperity of any society. Rather, the historical actors who should compel our attention are those who regarded themselves as Enlightened humanists; who came to find slavery and servitude abhorrent; who believed that all people should be equal in the eyes of the law and were capable of reform and self-improvement; who seemed most attuned to liberal ideals as to rights, political practice, economic activity, and progress; who looked forward in anticipation instead of backward with fear or longing. They should compel our attention because they were creating and shaping institutions designed to navigate a rapidly changing world, and while they were confident about human efficacy, they could also be blind to the deployments and meaning of power.

It was no accident that many of them found emancipation and penal confinement necessary and mutually supportive, saw free labor and harsh vagrancy laws as two sides of the same social coin, detested enslavement though viewed convict labor as desirable, and celebrated contract freedom even when it could produce near-servitude in the workplace. These were less contradictions in terms than parts of a coherent package of thought and class sensibility in which liberal optimism was yoked to visions of social order where power could be denied while being wielded. As purveyors of penal reform who were quick to accept penal servitude, as champions of slave emancipation who pressed for vagrancy laws, they envisioned a world of human capacity and agency while setting cultural and behavioral standards against which working people and poor folk, men and women of color, would be found wanting. And in each case, some type of expulsion and coercive discipline was viewed as the proper, and needful, remedy. Illiberal solutions always seemed the resort for liberal-detected problems. Thus, the nineteenth century was given over not so much to the transition from slavery to freedom as to the shifting boundaries of coercive practices, some old and sustained, others new and perhaps opaque, most retaining illiberal elements even as they were advanced by self-designated liberal advocates. We still live with what they left us.

Chapter Six

MODERNIZING
ILLIBERALISM

W HEN MARGARET SANGER FOUNDED THE AMERICAN
Birth Control League in 1921, she was eager to have Irving
Fisher join the board of directors. A Yale-trained economist and
student of William Graham Sumner's, Fisher's contributions to
the emerging field of neoclassical economics were such that Joseph
Schumpeter would describe him as "the greatest economist the
United States has ever produced," a judgment later seconded by James
Tobin and Milton Friedman. But for Sanger, Fisher was important for
his contributions to a different field: eugenics. In 1913, Fisher published a short book, *Eugenics*, and quickly became an active lecturer
for the cause. At the Second National Congress on Race Betterment
in 1915, Fisher reflected on the "race degeneration" taking place and
told his audience that "if I had my life to live over again, I rather think
I would devote myself preeminently to eugenics" because it "stands as
the foremost, as the most promising, means of redeeming the human
race." Two months before the First American Birth Control Conference, at which the League was founded, Fisher, who helped Sanger
organize the meeting, played an important role at the Second International Congress of Eugenics, convening, appropriately it turned out,
at New York's Museum of Natural History.[1]

It was no accident that Sanger came to work closely with Fisher or
that she also invited Lothrop Stoddard, author of *The Rising Tide of Color
Against White World Supremacy* (1920), to join the League's board. For
Sanger, birth control was not only a means of empowering women; it
was also a vehicle of population control and improvement. "The idea
in calling the conference," Sanger explained, "was to bring together,

not our old friends, the advocates of Birth Control . . . but new people . . . who have been working in social agencies and in other groups
for the same results as we, namely for a better nation and for the banishment of disease, misery, poverty, delinquency and crime." "Everywhere we are confronted by the fact that large families and poverty
go hand in hand," she continued; "We see the healthy and fit elements
of the nation carrying the burden of the unfit who are increasing in
number—an increase which threatens to wipe out the fit and healthy
population of our land." The League's goal was to "elevate the func-
tion of motherhood" so that "a race of well-born children" might be
"create[d]." To that end she advocated "research into the relation of
reckless breeding to delinquency, defect, and dependence," "sterilization of the insane and feeble-minded," and the "removal of state and
federal statutes that encourage dysgenic breeding."[2]

Margaret Sanger came to birth control and eugenics through the
avenues of socialism and working-class feminism. One of eleven children born to a family in the factory town of Corning, New York,
she trained in nursing, moved to New York City, and gravitated to
the social and political radicalism that percolated in Greenwich Village. In 1914, she began to publish the fiery magazine *Woman Rebel*,
whose masthead proclaimed, "no Gods no Masters," as I.W.W. organizers in Lawrence, Massachusetts, like anarchists before them, had
done in 1912 (Sanger was there too). In it, contraception was part of
a wide-ranging attack on "wage slavery," "bourgeois morality," and
"blackhearted plutocrats." Although her readership was a small one,
Sanger drew the attention of the United States Attorney's office; she
was issued a nine-count indictment for violating the nefarious Com-
stock laws banning the distribution of "obscene, lewd, lascivious, and
indecent" material. Fearing conviction and prison time, she fled the
country and, while in England, met the influential sexual psychologist
Havelock Ellis, whose work was already familiar to her. Ellis introduced her to eugenic ideas and the notion of scientific breeding. By
the time Sanger returned to the United States, eugenics had become
integral to the way in which she imagined birth control.[3]

Scientific breeding, later termed "eugenics" by Charles Darwin's
half-cousin Francis Galton, had American roots in communitarian

experiments of the mid-nineteenth century and a growing roster of supporters, including Victoria Woodhull, who wrote in 1891 that "if superior people are to be desired, they must be bred." By the early twentieth century, more and more states enacted legislation providing for eugenic sterilization, and in 1911 New Jersey governor Woodrow Wilson signed one such bill into law. In 1910 a Eugenics Record Office opened at the Carnegie Institution's station at Cold Spring Harbor, New York, and shortly thereafter Theodore Roosevelt told its director that "society has no business to permit degenerates to reproduce their kind." The World War One draft only seemed to dramatize the urgency of action; psychological testing, which laid the groundwork for IQ and SAT tests, suggested that more than half the American population was "feeble-minded."[4]

Margaret Sanger was particularly concerned with the "great problem of the feeble-minded," who, she believed, made for "degeneracy, crime, and pauperism." "The philosophy of Birth Control," she wrote in 1922, "points out that as long as civilized communities encourage unrestrained fertility . . . they will be faced with the ever-increasing problem of feeble-mindedness." There was no greater "menace to civilization," she insisted, than the "lack of balance between the birthrate of the 'unfit' and the 'fit,'" and no "more urgent problem [than] . . . the over-fertility of the mentally and physically defective." The First American Birth Control Conference thereby "mark[ed] a turning point in our approach to social problems" for it "made evident that . . . the most penetrating thinkers" now see "our problem as a fundamental necessity to American civilization." They are "coming to see that the qualitative factor as opposed to the quantitative one is of primary importance in dealing with the great masses of humanity." So it seemed. Supporters of and participants in the Birth Control Conference included *New Republic* editor Herbert Croly, Stanford University president David Starr Jordan, conservationist Gifford Pinchot, historian Will Durant, settlement house organizer Lillian Wald, novelist Theodore Dreiser, and future British prime minister Winston Churchill, together with Havelock Ellis, Lothrop Stoddard, and Irving Fisher.[5]

Eugenics is often treated as a sidebar to the dominant impulses

of the Progressive era, but its wide embrace, even among those associated with Progressivism's left wing, should give us pause. Indeed,
eugenics fit comfortably into a larger project of social engineering that began to engage scientists, intellectuals, and policy makers
during the last decades of the nineteenth century, and became compelling to more and more modernists during the first two decades of
the twentieth. Social engineering promised to tackle the enormous
challenges of post–Civil War industrialization, immigration, and
class conflict, and reorganize American economic and political life
around new institutions and sensibilities. The idea of social engineering proved to be the connecting tissue between corporatism, scientific management, political bureaucratization, racial segregation, and
imperialism. During the 1920s, it would propel prohibition, immigration restriction, and "hundred-percent Americanism." Although
many historians see in this period the emergence of a liberal state,
the scope of social engineering also gave rise to a reconfigured and
even more formidable illiberalism, one in which social hierarchies
were lent scientific support, rights became increasingly contingent,
human populations were organized into categories of intelligence
and capacity, and the levers of the state were deployed in newly coercive, and restrictive, ways. Viewed internationally and combined with
anti-radical and anti-immigrant violence at the grassroots (discussed
in the following chapter), the United States was, by the early 1920s,
carving a path that bore resemblance to the European fascism then
taking hold.

I

THAT THE NEW YORK Congress of Eugenics was deemed "international" suggests the scope of concerns and fears that fed eugenic
thinking. Attendees and discussants came from Great Britain, continental Europe, and Mexico, and societies devoted to advancing
eugenic policies were being organized across both the Pacific and
Atlantic worlds, all to be coordinated by an International Federation
of Eugenic Societies founded in 1921. Availing itself of the new pres-

tige of scientific investigation and the demands to meet the social challenges of modernization, eugenics seemed to offer an approach that enlightened elites and an educated public could value. Eugenics incorporated ideas about heredity that had been pioneered in the nineteenth century by Gregor Mendel and, to a lesser extent, Jean-Baptiste Lamarck in the eighteenth, and it encouraged the belief that a marriage of science and state policy could steer a course away from conflict and immiseration toward human betterment. Not surprisingly, the growing esteem accorded eugenics went along with new thinking about race and "race relations," a sense that racial hierarchies could be managed and racial interactions choreographed so that turmoil might be avoided, both at home and in colonial settings. To be sure, eugenics and related projects of social engineering were shaped by the political contexts in which they emerged, but almost everywhere they reflected disenchantment with the liberal dispositions of the Enlightenment and the nineteenth century that followed. Although the focus has often been on France, Italy, and especially Germany in this regard, the United States provides a comparable if unsettling example.[6]

Whether from the left or the right, the social critiques of the Gilded Age (roughly 1877–1896) took aim at liberal ideas and liberal society: at the celebration of individualism, the competitive relations of the marketplace, the pursuit of self-interest, and the system of representative governance. Burgeoning movements of workers and farmers, calling themselves "producers," denounced the "monopolization" of wealth and power, railed against the "wages system" that resulted in "wage slavery," and heaped scorn on the corruption of the political process by the "moneyed men" and their minions. "Robber Barons" and "Money Kings" were the royalist and aristocratic epithets they hurled at their enemies; they rallied instead to the goal of a "cooperative commonwealth." For their part, members of an older upper class—the declining regional elites who saw their places and prerogatives being overtaken by new classes of industrialists and bankers, soulless cities, and masses of poor immigrants—turned against modern culture and much it seemed to herald. They saw liberalism's autonomous self as an illusion and its notions of authority as illegitimate. Some longed for a preindustrial world of organic hierarchy, artisanal handicrafts, pastoral simplicity, and even medieval combat for the "authentic" experience that modernity appeared to expel.[7]

Yet the most consequential and enduring of the critiques came from new social groups that liberal, industrializing society itself produced. These were men and women, many born in mid-century to Protestant, middle-class families, who benefited from advanced educations, often traveled or studied in Europe, and played important roles in the developing professions and reform organizations. Too young to have participated in the Civil War, they came of age amid the disappointments of Reconstruction, the deep economic depressions of the 1870s and 1890s, and the violent conflicts that industrial capitalism was provoking. They were economists and social scientists, social reformers and ministers of the Social Gospel, engineers and chemists, philosophers and educators, business and labor leaders. However else their views may have differed, they shared a sense that the values of the nineteenth century were inadequate to the demands of either the present or the future.[8]

Society, they argued, was composed not of atomized individuals but of groups formulating and pursuing their goals. Competition produced not social and economic advancement but waste, conflict, and inefficiency. Political leaders at all levels were motivated not by a notion of the public good but by the prospect of power, place, and preferment. While denunciations of "pools," "trusts," and other combinations might have been rife among some of them, for the most part they accepted the trend toward large-scale economic institutions—corporations and other big businesses—but hoped that they could be effectively managed with the aid of an administrative state. They regarded scientific method and social experience as critical to progress, and most eagerly embraced ideas of social evolution. They saw cooperation—"association" some termed it—as a goal of public life, and nonpolitical experts, managers, and innovators as the key players to replace corrupt politicians beholden to their greedy and parochial constituents. A good many had been influenced by socialism and socialist projects, but, like social democrats more generally, they did not call the private ownership of productive resources into question nor did they hope to empower any social groups that might do so themselves.[9]

Few intellectuals or professionals captured the logic of these sensibilities more fully than Herbert Croly, a peripatetic writer and political thinker who would be one of the founding editors of *The New Republic* in 1915. Six years earlier he had published *The Promise of American Life*, which catapulted him to great prominence among Progressive policy makers and leaders, not least Theodore Roosevelt. Croly's was a wide-ranging critique of the condition of the country at the turn of the twentieth century as well as a blueprint for a reorganization to serve what he called the "national purpose." He recognized that the dynamics of the Gilded Age had led to the "concentration of wealth and financial power in the hands of a few irresponsible men." This, he believed, was not only subversive of the American economy but also "inimical to democracy." But he blamed the circumstances on "the inevitable outcome of the chaotic individualism of our political and economic organization" rather than on anything fundamental to the economic and political system itself. Here he saw the results of a deeply rooted Jeffersonian tradition, and called for the "subordination of the individual" to the demands of an "American state" which alone could make for a "morally and socially desirable distribution of wealth."[10]

Croly was a new type of nationalist. His was not just a nationalism of spirit and personal identity but also one of organization and purpose. He did not assume that "the fulfillment of our national Promise" was "inevitable"; it required a "conscious" effort based on "a certain measure of discipline . . . [and] a large measure of individual subordination and self-denial." Loyalty to the American state had to be cultivated through "positive service," and this would involve "the regulation of commerce, the control of corporations, and the still more radical questions concerned with the distribution of wealth and the prevention of poverty." States and municipalities, whose local power and influence he regarded as problematic, could carry out these services though only "as agents of the central government."

A good many Americans, Croly acknowledged, might consider

his "reconstruction policy" to be "flagrantly socialistic," but this
did not bother him, nor was he interested in "dodging the odium
of the word." Like many other Progressives, Croly imagined socialist ideas as part of the mix of social transformation while insisting
on "the preservation of the institution of private property in some
form." It was Hamilton rather than Marx who exemplified the sort
of purpose Croly had in mind, and he celebrated Theodore Roosevelt for "reviv[ing] the Hamiltonian ideal of constructive national
legislation." With his "new Nationalism," Roosevelt "emancipat[ed]
American democracy from its Jeffersonian bondage," and endowed
"popular government . . . with larger powers, more positive responsibilities, and a better faith in human excellence." By giving "men of
special ability [and] training . . . a better opportunity to serve the public," Roosevelt founded "a new national democracy," and insofar as
that democracy "must stand or fall on a platform of possible human
perfectibility," it was important to "improve the methods whereby
men and women are bred."[11]

II

HOWEVER HERBERT CROLY DERIDED the "existing concentration
of power in the hands of a few irresponsible men," he was no advocate for the small manufacturer or small producer. It was the corporation that represented his developmental ideal. National instead of
local in their horizons and reach, integrated instead of decentered in
their organization, "huge corporations . . . contributed to economic
efficiency" and constituted "an important step in the direction of the
better organization of industry and commerce." Indeed, Croly argued
that corporations "substituted cooperative for competitive methods,"
and this "process of industrial organization should be allowed to work
itself out" with the regulatory oversight of the "central government"
rather than "the states." The corporation was an institution "framed
in the national interest" and would offer "men of exceptional ability
[the opportunities] to perform really constructive economic work."

As for "the smaller competitor of the large corporation," should he be "unable to keep his head above water with his own exertions, he should," Croly scoffed, "be allowed to drown."[12]

Croly was hardly alone in expressing these views. He rather melded a number of currents of thought that were flowing in the early years of the twentieth century and joined the activities of private associations, lobbying groups, informal networks, and personal alliances—a social movement of sorts—among some of the country's most prominent industrial and financial capitalists. Recognizing the political dangers that capitalist excess had produced and chafing at the legislative pressure from "populist" and "provincial" constituencies that resulted in a morass of state regulations, they looked to advance the property rights, judicial rules, and class relations of a new political economy. Although they fought among themselves over the terms and balances, and would continue to do so, they could all gravitate to a banner that might be inscribed with "corporate capitalism and the administered marketplace."[13]

The corporate form was of relatively recent vintage, and the emergence of "huge corporations" even more so. Before the late nineteenth century, ownership of manufacturing establishments, even those becoming large and increasingly integrated, rested with individuals, families, and partnerships. They raised capital by tapping personal resources, reinvesting profits, or borrowing from commercial lenders, and often depended on local merchants for distribution. Efforts to expand their market power had encouraged the use of legally dubious and politically suspect "pools" and "trusts," and the growing ties between industrial and financial capital rendered the proprietary nature of manufacturing and related concerns less and less useful. Pioneered by the railroad industry and aided by decisions of the high courts as well as the generosity of some of the states, the corporate form not only addressed many of these problems: it represented a new form of capitalism.[14]

New was the creation of social relations and property rights that invested corporations with unprecedented powers, prerogatives, and protections. Ownership was effectively "socialized" among shareholders, liability was limited, and boards of directors not only gained legal standing but, owing to favorable incorporation laws in states like New Jersey and Delaware (there were no federal incorporation laws), they could hold stock, and thus ownership, in other corporations. As might then be expected, by the early twentieth century the great majority of large corporations were incorporated in New Jersey wherever else they did their main business, and what were known as "holding companies," corporations that existed for the sole purpose of gaining ownership in other corporations, could for a time claim a legal basis. When it came to raising capital, corporate managers looked to new institutions either born or strengthened by the financial exigencies of the Civil War. They were the stock and bond markets, brokerage houses, and investment banks rather than personal or company coffers. Corporate assets could far exceed the value of their plants and equipment.[15]

The foundations of corporate power were laid by the U.S. Supreme Court in cases concerning political liability and economic monopoly. In an 1886 case (*Santa Clara* v. *Southern Pacific Railroad*) involving taxation, the Court declared that corporations had the same due process rights as "natural persons" under the Fifth and Fourteenth Amendments. Congress quickly followed that guidance in crafting the Sherman Anti-Trust Act (1890), stipulating that "the word 'person' or 'persons,' wherever used in this act, shall be deemed to include corporations and associations." Corporations would thereby enjoy protections from aggressive regulations and taxes imposed by the states to which individuals were not subject, together with the status of a discrete type of property that "natural persons" could not hold. In addressing the meaning of "restraint of trade," furthermore, the hinge of anti-trust legislation, the Court came to embrace the "rule of reason," which distinguished between "reasonable" and "unreasonable" restraints. Neither the size of a corporation nor its market share would, in themselves, now be evidence of an illegal combination. The tsunami of corporate mergers between 1897 and 1904, which put half of the nation's manufacturing capital under the control of the three hundred largest corporations, did not therefore hit a restraining wall of lawsuits and legislation. When the tide of consolidation receded, U.S. Steel, General Electric, Standard Oil, Du Pont, and American Tobacco were among those newly standing.[16]

The corporate vision extended well beyond the boardrooms and shareholders, most notably to the workplaces where ideas of social engineering proved especially robust. The labor struggles and intense competition of the late nineteenth century encouraged managers to make the production process more efficient and, in important respects, challenge the power of skilled laborers and craftsmen who worked on the factory floors and possessed the technical knowledge integral to the organization of work. Mechanization, specialization, and homogenization were some of the ways forward, replacing skilled workers with semiskilled operatives. But even more appealing was "scientific" or "systematic" management, which revealed the growing connections between science and industry and an interest in bringing order and efficiency to the ways in which manufacturing was done. Here, machinist-turned-engineer Frederick Winslow Taylor pointed the way through time and motion studies, standardization of methods, and enforced cooperation, commonly called "Taylorism," which helped shift the control of production from the workers on the shop floor to the managers who supervised them.[17]

Yet the "labor question" that corporations confronted was not only about who held the knowledge to run the operation. It was also about the relative power that labor and capital could claim. Deeply hostile to fledgling labor unions—and fortified by the courts, which generally viewed unions and collective bargaining as violations of contract freedom and illegal restraints of trade—corporations had been resorting to wage cuts, injunctions, firings, strikebreakers, and paramilitaries to protect their property and interests. But new sensibilities were sprouting among some corporate leaders who imagined more of a cooperative than an antagonistic relationship to labor. Herbert Croly helped to articulate it.

Although he vilified "militant unionists" who "talk and believe as if they were at war with the existing social and political order," Croly had nearly equal contempt for the "non-union laborer," an "industrial derelict" who has "gone astray . . . prefer[ring] his own individual interests to the joint interests of himself and his fellow laborers." For Croly, rights to collective bargaining and union organizing were imperative for an efficient economic order, and worker demands for a minimum wage and workday needed to be met. "The labor unions deserve to be favored," he wrote, "because they are the most effective machinery . . . for the economic and social amelioration of the laboring class." Their recognition was entirely "justifiable," a key component of an economy organized along corporate-collective lines, and the only way "an effective fight" could be made against "unjustifiable demands" such as "the maximum amount of work and pay." But Croly, who had sympathies for the syndicalist leanings (embracing the workplace as the basis of social and political organization) of some working people, also distinguished between "good" and "bad" unions, and endorsed the refusal of employers "to recognize a union which establishes conditions and rules of labor inimical to a desirable measure of individual economic distinction and independence." In those cases, employers would do well to organize what Croly called "counter-unions"—effectively company unions—so that the organization of labor and capital could gradually "be fitted into a nationalized economic system."[18]

Some of Croly's ideas found earlier expression in the National Civic Federation, established in 1900 and tasked with bringing together leaders from business, labor, and the "public" to address the crises of American industrial capitalism. The membership included trade unionists like Samuel Gompers (American Federation of Labor), John Mitchell (United Mine Workers), and Daniel Keefe (International Longshoremen), as well as a cross-section of journalists, ministers, educators, and political luminaries like William Howard Taft, Grover Cleveland, Columbia University's Nicholas Murray Butler, and Harvard's Charles W. Eliot. But it was dominated by industrialists and bankers from some of the largest corporations in the United States—August Belmont, Andrew Carnegie, Charles Francis Adams Jr., Cyrus McCormick, several partners from J. P. Morgan's investment house—and headed up by Mark Hanna, the Ohio senator, political operative, and business magnate, whose biography Croly would write (1912). The NCF hoped to steer a path between labor radicals and socialists on the left and smaller industrialists represented by the National Association of Manufacturers (occasionally belittled as "anarchists") on the right by experimenting, in good pragmatic fashion, with new approaches and marshaling the power of the state for reform and reconstruction. Like Croly, they were interested in a "national" perspective on the problem of anti-trust and corporate regulation and sought to educate both legislators and the public on the wisdom of their views. At times, they drew up model bills and eventually contributed to the making of the Clayton Anti-Trust Act (1914), the Federal Trade Commission Act (1914), and the Federal Reserve System (1913).[19]

Still, their major concern was the labor question and, like Croly, some of the NCF members had come to accept the need for conservative unionism or, at the very least, informal methods for mediating disputes. Hanna hoped "to have organized union labor Americanized in the best sense and thoroughly educated to an understanding of its responsibilities" so it could be "an ally" rather than a "foe" of the capitalist. To that end, the NCF established an "Industrial Department" to promote collective bargaining, and took up issues of workmen's compensation, child labor, industry-wide contracts, and corporate responsibilities to workers in an effort to encourage cooperation between labor and capital as well as uniformity in regulatory legislation. President Theodore Roosevelt's intervention in a massive anthracite coal strike, mounted by the United Mine Workers in eastern Pennsylvania in 1902, which forced the coal operators to the table and was cheered on by Hanna, seemed to be an example for the future. Although few industrialists were yet ready to accept any form of collective bargaining or union recognition, the outlines of a corporatist vision, of social engineering on an industrial scale, were unmistakably taking shape.[20]

III

HERBERT CROLY REGARDED HIMSELF as a defender of modern democracy, one national in its energy and reach, propelled by large institutions, well-educated men and women, and a popular sovereignty expressed in the form of a "collective purpose." He was also a great critic of the Jeffersonian democracy that, in his view, prevailed during the nineteenth century and empowered individuals and localities, resulting in parochialism and corruption. Skeptical of the efficacy of some political reforms, such as the Australian (secret) ballot, direct primaries, and civil service reform, Croly imagined a national government run by competent and nonpartisan administrative bureaucrats and bolstered by popular loyalty. On the local (municipal) level, where corrupt practices were most in evidence, he believed a solution might be found in a chief executive "elected for a comparatively long term," an executive council "appointed by himself," and a legislative council "elected from large districts and . . . by some cumulative system of voting."[21]

Croly captured the temper of much Progressive political reformism, which saw democracy in terms similar to the corporation: emphasizing efficiency, expertise, good management, and institutional loyalty, while deriding signs of corruption, fraud, and incompetence. Proper democracy was best revealed when knowledgeable citizens attuned to a national purpose selected candidates for office who were well trained for the tasks of governance. Since this did not describe the workings of the American political system at any level, Progressive reformers looked to the establishment of nonpartisan commissions, at-large elections, top-heavy administrations, and the whittling of the electorate so that the uneducated, irresponsible, and disloyal would be deprived of the right to vote.

To be sure, elite concerns about the dangers of popular democracy were evident at the birth of the republic. And while they subsided during the first decades of the nineteenth century when adult white men were almost universally enfranchised, they ramped up during the 1840s and 1850s as thousands of poor, Irish Catholic immigrants swelled the ranks of the unskilled working class and gravitated to the Democratic Party. Nativist legislation spearheaded by Whigs and Know Nothings, especially in the Northeast, erected barriers to their political participation and laid the groundwork for renewed antidemocratic agitation once the Civil War ended and the revolutionary political empowerment of Black men in the North and South had run its course.

The alarms were sounded most loudly by Protestant elites who fretted about a political world they had lost and a worrisome new one they seemed to be inheriting, one in which "tens of thousands of restless workmen, foreigners for the most part," were overrunning the country. Those elites were joined by former enslavers in the South and land barons, developers, and even white workingmen in the West who cast hostile eyes on the Black and ethnically diverse populations around them, Mexicans and Chinese workers in particular, who were seen to be contaminating the ballot box and by extension the body politic. In so doing, they called into question the idea of "universal suffrage" as nineteenth-century Americans understood it, threatened, they believed, by ignorance and vice. The electorate needed to be "cleansed" and the ballot box "purifyed" so that "educated men" could be returned to their proper place in governance.[22]

For all their wealth and stature, these elites, including "liberal reformers"—Republicans who had come to detest the overreach of the government in supporting working people of various ethnicities— had tough rows to hoe. In industrial cities and towns, working-class political power, sometimes harnessed by urban machines, had gained traction through the Democratic, Greenback-Labor, or independent labor parties and demonstrated their ability to win offices and enact policies favorable to their constituents: early versions of "gas and water socialism," which looked to municipal ownership of utilities. In the former slave South, enfranchised freedmen, aided by the Union League and Reconstruction Republican party, shifted the balances of power in the plantation districts away from the big landowners and in some places withstood the onslaught of white paramilitaries to remain politically active and consequential. Even as Reconstruction governments were overthrown, the Fourteenth and Fifteenth Amendments complicated white efforts to destroy their power by guaranteeing the equal protection of the laws and prohibiting disfranchisement on the basis of "race, color, or previous condition of servitude." At least so long as congressional Republicans were prepared to pounce.[23]

A period of experimentation designed to make voting and citizenship more difficult to attain commenced, though with mixed results. It was the social and political explosions of the 1880s and 1890s—international in scope—that gave the momentum for political "reform" the decisive push. Indeed, it was not only the great labor strikes of the 1880s or the political insurgencies of the 1880s and 1890s, including Populism, which at times involved interracial alliances, that proved crucial; it was also the crushing defeats inflicted on them, often with lethal military and paramilitary violence, that enabled more success. Although the most brutal repression and sweeping disfranchisements came in the South—poll taxes, literacy tests, understanding clauses, and the empowerment of white registrars, all directed against the Black man's "habits and weaknesses"—a new political "reconstruction" was nationwide. By the late nineteenth century, Black suffrage was under attack outside of the South, first by liberal reformers and then nascent Progressives like the labor economist John R. Commons, the sociologist Edward A. Ross, and the young Woodrow Wilson, who all believed that Black men were unprepared to exercise the franchise and therefore major sources of corruption. They were "unpracticed in liberty, unschooled in self control, never sobered by the discipline of self support, never established in any habit of prudence," Wilson wrote in the *Atlantic Monthly* (1901). The Supreme Court, dominated by northern justices, lent validation to the southern approach in *Williams* v. *Mississippi* in 1898, which upheld the poll tax, literacy requirements, and other devices of racial disfranchisement.[24]

Yet the anti-democratic vision of political reformers was far wider. Earlier liberal fears of what Theodore Roosevelt would term "radical democracy" had won growing intellectual legitimacy from the technocratic and modernist currents of Progressivism. Universal suffrage and popular democratic politics were increasingly seen not only as dangerous but also as cumbersome and inefficient. They played to the emotions and narrow self-interest of voters and allowed the uneducated and inexperienced to get hold of the levers of power. As Croly might have put it, venality and mismanagement reigned supreme, the public interest, or "national purpose," was ignored, and conflict rather than cooperation prevailed. Partisanship itself, one of the main features of nineteenth-century political culture and the source of high levels of voter turnout, became an object of suspicion, an example of what made politics into a mass spectacle driven by greed and corrupt dispositions. Like liberal reformers, many Progressives wondered if popular democracy was conducive to the successful management of large polities. But rather than summoning an older governing elite, they sought, something in the manner of Croly, the rule of expertise, men trained to tackle social and political affairs, those not bound to particular constituencies and able to stand above the fray of party and patronage.[25]

Not surprisingly, especially in the industrial belt of the North, they availed themselves of some of the disfranchising devices that southern elites were deploying, liberal reformers had offered up, and nativists of the 1850s had previously unveiled. These included literacy and residency requirements; the exclusion of paupers, aliens, and felons; and taxpaying provisions for the exercise of the municipal franchise. Other initiatives had the virtue of appearing more modern and rational, more likely to promote political independence and combat fraud, more compatible with good governance. Thus, almost everywhere in the decades after the Civil War, voter registration systems were devised (varying from state to state in their particulars), ostensibly to prevent the ineligible from casting ballots and reduce chaos at polling places, though plainly in an effort to make the voting process more difficult. In large cities, especially where immigrants were able to elect their candidates to the municipal council or mayor's office, reformers pressed for redistricting and at-large elections to weaken political machines and bolster the prospects of office-seekers who could represent the "entire" city instead of smaller wards within it. Some reformers went further to advocate the adoption of "city managers" who would be appointed rather than elected, replacing mayors who stood for election, and who presumably would not be dependent on any one political party or social group. Once the Australian (secret) ballot was initially used in 1888 (in Louisville), it was widely adopted to enable voters to register choices and prevent interference from partisan operatives or coercive employers, though it also hindered illiterate voters who needed assistance at the ballot box.[26]

By the 1920s, this project of political reconstruction, or engineering, established many of the features of American politics that would prevail across the twentieth century and down to the present. These included the waning significance of partisan identification, the bureaucratization of political parties and institutions of government, the increasing importance of nonelected officials in policy-making positions, and the use of discriminatory registration procedures. As a consequence, popular participation in elections, at all levels, declined dramatically. The decline was steepest in the Deep South. African Americans were wholly driven from the public political arena, while many white voters either failed to qualify or chose to avoid the potential humiliation of registration. At all events, what one scholar calls "authoritarian enclaves," notably in the plantation belts and small towns, were reinforced. But even in the North and West, the drop in voter turnout was substantial: from over 80 percent in 1896 to about 65 percent in 1916 down to around 58 percent in 1924 for presidential elections, and lower still in off-year and local elections. Representative institutions remained in place, and most executive offices, from mayors to governors to presidents, remained elective. Yet the bureaucratization of the political system and the efforts to scale down the size of the electorate dimmed the meaning of popular sovereignty. Power was shifting away from grassroots constituencies where, for several decades after the War, it could be deployed against the designs of local elites. And although woman suffrage was finally enacted across the nation in 1920 with the Nineteenth Amendment, thanks to nearly a century of struggle, the political rights of Black women were ignored and the turnout rates among white women would prove no better than among white men. The scaffolding of a modernized "illiberal democracy" was coming into place.[27]

And one with corporatist dimensions. Political engineering of the sort that was reconstructing American politics, like social engineering more generally, demanded new roles for the government. "Purifying" the ballot box and political process required, something in the manner of eugenics, legislation at state and local levels together with the construction of new bureaucratic institutions to manage affairs for political parties and the public. There would be investigative commissions, boards of election, direct party (and in the South, white) primaries, and state officials tasked with election supervision (usually the secretaries of state). This was part of a larger political shift that looked to the state, and especially the national state, as a new administrative and regulatory power.

The impetus for this shift had come from a number of directions and, certainly before 1900, chiefly from the ranks of small producers and the anti-monopoly movements. Greenbackers demanded federal control of the money supply. The followers of Henry George demanded a "single tax" on land rents. Populists demanded a federally backed "subtreasury system" of cooperative marketing and credit and went so far as to demand federal government ownership of the railroads and telegraph. The social movement of corporate capitalists took shape in response to these demands, but rather than wholly reject them, they sought to channel them into new government-administered policies that could discipline business excesses in the name of the public interest while providing an environment for corporate activity marked by stability, security, and legal uniformity. This was an aspect of the "national purpose" that Herbert Croly imagined.

The Interstate Commerce Act (1887) and the Sherman Anti-Trust Act (1890) represented early and generally unsatisfactory forays in the regulatory direction, targeting as they did monopolistic practices on the railroads and other business enterprises and having few means of enforcement. But the sensibilities of political and corporate leaders began to change by the turn of the twentieth century once radical popular insurgencies had been defeated and the massive merger movement gained steam. The corporate form and the development of other large institutions were increasingly accepted as part of the natural evolution of society, and the issue was less whether the federal government should construct a regulatory apparatus than how it should be done and where regulatory power should reside. The triumph of the Republican Party in national politics in 1896 after two and a half decades of closely contested elections was of enormous importance—as was the drubbing of the Democratic Party's provincial agrarian wing—because prominent party leaders shared the corporate outlook and, like Theodore Roosevelt, who ascended to the presidency in 1901, believed that the power of the

"National Government was either not exercised at all or exercised with utter inefficiency."[28]

Roosevelt aimed to change that. For a time, he toed a line between asserting federal authority over the corporate sector and using government levers to discipline business abuses while at the same time providing corporations with a less cumbersome national arena in which to operate. He was in close touch with the National Civic Federation. Thereafter, Roosevelt moved in a statist direction, acknowledging private ownership while regarding corporations more as public utilities requiring strict accountability and subordination to federal oversight. Touting the wisdom and political gifts of icon Abraham Lincoln, as Croly had done in *The Promise of American Life*, and devising a Croly-esque "New Nationalism" as an alternative to the "country [being] divided into two" antagonistic parties and to the "extreme and radical democracy" that might ensue, Roosevelt envisioned a managerial government and a society organized principally along corporate lines. By the time he established the Progressive (Bull Moose) Party—some call it an "anti-party"—in 1912, the Democrats had made their own shifts in course. They had eschewed their agrarian for their corporate and cosmopolitan wing and nominated Woodrow Wilson for the presidency, a candidate, unlike perennial standard-bearer William Jennings Bryan, who saw "business as the foundation of every other relationship" and recognized the corporation as a fundamental component of a modern society. Much has been written about the battle between Roosevelt's "New Nationalism" and Wilson's "New Freedom," but, as political theorist Jeffrey Lustig has insisted, the real contrast was "not between Roosevelt and Wilson, but between both of them and what had gone before."[29]

The Wilson administration, in fact, played a critical role in giving corporate capitalism a strong institutional basis and sketching the dimensions of a political corporatism. The achievements were all the more impressive in view of the hostility with which the labor and agrarian constituencies aligned with the Democratic Party regarded big capital. During Wilson's first term, Congress dramatically lowered tariff rates (a victory for internationally oriented corporate interests), enacted an income tax (secured by a constitutional amendment) that provided the federal government an alternative source of revenue, created a Federal Reserve System staffed mainly by bankers and industrialists with the power to alter discount rates and accumulate reserves, and passed the Clayton Anti-Trust and Federal Trade Commission acts that together embodied the vision of a market administered directly by corporate and other private sector parties and subject to indirect government policing.[30]

The mobilization for American entry into the First World War, against which Wilson campaigned for reelection, took the corporate-inflected, administrative national state to a new level. With nonpartisan, expert-staffed commissions as a model, Wilson established a number of new federal agencies designed to oversee a wartime economy. Perhaps the most consequential was the War Industries Board, headed by Wall Street financier Bernard Baruch, which was to maximize production through industry agreements, adjust pricing, promote the conservation of resources, and coordinate military procurement. Seeking to avoid unnecessary conflicts or disturbances, the board also encouraged employers, much as the National Civic Federation had suggested, to accommodate labor's interests, especially as to organization. Some of these activities were channeled through a Price Fixing Committee and a National War Labor Board, as well as a Food Administration (headed by mining engineer Herbert Hoover), a War Trade Board, a War Finance Corporation, and a Fuel Administration. Without hint of contradiction, the director of the related Council for National Defense could describe the War Industries Board as "an industrial dictatorship without parallel" and as "the town meeting of American industry curbing, disciplining, and devoting itself."[31]

To these new federal agencies may be added the Selective Service Administration, a euphemism for conscription, the first since the Civil War, which not only supplied the military with manpower for the war but also provided deferments to the men local draft boards regarded as essential workers or in need of their direct supervision, such as Black men in the South. Here, too, intelligence testing devised by eugenically inclined psychologists would be administered to millions of recruits. Known as "Army Alpha" and "Army Beta" tests, they were meant to screen for "intellectual deficiencies, psychopathic tendencies, nervous intangibility, and inadequate self-control," and contributed to the development of the widely administered IQ tests. Nothing better showed how the impulses toward social engineering were both consolidated and advanced.[32]

To the disappointment of many who served, President Wilson dissolved the War Industries Board shortly after the Armistice ended the fighting in November 1919. But Grosvenor Clarkson of the Council for National Defense pronounced a fitting epitaph. The War Industries Board, he argued, "literally brought business into the business of Government. If we had a Government business manager with a free hand to run the business side of Government, we should have a successful Government of business." Perhaps, he imagined in his history of *Industrial America in the World War* (1923), "it may occur to some President to apply the organization scheme of the War Industries Board to Government." Less than a decade later, in the midst of the Great Depression, it did.[33]

IV

THE ADVENT OF JIM CROW'S regime of segregation, racial repression, and disfranchisement, which occurred at this time, has been easy to see as a throwback to the older order of enslavement, as the triumph of a white supremacy that slavery's history had nourished and demanded and that state and local governments would again impose where the personal power of whites did not suffice. The horrific violence visited on Black people in the years after emancipation—on religious leaders, political organizers, men and women refusing to submit, and young migrants passing through localities where they had not been before—has widely been reckoned an effort to re-enslave them and reassert the prerogatives of the white, especially male, southerners. Indeed, the dynamics of lynchings, which would claim the lives of thousands of Black men and women between the 1880s and the 1930s, showed many of these features, expressing the lethal "will of the community."

Lynchings tended to occur in cotton-growing counties where

whites and Blacks resided in near equal numbers amid demographic volatility. They targeted Black outsiders who did not have local white people to vouch for them, and were often provoked by alleged violations of the fabric of community life. That accusations of rape and miscegenation became central to the discourse of lynching—and not only in the South—suggests what participants in lynch mobs saw at stake. They sought to reestablish the boundaries they believed were being traversed, crush the attacks and violations they could associate with the weakening of their authority, and reject the notion that all people should be subject to the rule of law instead of the direct domination of the community. Many lynching victims had already been arrested and charged and, in some cases, convicted and sentenced to summary punishments when they were hauled out of jail, often with the sheriff looking on, and then "dispatched" or "launched into eternity." Not infrequently, what were effectively community executions drew crowds in the many hundreds and were accompanied by bloodthirsty and sexualized rituals of dismemberment.[34]

Yet the surge in racial violence was not an exclusively southern affair. Ever since the early decades of the nineteenth century, Black people who resided outside the South had been subjected to the expulsive and often lethal designs of white or ethnic mobs in urban areas large and small. The draft riots that consumed New York City over three days in July 1863—fired by a cross-section of native-white and Irish workers—claimed the lives of more than one hundred Black New Yorkers and left the Colored Orphan Asylum, along with many Black homes and businesses, in ruins. Other race riots and politically motivated attacks erupted sporadically during the post–Civil War decades in Philadelphia and Chicago as well as in Akron, Ohio, and Springfield, Illinois, as their Black populations grew even before the Great Migration of the early twentieth century. Some of the worst came immediately after the First World War—in East St. Louis, Chicago, Houston, Detroit—and often targeted returning Black veterans. In 1921, white fury exploded in Tulsa, Oklahoma, where a thriving and prosperous Black community known as Greenwood was immolated.[35]

In the Pacific Northwest, the hands of lethal expulsion turned against Chinese laborers, who had already been prohibited from immigrating to the United States in 1882. Mobs of whites, composed mainly of workingmen who feared for their economic security, attempted to drive the Chinese out of several towns in California, Washington, and Wyoming during the 1880s. Anticipating Tulsa, twenty-five Chinese men died in Rock Springs, Wyoming, when their section of the town was torched and left smoldering. Along the Texas-Mexican border, the disruptions caused by the unfolding Mexican Revolution (1910–1920) and the influx of Anglo landowners and ranchers doomed what had been an ethnically fluid district (the Nueces "strip"), and led to the lynching of suspected cross-border revolutionaries and the terrorizing of the Tejano (Texas/Mexican) population more generally: carried out by an alliance of Anglo vigilantes and Texas Rangers, the long-established policing and Indian-fighting force.[36]

Even so, the developing impulse among the more progressively minded, legitimated by new scientific theories of heredity and innate racial difference, was in the direction of social separation. Laws against interracial sex and marriage, which had long histories in North America, were reenacted in more comprehensive fashion after the Civil War, especially in the South and West. In the southern states, the laws barred marriage between whites and Blacks and thereby helped define the "one-drop" (any Black ancestry) rule of racialization, a contrived method of trying to bring clarity to an inherently opaque concept. In the West, and particularly the Far West, miscegenation and marriage laws would be far more capacious, encompassing the Chinese, Japanese, Kanakas (Hawai'ians), Malays, Mongolians, and Native peoples as well as Blacks. Although all these laws violated the equal-protection clause of the Fourteenth Amendment, to say nothing of freedom of contract, they were generally upheld by judges who instead invoked the "laws of nature" and the "police power of the State." Herbert Croly, revealing a eugenic mindset, went further still in his concern about the "steady increase in both crime and insanity," asking whether a "regenerated state government . . . might have the hardihood to inquire whether the institution of marriage . . . does not in its existing laws have something to do with" the problem. "Enforced celibacy of hereditary criminals and incipient lunatics," he suggested, "would make for individual and social improvement."[37]

As part of the effort to organize and temporize the interactions of different racial groups, the idea of "race relations" entered the discursive vocabulary. Focused chiefly on white and Black, "race relations" was meant to address, in ways dispassionate rather than violent, what was described as the "Negro problem": not simply their very presence in the United States (the "problem" as Jefferson understood it) but their ongoing demands for a meaningful freedom. The goal was to "choreograph" the terrain of race now that the submissive etiquettes and expectations of enslavement were gone and the struggles to create new ones proved increasingly explosive. Here, categorization and separation or "segregation" proved particularly appealing to white southerners who resided in growing urban centers and believed themselves well informed about the trends of the day and the "habits of the Negro." Indeed, segregation appeared as a very "modern" alternative to violent encounters on the one side and the possible empowerment of those regarded as "inferior" or "backward" on the other.[38]

Segregation also proved a central component in the formation of reorganized states. The almost simultaneous emergence of state-mandated segregation in the American South and South Africa is illustrative. Although the components of policy differed, in both places segregation developed most thoroughly in newer cities, tied to newer industries, where newer states sought to extend their reach. In South Africa, segregation statutes came quickly after the establishment of the Union of South Africa (1910) and were concentrated in the gold- and diamond-mining districts of the Transvaal to satisfy the escalating demands for labor while mediating potential conflicts between African and Afrikaner workers. In the American South, segregation followed the restoration of Democratic "home rule" and could be seen in its most aggressive forms not in the older cities of the Atlantic seaboard and Gulf Coast but in the industrializing and commercializing towns of the interior—Charlotte, Durham, Spartanburg, Atlanta, Birmingham, and Nashville—and on the transportation lines between and within them. Correspondingly, *de jure* segregation initially came to two of the institutions that typified the South's lurch toward modernity and the "promiscuous" (males and females in close physical proximity) social settings that they entailed: to the public schools established by Reconstruction governments and then the railroads and streetcars that steadily traversed the region during the 1880s and 1890s. Segregation ordinances then spread to nearly all areas of public life, snowballing during the late 1890s and opening decade of the twentieth century, once Black men had been disfranchised and the U.S. Supreme Court had issued its "separate but equal" ruling in *Plessy* v. *Ferguson* (1896).[39]

As Herbert Croly's remarks about how marriage policies might limit criminality and insanity implied, Progressive reformers generally greeted racial segregation in a favorable if not enthusiastic way. After all, segregation represented social engineering and the political deployment of scientific thinking on a grand scale. It was a rational, state-mandated alternative to terrorized submission, and one that would enable Black people to attain the levels of civilization that their capacities allowed. Alabama minister Edgar Gardner Murphy, deeply disturbed by the racial violence that afflicted the rural and small-town South, helped frame the perspective for southern and non-southern audiences alike. Although he viewed Black people as a childlike race in need of guidance, he rejected terror as the means toward their submission. Blacks, he believed, showed a "preference for amnesty" and an instinct for "self-preservation" when faced with the power of whites. Racial separation both recognized the boundaries of their prospects and encouraged racial pride, especially if it was accompanied by treatment and education that promoted friendship and cooperation.

As might be expected, Murphy saw Booker T. Washington as the model of Black leadership and foresight—"the greatest man save General Lee, born in the South in a hundred years"—while winning an appreciative reception in northern progressive circles where reformers had been searching for a new approach to "race relations." Some viewed Murphy as "a prophet, a reformer, a historian," as a counterpoint to the "sectional fanaticism" of the South. Progressive journals and newspapers published his writings and lent him high praise. Walter Rauschenbusch, a leader in the Social Gospel movement who had thought the "Negro problem . . . tragic and insoluble," could then regard it as the duty of whites to take "our black brother by the hand [and] urge him along the road of steady and intelligent labor, of property rights, of family fidelity . . . and of pride and joy in his racial achievements." President Roosevelt, who provoked controversy when he invited Booker T. Washington to dine with him at the White House or appointed a few Blacks to patronage positions, consulted with Murphy in 1904 and soon touted him as "one of the men to follow in reference to the Negro question."[40]

De jure segregation was, of course, always bolstered by the threat of violence against those who objected or refused to obey, and the trends outside the South suggested further that the line between *de jure* and *de facto* segregation could be fuzzy at best and perhaps misleading in the main. While northeastern and midwestern segregationism did not move forward with the legal torrent evident in the South, it nonetheless became encompassing and hard-fisted. Building upon the ethnic and racial enclaves that dotted industrializing cities for several decades, neighborhood protective associations, insurance companies, banks, and real estate interests, rather than state and local statutes, constructed a landscape of segregated housing, learning, and social life. They played upon concerns about declining property values, crime, and the transmission of disease, and fashioned restrictive covenants that were always enforced by the threat of personal violence. They also left their imprint on schools, which appeared as segregated as those in the South, while restaurants, theaters, and hotels, which remained beyond the reach of the Fourteenth Amendment according to court rulings, simply refused to serve Black people. By the second decade of the twentieth century, during the administration of President Wilson, a Progressive with southern roots, the federal bureaucracy segregated the African Americans who managed to escape dismissal. Other than those who were the targets, few registered any objections to the new organization of race relations that modernity was ushering in.[41]

V

WHEN THEODORE ROOSEVELT SAILED to the Panama Canal Zone in the fall of 1906, he became the first U.S. president to visit a "foreign" country while in office. Impatient to arrive, pacing the steamship for days, he stepped onto the dock with enormous enthusiasm despite a torrential rainstorm and would quickly marvel at the "epic feat" he was witnessing. Here, after failed efforts by the French and English and a multitude of scandals and missteps, the Americans could demonstrate their imaginative and technological superiority, their ability to tame nature in its most challenging guises. With massive machines and strenuous labor combined in their might, Roosevelt could reckon the canal-in-progress an unprecedented example of mechanical and physical engineering. Small wonder that he took the first opportunity to climb into the cab of a ninety-five-ton steam shovel and pose for photographs, ostensibly directing operations and digging the canal himself.[42]

Yet, as Roosevelt toured the Canal Zone, he was nearly as impressed with the social engineering in evidence. "With intense energy men and machines do their task," he observed, "the white men supervising matters and handling the machines, while tens of thousands of black men do the rough manual labor where it is not worthwhile to have machines do it." He soon found that a complex social hierarchy, based on race and national origins, had been put in place and contributed to the efficiency he extolled. The white employees, roughly 6,000 in number, were mostly Americans: "young, vigorous men energetically doing their duty" chiefly as engineers and conductors, machinists and carpenters, timekeepers, superintendents, and foremen. Many "brought down their wives and children" while the "bachelors" often shared rooms with one another. In all cases the "accommodations were good," the rooms "neat and clean, usually having books, magazines, and small ornaments," and provided free of charge.

Further down the ladder were nearly 20,000 laborers—unskilled and semi-skilled—composed, in part, of "a few hundred Spaniards" and "some Italians" employed largely in the drilling. The vast number, however, were West Indians, mainly from Jamaica, Barbados, "and other English possessions," who were "fairly, but only fairly, satisfactory." A few managed to become foremen, skilled mechanics, or policemen, and many of the "ordinary day laborers are good." But thousands "who are brought over under contract" go off to the jungle to live, loaf around the towns, and generally worked badly. Roosevelt thought the housing and food offered the Black laborers adequate, perhaps more so than they could expect back home, and made only indirect mention of the racial segregation that suffused the social worlds of the Canal Zone. He said nothing of the system of payment that reinforced the labor and racial hierarchy. White American workers and managers were paid with gold currency while the Afro-Caribbeans and others of the "alien" unskilled received devalued Panamanian silver. African Americans, relatively few in number and largely from the rural South, were deemed American citizens though placed on the "silver" payrolls.[43]

But how "foreign" was this country and to what extent did the organization of the Canal Zone reflect the tendencies of the age, especially in their imperial form? Panama had only recently gained its independence from Colombia, with no small assistance from the Roosevelt administration, and immediately granted the United States complete and perpetual control, as "if it were the sovereign," over the strip of land where the canal was to be built, for $10 million "in gold coins" and annual payments of $250,000. A governor was to be appointed, as in a U.S. territory, but in this case to head the Isthmian Canal Commission, and supplied with a great deal of power. Engineer and army veteran George Washington Goethals, tapped for the assignment, was ready. He ruled with a stern hand, showing little concern for democratic forms or tolerance for labor unrest. Unlike an American territory, the Canal Zone had a separate judicial system closely tied to the governor, with no jury trials or judicial review. The legal culture was, in fact, a hodge-podge of Colombian, Panamanian, and American procedures and practices. Workers arrested for various infractions were usually set to hard labor in one of the zone's penitentiaries, and could only appeal their sentences to the embassies of their home countries, with little prospect of success. Rather than an American territory within an otherwise sovereign country, the Canal Zone was an effective launching pad for the extension of American power over Panama itself.[44]

In important respects, the Panama Canal Zone fit comfortably into a new status the Supreme Court had been sketching out over the first ten years of the twentieth century. It was an "insular" territory, "unincorporated" and left to the authority of Congress. Which, in the Court's convoluted language, meant that the zone was not a "foreign country" in "an international sense," but was still "foreign to the United States in a domestic sense . . . merely appurtenant thereto as a possession." The zone, that is, was "insular" as to governance, not subject to any territorial precedent, while remaining under the sovereign power of the United States. In practical terms, the non-American denizens had certain "fundamental" rights, although they were not spelled out, but nothing like the rights of citizenship provided by the Constitution. Asked whether, after one of the Supreme Court's "insular" rulings, "the Constitution would follow the flag," Secretary of War Elihu Root cleverly responded that "the Constitution indeed followed the flag, but it doesn't quite catch up."[45]

The "insular" cases, ruled on by the same Supreme Court justices who handed down *Plessy* v. *Ferguson* in 1896, came in response to the issues raised by American conquests and annexations during the so-called Spanish-American War (it was, more accurately, a U.S.-Spanish, Cuban, and Filipino War). In effect, they proclaimed both separation from the American body politic and civil inferiority as to federal jurisdiction. But the logic of the insular cases and the status of the Panama Canal Zone fed off decades of experimentation within the formal boundaries of the United States, in efforts to define the place and prospects of racial and ethnic groups whose rights claims were partially or fully rejected: people of Native, African, Mexican, and Chinese descent chief among them. The experiments dated to the early nineteenth century and, over time, included expulsion, exclusion, deportation, extended federal territorialization, the creation of domestic homelands (reservations), segregation, civilizational uplift, and restrictions on participation in the formal arenas of political life, all backed by the often-unacknowledged use of violence. It was a highly repressive and illiberal mix, to say the least.

These experiments, carried out mainly in the West and the South, framed the arguments American political leaders made for warfare against Spanish colonizers and nationalist insurgents in Cuba and the Philippines in 1898. There was, of course, access to Asian markets and the protection of hemispheric investments that seemed all the more necessary after the steep economic depressions of the 1870s and 1890s and the popular turmoil they helped unleash in the United States. Still, policy makers also imagined a tutoring mission for populations that could not adequately fend for themselves, govern their own people, respect private property, or behave in a "civilized" fashion. Roosevelt, who had written a multivolume history of the American West, regarded the people of Cuba and especially the Philippines as "barbarous and semi-barbarous." He found it easy to liken them to rebellious Native Americans and see in Filipino insurgent Emilio Aguinaldo the image of Sitting Bull. "To grant self-government to Luzon under Aguinaldo," Roosevelt insisted, "would be like granting self-government to an Apache reservation under some local chief." Many of the officers in the Philippines were veterans of the Indian Wars in the American West, while most of the troops on the ground had been recruited from the western states and territories. Like Roosevelt, they were quick to draw the same comparison. According to one account, Major General Adna Chaffee, who spent years fighting Native peoples of the Plains and Southwest, "brought the Indian Wars with him to the Philippines and wanted to treat the recalcitrant Filipinos the way he had the Apaches in Arizona—by herding them onto reservations."[46]

When Roosevelt turned to the Western Hemisphere, in his famed "corollary" to the Monroe Doctrine, he elaborated a vision of racialized protectorates under the watchful eyes of the United States. Denying any interest in territorial "aggrandizement," he nonetheless warned newly independent countries, especially in the Caribbean basin, as to the consequences of "chronic wrong doing" and a "general loosening of the ties of civilized society." They would be permitted self-rule and their citizens the rights their governments accorded. But "instabilities" and "impotence" would "ultimately require intervention by some civilized nation," and in the Western Hemisphere, the United States, by virtue of the Monroe Doctrine, would be forced "to the exercise of an international police power."[47]

Roosevelt's vision of American expansion and imperial uplift, of extending the reach of civilization and reordering the world near and far from American shores, was part of an even larger project of social engineering. For he also looked to transform the outlooks and sensibilities of a new national ruling class in part by encouraging those from his own class background—regional and aristocratic elites who had come to scorn the ways of modernity—to take up the challenges that modernity itself was presenting and American power in a changing world required. "I wish to preach," Roosevelt, then governor of New York, told a Chicago men's club in the spring of 1899, "the doctrines of the strenuous life . . . that the highest form of success comes to the man who does not shrink from danger, from hardship, or from bitter toil, and who out of these wins the splendid, ultimate triumph." "The timid man, the lazy man, the man who distrusts his country, the over-civilized man who has lost the great fighting, masterful virtues . . . whose soul is incapable of feeling the mighty life that thrills stern men with empires in their brains," he warned, will "shrink from seeing us do our share of the world's work by bringing order out of chaos." Those who are "rich and worth your salt," Roosevelt implored, must "teach your sons that though they may have leisure, it is not to be spent in idleness" but rather in exercising "those virile qualities necessary to win in the stern strife of actual life."[48]

The "stern strife of actual life" was not an abstraction. Roosevelt took the occasion to emphasize the "responsibilities that confront us in Hawai'i, Cuba, Porto Rico, and the Philippines" and chide those who "fear righteous war." He had ached for war, believed that "the country needs one," and, as Assistant Secretary of the Navy in 1898, ordered, without presidential authorization, Admiral George Dewey to attack Manila at the first chance. Then, belittling the "half-castes and native Christians, warlike Moslems and wild pagans" who were "utterly unfit for self-government and show no signs of becoming fit," Roosevelt supported the annexation of the Philippines as a step toward "establish[ing] the supremacy of our flag."[49]

Those in the United States who stood in opposition to his project, generally known as "anti-imperialists," though really little more than "anti-annexationists," were of the very class whose cultural and political dispositions Roosevelt sought to reorient and invigorate. He described them, disparagingly, as "men of a bygone age," and his point was deeper than his language might suggest. Anti-annexationists, especially in Congress, comprised an odd coalition of New England patricians, some with strong antislavery credentials, white southern landowners, and local elites in the Midwest. Some had become liberal reformers; many more were Democrats. What they had in common were provincial outlooks and strong ties to the remnants of an agro-commercial economy being rapidly superseded. Annexationists, on the other hand, were not only concentrated in the Republican Party, but also represented the nation's growing metropolitan centers, with foundations of industry and finance. Many, like Theodore Roosevelt and Henry Cabot Lodge, themselves renegades from the provincial elites, were young, energetic, and "progressive," comfortable with a new role in the world for the United States, and eager to export what they considered a superior culture and set of institutions.[50]

Some of the anti-annexationists with progressive dispositions, like Jane Addams, doubted that annexation had any constitutional basis and believed "that the forcible subjugation of a people [represented] open disloyalty to the distinctive principles of our government." The United States would be turned, they worried, into a "vulgar, commonplace empire based on physical force." With Lincoln's "house divided" speech in mind, William Jennings Bryan maintained in 1900 that "no nation can long endure half republic and half empire." Yet even they shared the annexationists' view of potential subject populations as "peoples that sit in darkness," a "mess of Asian pottage," races who "could never amalgamate" and, certainly, could never exercise the responsibilities of American citizenship. Their battles would continue, in a variety of forms, into the second half of the twentieth century, punctuating American imperialism's seemingly inevitable triumph.[51]

The construction and political status of the Panama Canal presented no such problem. The canal was something of a progressive ideal, and even those on Progressivism's left wing looked on with interest if not admiration. The Canal, it appeared, was just the sort of project and partnership that they were trying to advance in the United States, linking an activist state, scientific and managerial expertise, and technological prowess and efficiency for all the world to see. The racial and labor hierarchies of the Zone that brought the Canal to completion ahead of schedule in 1914 troubled them little; most had come to accept segregation as sensible and necessary, the public construct of modernity. Indeed, they could see in the Canal Zone the symbol of an American empire that neither threatened the republic nor disgraced the Constitution, but vitally linked the foreign and the domestic, exemplifying the social experimentation and engineering they were so eager to carry out.

VI

THEODORE ROOSEVELT'S OBSESSION with warfare overseas and the virility it demanded was of a piece with his concerns about social degeneracy and "race suicide" at home. Together, as warnings and possible solutions, these challenges required the reconstruction of the American nation-state. Like Herbert Croly, Roosevelt saw the need for national purpose in a growing and increasingly complex society and believed that the state could play a critical role toward that end. Warfare he recognized as a great public unifier, a measure of strength and confidence, a sign of international ambition and resolve, a way of turning drift into mastery. Joined to an imperial engagement, it promised to extend civilization to those mired in backwardness, ignorance, ineptitude, and darkness.

At the same time, the marriage of science and eugenics suggested to Roosevelt and other political leaders that civilization could be advanced domestically in the face of crime, unrest, and cultural frictions. He was especially worried about the high fertility rates of new groups of immigrants, the declining birth rates among native-born whites, and the threats each posed to American destiny. "The chief blessing for any nation," he later argued, "is that it should leave its seed to inherit that land. [But] the greatest of all crises is sterility, and the severest of all condemnations should be that visited on will-ful sterility." "Americanizing" those who could assimilate, excluding those who could not, and surveilling social reproduction appeared the proper combination of initiatives, all of which would involve the state. Roosevelt himself signed laws, in 1903 and 1907, that barred the insane, the poor, the prostitute, and the anarchist from entry into the United States. The eugenic-minded like Croly and Margaret Sanger hoped to regulate marriage and procreation.[52]

State-formation and civilizationism cast an even wider net. Those committed to the national purpose and the centralization of author-ity, the use of science and medicine as a way to integrate and reconcile a sprawling country, set their sights on various regions that seemed to lag behind, needed economic and cultural uplift, and held popu-lations that showed the very marks of backwardness and incivility that could be seen in foreign colonies. The South in particular, for a half century after 1880, was increasingly depicted as a benighted section of the country, beset by economic sluggishness, enervating diseases, illiteracy, and cultural pathologies. And poor white people, perhaps even more than African Americans, seemed to epitomize the dilemma. The "Negro problem" became tied to the "Caucasian prob-lem" and both served as components of the "problem South."[53]

Although southern boosters like Atlantan Henry Grady attempted to identify signs of the post–Civil War South's social and economic progress and new urban vitality, northern observers and intellectu-als were more likely to see a world they associated with colonies and colonialism and in desperate need of help. Reformers interested in scientific agriculture often included the South on research itineraries that could extend to Puerto Rico, Hawai'i, the Philippines, and South Africa, fixed as they were on the social consequences of one-crop (like cotton) economies. The U.S. Congress held hearings in 1895 on the condition of cotton growers, and the U.S. Department of Agricul-ture dispatched agents to educate them on the techniques and advan-tages of crop diversification. Philanthropic foundations, influenced by eugenic discourses and fears of racial "degeneracy," focused on diseases such as hookworm and pellagra, rampant illiteracy, and the lack of basic sanitation, especially among poor whites, as challenges that had to be solved for the public welfare of the nation as a whole. In a sense, they hived off abolitionist depictions of the slave South to draw an updated set of contrasts between a dynamic and healthy industrial North and a laggard and sickly rural South.[54]

The idea of the "problem South," fortified as it was by social scientific investigations and the appeal of social engineering, helped set the agenda for an expanding federal government and turned regionalism into an enabler of, rather than an obstacle to, the growth of a national state. Still in the thrall of the Great Depression, President Franklin Roosevelt could term the South "America's Economic Problem No. 1" in hopes of enacting federal policies designed to advance southern economic development and replace the old plantation owners with new urban and commercial elites whose modern outlooks might represent the sort of reconciliation that the half century after the Civil War failed to achieve.[55] But nowhere in Roosevelt's vision of a modernized South were African Americans with full citizenship and political rights, let alone economic opportunities, to be seen.

Chapter Seven

FASCIST
PULSES

P RESIDENT WOODROW WILSON RETURNED TO THE
United States from six months at the Versailles peace conference
in July 1919, apparently having secured a reputation as a liberal internationalist. Even before the United States entered the war, Wilson
had called for a "peace without victory," and soon thereafter elaborated his "Fourteen Points" as a basis for American intervention and a
just peace. The president had envisioned a world of public diplomacy,
freedom of navigation, reduced barriers to international trade, substantial disarmament, adjusted colonial claims in which "the populations concerned must have equal weight," territories evacuated by the
invading Central Powers, territorial boundaries reconfigured in accor-
dance with "established lines of allegiance and nationality," "unham-
pered and unembarrassed" opportunity for Russia to determine "her
own political development and national policy," and a "general association of nations" created to "guarantee political independence and
territorial integrity." It was to be a world of nations based on popular
sovereignty and self-determination, connected, in turn, by free trade
and peaceful coexistence. Even colonized and stateless people across
the world could recognize Wilson as an advocate for their aspirations,
and in Egypt, India, China, and Korea his principles helped spark
anti-colonial and nationalist struggles.[1]

Almost immediately after his return, Wilson presented the Versailles Treaty with its controversial League of Nations to the Senate,
hoping to win ratification there. He reminded the senators that the
United States declared war solely "because we saw the supremacy,
and even the validity, of right everywhere put in jeopardy and free

government likely everywhere imperiled." The treaty he portrayed as "nothing less than a world settlement." Wilson then embarked on an exhausting eight-thousand-mile, twenty-two-day tour of the states to sell the treaty and the League to the American public. And, in what became the last of his speeches—in Pueblo, Colorado—Wilson not only touted America's long-standing support for "the equality of self-governing people" but also insisted that the treaty was "a great international charter for the rights of labor." "What we need to do with regard to the labor questions of the day, is tilt them into the light . . . [and direct it] upon the question of justice to labor," Wilson intoned. "Labor is going to have a forum such as it was never supplied with before, and men everywhere are going to see that the problem of labor is nothing more nor less than the problem of the elevation of humanity."[2]

Wilson's inspiring words about self-determination had already turned out to be remarkably hollow and easily ignored, buried by sets of illiberal impulses. On two occasions—1914 and 1916—he authorized the use of military force against Mexico, where large American investments had been encouraged by strongman Porfirio Díaz and then jeopardized by an increasingly radical revolution. U.S. naval forces first bombarded Veracruz and then, led by General John Pershing, a veteran of western Indian Wars and the Philippines insurgencies, U.S. troops chased Pancho Villa across the northern Mexican landscape for ten months before retreating without success. For such meritorious service Pershing was rewarded with command of the American Expeditionary Force in war-torn Europe. In 1915 Wilson commenced what became a two-decade occupation of Haiti, looking for "stability"—bows to Roosevelt's corollary—after the assassination of the country's president. And lest it appear that Wilsonian self-determination was chiefly a framework for Europe, he sent 13,000 American troops to Russia in July 1918 and kept many of them there after the Armistice, mainly to aid anti-Bolsheviks in seeking "self-government or self-defense." In Wilson's eyes, Bolshevism was simply incompatible with the world order he looked to advance.[3]

As for labor, Wilson, a Democrat, had curried working-class support and did sign the Clayton Anti-Trust Act, which offered organized labor some protection from the anti-trust litigation the earlier Sherman Act had enabled. During the war, in an effort to enhance industrial production, the Wilson administration appeared sympathetic to labor organizations and the rightful claims of working people. AFL president Samuel Gompers was not alone in seeing the opportunity to strengthen labor's hand by lending Wilson support. Yet labor's maneuvering room was limited, especially when unions veered toward independence or radicalism. As early as 1915, Wilson told Congress that the Industrial Workers of the World (IWW) "was the gravest threat to our national peace and safety," and encouraged a widespread crackdown that fully commenced after the federal Espionage Act, criminalizing activities that interfered with the war effort or aided the country's enemies, was passed in 1917. More than 10,000 U.S. troops then took over in the woods and sawmills of the Pacific Northwest, where the IWW had held sway, forming the nucleus of the 4L, the Loyal Legion of Loggers and Lumbermen, effectively the world's largest company (the War Department's) union. Indeed, Wilson's War Labor Board clearly regarded company unions as the most acceptable institutions for organizing workers, which the demands of efficient wartime production required. By the late 1920s, open shops and company unions had come to prevail across the industrial landscape.[4]

The IWW was hardly alone in its militancy. Between 1917 and 1920 unprecedented strike waves swept the United States, from copper and coal mines to steel and textile mills to shipyards and sugar refineries; even to police departments, as in Boston. On the table everywhere were not only issues of wages and working conditions but the right to sustain unions and bargain collectively. In Seattle, where the IWW had an important foothold, the AFL veered well left of Gompers, and socialism gained significant traction. A general strike then erupted in early February 1919 to support the struggles of striking shipyard workers. In a city of just over 300,000, more than 60,000 union members participated. And although the strike ended in five days as a police and military presence mounted, the strike committee had begun to establish dining stations, distribute milk and food, supply hospitals, and preserve the peace: begun, that is, to govern the city, restart the local economy, and safeguard the public health. For their part, the railroad brotherhoods, generally known for conservatism, called for government ownership of the railroads, while unionized coal miners (United Mine Workers) demanded the nationalization of the mines, the formation of a labor party, and the provision of health insurance.[5]

It was an international moment of radicalism and revolution that spread across the European continent, to the Western Hemisphere and Asia, reaching its pinnacle in Russia where the tsarist regime was toppled and the Bolsheviks soon took power. The Third International, or Comintern, was founded in 1919 and helped spark communist risings in Hungary and Germany, not to mention the Biennio Rosso in Italy, when the factories of Turin were seized and factory councils formed. But the heavy hands of political repression were quickly deployed everywhere, and in the United States they built upon government-sanctioned wartime attacks on socialists, anarchists, and "aliens" for their disloyalty and subversion; many of them were arrested and some deported. If anything, the Armistice saw the repression intensify. Wilson's new attorney general, A. Mitchell Palmer, created a General Intelligence Division in the Justice Department (headed by the young J. Edgar Hoover) in the summer of 1919 and conducted raids in November and January that targeted, often without warrants, the Union of Russian Workers and fledgling communist parties in more than forty cities and towns across the country. Well over 3,000 men and women were taken into custody, frequently after brutal beatings. At least 250 were subject to deportation.[6]

These episodes are widely known and represented as the "Red Scare" and "Palmer Raids," highly illiberal activities provoked by war-related demands for unity and a "hysteria" that came in the war's wake but receded with a return to "normalcy" in the 1920s. In truth, the repression of the war and immediate postwar years must be seen in a deeper and more extended context, one that began to take shape in response to labor radicalism in the late nineteenth century and then gained direction as a result of American colonialism, chiefly in the Philippines. The Bureau of Investigation, later the F.B.I., was established in 1908 on the orders of President Theodore Roosevelt and, by 1919, had 80,000 file cards on the activities of both "extreme anarchists" and "moderate radicals." Private security firms like the Pinkertons, founded before the Civil War, which broke strikes and harassed radicals, expanded rapidly in the early twentieth century so that by 1920 they had at least 10,000 offices and 135,000 employees. The Immigration Restriction League, looking chiefly to Europe, was born in 1894 and joined by the Asiatic Exclusion League in 1905, looking first to Japan and then to the Philippines. Veterans of American policing in the Philippines played central roles in establishing both the Military Police for occupied Europe and the Military Intelligence Division for domestic surveillance. An explosion of vigilance and patriotic groups, stretching back into the 1880s though energized by the war and labor radicalism, took aim, often in close association with federal agencies, at socialists, union leaders, and immigrant working-class communities.[7]

It all came to fruition in the 1920s with Prohibition, immigration restriction, the enormous expansion of the Ku Klux Klan, a new Protestant fundamentalism, and the campaign for 100 percent Americanism: forms of social engineering meant to fortify a nation of white Protestants and hobble those not fit to join. Illiberal, even protofascist, pulses were unleashed, and European fascists themselves would eagerly learn from the results. It may well be that the threads composing the fabric of Italian and German fascism were in earliest evidence in the United States.

I

AMONG THE "DOZENS OF ORGANIZATIONS" that surfaced in "various parts of the United States" in the early days of American entry into the First World War, according to Major General Ralph H. Van Deman and Emerson Hough, the American Protective League (APL) took pride of place. Founded in 1917 by Chicago businessman Albert Briggs and "never part of any state or national arm, service department or bureau," the APL was "devoted [chiefly] to the running down of spies." But it won sufficient government sanction to boast on its letterhead, "Organized with the Approval and Operating Under the Direction of the U.S. Department of Justice [and] Bureau of Intelligence." National in scope and quickly headquartered in Washington, D.C., the APL, with a membership eventually reaching 250,000, was also "scattered all over the United States and so placed that any important community of any size had a section of the organization." "A silent unknown army of more than a quarter of a million," it could be deemed "the largest company of detectives the world ever saw."[8]

For the most part, the APL recruited through networks of financial and corporate elites and, wherever one looked, the membership was male, white, and predominantly Protestant, unified by a fierce anti-Germanism and strong currents of anti-Catholicism and anti-Semitism. But local autonomy generally prevailed, and Emerson Hough, who wrote the APL's history, placed the organization in the long tradition of community-based law-and-order voluntarism. "What saves a country in need? Its loyal men. Its volunteers," he pronounced. "What saved San Francisco in the days of riot and anarchy in 1850? Its Volunteers for law and order. What brought peace to Alder Gulch [Montana, where gold was discovered] in 1863 when criminals ruled? Its Volunteers for law and order? . . . The line between formal written law and natural law is but thin at best."[9]

Signs of disloyalty and resistance to conscription stoked APL activism. "Slacker raids" brought thousands of "evaders" to the attention of military authorities and as many as three million cases of disloyalty to government officials. Yet, while its national leaders insisted that the APL rejected vigilantism or violence, matters were very different on the ground. "Today in Iowa there is a veritable reign of terror," a state agricultural journal could report. "More harm is resulting from this assumption of authority by private individuals than by all the pro-German propaganda or real disloyalty in the State. . . . Already this rule of passion freed from restraint has resulted in the excess of mob violence [as] men in positions of leadership and responsibility are fomenting and encouraging this spirit of mob rule and terror." Indeed, the APL took the opportunity of wartime policing not only to strike out against suspected Germans and other "aliens," but also to attack labor unions, socialists, and, especially, the IWW. In many places the APL joined forces with local vigilantes such as the Home Guards in South Dakota (referred to by a U.S. attorney as the "Ku Klux Klan of the Prairies") and the Citizens' Protective League in Bisbee, Arizona, to drive unionists, often the IWW, from the wheat fields and copper mines. In New York City, an APL operative formed what one historian describes as a "private free-lance intelligence bureau of ex-policemen" disposed to strong-arm methods. In St. Louis, a chapter called for detentions without the benefit of *habeas corpus* and publicly justified the lynching of a suspected subversive in nearby Collinsville, Illinois, because the government had failed to suppress "pro-German utterances." Throughout, the APL pressed for tougher restrictions on civil liberties. "At the crack of war," Hough crowed, "certain hundreds of dangerous aliens were interned at once. They simply vanished . . . behind the walls of camps or prisons." "We did not kill a single spy, a single traitor, we did not shoot known spies," he added, "but we garroted them in the dark and hurried them to jail."[10]

The eyes of suspicion were cast very quickly on African Americans, regarded as especially vulnerable both to German propaganda and political radicalism. Wilson himself believed that Blacks could be the "greatest medium in conveying Bolshevism to America," and already by the fall of 1917 Major General Van Deman of the Military Intelligence Division reported that "two extremely capable and reliable Negro men" were tasked with circulating "among the various communities where unrest was being reported among the Negro population." Lynchings spiked during the war years, and returning Black veterans, particularly those in uniform, were magnets for racist violence. Mississippi senator James K. Vardaman, a vocal white supremacist, warned about the dangers of Black military service and the "disasters" Black service members would inevitably inflict upon the South. "Impress the Negro with the fact that he is defending the flag [and] inflate his untutored soul with military airs," Vardaman thundered on the floor of the Senate, and he would soon demand that "his political rights be respected." On some occasions, white veterans provoked the lethal violence against their Black counterparts.[11]

What the Black writer and activist James Weldon Johnson called the "Red Summer" of 1919 was not just an explosion of nearly forty "race riots" in cities, towns, and rural districts across the United States. It was also an eruption of expulsive white nationalist vigilantism bent on destroying Black communities and businesses as well as punishing Black people, especially those accused of transgressing racial boundaries or agitating for their rights. The bloodiest and most murderous of them came in Elaine, Arkansas, when a union of Black tenants and sharecroppers was crushed by white plantation owners, leaving hundreds of Black people dead not long after the state's governor proclaimed that "there existed no twilight zone in American patriotism." Much like anti-abolitionist mobs in the 1830s or New York draft rioters in 1863, well-armed white men targeted entire Black residential and commercial districts in waves that began to rise in East St. Louis in 1917 and tore through Washington, D.C., Chicago, New York, Norfolk, Philadelphia, Memphis, and a multitude of other urban centers in 1919. The attacks and massacres did not crest until the Black neighborhood of Greenwood in Tulsa, Oklahoma (1921), and the Black town of Rosewood, Florida (1923)—both symbols of Black independence, wealth, and pride, and long-time affronts to white supremacists—were reduced to smoldering rubble.[12]

As many of the sites of anti-Black violence suggested, the beginning phases of the Great Migration of African Americans out of the South were already disrupting the tense boundaries of "race relations" all around the country, and marking new bases of Black community-building and political power. Although whites were invariably the instigators of violence, often in response to rumors of Black sexual predations or violations of racial "norms," Blacks pushed back and, in some places, armed themselves in self-defense. Fired as they were by new organizational initiatives—especially by the NAACP and Garvey's Universal Negro Improvement Association—and the experience of military service, they demonstrated that Jim Crow would now meet a formidable and militant response. The "New Negro" was hailed as early as 1917 by white as well as Black radicals who tried to capture the political and cultural sensibilities that the Great Migration was seen as fostering. With warnings of "Negro Uprisings" being articulated in the mainstream media, Attorney General Palmer had little doubt about what was afoot. "The Negro is seeing red," he fretted.[13]

Black organizational activity and militance simultaneously intensified the fascist pulses of the late 1910s and 1920s and, over time, helped limit their political impact. The UNIA, with its emphasis on Black collective rights and empowerment—on popular Black internationalism—emerged as the greatest of the organizations in terms of reach and membership, and the one with the largest mass base. It reflected a new political vocabulary and calculus shaped by ideas of race and empire, while provoking the ire of the nascent NAACP, which focused on civil and political equality even as some of its leaders sympathized with the socialist left. The rancor between Marcus Garvey and W. E. B. Du Bois over the direction of Black political struggle—almost as legendary as the earlier feud between Du Bois and Booker T. Washington—seemed to mark a nearly unbridgeable divide. Yet on the ground the divide was quite bridgeable, and local activists commonly belonged to both the UNIA and the NAACP. They joined forces against segregation in public life and in support of tenants' rights, the hiring of Black workers, and interracial labor unions. During the early 1930s, their influence would be crucial to the political fate of the country.

II

THE AMERICAN PROTECTIVE LEAGUE formally disbanded in February 1919, to the chagrin of many members, when the war that brought it into being came to an end. There was, in their view, lots of work still to do in advancing 100 percent Americanism and punishing those poised to threaten it, whether on political or ethnic accounts. A plethora of fraternal organizations, some, like the Brotherhood of Elks, already devoted to "Americanism," could, of course, absorb their energies, much like numbers of local patriotic societies, hatched during the war, which continued to meet and plan activities. But, in many ways, the APL agenda as well as its social composition was absorbed by the American Legion, a direct product of the war and destined to anchor a wing of the political right. The Legion, as one historian saw it, "stepped into the league's shoes as the guardian of national orthodoxy."[14]

Organized in Paris in March 1919 by officers of the American Expeditionary Force, the Legion first assembled stateside in St. Louis that May. Best recognized as a lobbying platform for returning World War I veterans, and eventually for all veterans, the Legion immediately aligned itself with a host of "patriotic" issues that had been fired up during the war even while insisting on its "nonpartisan" and "nonpolitical" disposition. In a series of resolutions in St. Louis, the Legion denounced "conscientious objectors," called for the deportation of alien draft evaders, and condemned the IWW, anarchists, international socialists, and other "Reds" for outbreaks of lawlessness. According to one of its spokesmen, the Legion stood for "nothing more nor less than 100 percent Americanism" and "opposed Bolshevism, anarchy and disorder, and every attempt to tear down the institutions of our country."[15]

The Legion's St. Louis gathering, or caucus, created a national structure, with state branches and local posts, that was supported by banks, national political leaders, and a congressional charter. By the summer of 1919 it had spread across the United States and boasted a membership in the many thousands. Although there were variations by state and locality, the Legion generally appealed to members of the white middle and upper-middle class. As many as three-quarters were professionals, managers, small businessmen, and salaried employees; fewer than one in five were skilled workers, and fewer than one in ten were unskilled laborers. The ability of Black veterans to join depended on the judgment of the state branches, but where they were admitted to membership, Black Legionnaires were to be found overwhelmingly in segregated posts regardless of their location.[16]

While national officials of the Legion focused on Congress and legislation to benefit veterans of the war, the state branches and especially the local posts had a good deal of discretionary authority in conducting their activities. "The posts themselves are qualified to speak on every question," a contributor to the *American Legion Weekly* took care to note. "These men should and will make themselves heard." That they did, often in the service of employers, the police, and their own notions of order and Americanism. A Stockton, California, Legion post targeted men who claimed and received military exemptions on the grounds that they were not citizens. Veterans in Detroit who had been among the U.S. troops deployed to Russia fashioned themselves as "Bolsheviki bouncers" to break up meetings of radicals. A post in Oakland, California, organized a force of two hundred veterans to assist the police in their efforts against the IWW, determined as they were "to see that no lawless element gets control of this city." State-level "commanders" in Montana, Idaho, Oregon, and Washington held a two-day conference to plan for combating the IWW "and other radical organizations." And the Utah Legion was "in the field against the local IWW and kindred Reds," informing all posts of the "spread of un-American activities."[17]

So widespread were the antiradicalism and vigilantism of Legion posts that the national office felt compelled to dispute stories in the press and proclaim the Legion's opposition to "mob violence." "If an agitator is mobbed by an ill-advised crowd," one *Legion Weekly* editor complained, "the enterprising reporter too often only sees a couple of Legion buttons on an olive drab shirt to fasten his account of the occurrence upon the American Legion." "Those unfriendly to the Legion have repeatedly pictured it as a self-appointed-police force whose chief aim is to spy on radical activities," another Legion official groused in the mid-1920s. Acknowledging "temptations aplenty . . . to demand an abridgement of those constitutional sanctions, liberty of utterance and liberty of the press," he nonetheless insisted that the Legion "confined itself to giving support to the agents of the government charged with keeping watch over radical activities."[18]

As might be expected, the Legion felt a strong affinity with allied war veterans in Europe, and, especially, with those in Italy who had rallied in support of Benito Mussolini and his Fascists. The *Legion Weekly* reminded readers in 1923 that Mussolini, "the most talked of man in Europe," was a "corporal in the Italian army" and sure to "approach army legislation with more intelligence" than some members of the United States Congress. That very year, the Legion's national commander, Alvin Owsley, invited Mussolini to the Legion's convention in San Francisco and, despite Il Duce's cordial decline, proclaimed that "if ever needed, the American Legion stands ready to protect our country's institutions and ideals as the Fascisti dealt with the destructionists who menaced Italy. The American Legion is fighting every element that threatens our democratic government—soviets, anarchists, IWW, revolutionary socialists, and every other 'red.'" "Do not forget," Owsley waxed, "that the Fascisti are to Italy what the American Legion is to the United States." Several years later, a Legion delegation visiting Rome met with Mussolini, who was eventually offered honorary membership in the organization and photographed wearing a cowboy hat.[19]

Owsley and other Legionnaires who admired the Italian fascists knew of what they spoke. The *squadristi* or *squadre d'azione*, best known as the Black Shirts, were, like the American Legion, organized in 1919 and composed heavily of veterans seething at the wartime disloyalty of socialists and other radicals. Black Shirts came to the aid of large landowners and other employers facing the demands of militant workers and turned their wrath on Socialist Party headquarters, newspaper offices, and the homes of socialist leaders, often putting them to the torch. They figured prominently in poet and protofascist Gabriele D'Annunzio's march on the Adriatic port of Fiume in September 1919; before long they occupied entire cities and then joined Mussolini's "March on Rome" in 1922, which secured the Fascist claim on power. Owsley's was an omen and thread that would continue to give the lie to the American military's official apolitical stance. "More directly than any other group," historian John Higham wrote, "the Legion perpetuated the corporate values of the war experience, the solidarity, the fellowship, the special identification with the nation."[20]

III

THE POLITICAL AND CULTURAL PULSES that animated the American Protective League, the American Legion, and a raft of more grassroots "patriotic" and "citizen's" clubs helped turn the Ku Klux

Klan into the largest and most formidable popular organization of the 1920s. Re-founded at Stone Mountain, Georgia, in 1915, decades after its Reconstruction forebear had unraveled, the Klan's reemergence resonated with a moment when Jim Crow had been sanctioned by the Supreme Court, the federal bureaucracy had been segregated, *Birth of a Nation* had premiered only miles away in Atlanta, and 100 percent Americanism was fast becoming the official bond of social cohesion. But it was not until the early 1920s that the Klan began to grow with exponential speed, not only in the states of the former Confederacy but across the entire country. Indeed, in many important respects, the Klan would be more powerful and consequential outside of the South than it would ever be in the region of its rebirth. In the eyes of a contemporary journalist, the Klan was "the most vigorous, active, and effective force in American life, outside business."[21]

The remarkable growth of the Ku Klux Klan owed both to its innovative recruiting techniques and its ability to tap into the currents of anti-Catholicism, anti-Semitism, antiradicalism, anti-modernism, and xenophobia, as well as anti-Black racism, already flowing across the United States. If anything, anti-Catholicism and antiradicalism proved most potent to the Klan's appeal in the North and West, and may help account for the distribution of membership, which tilted away from the South and toward towns and cities most everywhere. By 1921, the Klan was growing at a pace of 100,000 new members per week, and by the mid-1920s its membership reached at least two million; according to some, as many as four or five million. A reasonable estimate suggests that one white American in thirty may have belonged. Forty percent of Klan members could be found in the lower midwestern states of Indiana, Ohio, and Illinois, and another 8 percent in the upper midwestern and plains states, together comprising almost half. Nearly one-third of the members were in the Southwest and Far West; fewer than one in five were southerners. Of the ten states with the largest number of Klan members only two were in the South. Indiana, Ohio, Texas, and Pennsylvania boasted the greatest number of members, followed by Illinois, Oklahoma, New York, and Michigan. Perhaps even more surprising, roughly half of the Klan membership was to be found in metropolitan areas with populations of 50,000 or more, and about one-third in areas with populations of 100,000 or more. One student of the Klan describes Indianapolis, Dayton, Portland (OR), Youngstown (OH), Denver, and Dallas as "the hooded capitals of the nation." Chicago, longtime center of labor radicalism, site of large communities of southern and eastern European immigrants, and beacon for the Great Migration of African Americans, had the nation's largest Klan organization, with twenty "klaverns" and 50,000 members.[22]

Because the Klan did not keep official membership records and generally maintained a veil of secrecy, it is very difficult to know just how large it became or how closely connected it may have been with organizations like the American Protective League, the American Legion, or local patriotic and fraternal societies. But what we do know about membership and activities suggests that there was probably considerable overlap. Like the APL, the Klan was white and Protestant, and like the APL and the American Legion, the Klan's adherents came chiefly from the middle class and, to a lesser extent, the skilled working class, though in many places recognized community leaders joined and wielded influence. Small businessmen, including landowning farmers, composed the largest occupational group in the Klan followed by Protestant ministers (roughly 40,000) and white-collar employees. But, especially outside the largest cities, native-born skilled workers and industrial operatives, some of whom may have been union members, also joined in substantial numbers. To these may be added many thousands, particularly in areas where the Klan was active, who supported it even if they could not afford the dues (generally $10) or preferred not to pay them. Not surprisingly, many Klan recruiters were Freemasons and, when beginning a recruitment drive in any location, first made contact with fraternal orders and Protestant churches where sympathizers could best be found.[23]

Like the APL and American Legion, the Klan was devoted to 100 percent Americanism, which meant white Protestant supremacy and antiradicalism: "America First-ism" as they would describe it. Only native-born, white Protestant men could become members of the Klan, and the organization set its sights of vengeance on Catholics, recent immigrants, and internationalism of any variety. A Texas Klan leader, speaking at a July Fourth celebration in 1919, declared that

"I am for America, first, last, and all the time, and I don't want any foreign element telling us what to do." Klan vigilantism exploded everywhere, but especially in the lower Midwest and Far West, where Blacks, Asians, Mexicans, and Catholics suffered whippings, tarring-and-feathering, property destruction, arson, and lynchings. Earl Little, the father of Malcolm X and a Baptist minister and UNIA activist, was driven out of the family's Omaha, Nebraska, home in 1926. Elsewhere, Klan members marched or paraded brazenly in white robes—including in Washington, D.C.—and, as they did numerous times on Long Island, burned crosses at initiation ceremonies to intimidate Catholics, Jews, and Blacks.[24]

That Protestant ministers figured significantly among Klan members and enablers suggests the important cultural supports that religious faith provided. By the early 1920s, in a break with the dispensations of the past—most notably the Social Gospel and liberal Protestantism more generally—a fundamentalist pulse had ruptured the denominations and, for a time, emerged supreme. A powerful set of responses to the great social changes of the late nineteenth and early twentieth century, fundamentalism railed against the symbols and ethics of modernity, against reason and science, against the immoralities of urban life and cosmopolitanism. Instead, it demanded a return to religious purity and biblical truth. Taking their identity from a 1915 Baptist text entitled *The Fundamentals*, fundamentalists believed in the unerring validity of the Scripture, the inevitability of Christ's return to earth, and the story of Genesis, particularly humanity's descent from Adam and Eve. In part a product of intense theological struggle, fundamentalism also grew out of a larger cultural crisis that the war and widespread social conflict heralded, a sense that godly civilization was under attack from many directions and had to be defended before the second coming of Christ could occur. Sensibilities such as these gave Klan members both a community of like-minded believers and a set of tasks as religious warriors. The Imperial Wizard of the Klan, Hiram Evans, called "the spirit of Protestantism" an "essential part of Americanism; without it America could never have been created and without it she cannot go forward."[25]

The close ties between Protestant fundamentalism and the Klan show how much a part of ordinary, daily life the Klan could become. Klansmen were attracted by the male comradery and patriarchalism that the organization encouraged and many had experienced in fraternal societies and related clubs. Yet they also recognized the importance of women who shared their ideas of Americanism and were energized by woman suffrage, which the Klan generally supported: at least for white Protestants. Some of these women had undoubtedly been involved with the Women's Christian Temperance Union (WCTU), which the Klan admired, and the patriotic societies and auxiliaries that had blossomed during the war. By 1923, a separate Women of the Ku Klux Klan (WKKK) was established and drew in thousands of women, not all of whose husbands and fathers were Klansmen, especially where the Klan was robust. Overall, around half a million women joined the WKKK, and in some states they accounted for nearly half of the entire Klan membership.[26]

Many of the women who joined viewed the Klan as wielding a double-edged sword on their behalf. On the one hand, they saw the Klan as a vehicle to champion their conception of Christian morality against its detractors, and target the corruption they believed infested the political arena. At the same time, they imagined, and often insisted, that the Klan ensure the male protection that Klansmen perpetually vowed to provide, sometimes against their own dissipated husbands whose alcoholism "stings his family, degrades his wife, marks his children, and breaks the heart of his mother." What historian Linda Gordon calls "KKK Feminism" combined advocacy of women's rights, including employment outside the home, with acceptance of more traditional notions of gender and domesticity. It was an appeal that participation in church, reform, and charitable organizations had long nurtured. WKKK recruiters prominently asked: "Are you interested in the welfare of our Nation? As an enfranchised woman are you interested in Better Government? Do you not wish for the protection of Pure Womanhood? Shall we uphold the sanctity of the American Home? Shall we not interest ourselves in Better Education for our children? Do we want American teachers in our American schools?" A white Protestant woman living in northern Indiana later recalled that "store owners, teachers, farmers . . . the good people all belonged to the Klan. They were going to clean up the government, and they were going to improve the school books [that] were loaded with Catholicism." At all events, she added meaningfully, the Klan was "a way to get together and enjoy . . . a way of growing up," a part of the fabric and defense of community life.[27]

Although potentially bolstered by woman suffrage, the Ku Klux Klan never tried to turn itself into a political party. Over the course of the 1920s, however, it would have an outsized influence in the world of American politics. Klansmen were elected to office at the local, state, and national levels, and Klan support proved crucial in elections when Klan members themselves were not in the running. According to reliable assessments, sixteen Klansmen were elected to the U.S. Senate, twenty or more to the U.S. House of Representatives (the Klan claimed seventy-five congressmen), and eleven to state governorships. Two justices of the Supreme Court, Hugo Black and Edward Douglass White, had once been members. Rumor had it that President Warren G. Harding at least flirted with the Klan, so much so that he felt the need to publicly deny it, and, in the manner of Justices Black and White, Harry Truman joined up as a young man—he claimed he thought it just a "patriotic" organization—and subsequently quit. At the 1924 Democratic National Convention, the Klan supported William G. McAdoo, Wilson's treasury secretary and son-in-law, for the presidential nomination, and while McAdoo, initially the front-runner, failed to win, the Klan also managed to block the candidacy of New York's Al Smith, a Catholic, thereby strengthening its reputation as a political force to contend with.[28]

But it was on the state and local levels that the Klan's political influence was most pronounced. In Indiana, Oregon, Texas, Oklahoma, and Colorado the Klan reigned powerfully, and effectively controlled the city governments of Dallas, Fort Worth, Portland (OR), Portland (ME), and Muncie (IN), while winning elections in Des Moines, Akron, Columbus, Tulsa, Kansas City, and many other cities and towns in the country's mid-section and trans-Mississippi West. In Colorado where, according to one observer, the Klan "could well believe that they owned the state," the order dominated every city but Colorado Springs. Klansmen found their way into law enforcement, the criminal justice system, school boards, and town and county commissions even when they were not in full control. They or their sympathizers were elected as mayors, sheriffs, district attorneys, and judges. Where the Klan constituted a substantial portion of the electorate, they might hold their own primaries to identify candidates meriting their support. As a result, the Klan not only carved out a large field of force; it also had protection against the entreaties and resistance of opponents. When the American Civil Liberties Union approached the mayor of Enid, Oklahoma, about reported floggings, he told them that with fifteen hundred Klansmen and ten sympathetic policemen in town there seemed no point in conducting an investigation.[29]

With grips on legislatures and governorships in Oregon, Indiana, and Texas, and substantial legislative power in states across the country, the Klan was able to push forward an agenda that bolstered their notions of Americanism. Along with prohibition and immigration restriction, the Klan pressed for antimiscegenation and eugenic laws, the weakening or abolition of Catholic parochial schools, and control over the educational content in public schools. They also called for a national department of education at cabinet rank as a way to protect against Catholic influence, and, following their earlier opposition to the League of Nations, for rejection of U.S. membership in the World Court. Although the results were mixed, where the Klan did succeed politically their ideas comported closely with those of many other white Protestants who were not Klan members. In the words of historian Linda Gordon, the "Klan's program was embraced by millions . . . possibly even a majority of Americans."[30]

With their commitment to white nationalism and easy resort to—often celebration of—vigilantism and violence, the Klan of the 1920s clearly resembled the fascist movements of Europe, especially at the grassroots. Some Klansmen recognized the similarities in perspective and purpose. In 1922, the *Searchlight*, a Klan paper published out of Atlanta, saw in Benito Mussolini's seizure of power "a sign of political health in Italy and a guarantee against the crazy and experimental forms of government with which Russia is afflicted." Other Klan publications judged Mussolini's efforts to crush "communism and anarchy" a "worthy cause," while a Klan-aligned minister in California equated the "nationalistic movement" of the Klan with the "Black Shirts of Italy and the Grey Shirts of Germany." "The Ku Klux Klan," another minister insisted, much the way Alvin Owsley had spoken of the American Legion, "is the Mussolini of America," the expression of the "vast volume of discontent in this country with things as they are." The *Baltimore Sun* went so far as to report that in late 1922 the Klan declared its intention to create an "alliance" with Mussolini's fascists as part of a "European expansion program."[31]

This is unlikely. The Klan's nationalism and anti-Catholicism appear to have limited its interest in potential European counterparts and allies, especially in Italy, where fascism early surfaced, took power, and made amends with the Catholic Church. Yet for many American contemporaries, especially those who fought the Klan, the connection seemed obvious and palpable, another measure of the danger the Klan represented. Newspapers attempting to explain the "fascisti" to their readers often likened them to the Ku Klux Klan. Some, in fact, referred to the fascists as the "Italian Ku Klux Klan," and warned that the American Klan was also seeking "political power in the United States." As the *Tampa Times* put it, "The klan is the Fascisti of America and unless it is forced into the open it may very easily attain similar power." Although the Klan's organizational troubles and decline in the late 1920s may seem to set it apart from fascist and other right-wing movements in Europe that had more staying and did attain political power, critics were correct to see the Klan's fascist likenesses pulsing on an international stage and in ways the organization itself only partially directed. And one-time Klansmen and Klanswomen remained in their places of power and influence even after they put their robes and hoods aside.[32]

IV

AMONG THE FAVORITE TARGETS of Ku Klux Klan vigilantism were bootleggers, distillers, and others who facilitated the produc tion and distribution of alcoholic beverages. Although the Klan played a minimal role in the passage of the Eighteenth Amendment outlawing the "manufacture, sale, or transportation of intoxicating liquors" in the United States, or the Volstead (National Prohibition) Act meant to enable Prohibition's enforcement, Prohibition may well have been most responsible for energizing the Klan's explosive growth in the early 1920s. Simultaneously capturing the Progressive impulse toward social engineering and the Klan's ideas of 100 percent Americanism, Prohibition seemed to mark a clear divide, drawn by the federal government itself, between Protestant morality and white nationalism on the one side and the threats presented by immigrants, Catholics, radicals, and Blacks on the other—easily represented as a divide between lawfulness and criminality, between Americanism and alien saboteurs. Their vigorous defense of Prohibition brought the Klan respectability among white Protestants and power on the state and local levels where their influence could be most effective. It also showed how closely connected Klan objectives were with well-established American institutions and how many American communities accepted vigilantism in the service of their political ends. The Klan was, according to a journalist at the time, "the extreme militant wing of the temperance movement."[33]

Prohibition was the culmination of a century's long struggle, though it never wanted for substantial popular support. Beginning in the 1820s and 1830s and then rejuvenated in the 1870s, the movement for limiting or ending the sale and consumption of alcoholic beverages—temperance and prohibition respectively—attracted millions of, mostly, white, Protestant, and middle-class Americans who blamed alcohol for the impoverishment of families, the abusive behavior of husbands, and the soiling of political life. Like many social reform movements of the nineteenth century, temperance saw white, middle-class women play an especially prominent role, setting their collective sights on working-class saloons and southern "dives" frequented by "illiterate" whites and "negroes." Yet before the twentieth century these campaigns looked to state and local governments that could either pass the desired legislation or permit counties and townships to enact "local option" laws. For their work, helped along by the nationally organized WCTU and Anti-Saloon League, roughly half the population of the United States resided in jurisdictions where some form of liquor restriction prevailed.

But the other half did not. And they were most likely found in cities and towns with large immigrant, working-class populations, which were Catholic, Eastern Orthodox, Jewish, or non-evangelical Protestant and generally opposed—often strongly opposed—to either temperance or prohibition. "Alien illiterates rule our cities today," the WCTU's Frances Willard complained in 1890; "the saloon is their palace, the toddy stick their scepter." She might have added that they could be receptive to socialists, anarchists, and other radicals, further imperiling "Anglo-Saxon civilization." By 1913, plainly taking the measure of Progressive sensibilities, prohibitionists began to focus on the federal government and the prospect of a nationwide ban. It both made sense and had an urgency. The rural and small-town districts where temperance and prohibition sentiment proved strongest were overrepresented in Congress and state legislatures (they still are), and the 1920 census, which would show an urban majority for the first time, could demand significant reapportionment. Further availing themselves of the nationalism accompanying the country's entry into the World War, prohibitionists succeeded in winning congressional approval for the Eighteenth Amendment and quick ratification in the states. A sweeping and remarkable event it was: the first time the Constitution had ever been used to define acceptable cultural practices. It was the embodiment and harbinger of what the next decade would bring.[34]

This "war on alcohol," as historian Lisa McGirr terms it, was part of a larger and equally lengthy war on immigrants, at least on those who were not white Protestants from northern and western Europe or who suffered from mental or physical disabilities. From the early nineteenth century expulsionism against Irish Catholics, to the nativist movement of the 1840s and 1850s, to the attack on the voting rights of non-English speakers and their political machines, to the demands for the exclusion of Chinese workers, a growing racial nationalism cast fearful eyes on those who were not regarded as a part of American destiny. But until the late nineteenth and early twentieth centuries, there was relatively little effort—at least at the federal level—to obstruct the immigrant flow. Attention rather focused on restricting the rights and political power of those already in the country by extending naturalization requirements or limiting access to the franchise and officeholding. After all, those "swarthy" immigrants built the railroads and, with their labor, turned the United States into an industrial colossus.[35]

Signs of great change were in evidence by the late 1880s, however. The confluence of intense class conflict, surges in European immigration, a new respectability for science and social engineering, and an elevated race consciousness created openings for a new approach. Advocates of Chinese exclusion in the early 1880s tapped into deep hostilities against "coolies" and "heathens," and often deployed anti-slavery rhetoric to deny those of Chinese descent either citizenship or any form of belonging. Yet, much like white elites in the South who, wary of possible federal intervention under the Fifteenth Amendment, focused on the social conditions of African American life to disfranchise and segregate them, immigration restrictionists looked to poverty, criminality, mental illness, disease, and lack of education as justifications for closing the gates. In 1891, the year before Ellis Island opened, Congress passed a law that gave the federal government power to make and enforce immigration policy, sanctioned the deportation of aliens who entered the country illegally, and established categories for rejecting prospective immigrants. These included "all idiots, insane persons, paupers or persons likely to become a public charge, persons suffering from a loathsome or dangerous contagious disease, persons who have been convicted of a felony or other infamous crimes or misdemeanors involving moral turpitude, [and] polygamists." With the Immigration Act of 1891, the idea of the "illegal alien," developing since Chinese exclusion, gained firmer footing.[36]

Massachusetts senator Henry Cabot Lodge, a driving force in Congress for immigration restriction, made clear the goal. "The immigration of people of those races which contributed to the settlement and development of the United States," he wrote, "is declining in comparison with that of races far removed in thought and speech and blood from the men who have made this country what it is." His hope was to "sift the chaff from the wheat." And his device of choice was the literacy test, already in use to disfranchise Blacks and European immigrants, which he succeeded in getting through Congress before it met the veto of President Grover Cleveland. Congress kept at it for the next two decades only to encounter further presidential pushback, until the war eliminated all obstacles.[37]

The boom of wartime nationalism and the suspicions cast on any individuals or groups who might be considered "disloyal" gave further impetus to the restriction movement. Along with the Espionage Act, 1917 brought new immigration legislation that provided for a literacy test (Congress overrode Wilson's veto), imposed a head tax, created a massive "Asiatic Barred Zone," and added alcoholics, anarchists, prostitutes, and political radicals to the list of inadmissibles. But the groundwork for a quota system that both reduced the scale of immigration and sought draconian limits on certain national groups was laid in 1921 when the Emergency Quota Act focused on the likely arrival of postwar refugees. Washington State's congressman Albert Johnson, alarmed at the prospect of Asian and Eastern European immigration, chaired the House Committee on Immigration and Naturalization, and led the charge. With the eager assistance of Harry Laughlin, head of the Eugenics Records Office, Johnson's committee heard from numerous eugenicists including Lothrop Stoddard, whose *Rising Tide of Color Against White World Supremacy* (1920) had just earned him an international readership. Passed overwhelmingly, the Act was signed into law by President Warren G. Harding in May 1921.[38]

Harding may have vowed a return to "normalcy" but, in truth, his brief presidency, and that of Calvin Coolidge to follow, advanced a developing consensus on racial nationalism and the use of the federal government to secure what was increasingly called "Nordic" supremacy. Congressman Johnson had initially supported a temporary halt to all postwar immigration before embracing the idea of quotas. The wheels were now in motion for legislation that was neither temporary nor a matter of emergency but fundamentally altered American policy. With the enthusiastic assistance of eugenicists and the strong backing of the American Federation of Labor, the Ku Klux Klan, and the *New York Times* ("Preserving the American Race," the *Times* titled its editorial of support), the Johnson-Reed Act flew through Congress and onto Coolidge's waiting desk in May 1924. The *Los Angeles Times* exulted about a "Nordic Victory"; for Henry Cabot Lodge, the Senate majority leader who would be dead in six months, it was "one of the most important, if not the most important, [law] Congress has ever passed."[39]

The Johnson-Reed or Immigration Act of 1924 excluded Asian immigrants, dramatically restricted European immigration, and, equally significant, set quotas based on national origin. Favored countries—Britain, Germany, and the Scandinavian—were in northern and western Europe; those facing the greatest limitations were in southern and eastern Europe, where radicalism was thought to percolate and assimilation believed impossible. Funds for a border patrol were separately allocated that year as a bow to restrictionists angered by the lack of quotas for countries in the Western Hemisphere. "America of the Melting Pot Comes to an End," Senator David A. Reed of Pennsylvania, the act's cosponsor, concluded in the *New York Times*. Driven by racism, ethnocentrism, antiradicalism, and 100 percent Americanism, the Immigration Act of 1924 would remain in place for the next four decades, and showed just how entwined visions of Progressives and those of the Klan and other right-wing organizations were in the 1920s. Social engineering, and especially the engineering of a superior white, Protestant nation through the mechanisms of the state, brought them together. European fascists found much to admire and learn from.[40]

V

INTEREST IN AND ENTHUSIASM FOR FASCISM, especially for Italian fascism, were by no means confined to the American Legion or the Ku Klux Klan. After Mussolini's seizure of power in 1922 and before his invasion of Ethiopia in 1935, white Americans from many quarters looked to fascist Italy with favor and Mussolini with admiration as models of a future given over to experimentation, determination, economic energy, and strong authority. And as a formidable defense against Bolshevism. Needless to say, the Italian-American

press for the most part interpreted Mussolini's fascist regime glow-
ingly, as the culmination of the country's ideals, and Il Duce as the
reincarnation of the nineteenth-century nationalists Giuseppe Mazz-
ini and Giuseppe Garibaldi. But the American press, certainly by the
mid-1920s, widely joined in as well, "cautiously friendly and hope-
ful," as one observer described it. *Fortune*, the *Saturday Evening Post*,
and even *The New Republic* reported favorably on Mussolini and his
regime. Ida Tarbell, the famed "muckraker," was sent to Italy in 1926
by *McCall's* and wrote very positively not only about the new features
represented by the corporate state but also about what she called the
moral uplift in Mussolini's "world of work."[41]

The skepticism and hesitancy that greeted Black Shirt violence of
the very early 1920s appeared to evaporate once Mussolini ascended
to power. Business leaders quickly applauded the "remarkable recovery" and "splendid progress" Italy seemed to be making, and recognized Mussolini as a man who got things done. Elbert Gary of
U.S. Steel argued that "the entire world needs strong, honest men,"
and that the United States could "learn something by the movement
which has taken place in Italy." "Mussolini is a man every country
needs," the Wall Street financier Julius A. Basche wrote, and "autoc-
racy is the only solution to the world's problems," adding sarcasti-
cally "that is if we could only be sure that every autocrat would be a
good autocrat." Thomas Lamont, a partner at J. P. Morgan and Company, described himself as "something of a missionary" for Italian
fascism and became a business consultant for Mussolini, at one point
securing the regime a hundred-million-dollar loan. Even the advent
of the "corporate state" in 1926 drew little consternation from business elites. *Fortune* magazine later devoted an entire issue to it, high-
lighting the parallels between corporatism and the direction of the
American economy, especially with the rise of trade associations in
the late 1920s and then with the New Deal. To the editors of *Fortune*,
fascist and fascist-type movements had conquered most of Europe
and embodied the "ancient virtues" of "Discipline, Duty, Courage,
Glory, and Sacrifice." They were also reckoned as bulwarks against
the communist and socialist left.[42]

Corporatism was, of course, hardly unfamiliar to American business and political elites. The Progressive vision generally embraced the corporation and other large-scale economic institutions as both rational and more efficient, and many Progressives imagined a partnership between business, labor, and the public, administered by the state, as the desirable model of future development. Taylorist scientific management and its Fordist incarnations of the 1920s, combining mass production and mass consumption under expanded managerial control, in many ways anticipated fascist efforts to resolve the problem of class conflict through the "organic" unity made possible by a corporatist state. "Whatever the dangers of Fascism," Herbert Croly could write in 1927, "it has at any rate substituted movement for stagnation, purposive behavior for drifting, and visions of [a] great future for collective pettiness and discouragement."[43]

Mussolini himself was widely lionized and assimilated to a number of American values and icons. He was not only a "great man" but a "self-made man," the son of a blacksmith. And he seemed intent on affirming the virtues of "duty," "obedience," "loyalty," and "patriotism." The cult of personality that Mussolini nurtured played to an appreciative audience, and he, aware of the camera's eye and public fascination with feats of daring, drew comparison to the likes of Charles Lindberg, Lionel Barrymore, and Jack Dempsey. He was a man of action not words, a problem solver, a warrior, and a devoted Italian nationalist. The *Kansas City Star* marveled at the "thousands of youths" who had "flocked to Mussolini's banner" just as they had flocked to Garibaldi's army six decades earlier in a similar attempt to redeem Italy. Even more, "the Fascisti's ideals consist of 100 percent nationalism. They believe in applying patriotism with force; they not only have no patience with 50 per-cent Italianism, but they believe also in clubbing 50 per-centers." "What they want," the paper judged approvingly, "is the greatest well being and the maximum prosperity for the nation, not by class struggle, but by cooperation among the various classes."[44]

More than a few liberal intellectuals along with *The Nation* magazine expressed doubts and opposition to Italian fascism from the first, but the most organized resistance came from the ranks of labor. Although Samuel Gompers, who visited Italy shortly after World

War I, could suggest, reflecting a National Civic Federation perspective, that fascism was "capable of decisive action on a national scale" and "rapidly reconstructing a nation of collaborating units of usefulness," the AFL refused to join him, denouncing fascism as a menace to working people. At its annual convention in 1923, the AFL officially "abhor[red] and condemn[ed] every manifestation of fascism and call[ed] upon all affiliated unions to combat its importation into the United States." Instead, the AFL lent its "full moral support to the Anti-Fascist Alliance of North America," recognizing as it did "effort[s] to organize Fascisti groups in the United States." William Green, who succeeded Gompers as AFL president the following year, also dwelt in the anti-fascist camp and called upon workers and farmers to organize against it. As for the socialist and communist left, relatively little attention was paid either to Mussolini or his fascist regime before the 1930s and the advent of the popular front.[45]

For admiring Americans, Mussolini returned the favor. He lavished praise on the "original civilization" of America, its strenuous work ethic, and its contributions to the world's "mechanical and material" achievements, which were, in turn, enabled by a "magnificent spiritual activity." Here he claimed to be "thinking of William James, of Emerson, of Longfellow, of Mark Twain, and the great magician of the magnetic world, Edison." Mussolini, in fact, insisted that his intellectual development was shaped by William James, and although some doubts were expressed at the time, a number of American scholars saw in Mussolini and Italian fascism a strong pragmatic streak, an interest in scientific philosophy, a "hard-headed practicality," and an emphasis on "experience." Fascism's "philosophy is pragmatism," a Princeton professor proclaimed, "its sole guiding principle is that working principles are to be discovered in actual practice."[46]

Yet, far more than Benito Mussolini, it was Adolf Hitler and the Nazis who looked to the United States and its history as possible models. Writing *Mein Kampf* from his Bavarian jail cell in 1924, Hitler took keen note of the newly enacted American immigration law and especially touted its remedy—"the one state"—of refusing entry to "physically unhealthy elements, and simply exclud[ing] the immigration of certain races." Long fascinated by Westerns, Hitler also recognized the conquest of the American West and the destruction of Native peoples there as essential to the making of a "Nordic" society; by some accounts, the history of the American West, as Hitler understood it, influenced his views of *Lebensraum*, or German breathing space to the East. "One thing the Americans have which we lack," he later wrote, "is the sense of vast open spaces."[47]

In his views of the United States, Hitler was not alone among German Nazis, especially among their lawyers and scientists. "The most important event in the history of the states of the Second Millennium," one exclaimed, "was the founding of the United States of America," for there "the struggle of the Aryans for world domination . . . received its strongest prop." Special attention was devoted to American racial policies and, when drafting what became the Nuremberg Laws of 1935 denying citizenship to Jews and criminalizing their intermarriage, Nazi officials found much food for thought in antimiscegenation, immigration, and Jim Crow laws in the United States. This, they argued, was a state with a truly racial basis of citizenship and therefore an example for the Germans. "The U.S. too has racist politics and policies," a Nazi writer explained; "most states of the Union have special laws directed against the Negroes which limit their voting rights, freedom of movement, and career possibilities." "For a while," he added, "there was a plan to create a Negro reservation in the Southern states, similar to the Indian reservations," and he regarded "lynch justice" as the "natural resistance of the *Volk* to an alien race that is attempting to gain the upper hand." Remarkably, Nazis thought some of the American racial policies too harsh and rigid.[48]

Perhaps nothing was more significant in creating a community of scientific and policy interest between the United State and Nazi Germany than the international field of eugenics. German and American eugenicists were in touch from early in the twentieth century, and new American philanthropies, such as the Rockefeller Foundation, hoping to "save" German science after World War One, offered ample aid during the 1920s and 1930s to German institutions engaged in eugenic research. One of the beneficiaries of Rockefeller funding was Josef Mengele, later the camp physician at Auschwitz, and the Nazis took close measure of sterilization laws that eugenicist Harry Laughlin had helped some American states enact. "Now that we know the laws of heredity," Hitler observed, "it is possible to a large extent to prevent unhealthy and severely handicapped beings from coming into the world. I have studied with interest the laws of several American states concerning prevention of reproduction by people whose progeny would, in all probability, be of no value or be injurious to the racial stock." More than a few American eugenicists admired the work the Nazi regime commenced during the 1930s and took great satisfaction in the influence they may have had. As California eugenicist and board member of the Human Betterment Foundation, C. M. Goethe, put it to one of his colleagues, "You will be interested to know that your work has played a powerful part in shaping the opinions of the group of intellectuals who are behind Hitler in this epoch-making program. Everywhere I sense that their opinions have been tremendously stimulated by American thought."[49]

VI

WHATEVER FASCIST PULSES MAY have registered during the late teens and 1920s, most scholars recognize the New Deal and the political culture of the 1930s as veering sharply away from the dispositions of fascist and authoritarian regimes. They rather see the construction of a new liberalism that combined state activism in economic life with the protection of civil and political rights, with the maintenance of a liberal democracy. If anything, the "New Deal Order" that emerged in the 1930s, and endured in various forms for the next three decades, was as much of a social democratic experiment as the United States has ever pursued. Yet until quite recently the New Deal has not been placed in an international or comparative context, nor have continuities between the politics of the 1920s and 1930s been adequately noted. We need, that is, to do more looking out from the 1920s and early 1930s than looking back from the present day or from much of what followed. The results are, to say the least, disconcerting.[50]

The white nationalism, fundamentalist Protestantism, nativism, and racism that energized Prohibition, immigration restriction, and the Ku Klux Klan hardly dissipated in the late 1920s and early 1930s even as the organizational threads of the Klan frayed. Many Klan members and followers had fraternal or patriotic societies to engage them, not to mention local governance bodies to support their political agendas. They had, in many places, won those fights, sometimes resoundingly. Other former Klansmen joined self-styled "American fascist" organizations, like the Black Shirts and the White Band of Caucasian Crusaders in Atlanta, or the Khaki Shirts in Philadelphia, to intimidate or harm, in some cases murder, their enemies.[51]

The onset of the Great Depression further destabilized the political landscape, especially once the Nazis attained power in Germany. The Friends of New Germany, soon to become the German American Bund, was established in 1933 as a pro-Nazi paramilitary organization which would claim thousands of members. Before long the Bund was marching in the streets of New York City, filling its Madison Square Garden for rallies, and setting up military drill camps in New York, New Jersey, Pennsylvania, and Wisconsin. The Silver Legion, also known as the Silver Shirts—in imitation of Hitler's Brown Shirts—took form at the same time, hatched by William Dudley Paley in Asheville, North Carolina. Fairly quickly it could boast over 15,000 members with noteworthy activity in the Midwest and on the West Coast. Apart from the Bund and the Silver Legion, American Nazis and Nazi sympathizers were to be found across the country from North Carolina and Florida to California and Oregon to Michigan and Ohio, usually in cities large and small, often united in believing that Nazism embodied "True Americanism." The event in New York's Madison Square Garden in 1939, with more than 20,000 in attendance, had an immense, full-length portrait of George Washington, termed the "first fascist," unfurled behind the stage.[52]

The American Legion remained a self-appointed guardian of "Americanism." During the 1930s sections of the Legion served as a mass lobbying group subsidized by large corporations and the National Association of Manufacturers, and deployed vigilantes to break strikes and attack union organizers, especially as the Congress of Industrial Organizations (CIO) began to expand. Indeed, the

Legion was part of an extensive latticework of newer groups and well-established organizations through which fascist ideas could circulate and find receptive audiences. "Today there are innumerable shirt organizations, nightgown rackets, the Black Legion, the Friends of New Germany, the Americaneers, the Committees of 100, of 200, of one million, the Women's National Association for the Preservation of the White Race," journalist Benjamin Stolberg warned in 1938. "There are literally hundreds of such outfits. And this spirit reaches into the dark corners of the DAR, the ROTC, the American Legion, the Veterans of Foreign Wars, the Chamber of Commerce, the Lions, the Elks, the Eagles, the Moose, and the rest of the zoo of the small time Babbitry. It's all very dreadful and the Lord knows where it's leading to."[53]

The severity of the Great Depression created an immensely volatile political atmosphere that gave rise not only to new or revamped fascist and fascist-like networks, but to an array of popular movements that defied easy categorization. They all took on the challenges of economic suffering and inequality, as well as the vulnerabilities and deep disillusionment afflicting large sections of the middle and working class. And they all proposed solutions meant to readjust the economic imbalances and offer protections to the weak. Some, like Francis Townshend's "Plan" for old-age insurance and Upton Sinclair's End Poverty in California (EPIC) campaign, were clearly of the left, advocating higher taxes on the rich, pensions, and workers' and farmers' cooperatives.

Others combined redistributionist measures with authoritarian orientations. Huey Long, born and reared in politically renegade Winn Parish, Louisiana, came to power first as governor (1928–32) and then as U.S. senator (1932–35), railing against the oil and gas companies that were plundering the state and building a base among Louisiana's humble white folk; unable to vote, Black people widely admired Long as well. He hiked taxes on corporations; built roads, bridges, hospitals, and schools; established public works programs; and provided free textbooks for schoolchildren. Representing himself as the champion of local communities against outside interests bent on destroying them—like Standard Oil—Long earned both the loyalty of ordinary Louisianians along with the bitter enmity of big landowners and business interests identified with New Orleans. He also consolidated unprecedented power. Using strong-arm tactics and patronage, he quickly controlled the legislature, the courts, and the bureaucracy: pretty much the entire government of Louisiana. Then, as senator, he set his sights on Franklin Roosevelt and the New Deal, devising a "Share Our Wealth" plan truly breathtaking in ambition. He called for guaranteed annual incomes, pensions for the elderly, free college tuition and vocational training, healthcare, veterans' benefits, and a thirty-hour work week to be financed by higher taxes on personal fortunes, large incomes, and inheritances. Termed a socialist, a fascist, and a would-be authoritarian, Long insisted that he intended to "make every man a king."[54]

Much farther to the north, outside Detroit, Father Charles E. Coughlin developed his own brand of popular politics. Availing himself of the economic distress of industrial workers, many of whom were Catholic, and the new technology of radio, Coughlin drew in a mass following through weekly sermons that combined bitter attacks on international bankers with anti-communism. Pressing for the remonetization of silver, labor rights, and the nationalization of some industries, all flavored by a creeping anti-Semitism, Coughlin organized the National Union for Social Justice in 1934. It would attract several million members, some of whom went on in 1938 to form the right-wing Christian Front, which launched boycotts of Jewish-owned businesses, cooperated with the Bund, harassed radical union leaders, and participated in the Madison Square Garden rally of American Nazis.[55]

The Townshend Plan, Sinclair's EPIC campaign, Long's "Share Our Wealth" program, and Coughlin's National Union for Social Justice, which all debuted in late 1933 and 1934, indicated the travails that the country and the New Deal were enduring. Indeed, it is important to remember that however sweeping Franklin Roosevelt's election to the presidency and the Democrats' wresting control of Congress were in 1932, it was not at all clear where Roosevelt's New Deal would move. After all, during the campaign Roosevelt pledged to balance the budget. Early 1933 had witnessed the ascension of the

Nazis to power in Germany as well as Roosevelt's inauguration, and while Roosevelt sought to calm the nation by declaring that "the only thing we have to fear is fear itself," his address also included a sobering warning. Recognizing that "the Nation asks for action, and action now," Roosevelt declared that "in the event that Congress" should falter in its tasks and the "national emergency" remain "critical," he would "not evade the clear course of duty that will then confront me." That is to say, he would be forced to initiate a "temporary departure from that normal balance of public procedure" and "ask Congress for the one remaining instrument to meet the crisis—broad executive power to wage a war against the emergency, as great as the power that would be given me if we were invaded by a foreign foe."[56]

Here Roosevelt was only articulating ideas offered to him by a variety of intellectuals and opinion makers, often liberals themselves, who believed that decisive and unprecedented action was required. One suggested the construction of a "third road" between fascism and communism, accompanied by a "temporary dictatorship." Others believed that the use of emergency executive powers together with the weakening of Congress was necessary. Walter Lippman of the *New Republic* insisted that "strong medicine was required," including the suspension of the normal political process and the granting of extraordinary authority to the president that "the most liberal interpretation of the Constitution" might allow. "The situation is critical," Lippman told Roosevelt. "You may have no alternative but to assume dictatorial powers."[57]

The avalanche of legislation during the first hundred days of the Roosevelt administration was made possible by a remarkable aggregation of power by the president and his administration. Although Congress customarily drafted and enacted bills and then sent them to the president, the political vectors were now reversed. Virtually all the early New Deal legislation was drafted in the executive branch and then sent to Congress where, with large Democratic majorities in both houses, it was effectively rubber-stamped. By creating a host of new federal agencies lodged in the executive-linked bureaucracy (often called the "alphabet agencies") like the NRA and AAA, moreover, the legislation further empowered the president at the expense of Congress. So rapid and stunning were the changes that a reporter for the *New York Times* could describe the "atmosphere" in Washington at the time "as strangely reminiscent of Rome in the first weeks after the march of the Black Shirts, or Moscow at the beginning of the Five-Year Plan." A Republican congressman, with much distress, used a similar analogy in complaining that "the power . . . conferred upon the president . . . makes the distinguished dictator Mussolini, look like an Egyptian mummy." The political dynamic was not lost on the Germans. In May 1933, the Nazi Party newspaper, the *Volkisher Beobacter*, saw "Roosevelt's dictatorial recovery measures" as ushering in a new era in American politics.[58]

There was more to the analogy than the transfer of raw power. The signature New Deal legislation of the first hundred days was devised both to meet the crisis and win the support of the financial, large landowning, and corporate sectors, and thus maintain a complex coalition that had propelled the Democrats to electoral victory. The Glass-Steagall Banking Act, which separated commercial and investment banking, had the backing of newer investment and international banking houses looking to weaken the House of Morgan, whose hegemony rested heavily on the pillars of both. The National Industrial Recovery Act (NIRA), influenced by the War Industry Board of the 1910s and designed to stabilize the economy, suspended anti-trust litigation and called for the creation of industry-wide codes meant to set controls on production, pricing, wages, and employment. Trade associations that favored the largest companies in each industry—oil, electrical, automobile, and others—would create the codes, putting the lid on competition and bringing about what amounted to government-sponsored cartels. Although the NIRA also gave industrial workers the right to "organize and bargain collectively through representations of their own choosing," for the time being corporate leaders and other large-scale business interests gained the lion's share of power.[59]

The same was true for large landowners, especially in the southern states. Hoping to address the problem of crop overproduction, which had been depressing commodity prices, the Agricultural Adjustment Act (AAA) subsidized commercial growers to plow up acreage they had planted or refrain from planting altogether. But, owing to the influence of southern white elites in the Democratic Party and Roosevelt's need to court their support, the subsidies were administered by local planters and withheld from tenants and sharecroppers who composed most of the staple-growing labor force. For the first time since the Civil War, white southern landholders could benefit directly from the policies of the federal government, and they used the windfall to evict tenants and croppers, begin mechanizing their operations, and secure the "authoritarian enclaves" they had long ruled. In effect, the AAA initiated an enclosure movement that drove poor Black and white rural working folk off the land and demonstrated the powerful role that reactionary planters would have over federal policy for decades.[60]

That Congress marched so easily and quickly to the administration's drumming meant that Roosevelt had no need to embrace the emergency powers he warned of at the time of his inauguration. He did not move to suspend the Constitution, punish political opponents, infringe on civil liberties, postpone elections, or use the iron fist of military/police discipline. There was no American version of the Reichstag fire or the March on Rome. Roosevelt was clearly disposed to constitutionalism, as were those closest to him, and room was thereby created for the social mobilizations that pushed the New Deal to the left rather than to the right. They were mobilizations that made possible the unionization of the mass production industries under the auspices of the new CIO, paved the way for social security and unemployment insurance, and enabled Black people in northern cities to join the New Deal coalition and begin to force the Democrats to reckon with the meaning of Jim Crow.

Yet throughout the 1930s, what hovered over American social and political life was less the prospect of socialism or communism than the threat of fascism. Even as the Roosevelt administration and the New Deal seemed to suggest that a feared dictatorship was not in the offing, observers continued to reflect and worry that the United States had begun to travel down a fascist road, at an unpredictable pace, and that a distinctive, nationally branded form of fascism could well arise. A political scientist noted in 1935 that "attention has been drawn to the possibility of a Fascist Revolution in the United States," citing congressional committee testimonies, journalistic and cinematic exposés, the "revival of the 1918–20 'Red Baiting' spirit and technique," and the agitation of the League Against War and Fascism. Still, he argued that the danger was not the introduction of "a foreign brand of Fascism, but of an indigenous reactionary movement, disguised behind the façade of democratic ideology."[61]

The writer and critic Waldo Frank, addressing the question of "Will Fascism Come to America?" in 1934, similarly claimed that "the NRA is the beginning of American fascism. But unlike Italy or Germany . . . Fascism may be so gradual in the U.S. that most voters will not be aware of its existence. The true fascist leaders will not be the present imitators of the German Fuhrer and the Italian condottieri. . . . They will be judicious black-frocked gentlemen; graduates of the best universities; disciples of Nicholas Murray Butler and of Walter Lippman." Writing in the *North American Review*, Roger Shaw insisted that "the New Dealers strangely enough, have been employing Fascist means to gain liberal ends. The NRA with its code system, its regulatory economic clauses and some of its features of social amelioration was plainly an American adaptation of the Italian corporate state." "I am certain," a liberal wrote, "that in this country [fascism] will come dressed up in democratic trappings so as not to offend people." Or "wrapped in the American flag," as Huey Long may have said. As Sinclair Lewis's fictional dictator-in-the-making, Buzz Windrip, recognized in Lewis's 1935 novel *It Can't Happen Here*, "as warmly as [Windrip] advocated everyone's getting rich by just voting to be rich, he denounced all 'Fascism' and 'Nazism' so that most of the Republicans who were afraid of Democratic Fascism and all the Democrats who were afraid of Republican Fascism, were ready to vote for him."[62]

Sections of the business and corporate sector increasingly saw things differently, and their fears carried special and long-term consequences. In their view, the New Deal smacked not of creeping fascism but of creeping socialism, and they began to organize. Led by the Du Pont family and the National Association of Manufacturers, which had ceased being oriented solely to the concerns of small business, they looked to strike back. Roosevelt would lambaste them as "economic royalists," but they paid no mind. A bit later, they were joined by southern elites who worried that the New Deal threatened the racial order segregation and disfranchisement had been designed to solidify. The bipartisan American Liberty League, financed heavily by the Du Ponts and a handful of wealthy bankers and industrialists, looked to Republican Alf Landon in 1936 to pry Roosevelt out of office, and the southern congressional delegation, Democrats all, did its best to put the brakes on New Deal social and tax legislation as well as any talk of aiding Black men and women in the South.[63]

In the end, Roosevelt outmaneuvered them to keep his coalition intact and win an unprecedented third term. But by the late 1930s, the New Deal's social momentum seemed exhausted, and while Roosevelt rallied the public to aid the beleaguered British and prepare for another massive war, his opponents, a cross-section of conservative businessmen, white southerners, and a new group of "America first-ers" began to lay the foundation for a postwar political right. They had much on which to build.

Chapter Eight

THE "OTHER" NINETEEN-SIXTIES

O N 19 FEBRUARY 1964, GEORGE C. WALLACE, THE governor of Alabama, flew into Madison, Wisconsin, for a speaking engagement on the campus of the state university. It did not seem a likely destination. One year earlier, after a nasty, race-fueled campaign, Wallace was inaugurated governor, pledging to maintain segregation "now," "tomorrow," and "forever." Five months later, he stood in the "school house door" of the University of Alabama in an unsuccessful, though highly publicized, effort to prevent the federally supported integration of that institution. By the summer of 1963, after explosive demonstrations in Birmingham that left hundreds of Black civil rights' protesters injured by police dogs and fire hoses or jailed by the city police, Wallace seemed the embodiment of the battle against racial equality and for white supremacy. In Martin Luther King's eyes, Wallace was "perhaps the most dangerous racist in America today."

By the time he arrived at the University of Wisconsin, Wallace had already spoken at Harvard, Brown, Smith, and Dartmouth (Yale alone closed its doors to him), and, some weeks later, took his lecture tour to college campuses in the Midwest, Rocky Mountains, and Far West—maybe twenty in all. Although usually greeted by an assortment of civil rights protesters and activists, Wallace surprised audiences by bantering with hecklers, responding courteously to critical questions, and injecting humor into his presentations. Rather than discuss race or segregation, he focused on state rights, constitutional limits, and unbridled federal power. Issues of access to schools and other public accommodations or of open housing, he argued, were the province of states and municipalities, not the federal government. Somewhat bewildered, many of the students left with a more favorable opinion of Wallace, viewing him as thoughtful and reasonable. As the *Daily Cardinal*, the University of Wisconsin student newspaper, put it, "He came, he saw, he conquered."

Not long after, Wallace returned to Wisconsin and headed toward the heavily Republican Fox River Valley, hoping to attract its many conservatives. There, in the small town of Appleton—hometown of red-baiter Joseph McCarthy—Wallace announced, with little notice, his candidacy for the Democratic nomination for president, beginning with a run in the fast-approaching Wisconsin primary. Wallace made stops at other small towns like Manitowoc, Sheboygan, and Howard's Grove, but his most enthusiastic reception came on Milwaukee's southside, at Serb Memorial Hall, where working-class white ethnics had been angered by agitation for integration and fair housing. The seven hundred people who jammed into the hall, together with another three hundred left on the outside, heard Wallace denounce the Supreme Court for outlawing prayer in schools and encouraging the dropping of "God" from the Pledge of Allegiance. They also heard him launch an attack on the pending civil rights bill in Congress that would "destroy the union seniority system," "impose quotas," and make it "impossible for a homeowner to sell his home to whoever he chooses." "A vote for this little governor," Wallace concluded to thunderous applause, "will let the people in Washington know that we want them to leave our homes, schools, jobs, business[es], and farms alone." A week later, Wallace won one-third of the Democratic vote in the state and repeated the electoral feat in Indiana and Maryland, where he won sixteen of twenty-three counties, including Baltimore, before dropping out of the race. "Today we hear more state rights talk than we have in the last quarter century," Wallace crowed. "My mission has been accomplished."[1]

Wallace's paeans to state rights, political decentralization, local control, and individual freedom from the grasp of big government stood in marked contrast to the regime he was already building in Alabama. Like officials and police departments in many other states of the South, especially the Deep South, who sought to close ranks against civil rights activism by spearheading "anti-subversive" offensives, Wallace quickly moved to defend the "southern way of life." It all appeared another version of the state-established and -enforced Black subordination and humiliation that southern elites began to fashion after Reconstruction. But Wallace pushed even further to construct something of a personal fiefdom that harked back to the world of Huey Long, though without the populist dimensions. He created an interconnected set of repressive institutions run from the top and organized on a basis of personal patronage, rewarding acolytes and punishing those who dared stand in his way. Before he ever set off on his northern tour of college campuses, Wallace had the Alabama state legislature create a Peace Commission (something of a "star chamber" to harass and suppress dissenters), a Sovereignty Commission tasked with unifying and fortifying the state's struggle against the "federal juggernaut" of civil rights, and a Department of Public Safety meant to collect troves of materials on those, white and Black, seen as posing "threats" to the regime and the segregationist order. Northern white voters who rallied to Wallace's candidacy in 1964 paid no mind; they understood him very clearly and eagerly embraced his message.[2]

The early 1960s are widely viewed as the salad days of modern liberalism, when the social democratic impulses of the New Deal took on the challenges of Jim Crow, helped enact federal civil and voting rights legislation, and made possible Great Society programs designed, in part, to wage a "war on poverty," especially in the nation's inner cities where millions of African Americans faced social misery and isolation. The election of 1964, when Democrat Lyndon Johnson trounced Republican Barry Goldwater and Democrats won a Senate supermajority, seemed to symbolize not only the hegemony of a liberalism crafted during the 1930s but also the absence of serious opposition to it, save for the Deep South, already seen as a fading bastion of reaction. Indeed, some observers at the time were quick to pronounce the Republican Party and conservatism more generally in their death throes. The historian Richard Hofstadter puzzled, just before the election, as to the "development and prominence of a mind so out of key with the basic tonalities of our political life," and went on to speculate that while "it is always dangerous to predict the demise of a major party in our political system . . . Goldwater may have given the Republican party the coup de grace." Only the racially charged urban explosions of the mid-to-late 1960s together with the disastrous American defeat in Vietnam, many believe, marked the beginnings of the country's protracted turn to the right.[3]

Yet George Wallace's northern speaking tour in 1963–64, along with the unexpected levels of support he received in northern and border-state primaries that spring, should give us pause. Feeding off the lexicon of segregationist and white supremacist thought while fashioning a political language that subordinated race in a larger critique of federal overreach and the communist threat, celebrating state rights and local control while devising the instruments of repression, Wallace tapped a pulsing vein of illiberalism. The "will of the community" and its defense, long available for the purposes of exclusions and expulsions, were redeployed and invigorated to strengthen bonds of class, race, ethnicity, and locality. Between the end of World War Two and the early 1960s, the materials of political backlash against the federal government, its leaders, and its perceived clients—owing in large part to economic and demographic transformations of the time—were already percolating close to the surface of American political life. No one saw this more clearly or responded more energetically than George C. Wallace. And no one better anticipated the country's political direction.

I

THE ANGER THAT GEORGE WALLACE harvested among working-class white ethnics in Milwaukee could be found in many industrial cities stretching from Boston, New York, Philadelphia, and Baltimore to Chicago and St. Louis and then to Los Angeles. The wartime and postwar surge in African American migration from the South to the urban North and West exacerbated the housing shortages already bedeviling urban areas owing to returning war veterans. And they quickly pressed upon the residential racial boundaries that the earlier migrations (1915–1930) had carved. Between 1950 and 1960, the Black population of Philadelphia grew by 41 percent, Baltimore by 45 percent, Detroit by 58 percent, Chicago by 65 percent, Gary, Indiana by 72 percent, Los Angeles by 112 percent, and Milwaukee by a remarkable 187 percent. At the same time, federal benefits expanded white working-class homeownership, giving residents an even deeper stake in their neighborhoods and the local schools and churches attached to them.[4]

White working-class neighborhoods of the industrial North and West were generally composed of second- and third-generation European immigrants who were often predominantly Catholic and socially conservative, or of migrants from the South and Midwest who had embraced or been touched by Protestant evangelicalism. Bound together by their parishes and churches, shared blue-collar work experiences, (sometimes) union membership, and American patriotism, they had been reliable supporters of the New Deal and the postwar Democratic Party. Programs devised by the Roosevelt and Truman administrations had provided access to low-interest home mortgages and higher education. Cold War–inspired fears of the left, together with robust union mobilizations, had pushed employers, especially in the mass production industries, to accept collective bargaining and offer steady wage increases, health insurance, and pensions: in part as alternatives to worker co-management that the left wing of the CIO had pursued. The accoutrements of middle-class life were newly available although a sense of their precarity lingered.[5]

Like many neighborhoods and communities, those of the northern and western white working and lower-middle class were always sensitive to outsiders who might traverse their boundaries. But the prospects of Black families moving into single-family homes and apartments, or of public housing being constructed nearby, flipped a switch of hostility and activism that had few precedents. Very quickly, white homeowners and renters formed neighborhood organizations that, something in the manner of "taxpayer" and "people's" parties of the nineteenth century, sought to disguise their purposes under race-neutral rubrics. They were called "civic associations," "homeowners' associations," "protective associations," and "improvement associations," all devoted to patrolling their neighborhoods and influencing the politics of city government to block the spatial transformations underway. Between 1945 and 1965, whites in Detroit established nearly two hundred of these associations, which played a critical role in unifying white ethnics and articulating shared ideas about defending communities, families, homes, women, and children. There was, to say the least, a kinship with segregationists and even lynchers in the South who saw themselves policing the most intimate spaces from the violations of blood- and sex-thirsty inferiors. Not surprisingly, many of the northern whites, especially in blue-collar areas, were favorably disposed to racial segregation, particularly to residential segregation, as George Wallace plainly sensed.[6]

As this geography of illiberalism suggests, white neighborhood activism was not only concerned with political mobilization and lobbying; it commonly had paramilitary components. Almost invariably, Black families who attempted to move into these neighborhoods were greeted with expulsive harassment and violence. Much like episodes of community-sanctioned violence in the past, these were well orchestrated. Teenagers might serve as sentries or boundary watchers and bring news of an "invasion" to the attention of adults. The adults, in turn, might first make threatening phone calls or drive slowly past the newly purchased property, surveying the scene and implicitly warning the Black occupants of what was to come. Then, perhaps later that evening or on a subsequent evening, a crowd would gather, sometimes in the tens, sometimes in the hundreds, and begin by screaming insults and epithets before hurling rocks and bricks or setting fires, meant to defile the house and degrade the Black family, demonstrating as clearly as possible that there were no circumstances under which they could remain. Although the violence was mostly directed against property rather than persons, that line was indistinct at best. In Los Angeles, scene of more than one hundred such incidents between 1950 and 1965, crosses were burned and homes dynamited, in one case killing an entire family.[7]

For the most part, as in the Jim Crow South, the police either looked away or served as abettors. Often from these very communities themselves, police and other local officials sided with the white rioters and rarely attempted to make arrests; if they did, the cases were quickly scuttled. The "sympathy for the white rioters on the part of the average policeman," as an observer in the South Deering neighborhood of Chicago put it, "was extreme," a good reflection of the view taken by the chief of the district police. "It is unfortunate," he told a meeting of the South Deering Improvement Association, "that colored people chose to come out here." Small wonder that when Martin Luther King Jr. launched an open-housing campaign in Chicago in 1966, he was aghast at his reception: "I have never seen, even in Mississippi and Alabama, mobs as hateful as I've seen here in Chicago."[8]

Especially revealing was how white residents frequently discussed the nature of their resistance to racial integration, even on a small scale. Most widely and vividly, they spoke of "defending their neighborhoods," securing their community institutions, schools, and families against degraded outsiders who would threaten their well-being and diminish the value of their homes. They saw their neighborhoods as the very basis of rights as they understood them. As a Black journalist in Detroit put it, "The white population . . . has come to believe that it has a vested, exclusive, and permanent 'right' to certain districts." Others might elaborate and refer to a set of "homeowners' rights," a "right to privacy" and a "right to freedom from interference with their property," a right to freedom of assembly and association, all of which composed a basic notion of citizenship. Not in the abstract but in a neighborhood context did citizenship and the rights related to it became palpable, grounded in recognizable ways, particularly if linked to the stakeholding that homeownership symbolized. The rights of Black people and other minority groups might be acknowledged—whether to jobs, housing, or recreational activities—though only if they remained in their own neighborhoods and did not trespass beyond them. These ideas had very extended genealogies, as we have seen, fortified over time by traditions of localism and community control usually bounded by racial and ethnic identities, not to mention by the courts, which ruled in ways that limited federal power.[9]

Often on the front lines of neighborhood defense were women of working-class or lower-middle-class households. Understanding their domestic roles as foundations of family and community life, availing themselves of postwar prosperity and government programs, creating networks of housewives and mothers through the church and informal activities, they valued their homeowning security and proved especially sensitive to potential threats lurking at the boundaries. Taking a page from the ideology of domesticity and separate spheres so important to the emerging middle class of the early nineteenth century, they saw themselves, and were seen by many neighborhood men, as the custodians of local morality, traditions, institutions, and health who were quite ready to lay down the gauntlet. If a Black family sought to overstep the imagined borders of neighborhood, women were generally first out to mobilize and register their dissent. They set up picket lines, handed out leaflets, organized stroller protests with infants and toddlers in tow, spoke out at public meetings, and made harassing phone calls to the new Black property owners or the real estate agents who coordinated the sale. "My home is my castle, I will die defending it." "We don't want to mix." "The Lord separated the races." Such were the placards these women carried to voice their resistance and dramatize their efforts to protect themselves, their children, and the sanctity of their homes. Guardians of morality they claimed to be, with a class-inflected toughness that distinguished them from middle- and upper-middle-class counterparts, though they had formidable predecessors among white women of the Jim Crow South.[10]

Housing and "defended neighborhoods" were not only priorities for the white working class. The rapid growth of postwar suburbs, and especially suburban tract developments, became flashpoints too, as aspiring middle-class whites sought the affordable homeownership that was either unavailable or racially compromised in the city. And almost invariably, the developers included restrictive covenants— backed by the policies of insurance companies, the Federal Housing Administration, and the strong preferences of white purchasers—to keep Black families out. William Levitt, who pioneered single-family developments on Long Island and in Bucks County, Pennsylvania, prohibited the sale of his properties to Blacks because, as he put it, "white people refuse to live in a community to which Negroes will be admitted." It was, in language all too familiar, a business decision: Levitt "could not take the chance on admitting Negroes and then not being able to sell his houses." On one occasion, he went so far as to begin eviction proceedings against two white Levittown families who had the temerity to invite the children of Black friends to play in their yards.[11]

The Levittowns were hardly alone. If the late 1940s and the 1950s could be described as the era of the "crabgrass frontier," the crabgrass grew almost exclusively on the lawns of white-owned suburban homes. From coast to coast, suburbs new and old mobilized to deny Black families, even those of the professional middle class, an opportunity to buy in. Cicero, Illinois (Chicago), Dearborn, Michigan (Detroit), Lincoln Village, Ohio (Columbus), and South Gate, California (Los Angeles), were among the many suburbs that used a variety of devices, including violence and cross-burnings, to maintain their whiteness. Even relatively liberal, Quaker-dominated Swarthmore, Pennsylvania, used zoning and other legal harassments to prevent "open occupancy" subdivisions or single-family home sales to Blacks. "We do not want Swarthmore to become a laboratory in which to try out this or other schemes which have no assurance of success," the Swarthmore Property Owners' Association declared. "It is a cold, hard economic fact," twenty-two Quaker homeowners lectured, "that property decreases in value when Negroes move into the neighborhood." Their words were directed at another Quaker couple who hoped to advance integration by listing their home for open-occupancy sale.[12]

The fight against racial integration in housing could stir an entire state, with contradictory and foreboding signs. In 1963 the California Assembly passed a Fair Housing Act (also known as the Rumford Act for its Black sponsor, William Byron Rumford) that outlawed discrimination in the sale or rental of residential housing. Signed by then Democratic governor Edmund G. (Pat) Brown, the law put California at the forefront of open-housing legislation while generating a massive backlash. Within months, Proposition 14, which would amend the state constitution to give real estate owners absolute discretion as to who could buy, lease, or rent their properties, gained more than enough signatures to be voted upon in the November 1964 elections, which also determined state and national offices. When election day arrived, Democrat Lyndon Johnson easily defeated Republican challenger Barry Goldwater for the presidency with over 56 percent of the California vote. At the same time, Proposition 14 garnered a whopping 65 percent of the vote, sweeping all California counties save one and demonstrating that open housing brought out expulsive illiberalism among otherwise liberal-oriented Democratic voters.[13]

II

MANY OF THE DYNAMICS at play in the battles over open housing also surfaced, as might be expected, over the matter of school desegregation. Although the Supreme Court's landmark *Brown* decision of 1954 is generally understood as striking a blow against Jim Crow in the South, it had significant implications for many schools in the urban and suburban North and West that were highly segregated owing to long-standing racial discrimination in housing. The lead case in *Brown*, after all, came from a lawsuit brought in Topeka, the capital city of Kansas, and it was one of many actions taken by Black parents, usually in alliance with the NAACP, that targeted segregated schools in New York, New Jersey, Illinois, Pennsylvania, Ohio, and Michigan between the mid-1920s and mid-1950s.[14]

Here again the idea of "neighborhood," and "neighborhood schools" in particular, offered the conceptual rubric to galvanize opposition to desegregation whether within urban boundaries or in nearby suburbs, all the more so as civil rights agitation threw the explicit language of race into disrepute. To be sure, neighborhood was itself a social and cultural construction in a world of geographical mobility, an idea of stability and community when there was little of either to be found. The boundaries of neighborhoods were in regular flux, as were their social compositions; they often had a character that only residents recognized, especially when they coincided with racially marked areas of residence. But they did provide ideas of belonging as well as a rights vocabulary that tapped into deeply rooted localisms.

The most blatant response to the *Brown* decision in the South was "massive resistance," a defiant and ideological rejection of the authority of the Court and the premises that informed its ruling. This could include the state-mandated abolition of public schools or the withdrawal of funding from those schools choosing to follow some path toward desegregation. Virginia gained special notoriety here, but grassroots support for segregation was widespread across the South, often mobilized by white women. Elsewhere, the response to *Brown* may be termed either denialism or minimal capitulation. In multiplying metropolitan suburbs, patterns of residential segregation enabled school districts to fit easily within the boundaries of tract developments and thus strengthen the notion of a "neighborhood" school whose demographics raised few hackles. In older suburbs marked by race and class diversity, it required mobilizations by Black parents and their white allies to put segregated and dilapidated Black schools on the political table, much to the displeasure of white, generally well-to-do, residents. In Englewood, New Jersey, in 1962, civil-rights activist parents staged demonstrations, sit-ins, and school boycotts asking whether "the Englewood city fathers be allowed to continue to enforce apartheid in the public schools?" Few budged, either among the white homeowners or the local power structure. If anything, they dug in, joining in substantial numbers the newly created Save Our Neighborhood Schools (SONS). Only when the state commissioner of education stepped in, after months of protest, was the town school board told to desegregate.[15]

Although some civil-rights activists and even some state judges recognized that an equitable plan of desegregation would link suburban and urban school districts and reconfigure the racial compositions of schools within them (generally known as "metropolitan desegregation"), the burdens of desegregation often fell most heavily on working-class Black and white families. The results could be explosive. In Boston, where the Black population mushroomed in the two decades after the Second World War, the segregated and depleted condition of the schools in Black neighborhoods like Rox-

bury spurred a desegregation movement in the early 1960s that culminated in mass demonstrations and a Black-led boycott of Boston's
public schools in 1964. The Massachusetts legislature responded by
passing the Racial Imbalance Act in 1965 that required local school
committees to implement desegregation plans or risk losing funds
from the state.[16]

The white-dominated Boston school committee refused to com-
ply. From early on, the school committee, led by the fiery Louise
Day Hicks from the working-class neighborhood of South Boston,
rejected Black claims about the impact of de facto segregation and
refused either to carry out redistricting or build new schools on
the borders of Black and white neighborhoods. Hicks treated Black
demands, and especially the NAACP, with scorn while blaming the
problems they complained of on Black students and their families
rather than on the city's overcrowded, underfunded, segregated
schools or residential discrimination. With strong white support,
especially in the working-class districts, the Boston school committee
fended off the entreaties of the state until 1974, when federal district
judge W. Arthur Garrity Jr. pronounced the committee guilty of supporting a segregated school system and ordered the implementation
of a state-devised busing plan. It would involve between 17,000 and
18,000 Boston students and pair Roxbury and South Boston. Derisively termed the "Harvard Plan for the working class," the busing
plan provoked a notorious convulsion.[17]

Much has been written about that convulsion and the strident
anti-busing campaign led in good part by Hicks. It involved several
years of boycotts, racial violence, threats, and harassment that drew
heavily on more than a decade of growing hostility toward Blacks and
the "ghetto culture" they were thought to embody. This was a racism
that knew no class bounds but festered in neighborhoods like South
Boston (called "Southie"), whose residents lacked the resources to
follow middle-class whites out to the suburbs or to private schools
not subject to state jurisdiction. Yet it is also important to recognize
how anti-busers articulated their resistance. Hicks, one of a number
of women who played a prominent role in the pushback—a pattern
common to such movements in other cities—quickly fashioned a

name for the anti-busing group she led after the Garrity decision: she called it ROAR or Restore Our Alienated Rights.[18]

Neither Hicks nor her followers needed to be tutored as to what those "alienated rights" were. Like opponents of open housing, they rejected ideas about rights that could be carried by individuals and families wherever they traveled, rights that might be regarded as natural or at least conferred and protected by the state. Instead, they understood those rights as growing, cultivated, and defended in a community setting—whether the community was spatial, ethnic, racial, spiritual, or class—one built around notions of belonging and non-belonging, admission and expulsion, and especially around notions of local control and generational authority. The "alienated right" most heralded was that of choosing where children would go to school, the parental rights over the lives and educations of their children: a perspective easily attached to an array of school-related controversies, as recent complaints about curricula and the holdings of school libraries reveal.

Community control was not just a goal of aggrieved white people, whether working or middle class; it could also be regarded as a touchstone of security and welfare for Blacks and other minorities of color. Although the *Brown* decision was widely celebrated among African Americans, more than a few were apprehensive. Owing to the repressive strictures of Jim Crow, denying them admittance to schools with white students, they had spent decades building their own schools, their own corps of teachers, their own related community institutions, their own commitments to their students. What would happen now that separate schooling was deemed unconstitutional? What would happen to their towns and neighborhoods, the men and women who taught in those schools, and the students who could succeed there despite the poor resources available, the students who might be treated with racist contempt in a classroom with a white teacher?[19]

The idea of community control could also be embraced and demanded by Black activists in the wake of losing fights for desegregation. New York City proved to be an especially explosive battleground owing to well-entrenched patterns of residential segregation, the poor quality of schools in minority neighborhoods, and dissatis-faction with busing as a method of integration and reform. In 1968, a newly elected school board in Brooklyn's Black and Puerto Rican Ocean Hill-Brownsville neighborhood sought to avail itself of a pilot community schools program and strongly tethered threads of self-governance and popular nationalisms, by reassigning nineteen white teachers and administrators for underperformance: an assertion of authority over hiring, firing, and budget decisions. Objecting to the recircuiting of contract negotiations and what it regarded as union-busting, New York's powerful United Federation of Teachers called a massive strike in protest that involved over 50,000 teachers citywide. Eventually, an arrangement that toed the line between centralized decision-making and community control was put in place, one that effectively reinforced segregated schooling while stirring even deeper racial suspicions and hostilities. White families continued to head to the suburbs, further undermining the city's tax base and setting the stage for near bankruptcy and austerity a few years later.[20]

III

IN THE SPRING OF 1975, around fifty women from ROAR made their way to downtown Boston's famed Faneuil Hall where a rally in support of the Equal Rights Amendment, recently passed by Con-gress and moving through the states for possible ratification, was to take place. The rally never even started. The ROAR women shouted out against the ERA and would not allow any of the ERA's support-ers to speak. Instead, one of the ROAR leaders, Elvira "Pixie" Pal-ladino, read a statement excoriating the ERA as unrepresentative of Boston mothers and demanding a forum for women who opposed busing. Only a month before, about twelve hundred ROAR members had marched in the pouring rain of Washington, D.C., to call for a constitutional amendment of their own, one that would end court-ordered busing to achieve the racial integration of schools. "You're *our* guests, this is *our City* Hall," Palladino told an ERA rally organizer who asked them to leave. "No bunch of ladies from the suburbs is going to kick the women of Boston out of their own City Hall."[21]

For the ROAR women and many of the white working-class mothers of South Boston, the feminist demands that went into the making of the ERA were not entirely objectionable. With experience in the workforce and the multiple pressures of family life, they approved the idea of equal pay in the workplace, more available childcare, greater economic opportunities, and sharing household tasks with their husbands. Yet, as was the case with busing, they also regarded feminism and the ERA as products of class privilege and threats to the family and gender relations that offered the security and personal rewards they valued. Although the best-known narratives of the 1960s and early 1970s focus on the emergence of liberation movements and expanding rights demands, the episode in Boston and the subsequent defeat of the ERA demonstrate that opposition to feminism and the new forms of sexual expression it often heralded had been taking shape during the 1950s and 1960s and was ready for a showdown that could be won.[22]

It would have been hard to fathom the perils facing the ERA in June 1972 when the House and Senate passed the amendment and, within months, thirty states (thirty-eight states were required) had ratified it. Only a handful of opposition votes were registered in either house of Congress, and the leadership of both the Republican and Democratic parties was quick to offer their endorsement. So widespread was the embrace of the ERA that George Wallace and Strom Thurmond could be counted among the ranks of supporters, at least for a time. Support for an Equal Rights Amendment had, in fact, been part of the Republican and Democratic national platforms since the 1940s, and in 1960 Richard Nixon backed it with a written statement. The political momentum generated by the civil rights movement appeared to have put the wind at the backs of ERA advocates, and the spare language of the amendment itself, reminiscent of the Fifteenth Amendment on the right to vote, seemed relatively uncontroversial: "Equality of rights before the law shall not be denied or abridged by the United States or by any state on account of sex."[23]

Popular opposition to the ERA mainly flew under the radar of public discussion until congressional passage seemed imminent and, especially, in the months that followed. Before long, the momentum toward ratification began to shift again, and one of those most responsible for the shifting was a conservative Republican named Phyllis Schlafly. In early 1972, she wrote an essay entitled "What's Wrong with Women's Rights" for her monthly newsletter, the *Phyllis Schlafly Report,* and between July and September laid the groundwork for what she called a STOP (Stop Taking Our Privileges) ERA movement. Initially drawing upon networks of conservative women she had constructed through her involvement with the National Federation of Republican Women, Schlafly quickly gave the organization a national presence. By early 1973, STOP ERA could boast chapters in more than half of the states, with special strength in those that would be crucial to ratification. The impact was startling. The ratification process began to slow and then ground to a halt, with thirty-five states having ratified. Six states that had ratified the ERA turned around and voted to rescind their ratifications, a constitutionally dubious move but an indication of where things were headed. The amendment failed.[24]

Schlafly is so closely associated with the movement against the ERA and feminism more generally that it may be surprising to discover how late she came to the campaign. Born and raised in a conservative, Catholic family in St. Louis, Schlafly was energized by her work as a young researcher for the American Enterprise Institute and drawn to the Taft wing of the Republican Party with its deep suspicions of internationalists like Dwight Eisenhower. Schlafly made an unsuccessful run for Congress in the early 1950s and again in the late 1960s, but her activism focused chiefly on anti-communism and national defense. Like others on the Republican right, she believed the Cold War could be won, Soviet communism represented godless collectivism, and a strong defense was necessary to prevail. Few women or men were as conversant with the details of national defense, particularly strategic nuclear policy, as she (she coauthored three books on the subject) and, like many conservatives, Schlafly thrilled to the campaign of Barry Goldwater in 1964. Indeed, she wrote *A Choice*

Not an Echo, a blistering critique of the liberally inclined eastern establishment of the Republican Party—she called them the "secret kingmakers"—as part of a ringing endorsement of Goldwater. Over three million copies of the book were sold, and she was credited with helping Goldwater win the Republican nomination.[25]

Goldwater's resounding defeat in 1964 did not discourage Schlafly's belief that conservatism could find a winning base in the United States, but she devoted much of her time in the 1960s to writing and speaking on national defense, attacking liberal Democrats' conciliatory stance toward the Soviet Union ("the Democratic party has become the party of traitors," she railed), and supporting Richard Nixon's run for the presidency in 1968, even though she had serious doubts about his conservatism. As late as December 1971, Schlafly showed little interest in either feminism or the ERA, little interest in social issues more generally, but when she was invited to speak about the ERA by some conservatives in Connecticut (she preferred to speak on national defense), she read the material sent her and the light of activism switched on.[26]

STOP ERA served as a magnet for women who had already been involved with right-wing organizations in the 1960s. Many were, or had been, members of the John Birch Society, founded in 1958, whose vehement anti-communism traded in the conspiratorial thinking that Joseph McCarthy had previously made notorious. Even William Buckley of the conservative *National Review* denounced the Birchers "as far removed from common sense" (Robert Welch, the group's leader, had argued that President Dwight Eisenhower was a communist agent). Although it is not clear if Schlafly and her husband Fred ever joined, the Birch Society supported the Goldwater campaign, regarded the civil rights movement as a communist front, and opposed the Equal Rights Amendment. Experienced activists who gravitated to STOP ERA also came from a Birch Society–inflected organization established in Mississippi in 1962 in the face of James Meredith's integration of the state university: Women for Constitutional Government, which wrapped itself in Christian faith, free enterprise, and racial self-respect, urging white women to help preserve the good life for their children. But most characteristic of

STOP ERA activists and supporters was church membership. The Church of Christ stood out for its disproportionate influence, though opponents of the ERA came from a broad spectrum of religious denominations, including Southern Baptists, Mormons, Orthodox Jews, and Roman Catholics. The rise of sixties conservatism, driven by anti-communism and the defense of traditional families and communities, began a rapprochement between evangelical Protestants and Catholics that tempered the anti-Catholicism so central for so long to American political culture.[27]

A growing anti-abortion movement dovetailed with STOP ERA while cementing the alliance between evangelical Protestants and conservative Catholics. During the early 1960s, issues surrounding contraception and abortion elicited an assortment of views from denominational leaders, and few, save for Catholics, had clear positions on either. Some prominent clerics neither opposed the within-marriage sexuality that the newly available birth-control pill made possible nor the use of abortion before the second trimester. Conferences of theologians formally debated the point at which a fetus gained God's protection in ways that did not put all abortions into their crosshairs. It was rather in response to the success of state-level legalizations of abortion that an anti-abortion movement took shape, though at first, as might be expected, the energy came mainly from the Catholic Church. Then, in 1973, the Supreme Court's decision in *Roe* v. *Wade*, lending constitutional sanction based on a right to privacy, lit the fire for what became a large movement describing itself as "pro-life."[28]

Like the ERA, the question of abortion tapped into developing concerns about the liberalizing trends of the sixties and a sense of moral decline that seemed to be the result. Especially among Catholics, abortion raised searing personal issues about faith and the nature of life itself. Yet what linked the two movements was a belief that both the ERA and legalized abortion privileged the impulses and desires of individuals, particularly individual women, and represented frontal attacks on traditional families, family life, and the gender relations so integral to them. Both the ERA and abortion, opponents insisted, mocked childbirth and motherhood and thereby struck at the foundation of family structure and authority. Phyllis Schlafly's "What's Wrong with Women's Rights?" started by celebrating the many "privileges" American women already possessed and the "honored status" they occupied. She then charged "women's libbers" with "break[ing] the barriers of the Ten Commandments and the family," and "waging a total assault on marriage, on the family, and on children." "Why would women want more rights and privileges than they already have?" she asked, explaining that women in America "never had it so good" owing to the prosperity brought by the "free enterprise system" and the "financial benefits of chivalry." But Schlafly's most telling points came when she spoke of the "good fortune" women have to live in a world "which respects the *family* as the basic unit of society . . . ingrained in the laws and customs of our Judeo-Christian civilization." Not the individual, as liberalism understood rights-bearing, but the family with its hierarchies, mutual dependencies and obligations, clear roles as to gender and age, and truncated forms of power and responsibility. An illiberal patriarchalism resided at the heart of the society that Schlafly and her ardent supporters wished to defend. "Our respect for the family as the basic unit of society," she insisted, "is the single greatest achievement in the entire history of women's rights. It assures women of the most precious right of all—the right to keep her baby and be supported and protected in the enjoyment of watching her baby grow and develop."[29]

IV

IT IS COMMONPLACE TO REGARD the movements against the ERA and abortion rights as responses to the libertinism and new rights' demands of the 1960s, as backlashes that would gain wider traction owing to the economic crises of the 1970s and the failure of liberal Democrats, while preparing the way for the conservative ascendancy in American political life during the 1980s. There is, of course, more than a little truth to this. Yet such a perspective ignores how the 1950s and 1960s saw the growth of illiberal and radical right-wing ideas and activism in a variety of forms that fed much that was to follow. Here, deeply rooted threads of anti-communism, anti-statism, vigilantism, localism, and racism were strengthened by a newly politicized Protestant evangelicalism. From the outside looking in, Barry Goldwater's crushing defeat in 1964 reinforced the hegemony of modern liberalism and what some call the "New Deal Order"; from the inside looking out, Goldwater's nomination, whatever the general election results, marked one of the first victories of the illiberal right. Contrary to the political epitaph Richard Hofstadter pronounced, it would not be the last.[30]

The political right of the 1950s and 1960s found bases of support in the newly emerging American "Sunbelt," and, especially, in the fast-growing suburbs of the Southwest and southern Pacific coast. Stretching from North Carolina in the east through Texas and Arizona in the southwest, to southern California, this cultural and political belt was, ironically, produced by the policies of the federal government beginning with the New Deal of the 1930s, the military mobilizations of the Second World War, and then the defense industries and their affiliates of the Cold War. Engineers, technocrats, professionals, and small- to mid-size manufacturers and their families, nearly all of whom were white and Protestant, often became eager recruits to anti-communism and strident opponents of the visions of collectivism that communism, socialism, and even modern liberalism seemed to embody. As dependent as they were on the defense spending of the federal government and the benefits of homeowning that federal programs encouraged, they celebrated individual liberties (though not necessarily rights-bearing), free enterprise, and the local control of social and political life. By the early 1960s, many also gravitated to evangelical churches that harked back to the worlds of the small-town and rural South and Midwest (whence many came to the Southwest and West after the war) and adapted themselves quite well to a more modern, privatized, consumer-oriented way of life they came to embrace.[31]

Southern California, and particularly Orange County, was emblematic of the social and political forces at play. A fairly sleepy agricultural district before 1940, the population of the county boomed nearly sixfold during the next two decades, fed by migrants from the near South (Texas, Louisiana, and Arkansas) and the country's mid-section, most searching for the middle-class lives that homeowner-ship and good jobs made possible. Nearly three-quarters of county residents would find homes in exploding tract developments, while military bases and defense-related industries like electronics offered economic fuel and white-collar employment. And although many came from families who had once supported Franklin Roosevelt and the New Deal, their political sensibilities either were veering right or vulnerable to right-wing perspectives.

A confluence of events and institutions aided the rightward grav-itational pull. In 1961, Australian-born physician Fred Schwarz, who had launched a Christian Anti-Communist Crusade out of neigh-boring Long Beach, brought his "School of Anti-Communism" to Orange County for a five-day teach-in of sorts. It drew an audience of about seven thousand, many of school age. Schwarz left behind an Orange County School of Anti-Communism, supported by some of the county's men of wealth as well as by many of the public schools, part of a larger grassroots effort to contest what was seen as the liberal influence in education that threatened the "traditional American way of life." Men like Walter Knott, of Knott's Berry Farm fame, were especially important in driving the county's right-wing conservatism. He was aided by the work of local Baptist churches and the Orange County *Register*, the long-established newspaper well known for its anti-communism and general right-wing dispensation.[32]

One of the connecting tissues of developing right-wing activism, not only in southern California but in the Sunbelt more widely (and beyond), was the John Birch Society (JBS), commonly dismissed, by traditional conservatives like William Buckley as well as others, as a fringe extremist group. Yet the Society was one of the few organiza-tions to bridge both regional and ideological fractures on the right while providing a decentralized structure of belonging that gave local supporters a good deal of autonomy. Circulating the Birch Society *Bulletin* and founder Robert Welch's *American Opinion* magazine, estab-lishing chapters through the efforts of regional coordinators, and inviting correspondence through a "monthly messages department," Welch's Society warned of the dangers of communism, the tyranny of the state, and the inability of established political institutions to combat either, while crowing about free enterprise and the traditional family. In so doing, the JBS found common ground with right-wing organizations across a wide spectrum and lured more moderate conservatives worried about the changing political and cultural environment. The Birch Society was at the center of an intermixing brew of right-wing activity ranging from the Citizens Councils in the South, the Conservative Society of America (not by accident, the CSA, from the Civil War–era Confederate States of America), and Billy Hargis's Christian Crusade to Fred Schwarz's Schools of Anti-Communism and the campaigns for Barry Goldwater in 1960 and 1964.[33]

Estimates as to the membership of the Birch Society in the early 1960s vary from about 50,000 to 100,000, but there is little doubt that chapters spread out across the West and Texas. In Orange County alone, the Birch Society claimed thirty-eight chapters, and in the state of California as a whole it could claim around three hundred. There and elsewhere, the Society opened at least one hundred bookstores and succeeded in attracting about 27,000 paid subscribers for its *American Opinion* magazine. Although the Birch Society did not make formal political endorsements, it did attempt to generate broad campaigns, such as the one to impeach Supreme Court Chief Justice Earl Warren, a bane of the right given *Brown* v. *Board* and other rights-expanding jurisprudential decisions on his watch, while members gravitated to political campaigns like Goldwater's. Most commonly, chapters looked primarily to local issues and institutions, running slates of candidates for school boards to influence curricula and teacher hiring, or boycotting a newspaper or radio station deemed too liberal. The hope, according to the Society's "Leader's Manual," was to "provide our members with the opportunity to see tangible results of their efforts which can be a powerful factor in keeping the morale and spirit de corps of the chapters at a high pitch."[34]

Whatever the size and scale of the Birch Society, the membership hardly fit the description of those at the margins of American life, of "crackpots" as they were usually termed. They were white, from the middle and upper class, Republican, and a mix of Protestants and Catholics. They tended to live in less densely populated areas and in smaller communities than many other Americans, and, among the one-third who attended college, few went to elite institutions. Most who matriculated majored in engineering or business. One survey found the "typical" member to be a forty-one-year-old male, but women did more than play important roles in local chapters; they often brought their husbands in, much as was true among evangelical churches. "When Welch travels on speaking tours," two observers recorded, "he draws large audiences, most of them middle-aged and from the upper middle class. They are not unemployed malcontents or crackpots; they are patient and enthusiastic men and women, willing to wait on a line, four abreast, for an hour, to buy tickets to hear him." Reporters who interviewed them said that "many speak like educated people," and "from their dress and social poise most of them seem economically well off."[35]

The Birch Society's obsession with the threat of communism was shared by the Young Americans for Freedom (YAF), organized in 1960, well before the leftist Students for a Democratic Society (SDS), with which it is often compared. Stimulated by the anti-communism of the 1950s, the appearance of William Buckley's *National Review* (1955), the Goldwater campaign drive in 1960, and agitation for loyalty oaths, a group of 120 met at Buckley's Connecticut estate in September 1960. There they established YAF and issued the "Sharon Statement" (for Sharon, Connecticut, where Buckley's estate was located) outlining its principles and objectives. Like the "Port Huron Statement" of SDS two years later, the Sharon Statement began by declaring that the country faced a "moral and political crisis" requiring the energized activism of the "youth of America." Then it quickly veered in an ideological direction quite foreign to SDS. Attempting to encompass the traditionalist and libertarian strains of American conservatism, the statement "affirm[ed] certain eternal truths," which included "the individual's use of his God-given free will." Political freedom, the statement trumpeted, "cannot long exist without economic freedom," and the "purposes of government are to protect these freedoms through the preservation of internal order, the provision of national defense, and the administration of justice." The Constitution's chief role, according to the statement, was to restrain the

"concentration and abuse of power" and "reserve primacy to the several states, or to the people." But if this appeared just another declaration in support of state rights, the statement went on to proclaim that
"the forces of international Communism are, at present, the greatest
threat to these liberties," and the "United States should stress victory
over, rather than coexistence with, this menace": a dramatic call for
the empowerment of the federal government to establish a certain
type of international order.[36]

The Sharon Statement, quite brief in form and substance, made no
mention of rights-bearing beyond individual "liberty." There was nothing on popular participation in politics and decision-making, democracy, due process and the equal protection of the laws, or the issues
raised by a civil rights movement—which advanced a very different idea
of "freedom"—that just months before had challenged the segregated
lunch counters at Woolworth's department store in Greensboro, North
Carolina. M. Stanton Evans, who drafted the statement, suggested why
that may have been. "The conservative," he wrote at the time, "believes
ours is a God-centered, and therefore an ordered universe; that man's
purpose is to shape his life to the patterns of order preceding from the
Divine center of life; and that in seeking this objective, man is ham-
pered by fallible intellect." It was a view closely matching Russell Kirk's
The Conservative Mind (1953), which emphasized not only divine intent
but also the need for order and constraint, the importance of property
as a foundation of freedom, and opposition to "equalitarianism."[37]

Yet however much their ideology looked back to a more ordered
and hierarchical world, one in which the only universal was submission to God, YAF and its followers had no shortage of idealism and
determination to achieve power. They quickly launched a monthly
called *The New Guard*, established YAF chapters on college campuses across the country, and began to raise money from conservative sources to finance their operations. Although operating with a
top-down hierarchy for the conduct of policy and related business,
YAFers nonetheless saw themselves as rebels. "My parents thought
Franklin D. Roosevelt was one of the greatest heroes who ever lived,"
YAF chairman Robert Schuchman told *Time* magazine in 1961. "I'm
rebelling against that concept." Tom Hayden, then a student at the

University of Michigan, recognized what was afoot among the "new conservatives" a year before he drafted the SDS founding Port Huron Statement. He warned those on the left that the new conservatives "are not disinterested kids who maintain the status quo by political immobility. . . . They form a bloc. They are unashamed, bold, and articulately enamored of certain doctrines: the sovereignty of individual self-interest; extremely limited government; a free market economy; victory over, rather than coexistence with, the Communists." "What is new about the new conservatives," Hayden observed, "is their militant mood, their appearance on picket lines." More than a few of the YAF leaders—not only Evans but Pat Buchanan, Richard Viguerie, Dana Rohrabacher, Terry Dolan, Richard Allen, Howard Phillips, and Paul Weyrich, among others—would go on to play important roles in the Nixon and Reagan administrations, as well as in the founding of Jerry Falwell's "Moral Majority" (1979) and the Conservative Caucus.[38]

Regarding itself as an umbrella organization of the right, Young Americans for Freedom faced an assortment of challenges, especially from the John Birch Society. Although favoring free enterprise, individualism, limited government, and anti-communism, the Birchers had a well-deserved reputation for extremist views that frightened many in established Republican circles. Early on, the problem surfaced when YAF lent support to John Rousselot, a Republican congressman from East Los Angeles. Known for his easy equation of liberalism with socialism and militant anti-communism, Rousselot was also a member of the Birch Society and never disavowed either the racial segregationism or the conspiracies about left-wing subversion that Birchers widely accepted. The leadership of YAF was closely aligned with the Goldwater wing of the Republican Party and Goldwater's rightist ideas. But YAF also had Birch Society sympathizers who hoped to play a more consequential role, together with some in the moderate, internationalist Nelson Rockefeller wing, whose allegiance would be crucial in presenting conservatism to college-age students and young adults. William Rusher of the *National Review*, the publication closest to YAF, recognized the political dilemma. On the one hand, like Buckley, Rusher feared association with the Birch Society and thought those concerns should be made public. On the other hand, an "injudicious editorial . . . dissociating *NR* from Welch" risked alienating the very grassroots forces necessary for the right to win power. "The great bulk of our readership, of our support, and of the warm bodies available to us to lead in any desired direction," Rusher revealingly told his *National Review* colleagues in the spring of 1961, "lies in the more or less organized Right, and large segments of that Right are more simplistic than we are, or that we can perhaps in time bring them to be, and also far more closely tied to the John Birch Society than we are."[39]

Rusher knew of what he spoke. Democrat John F. Kennedy's inauguration as president in 1961 led to a great upsurge in Birch Society membership, and by the end of the year former Democratic senator Herbert Lehman of New York could ring alarm bells about the more than two thousand rightist groups in the country with as many as eight million members, perhaps sixty thousand of whom were to be found in the Birch Society. In places like the Texas panhandle, the Birch Society not only grew but quickly gave decisive shape to local politics. Birchers set their sights on the Parent-Teacher Associations and the local school boards, focused as they were on the educational values to which their children were exposed. They then threw strong support to the senatorial campaign of John Tower, Lyndon Johnson's replacement (when he became Kennedy's vice-president) and the first Republican to represent a southern state in Congress since 1913. They appreciated Tower's commitment to individual freedom, entrepreneurial capitalism, and traditional "community" values, commitments they also saw in Barry Goldwater in 1964.[40]

Among the many rightist groups to form in the early sixties were small-scale militias, some predicting a communist takeover of the United States in the near future and vowing armed resistance. One of these, the Minutemen, founded in 1961, was especially active in southern California though its leader claimed to have done organizing work in a number of cities on the East Coast and in the Midwest. Along with printing and circulating literature denouncing both communism and the United States government, they formed small cells, each with a good deal of autonomy, and advocated the paramilitary weapons training and the survivalism thought necessary in the event of communist-inspired domestic tyranny. On occasion, individual cells also plotted or carried out bombings against supposed communist targets. Not surprisingly, Minuteman founder Robert DePugh initially joined the Birch Society to express his interests in unfettered capitalism, nationalism, and Christian heritage but soon left the organization complaining that little was done to advance these goals. Still, DePugh and the Minutemen did not entirely sever their connections with electoral politics. They enthusiastically backed Goldwater in 1964 and then, in 1966, with four hundred supporters in attendance, established what DePugh called the Patriotic Party. The next year, at a meeting in Kansas City with nearly the same number of delegates, the party nominated George Wallace for the presidency.[41]

V

PLANS FOR ANOTHER WALLACE presidential run were already underway. In early 1967, about two dozen of his supporters gathered at the Woodley Country Club in Montgomery, Alabama, to plot out a strategy. They included members of the Klan, the White Citizen's Council, and other ardent segregationists from the Deep South, together with representatives of far-right groups such as Schwarz's Christian Anti-Communist Crusade, evangelist Hargis's Christian Crusade, and the Birch Society. This time, Wallace would not seek the nomination of either the Democratic or Republican Party but rather head up the newly formed American Independent Party, hoping to win enough popular and electoral votes to throw the 1968 election into the House of Representatives, where he might either prevail or become something of a "king maker."[42]

The presence of delegates from Schwarz's and Hargis's organizations suggests the growing importance of Christian fundamentalism to the politics of the far right. Well before the rise of Jerry Falwell's Moral Majority in the late 1970s, fundamentalists and their churches began moving from the sidelines of politics and political engagement into association with conservatives on the right who shared their concerns about the threat of communism and the interference of the liberal state, all the more so after the Supreme Court ruled, in *Engel v. Vitale* (1962), that school prayer violated the establishment clause of the First Amendment. Indeed, anti-communism, and the related critique of modern liberalism, helped evangelicals celebrate free enterprise and local control as necessary alternatives to the tyranny of the godless state. Often from the Southeast or the near-south of Texas, Oklahoma, Louisiana, and Arkansas, the evangelical pastors either found their way to the West Coast, as did many thousands of migrants and members of their congregations, or set up in parts of the booming Sunbelt. They soon developed or availed themselves of a rapidly expanding network of evangelical colleges, publishing houses, and especially radio and television outlets to spread their messages, raise money, and win a growing audience. For Wallace, who had been interested in Billy Hargis since the mid-1960s, the fundamentalist movement offered occasional appearances on their broadcasts and help in constructing his own direct-mail fund-raising program. Themes of the religious right soon found their way into Wallace's speeches attacking liberal "elites" and defending American traditions and values, elaborating on the issue of school prayer he had invoked back during the 1964 Democratic primaries.[43]

Wallace needed all the help he could get. The American Independent Party was a new creation without any sort of grassroots operation, and the first and largest task was simply to get on the ballot in all fifty states. It was not easy. Requirements to qualify for the ballot varied enormously across the country: from a few hundred signatures in Colorado, to nearly seventy thousand in California, to about half a million in Ohio; in some states the signatures needed to be collected and validated months before the election itself. Right-wing media, evangelical and otherwise, played a role in getting Wallace's message out, and Wallace traveled extensively, especially in California, holding rallies at stockcar tracks, high school football stadiums, fraternal societies, American Legion posts, and drag-racing strips, sometimes fronted by local country music bands. But it was local organizers and activists, many from the Birch Society, who did the hard work on the ground. Quite remarkably, and as an indication of how widespread and committed the radical right had become, Wallace's American Independent Party made it onto the ballot in every state, and, by one estimate, gathered well over two and a half million signatures in the process.[44]

The time seemed ripe for such a Wallace candidacy. The summer of 1967—"the long, hot summer" as some termed it—witnessed more than 150 Black uprisings across the country, with especially violent and destructive ones in New York, Newark, and Detroit. Although the Kerner Commission, established at the time by President Johnson, later concluded that the unrest was owed chiefly to economic inequality, racism, police brutality, and poor social services for communities of color, white Americans decisively rejected the assessment. Many, in fact, increasingly inclined to the hard-line views expressed not only by Wallace but also by big-city mayors like Chicago's Richard Daley and police commissioners like Philadelphia's Frank Rizzo (soon to serve as mayor there), all Democrats with substantial blue-collar and lower-middle-class white support. The next year, 1968, made 1967 appear just the warm-up. It started with the disastrous Tet offensive, which spelled the doom of American strategy in the Vietnam War. It was followed in short order by Lyndon Johnson's withdrawal from the presidential race (March), the assassinations of Martin Luther King Jr. (April) and Robert Kennedy (June), and urban rioting in the wake of the King assassination. Then came the fractured and violence-laden Democratic National Convention (August), which met in Chicago and nominated for the presidency Hubert H. Humphrey, Johnson's vice-president, who hadn't run in any of the presidential primaries during the winter and spring. Those who had backed Kennedy or Eugene McCarthy, the first insurgent in the race that forced Johnson out, fumed at the outcome. Many threatened to abstain in the fall election.[45]

No one saw the handwriting on the wall better than Richard Nixon, who had coasted to the Republican presidential nomination after nearly a decade in the political wilderness. Ever the paranoic who nonetheless prided himself on political acumen, Nixon, quickly leading in the polls by fifteen points, worried not about a Humphrey resurgence but about the threat of Wallace. Having recalibrated the language of race and honed that of local control and "law and order"—long nostrums of the Birch Society—Wallace could easily sweep the Deep South and deprive Nixon of electoral votes in a number of closely contested states in the border South and Midwest, where Wallace had previously demonstrated popular appeal. Either Humphrey might squeak through outright or, if the election was left to the House of Representatives, the substantial Democratic majority there would award it to him. Nixon, once imagining that moderate white voters in the southern suburbs would turn to him rather than a Democrat, and possibly tip the outcomes in a number of states—his "Southern Strategy"—now recognized that Wallace altered the game plan.[46]

In this case, there was little paranoic about Nixon's concern. Polling into early October showed Wallace receiving roughly 20 percent of the vote nationally together with majorities in the lower South and near pluralities in the border states of Virginia, Kentucky, and Tennessee that Eisenhower had won in 1956, first breaking into the "solid Democratic South" made by Jim Crow disfranchisement at the turn of the twentieth century. In September, *Life*, *Newsweek*, and *Time* magazines all did cover stories on Wallace, who was drawing crowds as large, and "twice as enthusiastic," as Nixon's and Humphrey's. Some in the media insisted that "not since Theodore Roosevelt's Bull Moose Party emerged in 1912 has a third party so seriously challenged the two party system." They stoked the fear of an election decided by the House for the first time since 1825.[47]

Nixon did not sit idly by. And his moves demonstrated how Wallace helped shift the Republican Party, and white ethnics who had previously voted Democratic, rightward to an extent that Goldwater's defeat in 1964 made difficult to conceive. Nixon cultivated the support of Strom Thurmond, one-time Dixiecrat and segregationist Democrat now turned Republican, in an effort to win the state of South Carolina and assure the segregationists there and elsewhere in the South that as president he would do the least possible to carry out the rulings of the federal courts or "to satisfy some professional civil-rights groups." As for the issue of "law and order," Nixon not only spoke about it almost continuously during the campaign—"the first requisite of progress is order" he told the Republican convention that nominated him—but, perhaps even more consequentially, chose for his running mate Spiro T. Agnew, Maryland's tough-minded governor. Agnew had won Nixon's notice by dressing down Baltimore's Black leaders for their silence, for "breaking and running," after destructive riots that followed King's assassination in April. "You were beguiled by the rationalization of unity," he scolded them, "you were stung by insinuations that you were Mister Charlie's boy, by epithets like Uncle Tom," and failed to condemn the "circuit-riding Hanoi-visiting . . . caterwauling, riot-inciting, burn America down type of leaders," like Stokely Carmichael and H. Rap Brown, whom Agnew blamed for the upheaval. The Black leaders promptly walked out of the meeting, currying further notoriety for Thurmond as well as Nixon.[48]

For a time, it appeared that Nixon's effort to outflank Wallace would fail. In late September and October Wallace drew crowds ranging between ten and twenty thousand at rallies in Detroit, Pittsburgh, San Diego, Phoenix, and Minneapolis. According to some reports, well over twenty thousand came to hear Wallace speak on the Boston Common, and less than two weeks before the election another twenty thousand packed into New York's Madison Square Garden, one of the largest political rallies held in the city since the 1930s (when the German Bund rallied there). In Boston, one of his supporters held a sign reading "In your heart you know George Wallace is right," a prominent slogan in Goldwater's 1964 campaign. The director of the AFL-CIO's political action committee, who hoped to give the Humphrey campaign a boost, complained of the "Wallace infection" after an internal poll suggested that one member in three and, according to the Chicago *Sun-Times*, more than four steelworkers in ten backed the Alabamian.[49]

But national polling showed slippage in support for Wallace by mid-October that continued unabated, much of it coming in the North and the border states. Wallace's selection of General Curtis LeMay as his running mate didn't help him. A hard right-winger in the Air Force, who was favorably disposed to the use of nuclear weapons—he served as the model for one of the comically noxious characters in Stanley Kubrick's film, *Dr. Strangelove or: How I Learned to Stop Worrying and Love the Bomb* (1964)—LeMay raised serious questions about Wallace's judgment and intentions when it came to the war in Vietnam. Democratic candidate Humphrey's late September decision to break with Johnson on the war—he announced that he would stop the bombing of North Vietnam—in an attempt to win back the party's antiwar wing, also changed the election's dynamic, boosting Humphrey's fortunes and closing the gap with Nixon. Even some Wallace supporters worried that voting for him would give Humphrey the presidency.[50]

When election day finally arrived, Nixon edged out Humphrey in both the popular and electoral votes, and Wallace finished a distant third. He won nearly ten million popular votes, but that was only 13.5 percent overall, well short of his polling apex, and the electoral votes of four Deep South states along with Arkansas, totaling forty-six. Despite some projections that he would emerge as the most formidable third-party or independent candidate in American presidential history, he in fact ranked third at the time and fourth to this day: bested historically by Know Nothing Millard Fillmore in 1856, Bull Moose Theodore Roosevelt in 1912, and later independent Ross Perot in 1992 (though Perot won no electoral votes and Fillmore won a mere eight). Needless to say, the election's outcome fell well below Wallace's aspirations and, until pretty late in the game, expectations. Still, Wallace did win more than 20 percent of the vote in eleven states (most of the states he lost but still received over 20 percent of the vote, were in the border South) and well over 15 percent in Kentucky. A relatively small shift in votes in Tennessee, North Carolina, Ohio, and New Jersey, moreover, might have deprived any candidate of an electoral vote majority and thrown the election into the House of Representatives.[51]

Disappointed as he was, Wallace recognized that he had tapped into a very deep well of discontent in the country and that voters responded to his critique of the liberal "intelligentsia," the counterculture, the "perverted" decisions of the Supreme Court, and the urban riot mongers. "We don't have riots in Alabama," he told one audience. "They start a riot down there, first one of 'em picks up a brick gets a bullet in the brain." Academics as well as the liberal-oriented media believed they saw this new political disposition too, and began to examine the "troubled American" and the angry and restive white working class together composing what Nixon would call the "great silent majority." And try as he might, Nixon as president could not steal back Wallace's political thunder. Successfully regaining the Alabama governorship in a divisive 1970 election campaign, Wallace again set his sights on the presidency, this time, as in 1964, as a Democrat rather than an independent or candidate of a third party. There is good evidence that he cut some sort of deal with the Nixon administration, no less worried about Wallace after 1968, which may have involved the dropping of a federal corruption investigation against his brother Gerald.[52]

Wallace was nonetheless happy to go after Nixon, and now he had an added issue to roil the Democrats and Republicans alike—busing. As he tried to cultivate an image as a supporter of "non-discrimination" in public schools and public accommodations generally, busing allowed him to harness the energy of white hostility to liberal methods of promoting social justice, which by 1972, according to polling, constituted majority opinion. Theodore H. White, who had become the establishment chronicler of presidential elections since 1960, saw the results, in his customary condescending manner, with "men in neckties and white shirts," "women in housedresses with their babies," and "old ladies with their gray hair sprayed into a blueish set" joining "gas station men" and "workers with muscular biceps" at Wallace events. In effect, busing enabled Wallace to find a clear lane among Democratic hopefuls, with cross-class appeal, while calling the Nixon administration to account, especially as to its mixed signals on school desegregation.[53]

The results were far more arresting in the spring of 1972 than they had been in the spring of 1964. In mid-March, Wallace won 42 percent of Florida's primary vote, beating out eleven other Democrats on the ballot; he was aided by a ballot referendum that called for a constitutional amendment banning busing and protecting neighborhood schools, which won the approval of 90 percent of Florida's white voters. In Wisconsin, Wallace finished second to George McGovern but ahead of both Humphrey and Edmund Muskie, who was on the 1968 ticket for vice-president and, for a time, regarded as the party's front runner. In Indiana, Wallace again ran second, this time to Humphrey, and did once more in South Dakota, where McGovern prevailed. By May, polling had Wallace in the lead for upcoming Democratic primaries in Maryland and Michigan, where labor leaders thought that he might carry nearly half of the state's union vote. "The rank and file just won't listen to us on this Wallace thing," a UAW official groused. "We just hope that they come back into the Democratic fold in November." Then, while campaigning at a small strip mall in suburban Maryland, Wallace was shot and grievously wounded by a Wisconsin man who had been stalking him, and Nixon, for months.[54]

Wallace survived the shooting and, as expected, won the Maryland and Michigan primaries. Left paralyzed from the waist down, however, he was forced to end his campaign. His consolation would be a speaking slot at the Democratic National Convention that he delivered from a wheelchair, and although he would make another primary run in 1976 and go on to serve four more terms as Alabama governor, Wallace's would-be assassin seemed to finish his career in national politics. Or maybe not. In Alabama Wallace appeared intent on making amends for his image and actions in the 1960s and 1970s. He announced that he had been born-again as a Christian and sought forgiveness, especially from Black Americans, to whom he apologized on numerous occasions beginning with an unexpected visit to Martin Luther King's Dexter Avenue Baptist Church in Montgomery in 1979.[55]

Yet Wallace's political legacy is much more profound than his losing campaigns and much more foreboding than would be recognized for decades. The harbingers were not only in Alabama or Georgia or North Carolina, or even in Wisconsin or Indiana or Maryland. They were in Michigan and New York as well, where urban as well as rural and small-town white voters, many but by no means all of them working- and lower-middle class, saw in Wallace a political figure willing to articulate their views and needs, one sensitive to their localist perspectives and fears of change, a brazen and possibly effective vehicle to challenge their perceived enemies and advance their vision for the country. In Detroit and especially in New York City, late in the campaign of 1968, thousands of supporters would wait, sometimes for two hours, to hear him speak, and then offer a "standing, screaming ovation of 20 minutes" that brought him to the front edge of the stage "at least eight times with each bow prompting increasing sound and fury." Scuffles with protesters invariably broke out, and Wallace was happy to warn his detractors about what was coming. "You better have your say now, I can tell you that," he lectured them, playing to the audience who "loved it as they do at every stop he makes," because "after November 5, you anarchists are through in this country."

The New Republic's political correspondent Richard Strout (TRB to the magazine's readers) drew a different sort of analogy for the "spectacle he encountered at [Madison Square] Garden" that "nothing had prepared him for." "There is a menace in the blood shout of the crowd," he recorded. "You feel you have known this all somewhere, never again will you read about Berlin in the 30's without remembering this wild confrontation of two irrational forces." Wallace, Strout insisted, was the "ablest demagogue of our time, with a bugle voice of venom and a gut knowledge of the prejudices" of his supporters. And although Strout did not fear that Wallace would win when the election was held, the "sympathy for him is another matter." Wallace was, as one of his discerning biographers observed, "the most influential loser in modern American politics." Little in the present day brings that judgment into dispute.[56]

Chapter Nine

NEOLIBERALS AND ILLIBERALISM

W HEN PRESIDENT BILL CLINTON SIGNED A PUNI-
tive crime bill on 13 September 1994, with uniformed police officers prominently in attendance, many in the media saw an attempt to outflank Republicans on the "law and order" issue they had long owned. Together with provisions banning assault weapons and lending increased scrutiny to domestic violence, the legislation created sixty new federal death penalty crimes, denied Pell grant support to inmates in higher education programs, encouraged the expansion of correctional facilities nationwide, and made gang membership a federal offense. It also enforced mandatory sentencing, including life imprisonment for a third violent felony conviction (a "three strikes and you're out" provision pioneered by California, New York, and Florida). But, draconian as the legislation was, Clinton hardly stood out among his Democratic colleagues in Washington. They had given him strong support in both houses of Congress and, along with Vice President Al Gore, were happily on hand at the bill signing ceremony.[1]

Clinton had been moving in this direction for more than a decade after appearing "soft on crime" cost him reelection as governor of Arkansas in 1980. Running for president in 1992, he called on Americans to unite around the crime issue and pledged to "take our neighborhoods back" in good part by "putting 100,000 new police officers on the streets." In January of that year, well before securing the Democratic nomination, he took valuable time from the campaign trail to fly back to Arkansas to sign the death warrant for an inmate who suffered from severe mental disabilities. For all intents and purposes, Democrats and Republicans were joining hands on the crime issue and only vied to prove who was tougher. Two years later, in another apparent effort to steal the Republicans' thunder, Clinton signed a welfare-reform act ending, he insisted, "welfare as we know it," by handing authority to the states, placing time limits on benefits, and requiring recipients to find work within two years.[2]

With the crime and welfare reform legislation, the Clinton administration seemed to be completing projects that the Reagan administration had begun during the 1980s with the "War on Drugs," large cuts to social welfare programs, and demeaning depictions of "welfare queens." It was a pattern to be found, as well, when it came to deregulation. Although he did not go so far as declaring government the "problem" rather than the "solution," Clinton and other Democrats, hoping to find a pathway to power, had come to believe in the liberating effects of the marketplace, especially when it involved new technologies, and the dampening effects of too much government interference. After his failure to carry through a healthcare reform package during his first year in office, Clinton, encouraged by Wall Street–connected advisors, embraced globalization internationally and deregulation domestically. He signed the North American Free Trade Agreement (NAFTA), the Telecommunications Act of 1996 (giving industry corporations the ability to consolidate control over their numerous sectors), and the Gramm-Leach Bill of 1999, which repealed the Glass-Steagall Act of New Deal vintage that had required the separation of commercial and investment banking. "Across his two terms," the historian Gary Gerstle writes, "Clinton may have done more to free markets from regulation than even Reagan himself had done."[3]

Pursuing economic deregulation while strengthening the punitive hand of the state may appear to be contradictory moves ideologically, but in truth they were very much part of a neoliberal package that the Clinton administration entrenched during the 1990s. That "package" of ideas and policy prescriptions had traveled a long and bumpy road, at times with little prospect for a serious hearing, let alone for achieving the near-hegemonic status it would come to occupy. First surfacing in central Europe (Vienna and Geneva most notably) during the 1920s and 1930s among a small group of economists and philosophers who bridled at what they regarded as the numbing, heavy-headed, state-regulated and -directed economies of the left and right, "neoliberalism" represented an effort to revive market values together with the individualism and freedoms of expression apparently tethered to them. Shortly after the Second World War, neoliberalism gained institutional expression with the founding of the Mont Pelerin Society (1947) in Switzerland, which brought together nearly forty intellectuals devoted to the cause including future luminaries and Nobel Prize winners in "economic science": Friedrich Hayek, Ludwig von Mises, Milton Friedman, Frank Knight, Karl Popper, and George Stigler.[4]

The prospects for the Mont Pelerin Society and neoliberalism more generally could not have appeared auspicious in the late 1940s and 1950s. However much the neoliberal critique may have meshed with some of the political threads of the Cold War, Keynesianism and social democratic or "third way" experiments reigned supreme on both sides of the Atlantic. If anything, the policies of the Eisenhower administration suggested that the New Deal framework of state activism in the service of economic growth and prosperity had achieved a bipartisan consensus while neoliberal perspectives—much like the classical liberal perspectives of the nineteenth century—could only be regarded as gasps from the past. Barry Goldwater's drubbing in 1964 and the ambitions of Lyndon Johnson's Great Society appeared to put any alternative to Keynesian statism to rest.

And yet, under the radar, neoliberal ideas were gaining traction both in prominent economics departments, like that at the University of Chicago, and in the growth of conservative/libertarian ideas within the Republican Party and the radical right. By the early 1970s, as declining corporate profits and fears about the future of free enterprise began to circulate among the business elite, new "think tanks" devoted to advancing neoliberalism and crafting related policies began to emerge. They included the Heritage Foundation, the Koch Foundation, the Manhattan Institute, the Cato Institute, and the Business Roundtable, not to mention the internationalist Trilateral Commission, a David Rockefeller initiative, established in 1973 to promote private enterprise and global trade.[5]

But the economic crises of the 1970s, and especially the new burdens of "stagflation," made for openings that only a few short years before seemed hard to fathom. On the one hand, it now appeared that Keynesianism as applied in earlier decades was inadequate to the economic challenges of the day, that the promises of such a statist and regulatory order were in serious doubt. On the other hand, neoliberals had a much better perch from which to argue that grinding stagflation was the logical outcome of a government-regulated economy rather than just a puzzling phenomenon. While demonizing organized labor, government overreach, and activist jurisprudence, they also touted the liberating effects of neoliberal reforms and perspectives.

By the late 1970s, the tide of economic thinking and power was already turning. The financial crisis in New York, which nearly forced the city to declare bankruptcy, discredited both the social democratic economy and generous social safety nets that had buoyed many New Yorkers since the 1930s and empowered bankers and other financial interests there who claimed to have "rescued" the city by imposing drastic austerity measures. At the same time, Jimmy Carter laced his administration with Trilateral Commission members (he was one as well) and began to move down the road of deregulation, especially in relation to the energy and transportation sectors. In Paris, the philosopher Michel Foucault could devote his "Birth of Biopolitics" lectures of 1979 in large part to "governmentality" and the genealogy of what he was already calling "neo-liberalism."[6]

The Reagan administration brought neoliberals and neoliberalism to power. Like his British counterpart Margaret Thatcher, Reagan early proved his mettle by crushing an air traffic controllers' strike (Thatcher crushed a lengthy miners' strike), and then cut personal income and capital gains taxes substantially, especially for the highest earners. He also advanced the deregulatory initiatives begun under Carter, celebrated supply-side economics, pressed for the repeal of the Federal Communications Commission's "Fairness Doctrine" (unleashing right-wing "shock jocks"), and appointed judges who took a dim view of expansive interpretations—allowing greater federal oversight—of the Constitution's "commerce clause." Although unable to make the level of cuts to social welfare and educational programs that Thatcher achieved, Reagan succeeded in stoking hostility to the public sector, the welfare services it provided, and the many people it employed, especially people of color, while championing neoliberal Reaganomics. So far-reaching did neoliberal sensibilities become during the 1980s that Mikhail Gorbachev in the Soviet Union and Deng Xiaoping in China initiated their own forms of market liberalization.[7]

Anticipated by the Carter administration but certainly accelerated by Reagan's landslide reelection in 1984, Democrats heeded the message in moving toward neoliberal principles and policy prescriptions. Led by Senators Gary Hart (CO), Paul Tsongas (MA), Bill Bradley (NJ), Al Gore (TN), and Massachusetts governor Michael Dukakis, as well as Bill Clinton, they believed that the party needed to shift to the center and embrace ideas that stepped outside the frameworks of the New Deal and Great Society. Often called "Atari Democrats" for their keen interest in the emerging hi-tech sector, they created the Democratic Leadership Council (DLC) and tasked it with refashioning the party's agenda and promoting candidates who were ready to move the party their way. The ending of the Cold War and the tottering of socialist/communist alternatives that had previously encouraged the construction of social welfare states in Europe and the United States further validated the neoliberal critique and widened the political lane for candidates like Clinton who rejected the pieties that had long been central to the Democrats' appeal. Although he initially staked his presidency on a major expansion of the social welfare system with a massive health-care reform bill (though one still based on private sector insurance), he quickly pivoted in the direction of deregulation, particularly to encourage the growing financial and tech sectors which had gained strong influence in his administration. "Not so long ago, we were all Keynesians," Lawrence Summers, one of Clinton's economic advisors, later reflected. "Equally, any honest Democrat will admit that we are now all Friedmanites."[8]

As this suggests, the ascent of neoliberal ideas was enabled, in part, by their appeal across a broad political spectrum, including to those in the United States and Europe who, during the nineteen sixties, were on the left or influenced by the counterculture. After all, neoliberalism spoke both to the emancipatory effects of an unleashed market-principled individualism and to suspicions about the intentions of the state, well cultivated by its repression of many popular movements at the time. Yet those who had embraced neoliberalism early on or found their way to it in the 1980s and 1990s were by no means libertarians or advocates of laissez-faire. Much like their nineteenth-century liberal predecessors, they understood the crucial role that the state would play in protecting the property regime and developmental ambitions of neoliberalism as well as in defending the security of the country in a globalized arena. And much like Progressive thinkers at the turn of the twentieth century, they believed decision-making was best carried out by trained experts and innovators rather than a voting public. That is to say, embedded in the neoliberal vision were reservations about political democracy and an openness to coercive, if not expulsive, measures to "ring-fence" the workings of the market economy against potential threats and enable the accumulation of capital: illiberal impulses at the heart of neoliberalism. More than almost anything else, the political economy of neoliberalism set the stage for the economic crises of the early twenty-first century and the political convulsions that followed.[9]

I

THE EXPLOSION OF MASS INCARCERATION in the United States that the Clinton administration helped to fuel coincided with the ascendancy and wide embrace of neoliberalism in many social and political quarters. It was no accident. Much like advocates of antislavery principles who promoted the penitentiary more than a century and a half before, the neoliberals of the 1980s and 1990s were quick to accept radical policing and expulsive remedies to maintain order and safeguard the relations of the free marketplace. Indeed, the role of the state, as they understood it, was precisely to protect the entrepreneurial energies and free range of capital that the neoliberal project claimed to embody. They had strong foundations on which to build.

Already in the early 1960s there was growing concern about the threats that Black populations in the country's largest cities posed for the maintenance of social peace. The Kennedy administration, under pressure from civil rights activists, saw fit to launch an attack on juvenile delinquency in the urban North, and, with the Youth Offenses Control Act (1961), developed programs to counteract the unemployment, poor housing, and inadequate education that appeared rife there despite the general prosperity in the nation as a whole. Yet the focus of concern was Black youth, and especially young Black males. And whatever the policy makers' intentions and acknowledgment of deep structural issues at play, they increasingly accepted the notion that a social and cultural pathology in Black communities, manifest in weak families and social isolation, bred criminality. To be sure, the association of Blackness with criminality has (as discussed earlier in this book) a history as long as that of the United States, and it has contributed to the unremitting repression that people of African descent have endured. But in the 1960s the notion of Black criminality so infused major urban reform initiatives that it quickly forced a retreat to the militarization of policing and eventually to preemptive measures aimed at those thought most likely to commit crimes.[10]

The confluence of political impulses, increasingly characteristic of mid-century liberalism, could be seen in how Lyndon Johnson's War on Poverty quickly morphed into his "War on Crime." Speaking to Congress in January 1964, only two months into his presidency, Johnson called for "an unconditional war on poverty" meant to "help replace despair with opportunity." He envisioned a "joint Federal-local effort to pursue poverty wherever it exists . . . not only to relieve the symptom of poverty, but to cure it and above all to prevent it." The metaphor of "war" was carefully chosen. And it was one that would be appropriated by Johnson's successors to describe the significance and formidability of the task at hand as well as the need for almost patriotic popular support that, in turn, cast the intended targets as domestic enemies. Not by coincidence did the Gulf of Tonkin Resolution and the ramping up of U.S. involvement in Vietnam's civil war occur at the same time. The early nineteen sixties initiated an era of "counterinsurgent" warfare that continues to this day and of which the mass incarceration of racial minorities is an important part.[11]

Although the idea of Black pathologies was well in place before-hand, the urban uprisings of the mid-1960s, especially the days-long rebellion in the Watts section of Los Angeles in August 1965, rein-forced it and encouraged policy makers to envision modernized policing as a critical aspect, in fact as a social service in its own right, of the War on Poverty. Even the Kerner Commission (officially the National Advisory Commission on Civil Disorders, headed by Illi-nois governor Otto Kerner), appointed by Johnson, which placed great emphasis on the structural foundations of poverty and unrest in its 1968 report, nonetheless deemed crime control in targeted Black neighborhoods as crucial to quelling the violent outbreaks that had become regular occurrences in big cities. The building blocks of what is widely called the "carceral state"—the institutions, personnel, social logic, and ideas of an expanding criminal justice system—were being put in place well before the surge of incarceration.[12]

Although it has been commonplace to blame conservatives and the Republican Party for turning law and order and retributive pun-ishment into salable political issues, there were, in truth, a number of currents at work by the mid-1980s that accounted for the wide embrace of a tough approach to crime. Interest in inmate rehabilita-tion, prison education, prisoner rights, and an end to the death penalty, which gained some public support in the 1960s (the Supreme Court briefly ruled the death penalty unconstitutional in 1972), gave way to more punitive perspectives by the mid- to late 1970s. The shift was enabled by a new attentiveness to "victims' rights" that law-and-order campaigns promoted, as well as by the women's movement's success in bringing rape and domestic violence to public consciousness—in each case fortified by the increasing association of drug abuse and criminality. New York's liberal Republican governor Nelson Rocke-feller is a good case in point. Once an advocate for rehabilitation and the expansion of social programs to combat crime, Rockefeller took a sharp right turn in 1973 by pushing through mandatory sentencing for drug possession and sale, even in small amounts. Two years earlier, he had dispensed with negotiations and ordered the violent suppres-sion of the prisoner rebellion at Attica. Plainly cultivating a "tough on crime" image to run for the presidency in 1976, he demonstrated

the ease with which those of liberal, and soon neoliberal, dispositions grasped the punitive hand of the state when disorder seemed to
intensify, how they became servants of "public opinion" when property and person appeared to be at stake. Rather than paying heed
to data that presented a complex picture of violent crime and drug
abuse rates in an effort to deter a stampede to vindictiveness, liberals
like Rockefeller found reinforcement in their assumptions about the
pathologies of the poor and the Black, and in lending priority to the
alleged victims, politically popular as it was.[13]

The Reagan administration added accelerants to the drive against
crime. The surge in crack cocaine use in targeted neighborhoods
of color, itself a manifestation of the economic devastation African
Americans and Hispanics were enduring, provided evidence and justification. Federal funds for drug enforcement grew almost tenfold,
and mandatory sentencing for drug use won overwhelming support
for national legislation. A Comprehensive Crime Control Bill in 1984,
the first major revision of the U.S. criminal code in nearly a century,
established the framework. And the media drew direct lines between
crack cocaine, the explosion of gang warfare, the increase in violent
crime, and the birth of "crack babies" whose mothers were addicts,
burdening hospitals and the welfare system. Los Angeles police chief
Daryl Gates gained notoriety when he told a U.S. Senate Judiciary
Committee hearing that even casual drug users were committing
"treason" and "ought to be taken out and shot." But support for the
drug war and the criminal crackdown included most Democrats and
many Black community leaders who worried about what was happening in their streets. Although incarceration rates began to climb
in the late 1970s and whites were using drugs in the same proportion
as Blacks, incarceration—and overwhelmingly of people of color—
began its steep climb in the mid-1980s. In the century following the
Civil War, a total of 185,000 Americans entered state and federal prisons; in just two decades after 1965 another 250,000 were added to
the prison population; and when Bill Clinton took office, the population had surpassed 1,000,000. By the time Clinton finished his two
terms, partly as a consequence of his crime bill, the number of incar-

cerated people in the United States neared 2,000,000 and was still climbing sharply.[14]

The dramatic growth of incarceration, which by the turn of the twenty-first century made the United States the world's leader both in the number of inmates and in the proportion of its total population behind bars, led to a crisis of overcrowding and calls for the building of new penitentiaries. This clearly registered in Clinton's 1994 crime bill along with increased funding at the state level, often at the cost of spending for higher education. Yet, as a measure of the neoliberal thinking involved, there was a surge in the construction and operation of private prisons—a true novelty though an example of the broader privatization of public sector responsibilities—beginning in the 1980s and continuing into the early 2000s. The logic was, of course, public expense savings in the service of detention and expulsion, which played well for lawmakers and the general public alike. The lure for investors was more limited governmental scrutiny and freer hands in modes of discipline and surveillance, not to mention healthy profits. The inmate population in private facilities, mostly likely to be found in Sunbelt states, with Texas holding a large lead over all the others, increased exponentially between 1985 and 2000, and then continued to grow until about 2012. As of 2016, privately run prisons held nearly 130,000 inmates, about 85,000 of whom were incarcerated by states rather than the federal government.[15]

Sizable as it was, the number of inmates in private facilities represented only about 9 percent of the total population of incarcerated people in the United States. Publicly run and financed penitentiaries and jails far exceeded their privatized counterparts in number and share of inmates. And enthusiasm for privatization began to wane as it became clear that costs were greater than anticipated, the finances of many facilities more precarious, and the desperate conditions inside some of them had come to public attention. Private prisons were less drivers of mass incarceration than parasites on it, feeding off its growth and doubts about the effectiveness of the public sector. But, together, the explosion of public and private incarceration symbolized the entanglement of neoliberal economic policies and illiberal solutions to the threats of racial unrest: unleashing the market on the one side and expelling those most likely to interrupt the process on the other.[16]

II

CHANGES IN URBAN POLICING were crucial to the expulsion and confinement of threatening populations. From the 1960s, and especially from the 1980s, police departments across the country began to appear and conduct operations much like the military: in their dress and armored protection, the high-grade weapons they carried, their transport vehicles, and their tactics. The relationship between police departments and the military became closer and more interdependent, stimulated by the language of warfare used to describe the challenges of domestic criminality and the international context in which it occurred.

This was very new. Historically, the police and the United States armed forces had little to do with one another. Professional police departments took shape in large American cities during the mid-nineteenth century, replacing informal night-watch patrols, and were tasked with keeping order on city streets. For a time, they were unarmed and even lacked uniforms, but quickly became part of the patronage apparatus of local political machines. Before long, city governments deployed the police to break strikes, arrest labor leaders and other "radicals," and disrupt political demonstrations, as was the case in Chicago's Haymarket in 1886. In the southern and southwestern states, policing initially took the form of slave patrols and, later, mounted units like the Texas Rangers, who played major roles in the repression of African Americans, Mexican Americans, and other immigrant groups. The enslavement of African Americans gave policing a national basis through the Fugitive Slave Acts and the federalization of slave catchers and their posses.[17]

The role of the U.S. military in policing was complex. Although focused on national defense, much of its activity through the nineteenth century was directed toward containing and suppressing domestic dissent (like strikes) and crushing rebellious Confederates in the South and Native peoples in the West. Still, the maintenance of domestic order was, for the most part, left to county or municipal police, or to the National Guard (organized in the early twentieth century), which served under the control of state governors. But the interconnections began to change in the 1960s.[18]

The urban rebellions of the decade were pivotal in convincing public officials that a new approach to policing was necessary, but their perspectives—as was true earlier in the century—were informed by developments overseas. Cold War experiences of counterinsurgency in the Third World, where police work was increasingly seen as one of the best means of defeating "communist subversion," proved especially influential. The Office of Public Safety (OPS), created in 1962 as part of the U.S. Agency for International Development, helped train police forces in nearly eighty countries over the following decade. Testifying before the Kerner Commission in 1967, OPS director Byron Engle spoke of the Cold War lessons that could serve domestic purposes. "The Communists have had long experience in utilizing disturbances, riots, terrorism, as political action tools," he told them, and "we have put a lot of emphasis on non-lethal riot control. We have found there are many principles and concepts which apply, whether it is Asia, Africa, or South America," adding that "those same principles would apply in the United States." The Safe Streets Act, passed the next year as part of Johnson's crime war, allocated more than $20 million to programs aimed at modernizing police departments through riot-control training and the use of military-grade weaponry (AR-15s and M4 carbines), steel helmets, batons, masks, armored vehicles, and tear gas.[19]

Some of this was already underway when, in 1964, the Philadelphia police department established a Special Weapons and Tactics (SWAT) team. Soon picked up in Daryl Gates's Los Angeles and eventually by other cities, SWAT was commonly viewed as an "urban counterinsurgency bulwark." By the mid-1980s, as part of funding for the Reagan-declared "drug war," almost every city in the country with a population over 100,000 had a SWAT team, while smaller cities looked for ways to establish them. Indeed, the militarized, coun-

terinsurgency dimensions of SWAT became something of a model
for many police forces in general, and one that both Republicans and
Democrats had little problem encouraging. In 1981, Reagan won congressional approval for a Military Cooperation and Enforcement Act
that permitted the armed forces of the United States to give police
departments access both to its bases and military equipment, part
of a larger framework of assistance. The following year, a Reagan-
sponsored crime bill, which Democratic senator Joe Biden criticized as
too lenient, especially on drug-related crime, passed the Democratic-
controlled Senate by a vote of 95–1. Four years later, when he signed
National Security Directive 221 declaring illegal drugs a threat to the
country's security, Reagan involved the CIA and State Department
and ordered the U.S. military to aid law enforcement agencies "in
the planning and execution of large counter-narcotics operations." In
1987, a like-minded Congress then alerted police forces to the availability of surplus military equipment. All along, talk circulated of setting up detention centers for drug offenders or sending them into
exile—an internationalization of expulsion not seen since the colonization movement of the antebellum and Civil War eras. Even so,
politicians from both parties continued to complain that the federal
drug war was "lackadaisical" or ineffective.[20]

Although some in the drug reform community hoped that Bill
Clinton's election to the presidency would turn federal drug policy
in a less aggressive and militaristic direction—he was, after all, an
admitted drug user—this was not to be. Clinton inherited not only
the wide use of no-knock search warrants, which were routinely
endorsed, often with little scrutiny, by district attorneys and judges if
they involved drugs, but also the deployment of the National Guard
for antidrug surveillance and to assist in local drug raids. "When you
have the equipment and trained personnel," a Massachusetts Democrat on the congressional Armed Services Committee maintained,
"you might as well put them to work." In 1992, the Guard took part
in almost 20,000 arrests nationwide and conducted thousands of
searches without warrants. Once in office, the Clinton administration had the Justice and Defense Departments enter into technology-
sharing agreements. Attorney General Janet Reno explained the

logic. "So let me welcome you to the kind of war the police fight every day," she told one group of defense and intelligence specialists. "And let me challenge you to turn your skills that served us so well in the Cold War to help us with the war we're now fighting daily in the streets of our towns and cities across the nation." To better wage that war, Congress passed and Clinton signed the National Defense Authorization Security Act (1997) which, as journalist Radley Balko put it, "further grease[d] the pipeline through which hardcore military gear flows to civilian police agencies." As a result, nearly $750 million worth of equipment was doled out by the turn of the twenty-first century, including 253 aircraft (Black Hawk helicopters among them), 7,856 M-16 rifles, 181 grenade launchers, 8,131 bulletproof helmets, and 1,161 pairs of night-vision googles.[21]

Much as he prided himself on his admiration for civil rights leaders and ease with Black audiences, Clinton had little patience for the most vulnerable among them when it came to drugs. His zero-tolerance approach extended well beyond sentencing. Residents of federally funded public housing—chiefly African Americans and other poor people of color—faced eviction for any violent or drug-related crimes they committed there, whether or not they were household members: a "one strike and you're out" policy that could expel entire families even for the offenses of a guest. Even Clinton's efforts to promote a Community Oriented Police Services (COPS) program with more than a billion dollars in grant money—which Barack Obama eagerly brought back to life after the Bush administration phased it out—ended up pumping more money into the prevailing system. For the most part, the grants were used to hire more police officers and to start up and fund new SWAT teams.[22]

The criminal justice system reflected neoliberal perspectives on public policy in other ways as well, some insufficiently grasped. Court fines and fees have long been part of the system both to offer an alternative to incarceration (or a burden added to incarceration) and to discourage frivolous prosecutions, since the losing side would have to pay the court for its services. But since the 1980s, and especially since the Great Recession of 2007–2009, a new chain of punishment has come into use. With county and municipal budgets under growing strain, all the more so as the war on drugs swamped court dockets, and with politicians reluctant or unable to raise taxes, the imposition of an assortment of fees on those accused or convicted of crimes has offered a solution, especially in smaller towns and rural counties. Those fees are not just for "court costs"; they are known as "board bills" or "pay-to-stay" bills that charge people for the time they serve, often beginning with arrests if the accused lack the resources to make bail and have to suffer incarceration until trial—even in cases of petty theft or other misdemeanors. In some places the daily rate is low; in Rapid City, South Dakota, it has been $6 per day. But in other places, like Riverside, California, the rate can be near $150 per day. "Over time," a former judge recognized, "lawmakers started to use the courts as piggy banks."

User fees such as "pay-to-stay" are not waived upon release. They have to be paid, and either they leave a former inmate with long-term debt or can result in reincarceration if the former inmate effectively defaults. Most of the men and women who find their way into the court system are poor, and nearly eight in ten have committed misdemeanors and other small crimes. Court and jail-time fees not only require payment but usually force the offender to show up in court every month regardless of other obligations, including a job. The disproportions can be staggering. Brooke Bergen, a poor white single mother, spent a year in rural Missouri's Dent County jail for shoplifting $8 worth of mascara from a local Walmart. Her bill for occupying the mold-infested jail cell was $15,900, which she was attempting to pay back as best as she could, hoping to scrape together $100 each month (at that rate it would take her thirteen years). Her probation was then supervised by a private company (a common phenomenon) that, among other things, administered regular drug tests, the cost of which would also be left to Bergen. And when Bergen's failure to answer a phone call about a random drug screening was reported as a probation violation, she was sent back to jail for ten days as a penalty and then billed for more than another $900. Imprisonment for debt was outlawed across the United States during the first half of the nineteenth century; it now seems to have been reinstituted, part of what some observers call the "criminalization of poverty."[23]

There is more to the story, with even broader implications. Under Missouri law, Brooke Bergen may have retained the right to vote because she served time for a misdemeanor rather than a felony. But in Missouri, as well as in many other states, convicted felons suffer disfranchisement not only while they are incarcerated but until they complete their parole or probation. Indeed, twenty-six states follow Missouri's example in denying voting rights to felons until they fully serve out their sentences, and some of them (Florida is an example) continue to deny voting rights until all costs and fees are fully paid. The impact is consequential to the number of eligible voters in the United States. According to The Sentencing Project, as of 2020 more than five million Americans were disfranchised for felony convictions; more than half of them were no longer incarcerated. And although reformers in some of the states are fighting to limit the reach of penal-related disfranchisement, the results vary a great deal and their achievements can quickly be reversed. In Florida, voters strongly supported a referendum in 2018 that would restore the voting rights of felons who completed their sentences (including parole or probation); previously released felons had to endure a five- to seven-year waiting period. Yet in very short order the state legislature enacted a law that also required convicted felons to pay all their legal financial obligations before they could register to vote. As a result, in a state with a history of closely contested elections, almost 900,000 people who have not fully repaid their fines and fees remain disfranchised.[24]

III

IN MARCH 1975, Milton Friedman and his colleague Arnold Harberger, both from the economics department of the University of Chicago, flew off to Santiago, Chile, at the invitation of the Chilean government. Especially eager for their arrival was a group of economists at the Pontificia Universidad Católica de Chile, most of whom had studied with Friedman and Harberger before they returned to their home country. Their connection with the University of Chicago was so well known and touted that they were called the "Chicago Boys."[25]

Friedman and Harberger were well aware that their host Chilean government had come to power two years earlier in a brutal military coup led by General Augusto Pinochet—immediately installed as dictator—that overthrew the popularly elected socialist government of Salvador Allende, cost Allende his life, and led to the murderous repression of the Chilean left. But along with giving lectures and seminars, Friedman had a forty-five-minute meeting with Pinochet after which he offered an extended list of recommendations for moving the Chilean economy in a neoliberal direction even while acknowledging that he knew little about Chile itself. "Shock therapy," as Friedman termed it, involved massive cuts to government spending, painful austerity measures, a revaluation of the currency, the rapid liberalization of international trade, and the privatization of most government-controlled industries.[26]

Best known at the time for his book *Capitalism and Freedom*, Friedman was soon called to account by many on the left for the aid he gave a dictator and authoritarian government. "In spite of my profound disagreement with the authoritarian system of Chile," he replied, "I do not consider it evil for an economist to render technical economic advice to the Chilean government, any more than I would regard it as an evil for a physician to give medical advice . . . to help end a medical plague." It was, to say the least, a strained analogy. Friedman plainly did not see political liberalization as a prerequisite for the market liberalization that he urged, or as a likely outcome. Pinochet's chief economic minister, one of the prominent Chicago Boys who had been involved in planning the coup, was more direct. "The effective freedom of a person is only guaranteed by an authoritarian government," he insisted. Friedrich Hayek, who also visited Chile during the Pinochet regime and was favorably impressed, could be less defensive than Friedman. "Sometimes it is necessary for a country to have, for a time, some form of dictatorial power," he explained. "As you will understand, it is possible for a dictator to govern in a liberal way. And it is also possible for a democracy to govern with a total lack of liberalism."[27]

Around the same time, the newly established Trilateral Commission issued a report on what it called the "crisis of democracy." Authored by a distinguished group of academics, including Harvard political scientist and ardent defender of Western ideals Samuel P. Huntington, the report was concerned not with the undermining of democratic values and practices but rather with the challenges that the expansion of democracy posed to governability. Huntington and his colleagues noted the "pessimism" that abounded as to the "future of democracy," which "coincided with a parallel pessimism about the future of economic conditions," the "vague and persistent feeling that democracies have become ungovernable." The question they posed was direct and arresting: "Is political democracy, as it exists today, a viable form of government for the industrialized countries of Europe, North America, and Asia?"[28]

By "governability" the authors meant the "ability of governments to give [effective] direction to the economies . . . and political communities they govern[ed]" so that economic growth, global trade, and a stable international order could be achieved. The problems, as they saw them, were the expansion of democracy in many parts of the world during the 1960s, the "creedal passions" that accompanied it, and the "overload" of participants and demands consequently heaped upon governing structures. Huntington was particularly worried that "the vigor of democracy in the United States in the 1960s . . . contributed to a democratic distemper, involving the expansion of governmental activity, on the one hand, and the reduction of governmental authority, on the other."[29]

Europe, Asia, and the United States showed different dynamics and timelines of crisis, but Huntington was not alone in arguing that a "balance between vitality and governability" needed to be maintained or restored. In the United States, Huntington wrote, some of the challenges of governance derived from "an excess of democracy" which needed to be moderated. For one thing, he suggested that "the claims of expertise, seniority, experience, and special talents" could "override the claims of democracy as a way of constituting authority," a perspective that had enlivened social and political thinkers since the Progressive era. At the same time, Huntington observed that "the effective operation of a democratic political system usually requires some measure of apathy and noninvolvement on the part of some individuals and groups"—"marginal social groups" he called them—which, especially "the blacks," are "becoming full participants in the political system." The "danger" was that they would overload the system with demands while undermining its authority. "Democracy," he concluded, "is more of a threat to itself in the United States than it is in either Europe or Japan," and "limits to the indefinite extension of political democracy" needed to be established. "Democracy will have a longer life," Huntington asserted, "if it has a more balanced existence."[30]

The problems that democracy posed for stable governance not only concerned the internationalists for whom developing neoliberal ideas resonated powerfully. They also concerned some of those in the United States who were crafting neoliberal ideas and hoping to translate them into public policies. Indeed, while the members of the Trilateral Commission still seemed to value democratic practice and popular input as part of an approach to the political and economic instabilities of the time, a number of economic thinkers and families of great wealth had come to believe that their neoliberal objectives could never win the requisite popular support and would therefore demand a wholesale reassessment of political decision-making. In the process, they showed how neoliberalism could work to fortify the illiberal radical right.

Among those who played important roles in this regard were James M. Buchanan, a Chicago-trained economist and eventual Nobel laureate (for his work on public or rational choice) and the Koch brothers, Fred and Charles, right-wing billionaires based in Wichita, Kansas, who had been active supporters of the John Birch Society. All were great enthusiasts of neoliberalism, of freeing the market from government-imposed regulations, of the need to whittle down the role of the state to the limited functions of securing the national defense and protecting private property rights domestically. They waxed on about "liberty," but defined it chiefly in economic terms. All were connected with the international Mont Pelerin Society. All were involved in think-tanks and programs that the Koch brothers and others who shared their views were funding to groom intellectual and legal talent. And all had grave doubts about whether the constitutional order and democratic governance would allow for the achievement of their objectives. They saw Milton Friedman as a turncoat and "sell-out" for his willingness to work from within the governmental structure, to "make government work more efficiently" when he "should be tearing it out at the root." They scorned majority rule, admiring John C. Calhoun for his interest in defending the political power of minorities, such as slaveholders, and were not reticent about posing the "uncomfortable question": "If in fact we seek what many do not wish, will we be more successful if we take this into account and seek political institutions and policies that allow us to pursue our goals?" "Restriction of the franchise to property owners, educated classes, employed persons, or some such group," seemed especially advisable.[31]

As one might expect, James Buchanan also found his way to Chile—in his case a few years after Friedman and Harberger had been there—and had few qualms about the coup that brought Pinochet to power or how neoliberal shock therapy could be achieved and sustained politically. In a series of lectures, Buchanan advocated "severe restrictions" on the economic reach of the government, the importance of a "balanced budget," and the requirement of super-legislative majorities for any substantial changes in policy: this as a new constitution was being devised to secure Pinochet's rule, entrench the organized right in power, and utterly suppress labor unions and the left. In an important sense, the involvement of the neoliberal right in guiding the Pinochet government's economic goals and policies was another episode in a lengthy history of American efforts—in Cuba, the Dominican Republic, Haiti, Central America, Colombia, Bolivia, Brazil—to shape Latin American political economies and defeat the socialist and communist left.[32]

And, in an equally important sense, this was very much how the neoliberal right came to view the political struggle within the United States. Their opponents, their enemies, were not liberals or Democrats, New Dealers or designers of the Great Society. They were "socialists" because, as they saw it, socialism was the proper rubric for any system in which the government, with popular support, played a large role in a nation's economic and political life, creating policies that knit large sections of the voting public into its embrace. Even the "Reagan revolution" of the 1980s, which resulted in major tax cuts, wide-ranging deregulation, and a prominent discourse excoriating an activist federal government, failed to register as a real victory in good measure because entitlement programs such as Social Security and Medicare—programs that were extremely popular across the political spectrum—accounted for such a large share of the federal budget. Small wonder that interest in privatizing Social Security grew rapidly on the neoliberal right—nothing would better detach Americans from dependence on the government and shift billions into the pockets of private investors—as did a recognition that control of Republican Party would need to be contested. The Republican Party of Ronald Reagan was simply not up to the task.[33]

Nowhere in the United States were neoliberal ends yoked to illiberal means or efforts to take over the Republican Party more directly than in the developing movement of the Christian right or, even more accurately, Christian nationalism. To be sure, since the 1950s Christian fundamentalists had waxed enthusiastic about the "free enterprise system" in their attacks on "godless" communism and socialism, and saw religious and economic freedom as two sides of the same coin of Christian capitalism. Yet, beginning in the late 1970s, led at first by Jerry Falwell's Moral Majority, the religious right became a movement aimed at taking the nation back from its political secularism and establishing a state based on a biblical world view, on "bible law" advocating, among other things, the subordination of women to men and the rule of a spiritual aristocracy. The spark was not, as many inaccurately believe, the Supreme Court's *Roe* v. *Wade* decision legalizing abortion; it was hostility to public education and especially to attacks on the tax-exempt status of Christian academies that were racially segregated. The anti-abortion issue was taken on only in 1979 both to promote an alliance with conservative Catholics and provide cover for the Christian right's defense of segregated schools.[34]

Along with Catholic conservatives, the Christian right found an ally, much as Augusto Pinochet did, in Milton Friedman, who was a great supporter of school privatization even at the cost of bedfellows whose racism he claimed to disavow. Some in the movement looked upon Friedman with suspicion (he was Jewish), but most were happy to celebrate his economic and political ideas, which aligned closely with their own. God, they insisted, was "pro-private property" and against progressive taxation. In the view of one of their leading historians and organizers, "freedom, faith, and free markets" formed the three pillars of American civilization. Indeed, those of the Christian right expected their schools to teach a version of history in which the American nation was established by Christian founders, separation of church and state was only meant to keep the state out of religious activity, and ratification of the Fourteenth Amendment began the nation's downhill slide away from Christian principles. They also expected their students to learn that the "highest level of prosperity occurs when there is a free market and a minimum of government regulation." It was, as one journalist wrote, a fusion of hyper-capitalist ideology and hyper-Calvinist theology, or neoliberalism and illiberalism.[35]

Much like James Buchanan and the Koch brothers, Christian nationalist leaders understood that their agenda for taking power and building a state run by and in the interests of biblical Christians had no real chance of achieving majority support. But they saw the Republican Party as a vehicle for advancing their movement, and mapped a strategy to capture control of many state legislatures and governorships, together with local school boards (long a goal of the radical right) and seats in Congress. Toward this end, the Christian nationalists tapped the support of plutocratic families—the Olin Foundation, the Bradley Foundation, the foundations of Richard Scaife, the Mercer Family Foundation, and especially the DeVos/Prince family of Michigan—who were committed Christians, had little interest in democratic practice, and shared their economic aims. They also tapped into small donors at the grassroots through their churches and, with help from sympathetic data-collecting services, constructed an argument of victimization, depicting the federal government as targeting Christians and their institutions. The results were already in evidence by the mid-1990s when Republicans took control of both houses of Congress and many state legislatures, and Georgia Republican Newt Gingrich, who was close to the Christian right, became Speaker of the House. Two decades later, Donald Trump showed his loyalty by appointing Betsy DeVos to head the Department of Education, which she hoped to abolish, and filling many other cabinet positions with men recognized as committed Christians. By the spring of 2018, eleven of fourteen cabinet members were participating in a White House Bible study group. Trump did not attend.[36]

IV

ONE OF THE GREAT EVANGELISTS of the time who embraced a neoliberal vision of past, present, and future was the Silicon Valley founder of Apple, Steve Jobs. Business, he explained in the early 1980s, was "probably the best-kept secret in the world." As he saw it, the free market had propelled the tech boom in the Valley from the beginning, and was destined to make for a near utopia of innovative genius and consumer satisfaction. To be sure, he was hardly alone among the "people making it all happen," but as Esther Dyson, one of the early Wall Street trackers of the personal-computer business put it, "he is one of us in a bigger, alien world," and while there were "lots of stars" in the new industry, "only Steve had the charm and eloquence to be a star to the outside world."[37]

Jobs regarded the government as a chain to the status quo, a hurdle-maker in the way of creativity, and something of a warmonger on the international stage, producing high anxiety at home and abroad. In the post-Vietnam and post-Watergate United States it was not very difficult to view the federal government as a villain in need of restraint and discipline. Yet the narrative Jobs was rolling out— one already honed by white southerners and westerners who had vilified the federal government while benefiting from massive federal investments in their regions' economic development—neatly erased the foundational part the government had played during and after World War Two in advancing the new world of hi-tech, especially when it came to electronics and computers. Federal support and dollars that had flowed toward military-related research—the Manhattan Project only the best-known example—increased substantially in volume and direction after the war, in large part because of Cold War tensions and the arms race they generated.

Through the newly organized National Science Foundation, the Defense Department, and other federal agencies, millions of dollars in grant money were channeled to university-based research. Government contracts for aircraft and weapons systems boosted the rapidly expanding aerospace sector, much of it growing across the Sunbelt and, most notably, in California. Military procurement continued to bolster the Sunbelt economies through the 1950s and 1960s and, after some years of cuts during the 1970s, grew dramatically once more during the Reagan-directed buildups of the 1980s. Even as Steve Jobs touted the free market's nurturing of creative energies, the federal government was spending more and more money on computer science programs. Eventually billions of dollars would support academic research labs and engineering schools that were busily training the future employees at Apple, Microsoft, and a host of other hi-tech companies of the time.[38]

Probably no arena of economic activity drew such enthusiastic bipartisan support as did hi-tech. Although the early innovators and entrepreneurs in Silicon Valley and Route 128 around Boston leaned strongly Republican in their politics (David Packard, cofounder of Hewlett-Packard and long-serving chairman of the board at Stanford University, is a prominent example), by the late 1980s and 1990s centrist Democrats began competing for their support. Tennessee's Al Gore had been interested in high-speed telecommunications and computer development since the 1970s and became a leading congressional voice for the construction, with government support, of what he called the information "superhighway," later known as the "internet." For his part, Bill Clinton spent a good bit of time in the early 1990s attempting to persuade the big money in Silicon Valley that he was the presidential contender with their best interests at heart. Clinton told them that the American economy needed to be rebuilt around new, "sunrise" industries and that international trade policy had to be liberalized. As Clinton saw it, the information superhighway would be constructed, owned, and operated by the private sector; there would be none of the centralization of control that marked the advent of the telephone. The government's role would not be to supervise a private monopoly like AT&T, but to provide the regulatory apparatus, much of it involving deregulation in the area of communications more generally, that would encourage private investment and tech industry growth.

By most accounts, Clinton was a hit, though nothing proved more convincing to Silicon Valley than his choosing Al Gore as his running mate: an unusual and risky move, since both were southerners and party tickets customarily provide some geographical balance. But for the tech world the message was clear. Here were two leaders of a younger generation, both committed to moving the Democratic Party to the center and charting a technologically driven way forward. Clinton insisted that Gore would not just be a run-of-the-mill vice president, waiting quietly in the wings. Gore would carry a substantial policy portfolio and be deemed the country's "technology czar." That was more than enough. By the early fall, some of the leading Silicon Valley executives publicly endorsed the Clinton-Gore ticket, and did so with enthusiasm and money. "I am still a Republican," one of them crowed, "but I am voting for Bill Clinton because I don't believe American industries can survive four more years of President Bush." Not by accident was the Clinton-Gore campaign theme song Fleetwood Mac's hit "Don't Stop Thinking About Tomorrow."[39]

The Clinton-Gore team found an unlikely ally in Republican congressman Newt Gingrich, catapulted to the speakership after the 1994 midterms gave the Democrats a shellacking and Republicans control of the House of Representatives for the first time in more than four decades. Gingrich had played an important role in defeating the Clinton administration's healthcare plan and in rolling out the Contract with America, a set of policies designed to limit the federal government's power and reach, which seemed attractive to many voters at the time. Still, Gingrich had a deepening interest in the tech sector, not simply because of its vast implications for communications, but also because he believed that, by its nature, internet technologies would decenter power and weaken Washington, D.C.'s hold over the rest of the country. As technology-watcher Esther Dyson put it after an interview with Gingrich in 1995, "Newt seemed to value the Net not for its efficiency, but for its political implications. He saw it as a political actor—not as a vehicle for better government." Yet his idea that "we should be driving for as little regulation as possible," to "liberate the market and let the technologies sort themselves out," was not very far from the Clinton-Gore perspective or from that of many "Atari" Democratic supporters. Their vision of a neoliberal utopia may have differed—though Gingrich proposed a $40 billion tax credit so that the "poorest Americans" could buy a laptop and opposed efforts of the religious right to establish a "decency" code— but they seemed to envision a similar path to get there.[40]

What also linked the Clinton-Gore and Gingrich perspectives was a neoliberal sense of political economy in which the important players and power relations involved the government and tech entrepreneurs in one arena, and the entrepreneurs and consumers in another. Deregulation meant shifting power from the public to the private sector, where entrepreneurs would be liberated to create, responding to intellectual and financial incentives, with few of the constraints that government oversight could impose. The power relations between tech companies and consumers could then be imagined as reciprocal and mutually beneficial, as innovations that offered faster and wider access to information and communication networks at relatively low cost. Search engines could draw their revenues from advertisements and licensing agreements rather than requiring users to pay effective "tolls" as transportation infrastructures often do. And the apparent efficiencies that manufacturers, retailers, and warehousers would derive from computer-based technologies could be presented as further gains for consumers in terms of both cost and speed of delivery.

This bright picture of a neoliberal market obscures developing conditions at workplaces, where the power relations pit tech-savvy employers against increasingly atomized employees. Unlike the industrial shop floor that encompassed an array of power dynamics involving foremen, operatives, and possibly unions as well as bosses/ managers and workers—with various sites of collective decision-making and action—the tech-bounded workplace links employees chiefly as individuals to their employers who, in turn, have much greater ability to chart their work rhythms and productivity. This is a decentering of power rarely addressed by hi-tech cheerleaders from either political party, who tend to see the gig economy not as an example of increasing vulnerability in the workforce but as a sign that one-time employees have chosen to stop punching in and instead become entrepreneurs in their own right.

And for the many millions who must still punch in, their "shop floor" can be laced by a web of surveillance. The recent exposés of Amazon "fulfillment centers," where workers have been so ground down that they stay, on average, eight months, are only the most conspicuous examples. "Technology has enabled employers to enforce a work pace with no room for inefficiency, squeezing every ounce of downtime out of workers' days," a reporter who worked at such a center in Indiana observed. "The scan gun to do my job was also my own personal digital manager. Every single thing I did was monitored and timed. After I completed a task, the scan gun not only immediately gave me a new one but also started counting down the seconds I had left to do it. It also alerted a manager if I had too many minutes of 'Time Off Task.'" The weakening of unions during the past half century, under Democratic and Republican administrations alike, has left many workers with few recourses for pushing back other than the good offices of journalists. Small wonder that unionization drives at Amazon, Starbucks, and other such worksites have formed independent organizations rather than ally with well-established unions.[41]

The reach of workplace surveillance captures, too, those regarded as independent contractors—small-scale entrepreneurs as it were—together with employees who have long been accustomed to relative independence. Here, the role of the government, through legislation and the courts, has reinforced the surveillance power of companies and employers as well as the exposure and precarity of those who work for them. The "rideshare" industry, now led by Uber and Lyft, provides good illustrations. Presenting itself as a technology instead of a transportation company, Uber depicts its drivers not as employees but as entrepreneurs who have freedom and flexibility in their work schedules and, notably, as "consumers" of Uber's technology services much like Uber's riders. "Fundamentally," one of Uber's lawyers explained, "the commercial relationship between these drivers and transportation providers and Uber, is one where they are our customer, where we license to them our software, and we receive a fee for doing that." Among other things, this means that, under American labor law, companies like Uber are not then required to observe minimum-wage standards or provide benefits to the drivers. Like other gig workers, the drivers are effectively on their own, responsible for paying an assortment of taxes and unable to collect unemployment insurance in case of termination. Although this classification system is being contested by drivers in state courts—they insist on their status as employees—with some favorable decisions, "the battle," in the words of the *National Law Review*, "is not ending anytime soon" and will "remain at the forefront of employment and labor law concerns, particularly in the gig economy."[42]

Digital technologies, like the devices that enable Uber to manage thousands of drivers by means of algorithms, have found their way into the world of long-haul truckers, whether independent or employed by trucking companies. Ever since the 1930s, in order to monitor the problem of driver fatigue, the federal government has subjected drivers to "hours of service" regulations, limiting the number of hours they can drive each day and week without taking long breaks. Record keeping remained in the hands of the drivers themselves, tracking hours in logbooks that were open to inspection by law enforcement. Given the financial incentives to drive as long and as far as possible, the logbooks were frequently falsified. This changed in 2017 when the federal government required truckers to purchase and install "electronic logging devices" (ELDs) so that tampering would be more difficult. But the new surveillance is not only deployed by the government; it is also used by trucking firms to collect data about the truckers' bodies, behaviors, and hours on the road. As one of the industry's tech leaders recommended, "If you're a fleet manager it's important to make sure your drivers stay ELD compliant. But beyond compliance ELDs can also offer fleets a wide range of benefits that help improve fleet management and help streamline operations, a great way to improve overall fleet efficiency, and offers fleet managers more visibility into driver behavior."[43]

By the early 2000s, workplace surveillance formed only part of a much larger structure of surveillance and expropriation that organized the experience and dispositions of the very consumers who had been represented as digital technology's mutual beneficiaries. The turning point came in the wake of the collapse of the so-called dot-com bubble (the huge uptick in the value of tech stocks during the 1990s) between 2000 and 2002, which led to a wider recession. Needing cash and searching for new forms of revenue—and new models of accumulation—hi-tech companies like the search engine Google began to regard users not as consumers and customers but as sources of behavioral data that could then be sold in something of a behavioral data marketplace to manufacturers and other enterprises looking to target potential consumers of their own products. The goal is the harvesting of enough behavioral data—gaining access through the internet to individual tastes, desires, aspirations, expectations, to as much of individual experience as possible—so that it will have compelling predictive value for its purchasers. In effect, individual users of the internet are transformed into raw materials, little more than sources of behavioral data and, particularly, of behavioral data surpluses that can be sold on what is, for all intents and purposes, a behavioral futures market. There, behavioral data mined in real time can be used to anticipate, with high levels of certainty, what users will respond to at some future point.[44]

The dynamics of power in what Shoshana Zuboff calls "surveillance capitalism" is radically new and extremely disproportionate, although it bears more than a little resemblance to the finance capitalism that emerged powerfully in the 1980s and has played a central part in funding Silicon Valley ventures. On the one side, behavioral data harvesters like Google—soon followed by Facebook, Amazon, Microsoft, and other companies like them—gain access to personal information that users cannot fathom or are entirely unaware of, presenting the results as, ostensibly, of value to the users themselves. Accordingly, they compile immense troves of cultural knowledge that can be dispensed as they see fit. On the other side, the users have no ability or legal right to protect themselves and their privacy from such invasion or to monitor how their personal data is used; no contract is negotiated, even with small print on it, that may limit what can be brought into the behavioral data marketplace. There is no recognition of an exchange by which a user can be reimbursed. The companies insist that these conditions are the inevitable results of the technologies themselves, while cloaking their operations behind a veil of inscrutability. The users are left in near ignorance as to what is transpiring, generally intimidated by the apparent complexities of the system and technological apparatus, and thus their possible agency—for accepting, rejecting, or modifying—is rendered inert.[45]

Digital technologies would have emerged in recent decades, whatever political economy was in place, owing to the encouragement of the federal government and the creative energies of those whose projects received support during and after World War Two. But the social relations, economic logic, and political backing that have come to compose the hi-tech sector were products of the neoliberal context in which they did emerge. And together they offer disconcerting examples of how the organizational structures that neoliberalism enables can promote dangerous forms of legal and political illiberalism. The Googles, Facebooks, Microsofts, and Amazons may tout the information and communication networks they make available, yet they have no interest in the personal rights and sovereignties that liberal societies claim to rest upon. They have few concerns about individual rights to privacy often acknowledged elsewhere (in the European Union there is a legal "right to be forgotten") and become complicit in illiberal political campaigns because surveilling and excluding content threatens the very sources of their wealth and power. They do savor First-Amendment protections of "free speech," and have benefited from sympathetic judicial decisions that closely associate free speech and property rights, thereby using the institutions of the state to limit potential oversight and regulation. But their vision of the world is hierarchical and their impulse is toward total possession of the vast numbers of users who come within their grasp. It is, in truth, a totalitarian ambition all the more perilous because it is not advanced by a political party or explicit political ideology. It masquerades as promoting spaces of endless freedoms and choices. In a society that has long embraced forms of technological determinism and has even more widely equated technological innovation with social and political progress, this makes for a steep hill to climb out of potential darkness.[46]

V

BEGINNING IN 1997, as the Clinton-Gore administration commenced its second term and Vice President Gore looked toward a presidential run in 2000, Gore met monthly with top Silicon Valley executives in what came to be known as "Gore-Tech." Sometimes they met in the Valley and sometimes at the White House, but wherever they met, they focused on discussing the "new economy" over which they were presiding and public policies to solve problems that were bound to arise. Although under the radar screen in official Washington, the meetings made for one of the administration's most influential "brain trusts." Gore was invariably attentive, and there was no shortage of hubris on the part of the tech executives. "We're so conceited that we think what's in the best interests of our industry is in the best interest of the whole country," one of them remarked, channeling CEO Charles Wilson's 1953 view of General Motors's status in the country. The meeting organizer was venture capitalist John Doerr, who had just invested $40 million in a successful effort to defeat California's Proposition 211, which would have made it easier for shareholders to sue corporations and their directors for costly blunders. "What we've learned from this 211 fight," Doerr reflected, "is that if we're not in an ongoing conversation with elected officials, we'll get what we deserve."[47]

Gore was not yet raising money for his campaign, but the Gore-Tech meetings further burnished his reputation in Silicon Valley and ensured that he would have strong support there when the time came. He surely was a great advocate for the internet and the technologies connected with it, worked to enable its development and protect the interests of those most invested in its expansion, and saw a resulting world of economic growth and political cooperation. Without doubt, Gore regarded the internet as a vehicle of job training, upward mobility, and possibly democratic engagement.[48]

Yet, during the 1990s, the inequalities of wealth in the United States soared—especially the wealth of the top 1 percent—and the turnout of eligible voters in the election of 1996 was at its lowest point, under 50 percent, since the election of 1924. The next election cycle, when Gore was a candidate for the presidency, witnessed little improvement. It seemed a reflection of one of the little appreciated though highly significant dynamics of the neoliberal era: the reifying of economic entrepreneurialism and the personal enrichment it made possible together with the marginalizing of popular politics and political engagement—the restraining of democratic impulses—that Samuel Huntington and many members of the Trilateral Commission had advocated two decades earlier. The presidential electoral debacle of 2000, which focused attention on the consequences of state-level voting procedures, minority voter suppression, and the anti-democratic character of the electoral college—a debacle resolved by the branch of government least subject to popular influence—also disguised the extent to which so many millions of Americans had lost interest in the political arena.

Bill Clinton and Al Gore may have succeeded in auditioning for Silicon Valley's billionaires in the making, and they may have imagined that, in so doing, they were giving the Democratic Party a far better political footing than it had in the 1970s and 1980s. But in the process, power was shifting even more dramatically toward hi-tech and hi-finance where the mantras of neoliberalism veiled their ability to control a public simultaneously tantalized and dependent upon them, a public constituted, at best, as consumers, though increasingly as resources for a game played in a different arena. The illiberal consequences were becoming apparent even before the decade of the 1990s was out.

Chapter Ten

SPECTERS OF RACE WAR AND REPLACEMENT

I T WAS, BY ANY MEASURE, AN ASTONISHING EVENT. Barack Hussein Obama, a man of African descent, had not only won the presidential nomination of one of the two major political parties but was then elected to the presidency by a substantial margin, both in the popular and electoral votes. When his victory seemed certain on election night, a crowd estimated at nearly a quarter million came together in Grant Park, Chicago, to celebrate Obama and his family and to hear Obama speak—he would quote Lincoln and Martin Luther King—about this "defining moment" and the challenging "road ahead." A sense of genuine excitement seemed to spread across the country, enabling some who had voted for Obama's Republican rival to acknowledge a pride that such a result was possible in the United States, that the stain of racism had not soiled the election, indeed, that they might then be absolved of wearing what had become a noxious label.[1]

Anyone traveling abroad at the time, especially to countries that customarily looked upon the United States with suspicion or hostility, could feel a change in perspective, surprise mixed with questions and an unexpected warmth, an eagerness to know how the United States managed the feat: to become the first white-majority nation to elect a person of color to its highest office. On 20 January 2009, well over a million people—nearly two million by some estimates—filled the National Mall from the Capitol to the Washington Monument to witness Obama's inauguration while observers in the media began to wonder if—even to declare that—the United States had become a "post-racial" society. "Post-racial" was, according to news analyst Daniel Schorr of National Public Radio, the "latest buzzword in the political lexicon."[2]

Less than a month later, however, the fantasy of a "post-racial" society came into new and sobering relief. Following a rant against some of Obama's policies by a CNBC reporter on the floor of the Chicago Mercantile Exchange, a "Tea Party" movement emerged to contest the administration and its programs, soon helped along by Fox News and a number of right-wing funders and advocacy groups. Within weeks a far-right militia group calling itself the "Oath Keepers," to be composed of retired and active-duty members of the military and first responders, formed with the goal of "prevent[ing] the destruction of liberty by preventing a full-blown totalitarian dictatorship from coming to power." Neither the Tea Partiers nor the Oath Keepers claimed to be motivated by racist animus; they both explicitly denied it. If anything, they were energized by fears of "illegal" immigration and the prospect of Muslim jihadists within American borders. Yet there was also no doubt that the elevation of a Black man to the office and power of the presidency—a man whose race, name, and cosmopolitanism conjured wild rumors about his eligibility and intentions—stoked deeper concerns among conservative whites who already looked upon the federal government as a patron for people of color rather than for themselves.[3]

The speed with which this movement from the far right surfaced and spread was hardly expected. If anything, it was Obama who had ridden the wave of a grassroots movement, perhaps two million strong, that swept him into the White House and seemed determined to support the progressive politics and policies that Obama's rhetoric and apparent vision for the country had inspired among them. Some of Obama's advisors clearly recognized the need to keep his supporters mobilized outside of the institutional structures of the Democratic Party if he was to succeed. But well before Obama's inauguration, they had lost out to the seasoned political "pros" who had turned to the tasks of governing and believed that, at most, the activists had to be folded into the Democratic National Committee, where their aims would be subordinated to the good of the party. Obama's diverse coalition of the young, the Black, the brown, and the progressive was thus derailed. Instead, what rose to the surface—surprisingly and forebodingly—was a movement of the far right determined to regain the power they claimed to have been losing for more than a decade.[4]

A confluence of developments, some long-term and some short, conspired both to enable Obama's success and provoke a backlash that wed race to a view of government tyranny. The civil rights movement's great successes were to be seen in the expansion of the Black middle class, the development of a large and loyal Black constituency of support for the Democratic Party, and the growing number of Black officeholders—chiefly Democratic—at all levels of governance, especially in Black-majority cities and districts. Obama could thereby be promoted up the ranks from community organizer to member of the Illinois state senate to the United States Senate and then to the presidency, well positioned by a Harvard law degree and access to Democratic funders, first in Chicago and then nationwide.

At the same time, the deindustrialization of the Northeast and Midwest, the steady weakening of the labor movement, the decades-long stagnation of middle- and working-class incomes, the mass incarceration of poor people of color, and the empowerment of the financial sector together deepened the vulnerabilities and grievances of whites who were, by their lights, left behind and aside. The demographic drift that would make the country minority white by the middle of the twenty-first century added immediacy and intensity, and provided a space for far-right warnings of white subordination and "replacement."

White supremacist views and projects, in a variety of forms, had long been close to the surface of American political and cultural life, but they seemed to find new traction during the 1980s and early 1990s. A white power movement took shape in the wake of the Vietnam War, especially among former military veterans who bridled at the social changes that greeted them back at home and felt betrayed by the military and political leadership that made them cannon fodder in what turned into a losing cause. Before long, this movement found allies among neo-Nazis, Klansmen, and skinheads, and came to believe that white Christians were under duress, shrinking in numbers, and in need of a homeland in a new world organized around racial apartheid. Some would contest for influence and power through the electoral system, though for the time being most imagined an evolving race war and literal apocalypse that would require military training and survivalist skills. During the 1990s they were joined by a growing network of militia groups inspired by both white supremacy and hostility to the federal government itself.[5]

Fears of race war have been part of American political culture since settler colonialists encountered Native peoples they regarded as "savages," and enslaved Africans became a foundation of North American settler societies. Over time, those fears found new expressions that reflected changed historical contexts. The Haitian Revolution brought the bloody image of "Santo Domingo" into the discourse. Reconstruction conjured the dire threat of "Negro Rule." The urban rebellions of the 1960s created an image of rampaging arsonists targeting the police, white storeowners, and landlords in their own neighborhoods. Throughout, Blacks and other people of color were simultaneously denigrated as ignorant inferiors and imagined as barbarians seeking vengeance. Black men with guns, and the criminalized Black body more generally, have long been sources of terror. But beginning in the 1980s and moving through the three decades that followed, specters of race war, intensified by new patterns of immigration, fortified the illiberal right and brought it from the fringes into the mainstream of American politics.

The Republican Party, aided by an assemblage of self-constituted militia groups, increasingly shed what was left of its neoliberal globalism and came to be dominated by white nationalists conjuring enemies foreign and domestic. When Donald Trump, resurrecting a racist trope of the Reconstruction era, questioned Barack Obama's legitimacy to be president, called on his supporters to "make America great again," warned of an "invasion" of "illegal aliens" from the south, expressed sympathy for torch-bearing neo-Nazis who vilified Jews, told the white-supremacist Proud Boys to "stand back and stand by," and eventually insisted that his presidency was stolen by electoral corruption in America's multiracial cities, he validated fears of a race war being waged from the deepest recesses of the state and summoned them to fight back across a number of fronts.

I

THE WARNING FLAG WENT UP in Louisiana in 1989, and was raised by a far-right extremist who, quite improbably, found success in the state's electoral politics. For those, such as Democratic political consultant James Carville, who first encountered him at Louisiana State University in the late 1960s haranguing students about the threat of Jews, communism, and Black people, David Duke seemed like one of the many prophets and agitators who regularly form part of campus cultural life. The "campus Nazi," as Carville called him, Duke was, in fact, a sophomore at LSU at the time and had grown up in the Louisiana suburb of Metairie in the home of an absent father and alcoholic mother. He had attended a Christian academy and, before graduating, was drawn to National Socialism after reading *Race and Reason: A Yankee View*, a defense of scientific racism and segregation by Princeton- and Columbia-educated Carleton Putnam. It was a book that had won veneration in the Deep South after its publication in 1961. Hardly shy or reticent about his evolving beliefs, Duke draped his bedroom with Nazi flags and other memorabilia, sported swastika rings, and enjoyed showing off his copy of *Mein Kampf*, especially to his Sunday school class. He had the heart and soul of a Nazi and anti-Semite, to which his racism and white supremacy were tethered.[6]

Before very long, Duke left speechifying and embraced organizing, already recognizing that explicit identification with Nazism was a dead end toward his goal of building a popular far-right movement. Thus, in 1973 he formed the Knights of the Ku Klux Klan, with himself as "Grand Wizard." He looked to bring the KKK into the modern age, construct a "White political machine," and contest the "minoritization" of America by first smashing "Jewish power." In effect, Duke's intention was to nazify the KKK and thereby expand its appeal. As might be expected, Duke's new organization served as a magnet for a number of extremists who had college educations, often records of military service, prior involvement with the neo-Nazi movement, and shared interest in mainstreaming their views. Advancing Christian identity and Holocaust denialism through the pages of his newspaper, *The Crusader*, Duke also trained his eyes on the electoral arena in hopes, at the very least, of gaining media attention and more members for the Knights of the Ku Klux Klan. In 1975, and again in 1979, he ran for the Louisiana state senate from Metairie and Baton Rouge, winning as much as a third of the vote in one of the primaries.

But Duke's real success came in growing the Klan's membership and attracting the notice of the national press, some of it remarkably favorable. The *Los Angeles Herald Examiner*, in a multipart series, found Duke to be "an articulate, media-hip, Louisianan who prefers a finely tailored suit to a loose-fitting robe" and had "taken a dying hate group and tried to turn it into a mainstream 'movement of love' every bit as respectable as the Elks, Masons, or Rotarians." Plastic surgery and a new blow-dried hair style completed Duke's transition from a brown-shirted, swastika-bearing, Hitler-mimicking Klansman into a mediagenic political personality.[7]

And a viable candidate for elective office. Duke's defeats in the 1970s did not deflate his electoral ambitions even as his one-time colleagues in the Knights of the Ku Klux Klan headed underground, embraced violence, and formed new cadres like Tom Metzger's White Aryan Resistance (WAR). So far as Louis Bream, the leader of the Texas Knights of the KKK, could see, Duke's vision of "numberless masses marching behind the banner of the Ku Klux Klan" was sheer "illusion," and a poor substitute for "knives, guns, and courage." Undeterred, Duke continued his pivot toward politics. He organized the National Association for the Advancement of White People (NAAWP), switched his registration from Republican to Democrat, and, George Wallace-like, entered the 1988 presidential primaries to "send them a message." After garnering only 45,290 votes in all (his best showing was in Louisiana where he received 23,391 votes, or 4 percent of the ballots cast), he became the presidential candidate of the Populist Party, a far-right amalgam of neo-Nazis, skinheads, and white supremacists backed by William Carto, head of the Liberty Lobby and publisher of the anti-Semitic *Spotlight* magazine. Election day brought him 47,047 votes spread across twenty states (his best showings were, predictably, in Arkansas, Mississippi, Kentucky, and Louisiana), or .05 percent of the national total.[8]

Yet Duke's breakthrough was soon to follow. Once again switching party registration, this time from Democrat to Republican, Duke entered a special state legislative election in his nearly all-white hometown district of Metairie when the incumbent unexpectedly resigned to become a state judge. And, owing to a large infusion of cash from Carto's Liberty Lobby, he squeaked out a win (by 227 votes) over his better-known rival. The election had captured national attention even before the balloting, and the Republican leadership in Washington and almost everywhere else was quick to disavow any connection to Duke. But Duke was hardly discouraged. He hit the legislative ground running, introducing bills to abolish affirmative action and set-asides (it passed the Louisiana house), require drug testing for residents in public housing, and the implanting of birth-control devices in the arms of mothers on welfare, all while renouncing the Klan and other "youthful indiscretions." Instead of an explicitly racist language of inferiorities, he embraced the ideas of "racial difference," of "equal rights for all," and the preservation of racial heritage. In effect, he tried to appropriate the political language of Reagan and Bush and use it for his own purposes.[9]

Over the next three years, Duke launched campaigns for the U.S. Senate (1990) and the state governorship (1991), rallying support in the suburbs and rural districts even after a courageous Holocaust survivor successfully drew public attention to his Nazi past. More than a few observers and political pollsters warned that Duke was gaining ground on the established party candidates and feared he could win. It took a massive effort on the part of the Louisiana Coalition Against Racism and Nazism, organized soon after Duke won election to the statehouse, to stem the tide. The Coalition mobilized thousands of Black and white Democratic voters and forced the local media to acknowledge Duke's Nazi past. Black voter turnout proved to be extraordinary and decisive. Even so, in the Senate election Duke finished second to incumbent Democrat J. Bennett Johnson by about 150,000 votes out of more than 1.3 million cast.[10]

The following year, Duke entered the gubernatorial election and, in the first round, beat out the incumbent Republican governor Buddy Roemer and finished only two points, and 30,000 votes, behind Democrat, three-time governor, and corruption-plagued Edwin Edwards. The subsequent runoff, dubbed the "race from hell," came into the national spotlight and provoked a widespread sense of fear and political urgency. The Edwards campaign went so far as to use the candidate's misdeeds for political effect: a "Vote for the Crook: It's Important" bumper sticker (Edwards happily put it on his own car) likely enabled some Republican Roemer supporters to hold their noses and vote for Edwards. In the end, aided by another huge Black turnout, Edwards prevailed by a two-to-one margin.[11]

A collective sigh of relief could then be heard, accompanied by a sense that this was pretty much a local, and limited, affair. After all, Louisiana had a well-earned reputation as a political outlier, inclined toward extreme views and corrupt practices, given over to family dynasties such as the Longs (Huey, Earl, and Russell, among many others), more of an appendage of Latin America than fully a part of the of the United States. But the election results had troubling implications well beyond Louisiana's borders. In each of the elections between 1989 and 1992 in which Duke was a candidate, he won the support of more than half—and usually closer to three-fifths—of all white voters, and although he seemed to do best in the heavily white rural districts, he also won a substantial share of the college-educated, middle-class, suburban white vote. Indeed, in the 1991 gubernatorial primary, Duke received more votes from wealthy, suburban Jefferson Parish (where Metairie was located) than from thirty-five other parishes combined.[12]

The writer Walker Percy, who lived outside New Orleans in an area rife with right-wing extremism, had a different warning for Americans. "If I had anything to say to people outside the state," he presciently told a reporter from the *New York Times* after Duke's election to the Louisiana legislature, "I'd tell them, 'Don't make the mistake of thinking David Duke is a unique phenomenon confined to Louisiana rednecks and yahoos. He's not. He's not just appealing to the old Klan constituency, he's appealing to the white middle class. And don't think that he or somebody like him won't appeal to the white middle class of Chicago or Queens.'"[13]

II

BARELY A MONTH AFTER David Duke lost out to Edwin Edwards in the Louisiana gubernatorial election, Pat Buchanan traveled to New Hampshire to announce his candidacy for the Republican presidential nomination in 1992. Having worked in the administrations of Richard Nixon and Ronald Reagan and served as the "conservative" on network news talk shows like *Cross-Fire* and the *McLaughlin Group*, Buchanan would not have been regarded as a renegade. But the sitting president in pursuit of reelection was Republican George H. W. Bush, so Buchanan was challenging the party establishment from the right. Over the course of what turned into a losing campaign, Buchanan attacked Bush's globalist "New World Order" and called, instead, for a turn inward, a "new nationalism," a "new patriotism," and "America first." He wanted a rollback of foreign aid, the lowering of taxes, the dismantling of the welfare state, greater scrutiny of America's recent immigrant arrivals, and the fortification of America's borders—he called for building a border wall, a "Buchanan fence"—to halt the flow of undocumented immigrants who, he insisted, were contributing to high taxes, crime, social instability, and the weakening of a predominantly Caucasian and English-speaking society. In May 1992, Buchanan found his way to the U.S.-Mexico border and heaped scorn on the federal government for its failure to protect the country from an "illegal invasion."[14]

So resonant was Buchanan's voice and substantial his popular following that he was given a prime-time speaking slot at August's Republican National Convention in Houston. There he railed about a "culture war" being fought across the country, a war "as critical to the kind of nation we shall be as was the Cold War itself," a "war for the soul of America" in which the Democratic Party and its candidates Bill Clinton and Al Gore were on "the other side." The fight, as Buchanan saw it, was against the advocates of abortion, gay rights, multiculturalism, radical feminism, wholly secular schools, and rampant democracy at home as well as abroad. And it was a fight for a white world that had been lost, one of "clean streets, pretty shops, and gasoline stations with courteous attendants, movies that expressed morality, homes that were neat, [and] people polite." The fight may have been framed as a "culture war" but at heart it was a fight to save white Americanism; at heart it was a race war.[15]

Buchanan was hardly unaware of David Duke. Duke popped onto his radar screen in 1989 and Buchanan soon urged the Republican Party to "take a hard look at Duke's portfolio of winning issues; and expropriate those not in conflict with GOP principles." That portfolio included not only taxes and affirmative action, but also crimes committed by "the urban underclass" and the "illegal alien problem." The Republican Party took heed. For the first time, the party's 1992 national platform included a plank calling for a border wall— "structures" on the southern border it was termed—and in 1994 California Republican governor Pete Wilson tied his reelection to state Proposition 187, which would deny undocumented immigrants access to most state services. Both succeeded at the polls, Proposition 187 by a two-to-one margin. But Duke had beaten them to it by more than a decade and a half. In 1977, he and his Knights of the Ku Klux Klan turned up at the San Ysidro, California, border crossing and promised to patrol the length of it from there to Brownsville, Texas.[16]

For more than a century, American immigration policy was driven by racist and ethnocentric fears of alien "invasions." In the late 1870s and early 1880s, advocates of Chinese exclusion warned of an "unarmed invasion," and the U.S. Supreme Court later described the Chinese as "vast hordes of people crowding in upon us." In the early twentieth century, exclusionism turned toward the Japanese, the "Silent Invasion," and then more generally toward the "Asiatics," including the "Hindu hordes" who were menacing the blood and civilization of Americans on the Pacific coast. A similar depiction of southern and eastern Europeans—the "Chinese of Europe" they were derisively called—part Asian and semi-Mongolian, led first to the Immigration Restriction League and in 1924 to a sweeping immigration act that, for the first time, set quotas for European countries (very low ones for those of southern and eastern Europe), categorized most Asian immigrants as "aliens ineligible to citizenship," and established a border patrol.[17]

President Calvin Coolidge happily signed the act, remarking at the time that "America must remain American," while the *New York Times* exulted that the law would be crucial to "preserving the American race." In Munich, Adolf Hitler closely followed the debates over the immigration act from his jail cell, where he sat after his failed beer-hall putsch, marveling at how well the United States deployed scientific (eugenic) opinion toward the ends of racial suppression and expulsion. The quotas established in 1924 would later help doom thousands of persecuted European Jews who unsuccessfully sought refuge from Nazism in the United States during the late 1930s and early 1940s. Even so, immigration to the United States remained subject to the provisions of the 1924 act until 1965, when the Hart-Celler Act replaced it and its prescribed quota system. Although neither the act's sponsors nor President Lyndon Johnson, who signed it in the shadow of the Statue of Liberty, imagined a significant impact on "the ethnic mix of our society," the Hart-Celler Act, which included provisions for family reunification, potentially increased the flow of immigrants to the United States and opened the doors previously closed to those from Asia, Africa, and Latin America. That is to say, after 1965, as one historian put it, the "Third World" came to America. White supremacists would regard the 1965 immigration act as the beginning of America's descent into a despised, racially diverse, future.[18]

Immigration did indeed quickly spike and a backlash soon took shape. Perhaps unexpectedly, the opening salvo was launched by environmentalists who had begun to worry that the planet could not sustain the rapid increase in its population that was especially apparent in the "poorer countries" of what we now call the Global South. Especially influential was Paul and Anne Ehrlich's *The Population Bomb* (1968)—written with the encouragement of the Sierra Club's executive director—which predicted mass starvation and social upheaval if steps to slow population growth at home and abroad were not taken:

steps that included contraception, sterilization, political pressure on foreign food aid, and tax incentives to limit family size in the United States. Paul Ehrlich, trained as a biologist, followed by helping to establish Zero Population Growth, an organization devoted to educating the public and lobbying politicians on the dangers they faced and the need for action.[19]

Zero Population Growth (ZPG) did not at first embrace immigration restriction as one of its policy preferences. That only happened when it attracted the attention of John Tanton. A Michigan ophthalmologist with a deep interest in eugenics, Tanton was active in the Sierra Club and Planned Parenthood before he became president of ZPG in 1975. Four years later, he founded the Federation for American Immigration Reform (FAIR), which he sought to mainstream by inviting prominent national figures like Walter Cronkite, Eugene McCarthy, Gore Vidal, John Lindsay, Warren Buffett, and Saul Bellow to sit on the board. But Tanton also began to correspond with white nationalists and Holocaust deniers, and then took money from both the racist Pioneer Fund (founded in 1937 by Wickliffe Draper) and Cordelia Scaife May, heiress to the Mellon-Scaife fortune, who bankrolled environmental and immigration restrictions, population control, and English-only language movements. Concerned about the coming "Latin onslaught," Tanton established a Center for Immigration Studies and a publishing house that circulated racist and anti-Semitic literature. "I've come to the point of view," he reflected, "that for European society and culture to persist requires a European-American majority, and a clear one at that."[20]

Whatever their differences, the immigration laws of 1924 and 1965 together entrenched the category of the "illegal alien," one deeply racialized from the outset, and whose onus would come to fall most fully on those of Mexican descent. It was not destined to be so. The 1924 act paid little attention to the Western Hemisphere, and Mexican migrations to the United States, which substantially commenced in the early twentieth century, were not subject to quotas or regulations. For the most part, though roundups and expulsions of "unauthorized" immigrants flared, migration represented seasonal flows of labor from the mostly rural and village areas of northern Mexico to the agricultural fields of the American Southwest. Negotiations between the governments of Mexico and the United States, influenced by economic interests on both sides of the border, framed the process and led to the guestworker "Bracero" program, which started up in 1942 and endured until 1964. Thereafter, a complex dance involving agricultural employers, immigration services, and government officials sought to construct another framework, while the liberalization of border trade fueled surges in migration, owing in part to the weakening of the Mexican economy during the 1980s and in part to Reagan-era immigration policies (a response to what Reagan called an "invasion" of illegals) that did provide a path to legal status for long-term undocumented migrants as well as a Special Agricultural Worker program.[21]

In effect, the hot-button issues concerning the southern border of the United States serve as case studies of how neoliberal economic projects ended up laying the groundwork for illiberal remedies. During the 1980s and early 1990s, the southern border not only reflected the turmoil that was being created on both sides by the lead up to NAFTA, but was also increasingly militarized on the American side. The dynamic at play linked authorized Border Control agents with self-constituted border vigilantes in explosive violence directed against migrants from Mexico and—due to the decade's civil warfare in Nicaragua, El Salvador, Guatemala, and Honduras—increasingly Central America. The southern California border was especially active with vigilantism as the Alliance for Border Control organized hundreds of cars to shine their headlights into Mexico while a "Metal Militia" of San Diego high school students conducted what they called "war-games" to hunt down and rob migrants.[22]

The confluence of developments that made for the weaponization of immigration as a threat to the country's well-being was clearly in evidence in the early 1990s: David Duke's campaigns in Louisiana; Pat Buchanan's America firstism and calls for a border wall; Proposition 187 in California; and Operation Gatekeeper, a further militarization of the border (near San Diego in this instance) replete with walls, fences, surveillance cameras, hi-tech motion sensors, and floodlights. It was no accident that the very tough Illegal Immigration

Reform and Immigrant Responsibility Act pushed by the Clinton administration passed the same year—1996—as his welfare reform bill, which limited benefits even to legal immigrants, and two years after his crime bill, which clearly tied harsh sentences to international drug trafficking and culture. When Clinton delivered his State of the Union Address in 1995 after a battering in the 1994 midterms, he highlighted his crackdowns on undocumented immigrants and their enablers, his hiring of many more Border Patrol agents, and the great uptick in deportations for which he claimed credit. "All Americans," he explained, "are rightly disturbed by the large numbers of illegal aliens entering our country. The jobs they hold might otherwise be held by citizens or legal immigrants. The public services they use impose burdens on our taxpayers." The logic of Duke, Buchanan, and Proposition 187 was now being embraced by a Democratic president regarded as an enemy in the right's culture war.[23]

III

IN 1950, HARLON CARTER of Laredo, Texas, became head of the United States Border Patrol, promising to wage "all-out war to hurl . . . Mexican wetbacks back into Mexico" with an "army of Border Patrol officers complete with jeeps, trucks, and seven aircraft." He knew of what he spoke. Carter had worked for the Border Patrol since 1936, following in the footsteps of his father, but for all intents and purposes he earned his bona fides five years before that when he shot a teenaged Hispanic boy to death sometime after his family's car had been stolen (there was no evidence that the Hispanic victim had stolen it). For this, Carter was tried, convicted, and sentenced to a three-year prison term, though the conviction was overturned by a higher court owing to the original judge's failure to adequately explain "self-defense" to the jury. So little was Carter's record blemished by the murder that in 1961 he became director of the southwestern region of the Immigration and Naturalization Service, a position he held until 1970, when he retired.[24]

It's not certain when Harlon Carter first signed up with the

National Rifle Association (NRA)—perhaps as early as the 1930s—
but he did join the national board in 1951, and in 1965, while still
working for the INS, briefly became the NRA's president. By that
point the organization was nearly a century old, having been established in New York in 1871 by Union Civil War veterans interested in
seeing that "rifle practice" and marksmanship skills were maintained
in peacetime. For many decades thereafter, the NRA was relatively
small and, at times, nearly defunct, devoted chiefly to hunting, conservation, and the safe use of guns, especially among sportsmen and Boy
Scouts. For a brief time in the 1930s, when the federal government
responded to "gangland violence" by enacting a bill that required the
registration of specific weapons (like machine guns) and a tax on their
production and sale, the NRA pushed back. But nothing was said
about the Second Amendment, and opposition to gun control faded
from their national agenda for another quarter century.[25]

Fractures in the NRA began to appear in the mid-1960s. The political assassinations and urban unrest of the period, not to mention the
emergence of the Black Panthers who publicly embraced armed self-
defense, gave gun control a hearing for the first time since the 1930s
as well as a base of support among conservatives like California governor Ronald Reagan, who was alarmed at the sight of young Black men
flaunting guns. The NRA mobilized opposition and began to invoke
the Second Amendment. "Can Three Assassins Kill a Civil Right?"
the *American Rifleman* cynically asked. Pressure from NRA members
and their congressional supporters served to weaken the Gun Control Act of 1968 substantially, and one top official wrote in *American Rifleman* that "the measure as a whole appears to be one that the
sportsmen of America can live with." But by decade's end, the NRA's
membership had grown dramatically, as did a faction that intended
to take the organization in a new and radically different direction.[26]

That faction was led by Harlon Carter, who came to Washington, D.C., in 1975 as founding director of the NRA's Institute for
Legislative Lobbying and was keen on ramping up the NRA's fight
against gun control. "We can win it on a simple concept," he wrote
to the entire NRA membership. "No compromise. No gun legislation." Carter was aided by Clifford Knox, a recent graduate of Abilene

Christian College in Texas, who believed that gun control laws not only threatened foundational American freedoms but also aimed to wholly disarm the American public. At the age of thirty, Knox started *Gun Week* magazine and went so far as to suggest that the assassinations that took place in the 1960s "might have been created for the purpose of disarming the people of the free world." The problem, as both Carter and Knox saw it, was that the NRA leadership appeared committed to a mainstream, nonpartisan approach, one focused chiefly on marksmanship, rather than on fighting against gun control advocates. The leadership's decision to move NRA headquarters out of Washington to Colorado and build a New Mexico recreational facility called the National Outdoor Center seemed all the proof needed. And so, at the NRA's annual convention in 1977, this time in Cincinnati, the Carter-Knox faction organized a "coup," swept through the convention floor wearing orange-blaze hunting caps, and took charge. "Before Cincinnati," one of the NRA rebels observed, "you had a bunch of people who wanted to turn the NRA into a sports publishing organization and get rid of guns. . . . We created the whole grass-roots lobbying concept." Plans to move the headquarters to Colorado and build the recreation center were scrapped. The NRA would remain in Washington, D.C., and its lobbying component would focus on the right to "keep and bear arms" as protected by the Second Amendment.[27]

The NRA formally entered partisan politics in 1980 when it endorsed Ronald Reagan for president. It continued to cultivate close ties to the Republican Party even though Democrats who represented rural districts often came on board as well. Yet, perhaps more significantly, the NRA began to craft a multidimensional image and appeal that had little to do with sportsmen, hunting, or marksmanship. It rather linked gun rights to freedom, the Constitution, patriotism, opposition to government "tyranny," protection of family and community against roving criminals, and white masculinity. The timing could not have been more propitious. Bolstered by a conservative turn in American politics and feeding off public worries about drugs, crime, a porous border, and growing racial tensions, the NRA soon became a potent force in American political life. Already in the

1980s, the NRA was a leading voice for law and order and crime control, devoting almost half of its monthly editorials in *American Rifleman* to these issues, and supporting calls for militarized policing and toughened sentencing laws. Without question, the NRA played an important part in the surge of incarceration and the building of a carceral-state apparatus.[28]

But there was much more afoot. With close ties to—and financial support from—the firearms industry, the NRA not only fortified opposition to gun control measures and contributed to an enormous uptick in gun ownership; it also energized an emerging right-wing nationalism that joined the objectives of elites who had been fighting to drastically limit the economic reach of the federal government with those of middle- and working-class whites who saw African Americans and other people of color, including immigrants, benefiting at their expense. Gun ownership was increasingly associated with both a Pat Buchanan–like white world that was being lost and a means of securing what was left of it against their dark enemies and enablers. Shortly before the presidential election of 2004, NRA leader Wayne LaPierre thus explained to members what was at stake: "If President George W. Bush is driven out of office—or if the Senate or House changes hands, two men will claim the credit," he warned. "And they will stand firmly in position to change the cultural destiny of America and . . . [declare] war against those of us who believe in the Second Amendment." The two men were not the Democratic presidential and vice-presidential candidates but "globalist billionaire George Soros and agitprop filmmaker Michael Moore." Soros, LaPierre predicted, would use the United Nations to establish a global gun ban, "which fits with his larger plan to diminish, weaken, and subjugate the United States as a world player, to erode our sovereignty . . . to domestically erase the dominant traditional values of the American people, . . . [to] buy himself a U.S. Supreme Court, stacked with anti-gun justices," and sponsor a "nationwide voter registration [that] targets Michael Moore's angry, undiscerning, fan club." Laced with anti-Semitic references and alarms about an expanding multiracial democracy, LaPierre was channeling David Duke and Pat Buchanan, but these would soon be talking points of right-wing Republicans redefining the party's mainstream.[29]

At the time of LaPierre's diatribe, the decade-old assault-weapons ban, enacted as part of Bill Clinton's 1994 crime bill, had just expired, not to be resurrected, and private gun ownership was growing by leaps and bounds. By 2015, Americans owned 255 million guns, an increase of 70 million since 1994, or more than one gun for every adult in the United States. Between 1990 and 2020, moreover, nearly 25 million assault weapons were either manufactured in or imported into the country. While it is true that a majority of the American public, including a good many gun owners, support background checks and restrictions based on age and disability, there is less support for the creation of a national gun-data registry or for banning assault and high-magazine-capacity weaponry. But roughly one-third of all American adults own a gun, nearly half live in households where a gun can be found, and the demographic leaders for both metrics are white men, about half of whom own guns themselves. For their part, only a quarter of white women and nonwhite men are gun owners. Even more important, the NRA has built a robust membership that is far more ideological and politically oriented than the gun-owning public at large. Members rally around the Second Amendment, strongly oppose any effort to limit gun rights, regard themselves as the embodiments of American patriotism, and overwhelmingly (almost 80 percent) align with the Republican Party. Not surprisingly, somewhere between two-thirds and three-quarters of them are white.[30]

As the demographic and political profiles of NRA members suggest, racial fears and resentments have become central to the gun culture that the organization has promoted, a culture that extends well beyond the NRA itself. More than two-thirds (67 percent) of all gun owners in 2017 regarded "protection," instead of "hunting" (38 percent), as their main reason for owning a gun, a significant change since the late 1990s when only one-quarter (26 percent) cited "protection" and about half (49 percent) cited "hunting." This helps us understand how nearly forty states, prodded by the NRA, have passed open-carry laws for handguns, and even more have open carry laws for "long guns" or rifles and shotguns, regarded as symbols of white security and power. Some open-carry advocates were quick to demonstrate the meaning of their political victories. In 2014 they proclaimed their right to carry weapons anywhere and everywhere by brazenly parading through Black areas of downtown St. Louis, Missouri, brandishing handguns, long guns, and assault rifles. Apparently, they took Wayne LaPierre's advice, expressed earlier that year, to be on the watch for "terrorists [and] home invaders, drug cartels, carjackers, knock out gamers, and rapers, and haters."[31]

It is no accident that the partisan and nationalist turn of the NRA coincided with the Reagan administration's escalated wars on crime, communism, and federal power as well as with the emergence of a "white power" movement in the United States. Together they expressed deepening resentment at how the modern American state encroached on constitutional rights, raided the pocketbooks of taxpayers, and denigrated white people while drawing upon the support of racial minorities and new waves of immigrants. As Glenn Miller of the White Patriot Party put it in 1985: "The federal government abandoned white people when they rammed blacks down the throats of white people and the government forced integration, forced white boys to fight in the Vietnam War, allowed aliens into the country, allowed Jewish abortion doctors to murder children, and allowed blacks to roam the streets, robbing, raping, and murdering."[32]

The argument was hardly new. David Duke had already warned that "immigration along with non-white birthrates will make white people a minority totally vulnerable to the political, social, and economic will of blacks, Mexicans, Puerto Ricans, and Orientals" resulting in a "social upheaval . . . that will be the funeral dirge of the America we love." The Aryan Nations, with close ties to the deeply racist and anti-Semitic Christian Identity movement, had been organizing white supremacists nationwide around a racial homelands policy. And *The Turner Diaries* (1978), an apocalyptic novel depicting the overthrow of a Jewish-controlled American government and the waging of a global race war bent on the extermination of all non-whites, had been published and widely circulated among those on the radical right.[33]

Yet it was not until the early 1990s that the threads of racism, anti-Semitism, and hatred of the federal government came together and led to the organization and expansion of paramilitary militias. Although right-wing militias have a deep history in the United States and resurfaced in the late 1970s and 1980s, two events proved to be special triggers in the 1990s. The first was a 1992 federal assault on a white supremacist enclave, Ruby Ridge, in Boundary County, Idaho, based on charges of trafficking illegal weapons. It resulted in an eleven-day siege, a lethal shootout, and the death of two members of the Randy Weaver family (targeted in the attack)—along with a U.S. deputy—and to Weaver's arrest (he was acquitted of most of the charges and received over three million dollars in federal restitution for his family's deaths). The second, in 1993, was another arms-trafficking-related siege, this one brought against the Branch Davidian religious compound near Waco, Texas, that eventuated in an FBI-initiated attack, an explosive fire at the compound, and the deaths of seventy-six Branch Davidians, including many children and their leader. Very quickly, militias organizing in all fifty states had more than fifty thousand members and perhaps as many as five million sympathizers and supporters, drawn together by the rhetoric of government "tyranny" as well as by evolving rightist views on immigration, local sovereignty, land use, racial hierarchies, and gun rights.[34]

The retaliation came quickly. On 19 April 1995, a few months after the Republicans swept the midterms and Newt Gingrich became House Speaker, a massive explosion detonated at the Alfred P. Murrah Federal Building, a U.S. government complex in Oklahoma City, Oklahoma. The blast—which leveled the Murrah Federal Building, badly damaged structures within a four-block radius, and killed 168 people at the site, nineteen of them children—could be heard fifty miles away. Another 650 or more victims suffered wounds. It was immediately recognized as an act of terrorism and, to that point, the deadliest in American history.

A suspect named Timothy McVeigh was soon arrested, and although he claimed to be acting on his own, he clearly had become part of the white power and militia movements of the time. Like many other movement adherents, McVeigh was a military veteran who had come under the influence of right-wing extremists and racists while in the service. Once out of uniform, in 1991, he moved around a great deal, briefly joined the Ku Klux Klan in Arizona, and then became involved with the increasingly notorious Michigan Militia and, especially, Terry Nichols, one of its members, who had been his army platoon leader and was already interested in blowing up the Murrah Building. Concerned about the power of the federal government, taxation, and threats to gun rights, McVeigh traveled to Waco, Texas, at the time of the siege to show his support for the Branch Davidians and distribute pro–gun rights literature. Indeed, while McVeigh had been a member of the NRA, he quit the organization because he believed it was doing too little to protect gun owners. Driving to and from Oklahoma City, he kept a copy of *The Turner Diaries* in his car.[35]

McVeigh, Nichols, and another accomplice were arrested, tried, and convicted for the bombing. McVeigh was sentenced to death and the two others to lengthy prison terms. In the immediate aftermath, the militia movement was cast on the defensive and saw a decline in its organizational base and membership. In truth, Oklahoma City was both culmination and catalyst: a brutal example of right-wing paramilitarism and a magnet for further activity and recruitment that, after a lull, took off again following Barack Obama's election. As for Newt Gingrich and his Republican colleagues, they received fire from both sides. While the press and many Democrats called Gingrich to account for his divisive rhetoric and the "anti-government climate" he created, more than a few militia members regarded him as little more than a government shill. Both critiques were on the mark. Trading on fears of crime, multiculturalism, and government overreach, Gingrich's was the electoral side of the new forms of political warfare being waged, but for the far right he didn't go nearly far enough.[36]

IV

In August 2017 hundreds of far-right protesters descended on Charlottesville, Virginia, for what they termed a "Unite the Right" rally. The organizers included white nationalists, neo-Nazis, members of the Ku Klux Klan, neo-Confederates, and a variety of groups on the alt-right that embraced white supremacy and anti-Semitism. Among the attendees were militias from Pennsylvania, New York, and Virginia, along with David Duke. Their stated goals were both to bring together the country's far-flung white nationalist movement and mobilize against the impending removal of Robert E. Lee's statue from the city's Lee Park. Quickly, the rally spiraled into violent clashes with counterprotesters and the murder of one of them. Yet in many ways the most vivid and disturbing images to come out of it were torch-bearing young white men in khakis marching through the University of Virginia campus on the night before the rally chanting "blood and soil," "white lives matter," and "Jews will not replace us," all Nazi and white-supremacist slogans. President Donald Trump then shocked much of the nation—including some cabinet members and senior advisors who nonetheless chose not to resign—by refusing to condemn the rally and suggesting that there were "good people on both sides."

The torchbearers seemed to be hiving off the "great replacement theory," conjured by French intellectual Renaud Camus in 2012 as a warning to white Europeans of the "reverse colonialism" taking place among them as "Black and Brown immigrants . . . flood the Continent in what amounts to an extinction-level event." Earlier versions of the theory came in the form of French author Jean Raspail's dystopian novel, *The Camp of the Saints* (1973), which depicted the destruction of Western civilization owing to mass immigration from what was then termed the Third World, and British writer Bat Ye'or's *Eurabia* (2006), which focused on the replacement of white Europeans by Muslims determined to expand the Caliphate and impose Sharia law. Together they shaped the perspectives of Europe's emerging far right and encouraged deadly attacks on Muslims and people of color the world over. They have also found a very receptive audience on the American far right, from Steve Bannon to Stephen Miller, and on right-wing media, most consequentially Fox News, though also on many far-right internet sites.[37]

The "great replacement" is, of course, only an updated take on the fears of "race suicide" that coursed through much of the Euro-

Atlantic world in the late nineteenth and early twentieth centuries, provoked by declining birthrates among white Protestants and the massive influx of southern and eastern Europeans who were regarded as poor, illiterate, untrustworthy, prone to violence and criminality, and extraordinarily fertile. Then immigration restriction was married to population control, and eugenics became the widely accepted solution to the destiny of the white race. Few in Progressive America, drawn as they were to the possibilities of social engineering on a large scale, would have rejected the logic, and strong advocacy came from the highest reaches of political and cultural life. It would be decades before the fears of race suicide and the eugenics mindset fell into disrepute. And there is no good way to understand how crime, race, and immigration became so effectively weaponized in recent years without recognizing the very deep roots that had been sunk more than a century before.[38]

The replacement idea has of late been closely connected to the issue of immigration and the "caravans" of "illegal aliens" heading to the U.S.-Mexican border, apparently determined to enter the United States. Beyond doubt, the idea has gained traction not only on the far, white-supremacist right but also among conservative Republican voters, regularly warned by media outlets like Fox News that the future of the country hangs in the balance. The argument is twofold: that the swelling number of undocumented immigrants is accelerating the demographic trend in the United States that will make white people a minority by mid-century; and that it is all being encouraged by Democrats who want unrestricted immigration to expand their electoral base and secure their power. Rather than making many white Americans more sympathetic to minorities in their midst, this prospect of white minority status has instead reminded them of the dismal fate they are bound to experience when the tables turn and one-time minorities become majorities and can exercise power accordingly. It is a fate they seem intent upon resisting, for some at all cost. "Nobody wants to be a minority," one far-rightist declared. "Look at how we've treated black people. Don't for a second think that they'll treat us any better."[39]

Yet, far more significant to the advance of the illiberal politics to which replacement theory appeals is the anti-government perspective that it fortifies: not so much a new version of race suicide than a simplified and highly arresting way of expressing popular unease with the workings and apparent alliances of the state. Instead of viewing federal and state governments as potential resources for communities undergoing social and cultural disruptions—as was true during the years between 1890 and 1930 when hostility to people of color, immigrants, and the ways of modernity could be legislated—growing numbers of whites came to see the state, especially the federal government, as an enabler of those disruptions, concerned less about white people and their communities than about the new clients that civil rights struggles and then new patterns of immigration had yielded. What was being replaced was not yet white numerical dominance but rather the privileges and access they remembered enjoying—the relatively unquestioned deference and acknowledgment accorded the will of their communities. This is what George Wallace saw as he began his national campaigns in 1964. He understood that there were constituencies of white voters who were coming to fear federal power as a solvent of the communities they wished to defend, communities founded on exclusions and hierarchies that the government was rejecting and rendering illegal. Wallace was a product of the white "authoritarian enclaves" that had ruled the South for more than eight decades and were struggling to hold on, and he crafted a language that resonated with white enclaves outside the South that were also struggling to hold on or, in fact, to reconstitute themselves in the face of change.[40]

The taxpayer revolts, attacks on busing and the ERA, the demonization of government power, and growing alarm about "illegal" immigration gave voice to deep-seated fears of replacement. And they most certainly fed currents of illiberal politics, already gaining force in the 1960s. Yet by the early twenty-first century it was not the white-supremacist militias who channeled those currents into the mainstream of American politics. It was the Tea Party movement that burst onto the scene so quickly after President Obama's inauguration.

The Tea Party crippled his congressional support, put many state legislatures in right-wing Republican hands, and developed perspectives that set the direct path for Donald Trump.

Those who joined local Tea Party groups or identified politically with the Tea Party movement did not have uniform views on social, economic, or cultural life. Some were libertarians and some nationalists; some were hawkish on foreign affairs, and some leaned toward "America firstism"; some were advocates of the free market and some suspicious of the business elites who strongly embraced it; some vigorously opposed big government programs and some were more selective in their support. Still, among Tea Party adherents, there was a political culture and set of sensibilities that most shared. They believed that the country they and their parents had worked hard to build, and one they claimed to have stored in their memories, was crumbling or being taken away. They feared that they were on a slippery slope of decline—demographically, politically, and culturally, with devastating consequences for their children and grandchildren. They wanted the government to stop "illegal immigration," with iron-fisted methods if necessary. They tended to view Blacks and people of color generally, especially immigrants, unfavorably, as "takers" rather than "makers," and while they supported Social Security and Medicare, they generally opposed government programs seen as helping people with low incomes. As for Democrats, they were viewed as collaborators with corrupt labor unions and allies of the immigrants and people of color in the process of replacing them. A great many Tea Partiers were church-goers and backers of government regulation of marriage and childbearing. That is to say, they generally opposed gay marriage and, at best, were dubious about reproductive rights. And they were pleased to see law enforcement and other state institutions deployed against their presumed enemies.

Most of all, Tea Party adherents detested Barack Obama and what they believed he stood for. That this movement erupted in the apparent afterglow of Obama's election and talk of America as a "post-racial" society suggests how visceral their fears and anger had become and how close to the surface they rested—triggered, it seemed, by no more than a rant on a television media outlet. Many Tea Partiers regarded Obama as "un-American," un-Christian (likely Muslim), difficult to comprehend, and a figure who truly embodied the cultural and demographic changes taking place before their eyes as well as the mechanisms used to favor people of color and illegal "aliens" over them. In effect, many assumed that Obama had been catapulted to the presidency by means of special race-based privileges and would soon be waving others like him to the front of the line, cutting in ahead of them. He was *their* president, not *your* president. The impulse was hardly new; it harked back to a well-worn Reconstruction-era racist reaction to the extension of civil and political rights to African Americans, one that rejected the legitimacy of Black equality and empowerment, whatever federal law and the Constitution demanded. The Tea Partiers took and ran with this well before Donald Trump began to publicly question Obama's place of birth.[41]

For many observers at the time and since, the Tea Party and its illiberal politics captured the grievances and resentments of the "white working class." Battered by decades of deindustrialization, betrayed by the Democrats who once rewarded their support, angered by the challenges and gains of minorities and feminists, and sedated with the Reagan-era bromides about immigrant "invasions" and "welfare queens," white workers appeared especially vulnerable to the narratives of decline, loss, and replacement that the Tea Party peddled. Especially in towns and counties that had at one time been the citadels of manufacturing might and organized labor power—like steel-making Youngstown, Ohio—the story of white "deprivation" (of power, stability, and well-being) and "minoritization" has been as pervasive as it is troubling. The same narrative has been animating support for the nationalist and nativist far right, at least since the 1990s, in the once-robust industrial zones of Britain, France, Belgium, and Italy, where labor, socialist, and communist parties had long ruled. It too has focused on cultural as well as economic issues.[42]

As it turns out, however, the energy for Tea Party illiberalism came not from the white working class, however that "class" may be reckoned, but from older (over forty-five on average) white women and, especially, men, who were relatively well educated, economically comfortable, heavily concentrated in the Sunbelt rather than the Rust Belt, evangelical in their religious dispositions, and sufficiently conservative in their politics to regularly place themselves to the right of the Republican Party. Many Tea Party men were veterans of the Vietnam War, much like those who formed the base of the white power movement in the late 1970s and early 1980s or were career military. Many more were small-business owners in sectors, like construction, that were hit hard during the Great Recession of 2007–2010 and long bitter about the taxes they had to pay for the sake of the "undeserving" Blacks and poor. About six in ten had guns in their homes, and a significant minority of them believed that violence against the U.S. government could be justifiable. Almost all described President Obama's policies, exemplified by the Affordable Care Act, as destined to move the country toward socialism. At least one-third were convinced that he was born outside the United States.[43]

The political leanings of the "white working class" are difficult to divine not just because election data is only available in aggregates (by districts and counties) but also because there is little clarity or agreement about what makes white men and women members of the working class to start with. For the most part, the metrics used are levels of education (no more than a high school diploma) and income, though both may be misleading. Bill Gates lacks a college degree, and many small-business owners have volatile incomes. What's more, while the two and a half decades after World War Two witnessed impressive material gains on the part of workers, especially in the unionized manufacturing sector, the past four or five decades have seen both a dramatic erosion of those gains and the slippage of substantial sections of the middle class into what can best be described as working-class life circumstances. That is to say, slippage into an economic life of job insecurity, wages rather than salaries, precarious benefit packages, and diminished personal savings and assets. The industrial working class of the past has shrunk dramatically, many of its berths moving overseas or to Latin America, replaced by the great expansion of service-sector employment (of myriad types) that is marked by low wages, few if any benefits, underemployment, and multiethnic workforces. As for the higher levels of the information economy—those with college degrees and related skills—consulting and contract labor is becoming the norm, with limited career tracks in places where affordable housing is hard to find. Institutions of higher education have exemplified this trend, depending more and more heavily on adjuncts who may hold masters or doctoral degrees but are generally paid by the course, deprived of a recognized status on campus, and usually denied any benefits.[44]

Even so, the political picture is not entirely clear. Despite Tea Party mobilizations, Barack Obama won reelection comfortably in 2012, holding on to most of the districts and counties he won in 2008. Many had been Democratic strongholds of white working-class and lower-middle-class voters. Indeed, what made Donald Trump's election possible in 2016 was his flipping of over two hundred counties, a remarkable one-third of Obama's 2012 total. And although white working-class men clearly broke for Trump in the end, sometimes in the face of their unions' blandishments, it would be a mistake to put them all in one political box. Working-class (auto manufacturing) Macomb County, Michigan, supported Trump in 2016 after supporting Obama in 2008 and 2012; working-class (steel manufacturing) Mahoning County, Ohio, which strongly supported Obama in 2008 and 2012, backed Hillary Clinton in 2016. Not a few of these voters, during the primaries and in the lead-up to the general election, either saw Bernie Sanders as a close second to Trump or preferred him outright. As one of them in rural Pennsylvania, who would ultimately vote for Trump, explained, Bernie "is just a down to earth guy. He's one of us. He's thinking about the people that work for a living. He's on the right track. The actual popular vote, I think Bernie would have had it."[45]

Thus, the picture is one of volatility, stirred by mistrust of established political institutions and "career politicians," as well as hostility toward those viewed as the "takers." Observers often simplify it all as rageful "populism" laden with conspiracy theories of many sorts, and the volatility surely can and has tipped to the illiberal right when little better is on offer. But the appeal of Sanders suggests a different type of opening and set of dispositions, as unexpected at the time as Trump's but also rooted equally deep in America's past.[46]

V

The road to the Trump presidency and the empowerment of right-wing illiberalism that he fired up and then availed himself of was not a sudden departure from "liberal democratic norms" or a thoroughfare of recently fomented racist rage. Long and winding, it has been paved for nearly three-quarters of a century by mainstream politics and sweeping transformations of the global economy and ecosystem. The road has been paved by public policies seen as threats to community autonomy and by the struggles and balance-tilting gains of African Americans and women. It has been paved by George Wallace's reconfiguring the language of race and local right, by the weakening of the American economy, and by the deindustrialization of its once thriving corridors. It has been paved by the political offensives of corporate capital against working-class gains and the "class-compromise" of the 1940s and 1950s, and later by the neoliberalism of the Reagan and Clinton eras and the dramatic economic inequalities it promoted.

The road to Trump and right-wing illiberal empowerment has also been paved by successive "wars" on crime and drugs and the militarization of domestic policing. It has been paved by the end of the Cold War and the destabilizations of the political alignments and perspectives it had brought into being. It has been paved by new patterns of migration the world over, set off by civil warfare, labor demand, and the aftermath of decolonization. And it has been paved by the hollowing out of welfare states and social democratic policies in the Euro-Atlantic owing in good part to the slowing of economic growth worldwide, as well as by the demographic transformations that came along with much of this. For a time, there was sufficient ballast remaining in the political orders created after the Second World War to stand against the conservative winds and the illiberal projects encouraged by them. But once the parties of the left and center-left—Democrat, Labor, Socialist—moved toward the middle and increasingly accepted the world that conservativism and neoliberalism was making, the road toward Trump and the far right had fewer obstacles.

The specters of race war and replacement that have been driving politics during the past few decades are at the very least Euro-Atlantic and could not have gained real traction otherwise. For much of the twentieth century, the United States stood out as an arena of organized and bloody racism; much of Europe, especially after World War Two, successfully confined racist violence to the colonies and thrived off its results without much disruption of life at home. The United States could appear as a special offender and Europeans could pride themselves on the absence of racial strife in their midst. It was Swedish-born Gunnar Myrdal who wrote the searing indictment of American race relations in 1944, *An American Dilemma: The Negro Problem and Modern Democracy,* suggesting how America's liberal "creed" and the long-term oppression of Black people could go hand-in-glove. Then the empire struck back. People of color from the Caribbean, Africa, and Asia began to swell populations across much of continental Europe and Britain, adding to their social and cultural complexity and, as Euro-American economies stumbled, seemed to weigh on the resources of social-democratic regimes and the expectations of their citizenries.

Parties of the right began to form in the 1980s and 1990s, but their appearance and growth were especially noteworthy during the first two decades of the twenty-first century. Most were organized around nationalism and opposition to immigration. The National Front (now National Rally) in France, though founded earlier, made its first major showing in the elections of 2002 when its presidential candidate Jean-Marie Le Pen made it to the final round of voting against Jacques Chirac. By 2014, the party was well represented both in France and the European Parliament, and in 2017 Marine Le Pen finished second in the national presidential election. Hungary's Fidesz Party, Christian nationalist and anti-immigrant, made a major showing in the 2004 European Parliamentary elections and then took power in Hungary in 2010, which it has held ever since owing to the constitutional revisions it pushed through.

The neo-fascist Brothers of Italy, in power as of 2022–23, was established in 2012, the hard-right Alternative for Germany (AfD) in 2013, the Spanish Vox party in 2013, and the Danish New Right

344 I L L I B E R A L   A M E R I C A

Party in 2015 (supplanting the Danish People's Party of 1990s vintage). Moving east, the far right is also a formidable presence, emerging since the end of the Cold War, growing in Serbia, the Czech Republic, Ukraine (before the Russian invasion), Georgia, Armenia, and, of course, holding power both in Poland (the Law and Justice Party) and Hungary. Founded in 1982, the fascist British National Party remained on the margins of political life until the 2000s; then it began to win seats in local governments and was boosted by its support, together with the Euro-skeptic United Kingdom Independence Party, for Brexit in 2016, which in many ways demonstrated political and economic nationalism at its most successful. Even as far-right parties have faltered in some recent elections, as in Austria and the Netherlands, they have made surprising gains elsewhere, in Sweden and especially in Italy. Quite clearly, the far right has become an integral part of the European political landscape, has sufficient popular support to pull centrist and conservative parties their way, particularly on issues surrounding immigration, and have infiltrated state institutions such as the military and police forces. Outside of Europe, the far right has near majority followings from the Philippines to Brazil, and commands power in India and Israel.[47]

However nationalist and anti-globalist the far right in Europe and America may be, transnational networks have been built, especially during the 2010s. One of the most important vehicles is the internet, which serves as a means of communication as well as one of camaraderie and alliance. There are personal contacts as well. American far-right leaders have traveled abroad to meet with their European counterparts, and some of their members have gone so far as joining European paramilitary groups, especially armed neo-Nazi groups in Eastern Europe. The European far right has in turn reached out to the American, and far-right parties like Vox in Spain are in the process of constructing a far-right network for the Spanish-speaking world, focused chiefly on Latin America.[48]

Perhaps most significant is a "mainstreaming" of these connections. In October 2021, Senator Ted Cruz spoke in a live video to a Vox rally in Madrid, arguing that "we all face the same challenges, including a bold and global left, that seeks to tear down cherished national and religious institutions." Only one month earlier, former vice president Mike Pence traveled to Hungary to speak at the biannual Budapest Demographic Summit, where he praised Viktor Orbán's government and others in central Europe for their pro-family (anti-abortion) policies. "For our civilization to prosper," he maintained, "if we're to pass on the rights and freedom and values that we cherish to the next generation, our highest priority must be to preserve, renew, and strengthen the families upon which our nations and our civilizations have been built." There Pence joined the heads of state of Poland, the Czech Republic, Slovenia, and Serbia together with French far-rightist Eric Zemmour, who would enter the French presidential race several months later. Pence was also photographed with Bosnian Serb leader Milorad Dodik, who has called the Muslim massacre at Srebrenica a "fabricated myth." A month before that, one-time Fox News star Tucker Carlson took his nightly show to Budapest for a week of broadcast, showcasing the authoritarian Orbán government and its achievements, most notably on issues of immigration and national culture. "If you care about Western civilization and democracy and families," Carlson told his viewers, "you should know what is happening here now." Taking the opportunity to fly over Hungary's fenced-off border, he insisted that "Hungary's leaders actually care about making sure their own people thrive. Instead of promising the nation's wealth to every illegal immigrant from the Third World they're using tax dollars to uplift their own people." Not to be outdone, the American Conservative Political Action Committee (CPAC) held a May 2022 conference in Budapest too; Orbán returned the favor that August, addressing CPAC's meeting in Dallas.[49]

Traveling to and bowing at the altar of Viktor Orbán's Hungary has become something of a ritual of the American far right in its various guises. Steve Bannon, Dennis Prager, Milo Yannopolous, and Jeff Sessions paved the way. Now it seems to be a required stop of right-wing authenticity. That is because Orbán's Hungary doesn't simply represent the aspirations of the far right; it is the embodiment and exemplar, a symbol of illiberal views and policies, a true success story, an indication of how they can win and rule. After all, Orbán is the longest-reigning head of state in Europe. He has used his power and that of his Fidesz Party not only to dominate politics and political society but also to organize Hungary's culture, playing to the nationalism of his supporters and harassing, repressing, or expelling his enemies. He has represented himself as an ardent defender of Western civilization under siege, a Christian nationalist in the face of Muslim onslaughts and Jewish money, a promoter of family formation for ethnic Hungarians, an opponent of multiculturalism in all its forms (including gender and sexuality), and a foe of immigration from outside Europe as well as an advocate of restrictive rights for those who enter. Perhaps more than anyone else in the Euro-Atlantic world, Orbán appears as the great warrior against the great replacement.[50]

But Orbán is not alone. When neo-fascist Giorgia Meloni, an acolyte of Mussolini and a hardliner on immigration (she claims to support a naval blockade against sea-borne migrants), swept to victory in Italy's national elections in September 2022, the American right greeted her with the greatest enthusiasm. "Spectacular," Ted Cruz exulted. "Buona Fortuna," crowed former secretary of state Mike Pompeo. "Italy deserves and needs strong conservative leadership." "Congratulations to Giorgia Meloni and the winners in the Italian elections," Arkansas Republican senator Tom Cotton declared; "we look forward to working with her and other Italian leaders who share our interests." While Georgia congresswoman Marjorie Taylor Greene described Meloni's victory speech as "beautifully said," Colorado's Lauren Boebert offered some rightist perspective. "This month Sweden voted for a right-wing government. Now Italy voted for a right-wing government. The entire world is beginning to understand that the Woke Left does nothing but destroy." "God speed to Italy's incredible prime minister," Arizona gubernatorial candidate (and eventual loser) Kari Lake chimed in. The Americans were joined in Europe by Marine Le Pen, Eric Zemmour, Polish prime minister Mateusz Morawiecki, and, of course, Viktor Orbán. As the Spanish Vox Party put it, Meloni's victory showed "the path of a new Europe of free and sovereign nations."[51]

Some saw such prospects even earlier. In 2012, David Duke traveled to Italy and set up in the northern town of Venas di Cadore, near the Austrian border, apparently intending to form "racist and anti-Semitic groups in Europe." Arriving with a visa and under an assumed name, Duke managed to go about his business undetected. But eighteen months later his cover was blown and he was expelled from the country, deemed by an Italian court as "socially dangerous due to his infamous racist theories" and his efforts to establish "an organization aiming to exterminate the black and Jewish races in Europe." Now, one would think, Duke could easily return and continue his work.[52]

CONCLUSION

O N   P R E S I D E N T ' S   D AY   2 0 2 3 ,   THE   FAR-RIGHT   CON-
gresswoman from Georgia, Marjorie Taylor Greene, one of the
most powerful Republicans in the House of Representatives, called
for a "national divorce." By this she meant the formal separation of
the "red states" from the "blue states," the shrinking of the federal
government, a much stronger embrace of state rights, and the prospect of escape from the "disgusting woke culture issues shoved down
our throats [by] the Democrat's [*sic*] traitorous America Last policies."
Although Greene said little about how such a divorce would come
about (she floated the idea of a "legal agreement") or how the borders
of these states would be determined, she disclaimed a "civil war" as a
means to her end while insisting "it's going in that direction, and we
have to do something about it." The important thing, as Greene saw
it, was that the divorce would enable citizens of red states to set their
own rules about rights, belonging, power, culture, religious faith,
and political dispositions—an illiberal state sovereignty—that, she
believed, expressed the vision of the country's founders. "Red states,"
Greene imagined, "can choose in how they allow people to vote in
their states. . . . [They] could propose if Democrat voters choose to
flee these blue states where they cannot tolerate the living conditions,
they don't want their children taught these horrible things, and they
really change their minds on the types of policies they support, well
once they move to a red state, guess what, maybe you don't get to vote
for five years."[1]

The idea of a "national divorce" drew the expected rancor from

Democrats as well as dismissive pushback from some Republicans. But polling at the time suggested that as many as one-third of the American electorate, and nearly half of Republican voters, were favorably disposed to some version of it. Critics, particularly historians among them, were quick to mark the worrisome parallels from the past: either the shaky political world made by the Articles of Confederation or, more ominously, the secession of the enslaving states in 1860–1861 that did lead to civil war. In truth, the "national divorce" conjured by Greene bears a closer resemblance to the idea of an "ethnostate," especially to white homelands policies, that began to surface in the 1970s with the founding of the Aryan Nations and has been carried forward by white nationalists, neo-Nazis, Proud Boys, and the alt-right more generally. David Duke was an early proponent. The "Unite the Right" rally in Charlottesville, Virginia, in 2017 was a threatening expression. Donald Trump happily hailed the leaders. And Greene plainly signaled her alliance with them by headlining a white nationalist conference in Orlando, Florida, in 2022, organized by Nick Fuentes, later a dinner guest at Trump's Mar-a-Lago.[2]

The national divorce, the growth of white nationalism, the upticks in anti-Semitism, the support for "America First," the successful attacks on well-established civil and political rights, the demonization of immigrants and people of color, the popularity of "independent state legislature theory" on the right wing, and the resurgence of the crime issue to fortify open-carry and stand-your-ground laws all exemplify the very dark illiberal moment in which we find ourselves. Mass shootings of children and adults have become regular occurrences. The expulsions of duly elected Black and transgender legislators, following fast upon the more generalized racial expulsions that partisan gerrymandering enables, have become features of our political system. To find an analogous era of illiberal darkness, we would have to go back at least to the McCarthyite repression of the 1950s or, more likely, to the government-endorsed fascist pulses of the 1920s.

Yet this should not suggest that illiberal influence and power rise and fall cyclically or swing pendulum-like, that illiberalism grows much like a noxious weed, able to be extracted by a liberal or progressive movement or shift, to rise again perhaps in the future when liberalism goes into crisis. Illiberal ideas, relations, practices, sensibilities, places of empowerment, cultural hierarchies, and political projects have been—as this book maintains—deeply embedded in our history, not at the margins but very much at the center, infusing the soil of social and political life, and often ensnaring or entangling much else that grows there. Illiberalism develops and changes, transforms and reconstitutes itself, finds new bases of support while displacing others, and is rarely distant from the levers of power. It is usually nourished by the "community" and expressed by the community's "will," however the "community" may be understood. Illiberalism's history is America's history.

I

BUT NOT ALL OF THAT HISTORY. American history has, from the first, swirled with political currents that do not course easily with either liberalism or illiberalism, even if at some point they flowed through or over both. Along with the feudal and neo-feudal visions that shaped North American colonization from the sixteenth century, or the liberal visions that began to emerge by the end of the seventeenth century, there were other challenges to ideas of political and spiritual belonging, even to the meaning of private property, that revolutionary England saw in the rise of the Levellers and Diggers or of the Quakers and Ranters, and that would move across and around the Atlantic world. Along with the anti-Catholicism, monarchism, and localism to be found in Revolutionary and Constitutional America, there were demands for ending the slave trade and enslavement, for an unvarnished republicanism, for a popular democracy well beyond what the founders could conceive, and for what we would later call "human rights." Together they composed the foundation of the new country and would remain there for later excavation.

This would be apparent in the many decades to follow. Along with the expulsions of Indigenous peoples, African Americans, Catholics, and Mormons that contaminated the 1830s, there were early organizations of working people, bold critiques of market relations and, on occasion, private property, the spread of producer cooperatives, and the rise of a radical abolitionism that could call into question many relations of power and authority. Along with the advent of the penitentiary and prison labor that, during the Civil War, limited the meaning of free labor and heralded an industrial capitalist order, there was the military defeat of enslavers, the uncompensated emancipation of four million enslaved people, the prospect of sweeping land reform, demands for women's rights, and the ratification of constitutional amendments that established birthright citizenship and the legal basis for later rights struggles. Along with the social engineering, corporatism, Jim Crow racism, and eugenic dispositions of the Progressive era, there was a nationwide expansion of socialism, experimentation with novel types of political representation (including one based on occupation), and the emergence of organizations—like the NAACP and UNIA—devoted to racial equality and empowerment. And along with the antiradical, anti-immigrant, anti-labor, Christian fundamentalist, fascist appeals, and corporatist policies of the 1920s and early 1930s, there was a newborn feminism, the Harlem Renaissance, a developing industrial unionism, and a project of social democracy determined to turn state power toward the end of a more inclusive and equitable society.

The outbreak of the Cold War threw many impediments in the path of that social-democratic project and helped stir cauldrons on the illiberal right, as we have seen. But anti-communism, vehement opposition to open housing, and backlashes against busing, affirmative action, and feminism demonstrated the power and impact social justice movements were having and how they forced the federal government to their side, however limited and short-lived that support proved to be. The dramatic empowerment of conservatives, the embrace of neoliberal policies, and the "wars" on drugs and crime that then consumed the 1980s and 1990s and fueled mass incarceration were accompanied by an international movement against nuclear weaponry, popular movements against the social and economic consequences of neoliberal globalization, and an unprecedented movement for gay rights (in part the result of the tragic AIDS epidemic) together with new perspectives on sexual orientation. Even the right-wing mobilizations around threats of race war and white "replacement," stoked as they have been by dimming economic prospects for large sections of the white middle and lower-middle class, saw the remarkable presidential campaign of a democratic socialist and the rise of a Black Lives Matter movement that mixed issues of racism, economic inequality, and sexual orientation so compellingly as to rattle the illiberal right at all levels.

An even wider and deeper historical journey would acquaint us with the social and gender relations, the spiritualities, and especially the very different ideas about enacting justice that Indigenous peoples across the continent developed and deployed not only well before white Europeans arrived but also in the face of Euro-American efforts to eradicate them. And throughout our history, men and women of African descent subjected to enslavement, Jim Crow, and persisting—and truly systemic—racisms have offered us, from the seventeenth century to the present, the most expansive conceptions of civil and political equality, the most sustaining ideas of freedom, and some of the most stunning examples of social movement building. It's true, of course, that ideas and projects that flowed at cross-purposes or disconnected from both illiberalism and liberalism could find themselves entangled by or making their peace with either. Yet, they would endure in ways that allow for their retrieval, reexamination, and reinvigoration.

It is also important to recognize that political categories are often unstable, and it is not uncommon for people and communities to move between them or use them for purposes that seem at odds with prevailing expectations. In the United States and in many other parts of the world, working people and rural cultivators have embraced Lockean and related liberal ideas, especially those linking productive use and property claims, to push back against their employers, their landlords, and their imperial overseers: to argue for a labor theory of value, for access to uncultivated land, for upholding common rights to unenclosed woodlands and pastures, and for laws to prohibit speculative engrossment.[3] Anti-monopoly politics in the United States, particularly vital between 1870 and 1900, advanced many of these arguments while demonstrating how some liberal formulas could be used to attack the "wages system" (often called "wage slavery") and construct a producers' commonwealth in its stead.

II

IN IMPORTANT RESPECTS, what we have come to call "populism" reveals much of this historical instability as well as political danger and possibility. In recent years, observers have generally regarded populism as a menace rather than a movement, a backlash rather than a program, and a rage-filled attempt to target domestic enemies rather than a rational response to disruptive change. Yet populism has had a lengthy and complex history in the United States, one that defies contemporary representations and suggests that political migrations can occur among those who may seem the least likely to migrate.

As early as the 1820s and 1830s, anti-aristocratic rhetoric and demands for democratic reform that some historians call "populist" accompanied the expansion of mass politics and the rise of new political parties. Much more significant was the People's or Populist Party that emerged during the 1890s and captured the popular radicalism that had become widespread after Reconstruction. This was a movement that named itself "Populist" and developed a program designed to reorient the political economy of the United States in the face of expanding capitalist relations and values. Populists attacked the concentrations of wealth and power and the denigrations of democracy at the hands of "robber barons" and "money kings." And they imagined a producers' republic and "cooperative commonwealth" as alternatives to a capitalism that was pushing more and more working people (rural and urban) into states of abject dependency.

In 1892, they organized the People's Party and constructed a platform designed to promote fundamental change. Most famously, the Populists demanded the free and unlimited coinage of silver for the purposes of monetary inflation, to lift the burdens of debt from the shoulders of producers. But they also demanded a "union of the labor forces" of the nation, public control of the money supply, a system of federally funded marketing cooperatives, government ownership of the railroads and telegraph, an eight-hour workday, a graduated income tax, and the direct election of U.S. senators who, since the ratification of the Constitution, had been chosen by state legislatures. In all these demands they built upon the political sensibilities of the Greenback Labor Party of the 1870s, the Knights of Labor of the 1880s, and the Farmers' Alliances of the 1880s and early 1890s. And in the southern states, they built upon some of the biracial politics of the Reconstruction and post-Reconstruction periods to threaten the dominance of plantation owners and their commercial allies. To this day, the Populism of the 1890s stands as the largest third-party movement in all American history.

By the turn of the twentieth century, the Populists had suffered defeat, and some of their supporters either made their peace with the prevailing two-party system or withdrew from political engagement. But others moved farther left, aligning with the Socialist Party that was established in 1901, spread rapidly across the United States in the 1910s, and had special prominence in Texas, Louisiana, Arkansas, and Oklahoma (what we now, for the most part, call very "red" states), as well as in the Dakotas, Minnesota, and Wisconsin. Socialists were elected to state and municipal offices there and made their presence felt in smaller cities and towns like Schenectady, New York; Ashtabula, Ohio; Kalamazoo, Michigan; Grand Junction, Colorado; Coquille, Oregon; and Watts, California. Moving along with them during the 1910s and 1920s were the Non-Partisan League and the Farmer-Labor Party of the upper Plains, which achieved political power and held on to it tenaciously for years. In the depths of the Great Depression, the legacies of 1890s populism were carried forward by many New Dealers along with the followers of both Louisiana's Huey Long and Detroit's Father Coughlin.[4]

Across the decades from the 1830s to the 1930s, and then in more recent times, "populism" in its various incarnations has shown a significant and historically notable continuity. It has had special appeal for certain social class constituencies: for petty property owners, rural producers, artisans and craftsmen, some skilled industrial workers, and small-scale employers who were almost invariably white, in part because the populist appeal, at any point, could also include suspicions of outsiders or people of color. Yet the continuities in the social base belie the volatilities of their political expressions. Populist politics, in the United States and elsewhere around the world, have exploded in unpredictable ways. They have trended left, right, and reformist; in some cases, they have been difficult to categorize. Scholars and other observers have, as a result, long debated how populism is to be defined, situated, and assessed, and they have often arrived at conflicting conclusions.[5]

But history reveals that change can unfold in surprising ways. One especially remarkable episode occurred in the cotton counties of East Texas—Grimes County in particular—during the last decades of the nineteenth century, under the leadership of Garrett Scott and Jim Kennard. Scott was hardly the picture of a radical or insurgent; he was from a family of white plantation owners who fought for the Confederacy during the Civil War and very likely enslaved Black men, women, and children. But hard times in the 1870s led Scott to the Greenback Labor Party, and when he decided to run for Grimes County sheriff in 1882, he discovered that local Blacks had already built a formidable Republican Party organization that could turn out the votes necessary to defeat the opposing, reactionary Democrats. And so he joined hands with Jim Kennard, the Black Republican leader, and formed an interracial coalition. Both won election in 1882, Kennard to the office of district clerk.

To be sure, the coalition began as a matter of expediency, and little is known about the personal dynamic that developed between Scott and Kennard. What we do know is that Scott and his followers recognized that their ability to gain and maintain power depended on Black votes, and, through Kennard, Scott learned a great deal about the needs of Grimes County's Black constituents. As a result, he appointed Black deputy sheriffs (a rarity in the post–Civil War South) and supported the county's Black schools and schoolteachers financially. In the process, Scott earned the trust of 80 to 90 percent of the county's Black voters while holding on to about a third of the county's white voters who, like Scott, inclined to insurgency. For most of the next eighteen years, the coalition, in Greenback, Independent, and then Populist phases, ruled the county.

Indeed, during the 1890s, as the Populist Party rose, flexed its muscles, and then spiraled down in defeat nationally, the coalition in Grimes County, now clearly labeling itself Populist, held on to power. Scott had been joined by white leaders J. W. H. Davis and J. H. Teague, and Kennard had been joined by Black leaders Morris Carrington and Jack Haynes, all experienced in struggling together against white Democratic foes. In 1896, the decisive year that saw the Populist national and Texas state parties begin to crumble, the Grimes County Populists were victorious. Two years later, when Populism was vanishing on the larger political stages, the Grimes County Populists seemed to cement their power; the maneuvers and machinations of local Democrats could not defeat them in good measure because Texas had not yet followed many of the Deep South states in formally disfranchising African American men by means of poll taxes, literacy requirements, and registration laws.

As the elections of 1900 approached, Grimes County Democrats laid down the gauntlet. They established the White Man's Union, pressured most of the county's white voters to support them, and unleashed a reign of terror on the county's Blacks, provoking an exodus that quickly changed the county's demographic balance. But the Populists refused to back down, and in the weeks before the election the White Man's Union turned to the method that had long sustained white supremacy there: lethal violence. They gunned down the Populist leadership, beginning with Jim Kennard and ending with a post-election shootout in the county seat of Anderson, where Garrett Scott and members of his family fell victims to the fusillade. Remnants of the bullet holes can still be seen in the walls of the white-washed county courthouse.[6]

So ended the biracial political coalition that brought together former Confederates and formerly enslaved people. The White Man's Union not only destroyed the Populist leadership and base in the county but commenced a more than fifty-year local rule that also expunged the memory of what had happened in the late nineteenth century among white and the remaining Black denizens alike. It thereby buried a stunning history of race and politics, much as the illiberal right is currently attempting to do for the country as a whole.

III

HISTORY IS A BURDEN and an inspiration. It is buried deep within each of us, and hovers over the worlds that have been made and the future for which many now struggle. It offers few clear or easy lessons or any real prospect of repetition, however much we may believe that the past speaks directly to the present. The Grimes County story shows what might be possible among people who could otherwise be at odds, but it shows, as well, how hard change is to achieve and how precarious change always remains amid gross imbalances of wealth and power. What enabled a coalition of white and Black rural people to rule in Grimes County was not only an experience of shared exploitation but also years of working together, mobilizing their supporters together, braving the risks of political insurgency together, and governing their small-scale republic together. The class and racial isolation and hostility that enslavement imposed and that emancipation failed to extinguish were surmounted by the need for some sort of cooperation and by the knowledge and trust that could be cultivated year by year, policy by policy, election cycle by election cycle. Yet in Grimes County as most everywhere else, political power, in the end, grew out of the barrel of a gun, and the Grimes County Populists lacked the ammunition to withstand the assault that the White Man's Union was able to inflict upon them.

Recovering the story of Grimes County Populists—an example of how historical excavation can cut through the fog of illiberal racism—reminds us of the moments that best capture the democratic and rights-bearing currents in American history, and reminds us that they are usually the work not of the founders or of their elite heirs but of ordinary people in many different contexts, who are capable of reconfiguring their own inner histories. The story reminds us too of the fragilities of those moments, and of the risks and costs of challenging those who hold power.

The British poet, artist, and political renegade William Morris (1834–1896) once reflected on the people who "fight and lose the battle, and the thing that they fought for comes about in spite of their defeat, and when it comes turns out not to be what they meant, and [others] have to fight for what they meant under another name."

Political and social justice struggles are ongoing, indeed neverending whatever successes or failures they may have because "what they fought for" at one point may veer off in directions unforeseen, and so others have "to fight for what they meant under another name." The worlds of William Morris and the Populists were of vibrant and conflict-ridden political cultures, and in the United States were marked by very high levels of participation in electoral politics and strong identifications with political parties and movements, whether Democratic and Republican or insurgent parties like the Populists, even if often scorched by illiberal bursts of coercion and repression. More than a century later, those political worlds are much more hollowed out, many of our collective resources depleted by the changing nature and distance of power. Little wonder that as profound and often existential crises face us, authoritarian solutions have an appeal—here and elsewhere—not seen since the early decades of the twentieth century. For those who find such solutions repugnant, who wish to make human rights and democratic practice the norms they are still imagined to be, William Morris and the Grimes County Populists have an enduring message. History shows us what we have had and can fight for. And, just as surely, it shows us what we are up against.

ACKNOWLEDGMENTS

THIS BOOK HAS BEEN VERY CHALLENGING TO WRITE, owing both to the scale of the subject and the many obstacles posed by the COVID-19 pandemic, during which much of the work was undertaken. So, I am especially grateful to a number of institutions for offering me the opportunity to move ahead, and to colleagues and friends who took precious time from the many challenges they were facing to help me think more clearly and deeply about what I was trying to do.

The idea for *Illiberal America* first took shape while I was the Rogers Distinguished Fellow at the Huntington Library in San Marino, California, from 2016 to 2017, where I was chiefly trying to bring another book project nearer to completion. Many thanks to research director Steve Hindle and his predecessor (and my friend) Roy Ritchie for their help and hospitality, and especially to my history colleagues there at the time who showed interest and asked hard questions, sharing as we did the special traumas of the 2016 election: John Demos, Scott Heerman, Woody Holton, and Beth Saler.

Most of this book was drafted during the academic year 2020–21, when I was a fellow at the Cullman Center for Scholars and Writers at the New York Public Library. COVID restrictions limited the contact that fellows could have with one another and also limited our access to many of the library's incredible resources. Even so, Cullman Center Director Salvatore Scibona and Deputy Directors Lauren Goldenberg and Paul Delaverdac, along with the library's staff, did remarkable jobs in enabling all of us to have the most productive experiences then possible while keeping us safe. To them I offer my sincere thanks. Sincere thanks, too, to some of the fellows I did come to know and who, despite the interactive limits that were imposed, made important contributions to the progress I was able to make: Barbara Demick, Hernan Diaz, Jennifer Mittelstadt, Caroline Weber, and Mason Williams.

Since the pandemic made it nearly impossible to "workshop" my book manuscript, I'm very grateful to friends and colleagues I called upon to read portions of it and who gave me invaluable help and advice. Their comments, criticisms, redirections, bibliographic suggestions, and encouragement enabled me to clarify my ideas, better organize the writing, take up issues I had ignored or insufficiently addressed, and advance arguments I was attempting to make. Deepest thanks then to Ed Berenson, Bob Blau, Kate Boo, Hernan Diaz, Ada Ferrer, Eric Foner, Harold Forsythe, Thavolia Glymph, Rebecca Goetz, Adam Goodman, Kevin Kenny, Kate Masur, Michael Meranze, Keri Leigh Merritt, David Oshinsky, Kim Phillips-Fein, Joe Reidy, Natalie Ring, Roberto Saba, Nikhil Pal Singh, Tom Sugrue, Emma Teitelman, and Barbara Weinstein. Special thanks to Greg Downs, Gary Gerstle, Rachel Klein, Jennifer Mittelstadt, Larry Powell, and Jonathan Prude, who read drafts of the entire book and discussed them with me at greater length than I could have expected. And thanks, as well, to my students in NYU's Prison Education Program, who enabled me to see the world in new and unsettling ways but who also uplifted me with their intellectual and artistic gifts, their determination to make better lives for themselves, their perseverance under the most difficult of circumstances, and their concerns for one another.

I was very fortunate to have Steve Forman, whom I long admired, as my book editor. And, if anything, my expectations have been surpassed. Steve is an extremely knowledgeable historian in his own right as well as a deft and perceptive editor, very much able to strike a balance between his vision of what the book could be and mine of what the book was becoming, a balance that really works. He very quickly understood what I was trying to do, recognized what was different about the book compared to other interventions in the American history field, and, chapter-by-chapter, helped me develop my arguments and interpretations. I am very much indebted to him.

I am indebted, as well, to my agent, Sandy Dijkstra, whose wisdom and foresight were so important when this book was just an idea.

My son and daughter, Declan and Saoirse, and my partner, Susan Wishingrad, were my strongest supporters and often my best critics from the start. They each brought their knowledge of the past, their concerns about the present, and their special eyes and ears to their readings and discussions with me. And, as I struggled along at times, I was invariably inspired by their own experiences of battling through and transcending major hurdles and setbacks, by the toughness and resilience that they, in their own ways, have shown. I'm quite certain that I could not have finished this book without them.

I'm not sure what Ira Berlin would have thought about the idea of this book. He spent his life as a scholar and teacher excavating and exploring the worlds of those—especially those of African descent— who were on the receiving end of what illiberal America frequently dealt out. But Ira always recognized that we needed to come to grips with the nature and workings of power if we were ever to construct a better, more democratic, and socially just world, and that doing so could be enlightening as well as dispiriting. As a dear friend and mentor, as an incredibly generous human being, Ira exemplified what I hoped this life could be all about, and he set a standard by which we could always measure ourselves. Despite his tragically early death, his example will long endure. I'd like to think that he would have cheered me on.

NOTES

INTRODUCTION

1. This, in some version, is the predominant perspective of historians. See, most recently, Jill Lepore, *These Truths: A History of the United States* (New York, 2019).
2. For important recent exceptions that have called the liberal tradition into question or fundamentally complicated it, see Rogers Smith, *Civic Ideals: Conflicting Visions of Citizenship in U.S. History* (New Haven, 1997); Aziz Rana, *The Two Faces of American Freedom* (Cambridge, MA, 2010); Gary Gerstle, *Liberty and Coercion: The Paradox of American Government from the Founding to the Present* (Princeton, 2015). Smith speaks of a "multiple traditions view of America," and clearly recognizes inegalitarian or illiberal traditions among them.
3. On illiberal democracy and its international following, see Marc Plattner, "Illiberal Democracy and the Struggle on the Right," *Journal of Politics* 30 (January 2019): 5–19; Isaac Chotiner, "Why Conservatives Around the World Have Embraced Hungary's Viktor Orbán," *New Yorker,* 10 August 2021; Timothy Garton Ash, "Europe Must Stop This Disgrace: Viktor Orbán is Dismantling Democracy," *The Guardian,* 20 June 2019; William Galston, "Viktor Orbán's Illiberal Cheerleaders," *Wall Street Journal,* 23 August 2022.
4. Thomas Hobbes, *Leviathan* (1651); John Locke, *Second Treatise of Government* (1689).
5. William E. Leuchtenberg, *Franklin Roosevelt and the New Deal, 1932–1940* (New York, 1963); David Kennedy, *Freedom from Fear: The American People in Depression and War, 1929–1945* (New York, 1999); Steve Fraser and Gary Gerstle, eds., *The Rise and Fall of the New Deal Order, 1930–1980* (Princeton, 1989).
6. Gary Gerstle, *The Rise and Fall of the Neoliberal Order: America and the World in the Free Market Era* (New York, 2022); Wendy Brown, *Undoing the Demos: Neoliberalism's Stealth Revolution* (New York, 2015); David Harvey, *A Brief History of Neoliberalism* (New York, 2005).
7. See, for example, Marlene Laruelle, "Illiberalism: A Conceptual Introduction," *East European Politics* 38 (March 2022): 303–27; Thomas J. Main, *The Rise of Illiberalism* (Washington, DC, 2022); Pippa Norris and Ronald Inglehart, *Cultural Backlash: Trump, Brexit, and Authoritarian Populism* (New York, 2019).
8. The historian Richard Hofstadter became increasingly interested in these tendencies though he saw them as subcurrents, brief eruptions, or "cyclical fluc-

tuations" against the predominant liberal tradition. See, especially, Hofstadter, *Anti-Intellectualism in American Life* (New York, 1962); Hofstadter, *The Paranoid Style in American Politics* (New York, 1965).

9. See, especially, Gary Gerstle and Joel Isaac, eds., *States of Exception in American History* (Chicago, 2020).

10. On reactionary conservatism and a powerful argument for it as the historical essence of conservatism, see Corey Robin, *The Reactionary Mind: Conservatism from Edmund Burke to Donald Trump* (New York, 2018). On anti-liberalism, see Stephen Holmes, *The Anatomy of Antiliberalism* (Cambridge, MA, 1993). Obvious examples of illiberal regimes of the left include the Soviet Union, Cuba, and the People's Republic of China.

CHAPTER ONE
THE INVENTION OF THE LIBERAL TRADITION

1. Fareed Zakaria, "The Rise of Illiberal Democracy," *Foreign Affairs* (November/ December, 1997): 22–43; Zakaria, "America's Democracy Has Become Illiberal," *Washington Post,* 29 December 2016. Also see William Grieder, *Who Will Tell the People: The Betrayal of American Democracy* (New York, 1992).

2. See, for example, Larry Diamond, "Is There a Crisis of Liberal Democracy?" *American Interest,* 13 October 2017; Steven Levitsky and Daniel Ziblatt, "Is Donald Trump a Threat to Democracy?" *New York Times,* 16 December 2016; "Trump, Putin, and the Threat to Liberal Democracy," Toronto *Globe and Mail,* 30 December 2016. Recent polling shows that as many as eight in ten Americans believe that the nation's democracy is under threat though there is disagreement as to what that threat is. See NPR, 15 December 2022; *Forbes Magazine,* 19 October 2022.

3. Sheri Berman, "The Main Threat to Liberal Democracy Comes from Within," *Washington Post,* 26 March 2016; Zakaria, "Rise of Illiberal Democracy"; Mark F. Plattner, "Illiberal Democracy and the Struggle on the Right," *Journal of Democracy* 30, no. 1 (January 2019): 5–19. Also see Mark Mazower, *Dark Continent: Europe's Twentieth Century* (New York, 1998); Helena Rosenblatt, *The Lost History of Liberalism: From Ancient Rome to the Twenty-First Century* (Princeton, 2018).

4. Diamond, "Is There a Crisis of Liberal Democracy?"; Zakaria, "Rise of Illiberal Democracy"; John Shattuck et al., "How Resilient Is Liberal Democracy in the United States" (Unpublished mss., Carr Center, Harvard University, 15 February 2018); Zakaria, "America's Democracy Has Become Illiberal." Also see Werner Sombart, *Why Is There No Socialism in the United States?* (Tubingen, 1906); Eric Foner, "Why Is There No Socialism in the United States," *History Workshop Journal,* no. 17 (Spring 1984): 57–80. Despite a voluminous literature, the New Deal has rarely been placed in an international context nor have scholars raised the question—explicitly—of why the United States did not follow many other societies (Germany, Italy, Japan, Argentina, Spain, and Portugal, to name a few) in turning toward fascist or authoritarian solutions to the crises of the 1930s. For important exceptions, see Ira Katznelson, *Fear Itself: The New Deal and the Origins of Our Times* (New York, 2013); Wolfgang Schivelbusch, *Three New Deals: Reflec-*

tions on Roosevelt's America, Mussolini's Italy, and Hitler's Germany, 1933–1939 (New York, 2006).

5. Cass Sunstein, ed., *Can It Happen Here? Authoritarianism in America* (New York, 2018).

6. On the "invention of tradition," see Eric Hobsbawm, "Inventing Traditions," in Eric Hobsbawm and Terence Ranger, eds., *The Invention of Tradition* (Cambridge, UK, 1983), 1–4.

7. See, for example, Stephen Nissenbaum, *The Battle for Christmas* (New York, 1997); Richard J. Ellis, *The Flag: The Unlikely History of the Pledge of Allegiance* (Lawrence, KS, 2005).

8. *The Liberal Tradition in America: An Interpretation of American Political Thought Since the Revolution* (New York, 1955).

9. There is an immense scholarly literature—already large in the 1950s—taking up the question of how feudalism may be defined and how it may have varied over time and space. Hartz did not engage with this literature, though he was clearly aware of some of it, but preferred to associate a feudal past with a number of social and political characteristics.

10. Daniel Boorstin, *The Genius of American Politics* (Chicago, 1953); Lionel Trilling, *The Liberal Imagination: Essays on Literature and Society* (New York, 1950); Richard Hofstadter, *The American Political Tradition and the Men Who Made It* (New York, 1948).

11. Richard Hofstadter, *The Age of Reform: From Bryan to F.D.R.* (New York, 1955). For Hofstadter's subsequent volumes, see *Anti-Intellectualism in American Life* (New York, 1963) and *The Paranoid Style in American Politics and Other Essays* (New York, 1965). Also see Alan Brinkley, *Liberalism and Its Discontents* (Cambridge, MA, 1998), 132–50. On Hofstadter, see David S. Brown, *Richard Hofstadter: An Intellectual Biography* (Chicago, 2006), especially 50–160.

12. For an excellent discussion, see Peter Novick, *That Noble Dream: The "Objectivity Question" and the American Historical Profession* (New York, 1988), 61–108. See also Thomas J. Pressley, *Americans Interpret Their Civil War* (New York, 1965); David Blight, *Race and Reunion: The Civil War in American Memory* (Cambridge, MA, 2002).

13. Frederick Jackson Turner, "The Significance of the Frontier in American History," *Annual Report of the American Historical Association* (1893) ; Frederick Jackson Turner, *The Frontier in American History* (New York, 1921); Charles A. Beard and Mary Beard, *The Rise of American Civilization* (New York, 1930); Charles A. Beard, *An Economic Interpretation of the Constitution of the United States* (New York, 1952); Vernon L. Parrington, *Main Currents of American Thought,* 3 vols. (New York, 1930); Carl L. Becker, *History of Political Parties in the Province of New York, 1760–1776* (Madison, WI, 1909); John Hicks, *The Populist Revolt: A History of the Farmers' Alliance and the People's Party* (Minneapolis, 1931); C. Vann Woodward, *Tom Watson: Agrarian Rebel* (New York, 1938); Arthur Schlesinger Sr., *The Rise of the City, 1878–1898* (New York, 1933). Arthur Schlesinger Jr. followed in his father's footsteps with, among other works, *The Age of Jackson* (Boston, 1945). For Hofstadter's perspective, see *The Progressive Historians: Turner, Beard, Parrington* (New York, 1968).

14. Arthur Schlesinger Jr., *The Vital Center and the Politics of Freedom* (Boston, 1949),

xviii–ix; *America and the Intellectuals, Partisan Review* Series, no. 4 (1953), 1–4, 14–15, 111–12; Richard H. Pells, *The Liberal Mind in a Conservative Age: American Intellectuals in the 1940s and 1950s* (New York, 1985). For a capacious picture of intellectual and cultural life in this period, see Louis Menand, *The Free World: Art and Thought in the Cold War* (New York, 2021).

15.   Schlesinger, *Vital Center*, 37–40. Schlesinger called progressives, especially supporters of Henry Wallace, "doughfaces," suggesting comparison with the southern-oriented northern Democrats of the Civil War period.

16.   See Hannah Arendt, *The Origins of Totalitarianism* (New York, 1951); Theodor Adorno et al., *The Authoritarian Personality* (New York, 1950); José Ortega y Gasset, *The Revolt of the Masses* (1930; New York, 1994); Carl Schmitt, *On Dictatorship* (1921; Cambridge, UK, 2014). Schmitt, who did important theoretical work, was himself a conservative and then supporter of the Nazi state.

17.   Pells, *Liberal Mind in a Conservative Age*, 117–83; Sarah M. Harris, *The CIA and the Congress for Cultural Freedom: The Limits of Making Common Cause* (New York, 2016); Patrick Iber, *Neither Peace Nor Freedom: The Cultural Cold War in Latin America* (Cambridge, MA, 2015); Christopher Lasch, *The Agony of the American Left* (New York, 1968), 61–114.

18.   Victor Navasky, *Naming Names* (New York, 1980); Pells, *Liberal Mind in a Conservative Age*, 262-345; *Mississippi Valley Historical Review* 32 (September 1945): 263–64; *American Historical Review* 51 (October 1945): 131–33.

19.   On McCarthyism, see David M. Oshinsky, *A Conspiracy So Immense: The World of Joe McCarthy* (New York, 1983); Ellen Schrecker, *Many Are the Crimes: McCarthyism in America* (Boston, 1998). Also see Michael Rogin, *The Intellectuals and McCarthy: The Radical Specter* (Cambridge, MA, 1967); Peter Viereck, *The Shame and Glory of the Intellectuals: Babbit Jr. Versus the Rediscovery of Values* (Boston, 1953).

20.   See, for example, the essays by David Reisman, Nathan Glazer, Richard Hofstadter, Daniel Bell, and Seymour Martin Lipset in Daniel Bell, ed., *The New American Right* (New York, 1955), expanded and updated as *The Radical Right* (New York, 1963); and the essays by Viereck and Daniel Bell in Bell, ed., *New American Right*.

21.   Henry Nash Smith, *Virgin Land: The American West as Symbol and Myth* (Cambridge, MA, 1950); Perry Miller, *The New England Mind: The Seventeenth Century* (Cambridge, MA, 1939); Miller, *The New England Mind: From Colony to Province* (Cambridge, MA, 1953); John William Ward, *Andrew Jackson: Symbol for an Age* (New York, 1955). Miller, it should be said, had a more critical view of the relation of Puritanism to either capitalism or liberalism. On the development of American studies, see Richard P. Horwitz, "American Studies: Approaches and Concepts," in George Kurian et al., eds., *Encyclopedia of American Studies*, vol. 1 (Bethel, CT, 2001), 112–18; Jerry A. Jacobs, "American Studies: A Case Study of Interdisciplinarity," *PSC Working Papers* 48 (2013). Among the important American studies works during the 1960s that show their influence were Leo Marx, *The Machine in the Garden: Technology and the Pastoral Ideal in America* (New York, 1964); and Alan Trachtenberg, *Brooklyn Bridge: Fact and Symbol* (New York, 1965).

22.   See, especially, Ulrich B. Phillips, *American Negro Slavery* (New York, 1918); Phillips, "The Central Theme of Southern History," *American Historical Review* 34

(October 1928): 30–43. Historians who challenged Phillips and his students before the 1950s included Luther Porter Jackson, W. E. B. Du Bois, and Herbert Aptheker.

23. Kenneth M. Stampp, *The Peculiar Institution: Slavery in the Antebellum South* (New York, 1956).

24. Stanley M. Elkins, *Slavery: A Problem in American Institutional and Intellectual Life* (Chicago, 1959); Alfred H. Conrad and John R. Meyer, "The Economics of Slavery in the Antebellum South," *Journal of Political Economy* 66 (April 1958): 95–130. Elkins was deeply influenced by the work of Frank Tannenbaum, who published one of the earliest comparative studies of slavery in the Western Hemisphere. See *Slave and Citizen: The Negro in the Americas* (New York, 1946). On the "natural limits," see Phillips student Charles Ramsdell, "The Natural Limits of Slavery Expansion," *Southwestern Historical Quarter* 33 (October 1929): 91–111.

25. Oscar Handlin, *The Uprooted: The Epic Story of the Great Migrations that Made the American People* (Boston, 1951), 5–6 and passim; John Higham, *Strangers in the Land: Patterns of American Nativism, 1860–1925* (New Brunswick, NJ, 1955). It should be said that this literature was, and for quite some time remained, Eurocentric in its perspective.

26. See, for example, William Appleman Williams, *The Tragedy of American Diplomacy* (Cleveland, 1959); Williams, *The Roots of Modern American Empire: A Study of the Growth and Shaping of Social Consciousness in a Marketplace Society* (New York, 1969); Walter La Feber, *The New Empire: An Interpretation of American Expansion, 1860–1898* (Washington, DC, 1963); Lloyd C. Gardner, *Economic Aspects of New Deal Diplomacy* (Madison, WI, 1964); Thomas C. McCormick, *China Market: America's Quest for Informal Empire, 1893–1901* (Chicago, 1967).

27. See Sarah E. Igo, *The Averaged American: Surveys, Citizens, and the Making of a Mass Public* (Cambridge, MA, 2008); Dorothy Ross, *The Origins of Social Science* (New York, 1991); David Easton, Luigi Graziano, and John Gunnell, eds., *The Development of Political Science: A Comparative Survey* (Oxfordshire, 1991); Peter C. Ordeshook, *Game Theory and Political Theory: An Introduction* (Cambridge, UK, 1986); Michael A. Bernstein, *A Perilous Progress: Economists and Public Purpose in Twentieth Century America* (Princeton, 2001). John Rawls's immensely influential *A Theory of Justice* (Cambridge, MA, 1971) also showed the marks of rational choice thinking.

28. Daniel Bell, *The End of Ideology: On the Exhaustion of Political Ideas in the Fifties* (Cambridge, MA, 1960).

29. See, for example, Novick, *That Noble Dream*, 415–68. The literature taking aim at the "liberal tradition" of American historical interpretation is far too large to reference here, but Novick identifies some of it.

30. See, for example, Eugene D. Genovese, *The Political Economy of Slavery: Studies in the Economy and Society of the Slave South* (New York, 1965); Eric Foner, *Free Soil, Free Labor, Free Men: The Ideology of the Republican Party before the Civil War* (New York, 1970); Sean Wilentz, *Chants Democratic: New York City and the Rise of the American Working Class* (New York, 1984). Of special influence here were the British historians E. P. Thompson and Eric Hobsbawm.

31. See, for example, Rogers Smith, "Understanding the Symbiosis of American

Rights and Racism," in Mark Hulliung, ed., *The American Liberal Tradition Reconsidered: The Contested Legacy of Louis Hartz* (Lawrence, KS, 2010), 55–89; Rogers Smith, *Civic Ideals: Conflicting Visions of Citizenship in U.S. History* (New Haven, 1997); William Julius Wilson, *The Declining Significance of Race: Blacks and Changing American Institutions* (Chicago, 1978); Richard Sennett and Jonathan Cobb, *The Hidden Injuries of Class* (New York, 1072); Aziz Rana, *The Two Faces of American Freedom* (Cambridge, MA, 2010). Rogers Smith has been especially compelling not only in identifying liberalism's dark underbelly but in drawing the very concept of a prevailing liberal tradition into question.

32. For assessments of the challenges and drawbacks of synthesis, see Thomas Bender, "Strategies of Narrative Synthesis in American History," *American Historical Review* 107 (February 2002): 129–53; Bender, "Wholes and Parts: The Need for Synthesis in American History," *Journal of American History* 73 (June 1986), 120–36; Eric H. Monkkonen, "The Dangers of Synthesis," *American Historical Review* 91 (December 1986): 1146–57; Philip J. Deloria, "American Master Narratives and the Problem of Indian Citizenship in the Gilded Age and Progressive Era," *Journal of the Gilded Age and Progressive Era* 14 (January 2015): 3–12.

33. See, for example, Lynn Hunt, ed., *The New Cultural History* (Berkeley, 1989); Victoria Bonnell, ed., *Beyond the Cultural Turn: New Directions in the Study of Society and Culture* (Berkeley, 1999). The work of Michel Foucault was especially influential and helped give postmodern scholarship an almost unprecedented interest in social and cultural theory.

34. Francis Fukuyama, *The End of History and the Last Man* (New York, 1992); Diamond, "Is There a Crisis of Liberal Democracy?" On recent developments, see Kevin M. Kruse and Julian Zelizer, *Fault Lines: A History of the United States Since 1974* (New York, 2019), 203–358.

35. The scholarship on slavery and capitalism has exploded in the last decade and has had a large impact not only on academic historians but on a larger public. For some of the best examples, see Sven Beckert and Seth Rockman, eds., *Slavery's Capitalism: A New History of American Economic Development* (Philadelphia, 2016); Sven Beckert, *Empire of Cotton: A Global History* (New York, 2014); Seth Rockman, *Scraping By: Wage Labor, Slavery, and Survival in Early Baltimore* (Baltimore, 2008). Also see Jonathan Levy, *Ages of American Capitalism: A History of the United States* (New York, 2020). The concept of "racial capitalism" is generally attributed to Cedric Robinson in his important book, *Black Marxism: The Making of the Black Radical Tradition* (London, 1983). Readers of Robinson's book will find a far more complex and nuanced historical account than is often represented.

36. Alan Gibson, "Louis Hartz and the Study of the American Founding," in Hulliung, ed., *American Liberal Tradition Reconsidered*, 175. Of all the essays on Hartz, only that of James Kloppenberg, the lone historian, places the publication of *The Liberal Tradition* in a specific historical context. See Kloppenberg, "Requiescat in Pacem: The Liberal Tradition of Louis Hartz," 90–124.

37. Hulliung, "What's Living, What's Dead in the Work of Louis Hartz," 267–73.

38. Nikole Hannah-Jones, "The 1619 Project," *New York Times* Magazine, 14 August 2019. If anything, the 1619 controversy raises questions about the usefulness—other than for partisan political purposes—of *any* "origin" story.

CHAPTER TWO
FEUDAL DREAMS AND COERCIVE POWERS

1. Richard Hakluyt (the Elder), *Pamphlet for the Virginia Enterprise* (1585), in E. G. R. Taylor, ed., *The Original Writing and Correspondence of the Two Richard Hakluyts*, 2 vols. (London, 1935), II, ch. 47; Richard Hakluyt (the Younger), "Discourse of Western Planting," in *Collections of the Maine Historical Society*, 2nd ser., vol. 2, 152–61. Also see Peter Mancall, ed., *Envisioning America: English Plans for the Colonization of North America, 1580–1640* (Boston, 1995), 1–49.

2. On capitalism coming in the first ships, see Carl Degler, *Out of Our Past: The Forces that Shaped Modern America* (New York, 1959), 2, though this is a view that is widely, if less explicitly, shared.

3. Daniel Richter, *Before the Revolution: America's Ancient Pasts* (Cambridge, MA, 2011), 68.

4. Hakluyt, "Discourse of Western Planting," 152–61. On the fifteenth- and sixteenth-century transformations of England and parts of Western Europe, see T. H. Aston and C. H. E. Philpin, eds., *The Brenner Debate: Agrarian Class Structure and Economic Development in Preindustrial Europe* (Cambridge, UK, 1985); Jane Whittle Hill, ed., *Landlords and Tenants in Britain, 1440–1660* (Woodbridge, UK, 2013); Fernand Braudel, *The Wheels of Commerce* (New York, 1982).

5. See, for example, Nicholas Canny, "England's New World and the Old, 1480s–1630s," in Canny, ed., *The Origins of Empire: British Overseas Enterprise to the Close of the Seventeenth Century* (Oxford, 1988), 157–58; Richter, *Before the Revolution*, 37–117.

6. See Canny, "Origins of Empire," 3–7; Jane H. Ohlmeter, "'Civilizinge of those Rude Partes': Colonization within Britain and Ireland, 1580s–1640s," in Canny, ed., *Origins of Empire*, 124–47; Richter, *Before the Revolution*, 108–9. Also see David Armitage, *The Ideological Origins of the British Empire* (Cambridge, UK, 2000), 24–60.

7. Ohlmeyer, "'Civilizinge those Rude Partes,'" 139–40; Richter, *Before the Revolution*, 101–12. See also Niccolo Machiavelli, *The Prince* (1531; New York, 1950), 8–9.

8. Although the data we have on Atlantic migrations in the seventeenth and eighteenth centuries has become increasingly detailed and sophisticated, we are still left with estimates. For the most careful and reliable pictures, see Christopher Tomlins, *Freedom Bound: Law, Labor, and Civic Identity in Colonizing English North America, 1580–1865* (New York, 2010), 21–66; Ira Berlin, *Many Thousands Gone: The First Two Centuries of Slavery in North America* (Cambridge, MA, 1998), 15–216; Philip Curtin, *The Atlantic Slave Trade: A Census* (Madison, WI, 1972); John J. McCusker and Russell Menard, *The Economy of British North America, 1607–1789* (Chapel Hill, 1989). These figures do not include about 55,000 convicts or prisoners of war who were sent to North America.

9. See Stuart Schwartz, *Sugar Plantations in the Formation of Brazilian Society, 1550–1835* (Cambridge, UK, 1986); Alexander Marchant, *From Barter to Slavery: The Economic Relations of Portuguese and Indians in the Settlement of Brazil, 1500–1580* (Baltimore, 1942); Richard Dunn, *The Rise of the Planter Class in the English West Indies, 1624–1713* (Chapel Hill, 1972); James Pritchard, *In Search of Empire: The French in the*

Americas, 1670–1730 (Cambridge, UK, 2007). A robust Indian slave trade developed along the Atlantic coast of North America during the seventeenth century. See Alan Gallay, *The Indian Slave Trade: The Rise of the English Empire in the American South, 1670–1717* (New Haven, 2001); Andrés Reséndez, *The Other Slavery: The Uncovered Story of Indian Enslavement in America* (Boston, 2016).

10. See, for example, Tomlins, *Freedom Bound*, 452–75; Berlin, *Many Thousands Gone*, 109–41; Edmund Morgan, *American Slavery, American Freedom: The Ordeal of Colonial Virginia* (New York, 1975). Figures on enslavement for the first half of the seventeenth century are quite scarce. In 1650, there were around 300 slaves in the Chesapeake, perhaps a couple of hundred enslaved people scattered across New England, mostly in Massachusetts, and somewhere between 100 and 500 slaves in the Mid-Atlantic, notably in Dutch Nieu Netherland, where they began to arrive in the late 1620s but started coming in greater numbers between 1650 and 1664. The year 1619 by no means marks the first appearance of people of African descent on the North American continent. Enslaved Africans were among the Spanish expeditions that explored Florida, the interior of the continent, and the southeastern coastline during the sixteenth century. I am indebted to my colleagues Rebecca Goetz and Susanah Romney for their insights.

11. See Morgan, *American Slavery, American Freedom*, 133–212; Allan Kulikoff, *Tobacco and Slaves: The Development of Southern Cultures in the Chesapeake, 1680–1800* (Chapel Hill, 1986), 23–77.

12. "The Social System of Virginia," *Southern Literary Messenger* 14, no. 2 (February 1848): 65–81; Warren Billings, *Sir William Berkeley and the Forging of Colonial Virginia* (Baton Rouge, 2004).

13. "The Fundamental Constitutions of Carolina, 1 March 1669," Avalon Project: *Documents in Law, History, and Diplomacy*, Yale University Law School; Tomlins, *Freedom Bound*, 432–35; Peter Wood, *Black Majority: Negroes in Colonial South Carolina from 1670 Through the Stono Rebellion* (New York, 1974), 13–34.

14. John Locke, *Two Treatises of Government* (London, 1689); Tomlins, *Freedom Bound*, 426–36. Historians have long tried to square John Locke's *Second Treatise* with his participation in the proprietary settlement of the Carolinas and his investments in enslaving activities. Some argue for hypocrisy, some for his role as a secretary for the Earl of Shaftsbury. Holly Brewer has suggested drawing a distinction between what Locke saw as legitimate and illegitimate forms of enslavement. See Holly Brewer, "Slavery, Sovereignty, and 'Inheritable Blood': Reconsidering John Locke and the Origins of American Slavery," *American Historical Review* 122 (October 2017): 1038–78; Brewer, "Slavery Entangled Philosophy," *Aeon* (12 September 2018). On liberalism's exclusionary impulses, see Uday Singh Mehta, *Liberalism and Empire: A Study in Nineteenth Century Liberal Thought* (Chicago, 1999). On the enslavement of captives in just wars, see Orlando Patterson, *Slavery and Social Death: A Comparative Study* (Cambridge, MA, 1982); David Brion Davis, *Inhuman Bondage: The Rise and Fall of Slavery in the New World* (New York, 2006); John K. Thornton, *Africa and Africans in the Making of the Atlantic World, 1400–1800* (New York, 1992); Reséndez, *The Other Slavery*.

15. See Kathleen Brown, *Good Wives, Nasty Wenches, and Anxious Patriarchs: Gender, Race, and Power in Colonial Virginia* (Chapel Hill, 1996); Philip Morgan, *Slave Coun-*

terpoint: Black Culture in the Eighteenth Century Chesapeake and Low Country (Chapel Hill, 1998); Berlin, *Many Thousands Gone*, 95–141; Tomlins, *Freedom Bound*, 428–75.

16. See, especially, Morgan, *American Slavery, American Freedom*, 238–70. See also James D. Rice, *Tales from a Revolution: Bacon's Rebellion and the Transformation of Early America* (New York, 2012); and especially Matthew Kruer, *Time of Anarchy: Indigenous Power and the Crisis of Colonialism in Early America* (Cambridge, MA, 2021), who offers a Native perspective on a complex series of events.

17. Berlin, *Many Thousands Gone*, 47–63; Lorenzo Greene, *The Negro in Colonial New England, 1620–1776* (New York, 1942); Tomlins, *Freedom Bound*, 476–504; Wood, *Black Majority*, 131–66.

18. This argument has been made with special power by Morgan, *American Slavery, American Freedom*, 295–388.

19. Aubrey Land, "Economic Base and Social Structure: The Northern Chesapeake in the Eighteenth Century," *Journal of Economic History* 25 (December 1965): 639–54; Morgan, *American Slavery, American Freedom*, 215–92; Kulikoff, *Tobacco and Slaves*, 40–50.

20. See, especially, Robert J. Steinfeld, *The Invention of Free Labor: The Employment Relation in English and American Law and Culture, 1350–1870* (Chapel Hill, 1991); Robert J. Steinfeld, *Coercion, Contract, and Free Labor in the Nineteenth Century* (New York, 2001), 29–84; Tomlins, *Freedom Bound*, 335–400.

21. C. S. Manegold, *Ten Hills Farm: The Forgotten History of Slavery in the North* (Princeton, 2010), 3–49; *Massachusetts Body of Liberties,* December 1641, in Edmund S. Morgan, ed., *Puritan Political Ideas, 1558–1794* (Indianapolis, 1965), 177–202.

22. John Winthrop, *Christian Charitie: A Modell Hereof* (1630), in Morgan, ed., *Puritan Political Ideas,* 75–93; John Smith, *A Description of New England* (1616).

23. *Mayflower Compact,* 1620, Avalon Project, Documents in Law, History, and Diplomacy, Yale University Law School. There are many questions surrounding Winthrop's "Modell," not least when or where it was written or if he ever delivered it to fellow migrants, whether before or during their voyage. Daniel T. Rodgers, in the most careful treatment, demonstrates that it took shape over a number of months and was not likely delivered at any public occasion, and so should not be regarded as a "sermon." See Rodgers, *As a City on a Hill: The Story of America's Most Famous Lay Sermon* (Princeton, 2018), 13–30; Abram Van Engen, *City on a Hill: A History of American Exceptionalism* (New Haven, 2020).

24. See Barry Levy, *Town Born: The Political Economy of New England from Its Founding to the Revolution* (Philadelphia, 2009), for a compelling argument that links transformations in England with the character of Massachusetts towns. For perspectives that emphasize the New England transition from "community" to "society," or from a more communal village to a more liberal and market-oriented social order, see Richard Bushman, *From Puritan to Yankee: Character and the Social Order in Connecticut, 1690–1765* (Cambridge, MA, 1967); Philip S. Greven Jr., *Four Generations: Population, Land, and Family in Colonial Andover, Massachusetts* (Ithaca, NY, 1970); Kenneth S. Lockridge, *A New England Town: The First Hundred Years, Dedham, Massachusetts, 1636–1736* (New York, 1970); Michael Zuckerman, *Peaceable Kingdoms: New England Towns in the Eighteenth Century* (New York, 1970).

25. Allan Greer, *Property and Dispossession: Natives, Empires, and Land in Early Modern*

North America (New York, 2018), 202–12. As Greer argues, this was by no means a regime of private, absolute property rights.

26. Edmund S. Morgan, *The Puritan Family* (New York, 1966), 62–77.

27. Levy, *Town Born*, 17–83. There are numerous editions of Winthrop's *Journal.* The most recent and most authoritative is Richard S. Dunn and Laetitia Yeandle, eds., *The Journal of John Winthrop, 1630–1649* (Cambridge, MA, 1997). Also see Morgan's *The Puritan Family*, 78–89. On the number of indentured servants migrating to New England and the Chesapeake in the seventeenth century, see Tomlins, *Freedom Bound*, 573, and on New England labor, 310–315. A forty-lash limit—commonly ignored—was included in numerous slave codes in North American colonies and later the United States as well.

28. See Levy, *Town Born*, 37–42, 84–89; Douglas L. Jones, "The Strolling Poor: Transiency in Eighteenth Century Massachusetts," *Journal of Social History* 8 (Spring 1975): 28–54. John Winthrop echoed the Dedham founders in 1637: "If we heere be a corporation established by free consent, if the place of our cohabitation be our owne, then no man hath right to come into us etc. without our consent . . . [and] it is worse to receive a man whom we must cast out againe, than denye him admittance." See Winthrop, "A Declaration in Defense of an Order of Court made in May, 1637," in Morgan, ed., *Puritan Political Ideas*, 145–46.

29. There are many depictions of Puritan theology and thought, but an especially powerful contribution that attempts to treat Puritanism as a coherent system is Perry Miller's *The New England Mind: The Seventeenth Century* (Cambridge, MA, 1939). Also see Morgan, *Puritan Family*.

30. Miller, *New England Mind*, 17, 48–53. For an especially interesting and provocative reading, see James Simpson, *The Permanent Revolution: The Reformation and the Illiberal Roots of Liberalism* (Cambridge, MA, 2019).

31. Winthrop, "Declaration in Defense of an Order," 146; Michael T. Winship, *Hot Protestants: A History of Puritanism in England and America* (New Haven, 2018), 85–90, 165–77. During the famed Putney Debates of 1647, Levellers pressed for the extension of the franchise to all Englishmen without property qualifications, although Levellers also made it clear that these rights were for native-born men and not for women or those in servitude. As the Leveller Thomas Rainsborough declared, "I think that the poorest hee that is in England hath a life to live, as the greatest hee, and therefore . . . every Man that is to live under a Government ought first by his own Consent to put himself put himself under that Government; and I do think that the poorest man in England is not at all bound in a strict sense to that Government that he hath not had a voice to put Himself under." See A. S. P. Woodhouse, ed., *Puritanism and Liberty, Being the Army Debates, 1647–49, From the Clark Manuscripts* (London, 1938). This was before the publication of either Thomas Hobbes's *Leviathan* (1651) or John Locke's *Second Treatise* (1689).

32. Levy, *Town Born*, 76–83. Also see John P. Demos, *Entertaining Satan: Witchcraft and the Culture of Early New England* (New York, 1983); Carol F. Karlsen, *The Devil in the Shape of a Woman: Witchcraft in Colonial New England* (New York, 1987); Paul Boyer and Stephen Nissenbaum, *Salem Possessed: The Social Origins of Witchcraft* (Cambridge, MA, 1974); Mary Beth Norton, *In the Devil's Snare: The Salem Witchcraft Crisis of 1692* (New York, 2002).

33. During the ninth century, Norse explorers sailed the north Atlantic, establishing settlements in Britain and making landfalls in Iceland and Greenland. Around 1000 CE they founded a colony (or colonies) known as Vinland in the far northeast of Atlantic North America, but before too long retreated to Greenland. The human catastrophe of contact was hemispheric, in some places leading to a decline of near 95 percent of the Indigenous population over the course of a century. See Alan Taylor, *American Colonies* (New York, 2001), 3–49; Charles Mann, *1493: Uncovering the World Columbus Created* (New York, 2010). For an impressive and imaginative perspective on early Indigenous experiences with and responses to Europeans, see Daniel Richter, *Facing East from Indian Country: A Native History of Early America* (Cambridge, MA, 2001).
34. See, most recently, Pekka Hamalainen's remarkable synthesis, *Indigenous Continent: The Epic Contest for North America* (New York, 2022). Also see Richard White, *The Middle Ground: Indians, Empires, and Republics in the Great Lakes Region, 1650–1815* (New York, 1991); Lisa Brooks, *Our Beloved Kin: A New History of King Philip's War* (New Haven, 2018); Colin G. Calloway, *New Worlds for All: Indians, Europeans, and the Remaking of Early America* (Baltimore, 1998); James Merrill, *The Indians' New World: Catawbas and the Neighbors from European Contact to the Era of Removal* (Chapel Hill, 1989); Elizabeth Ellis, *The Great Power of Small Nations: Indigenous Diplomacy in the Gulf South* (Philadelphia, 2022).
35. Hamalainen, *Indigenous Continent*, 3–110.
36. Richter, *Before the Revolution*, 113–17; Kruer, *Time of Anarchy*, 13–49.
37. John Winthrop, *Reasons for the Plantation in New England* (ca. 1628), Winthrop Society.com; Brookes, *Our Beloved Kin*, 17–20.
38. Greer, *Property and Dispossession*, 81–95. On long-standing practices of fencing crops and use rights to unenclosed land in rural America, see Greer, *Property and Dispossession*, 261–69; Richard B. Morris, *Studies in the History of American Law with Special Reference to the Seventeenth and Eighteenth Centuries* (Philadelphia, 1959); Steven Hahn, "Hunting, Fishing, and Foraging: Common Rights and Class Relations in the Postbellum South," *Radical History Review* 26 (1982): 37–64.
39. See, especially, the important arguments in Greer, *Property and Dispossession*, 81–95, 259–64. That Native peoples of North America did not raise domestic livestock helps account for their utter vulnerability to European transported pathogens.
40. Kruer, *Time of Anarchy*, 50–200.
41. Richter, *Before the Revolution*, 265–72; James D. Rice, "Bacon's Rebellion in Indian Country," *Journal of American History* 101 (December 2014): 726–50; Kruer, *Time of Anarchy*, 78–236.
42. For the most interesting and narratively expansive account of King Philip's War, which reveals the importance of the female leader and diplomat Weetamoo, see Brooks, *Our Beloved Kin*, 3–4, 17–71, 143–45, and passim. Also see Jill Lepore, *The Name of War: King Philip's War and the Origins of American Identity* (New York, 1998); Richter, *Before the Revolution*, 282–87; Taylor, *American Colonies*, 199–202.
43. James T. Lemon, *The Best Poor Man's Country: A Geographical Study of Early Southeastern Pennsylvania* (Baltimore, 1972).
44. Tomlins, *Freedom Bound*, 181–83; 276–93; Berlin, *Many Thousands Gone*, 47–63, 177–94.

45. Brendan McConville, *These Daring Disturbers of the Public Peace: The Struggle for Property and Power in Early New Jersey* (Ithaca, NY, 1999), 11–27; Thomas Summerhill, *Harvest of Dissent: Agrarianism in Central New York in the Nineteenth Century* (Urbana, IL, 2005).

46. Peter Silver, *Our Savage Neighbors: How Indian War Transformed Early America* (New York, 2008), 3–14; Taylor, *American Colonies*, 271–72.

CHAPTER THREE
THE POPE, THE KING, AND THE REPUBLIC

1. Governor Bernard to Lord Halifax, 15 August 1765, and Thomas Hutchinson to Richard Jackson, 30 August 1765, both in Edmund S. Morgan, ed., *Prologue to Revolution: Sources and Documents on the Stamp Act Crisis, 1764–1766* (New York, 1973), 106–9; Alfred F. Young, "Ebenezer Macintosh: Boston's Captain General of the Liberty Tree," in Alfred F. Young et al., eds., *Revolutionary Founders: Rebels, Radicals, and Reformers in the Making of the Nation* (New York, 2011), 15–17.

2. Edmund S. Morgan and Helen M. Morgan, *The Stamp Act Crisis: Prologue to Revolution* (Chapel Hill, 1953), 157–204; Peter Shaw, *American Patriots and the Ritual of Revolution* (Cambridge, MA, 1981), 177–225.

3. Dr. Thomas Moffat to Joseph Harrison, 16 October 1765, and Hutchinson to Jackson, both in Morgan, ed., *Prologue to Revolution*, 109–13; Bernard Bailyn, *The Ordeal of Thomas Hutchinson* (Cambridge, MA, 1974), 109–55.

4. On Pope's Day rituals, see Brendan McConville, "Pope's Day Revisited, 'Popular' Culture Reconsidered," *Explorations in Early American Culture* 4 (2000): 258–80; Francis D. Cogliano, "Deliverance from Luxury: Pope's Day, Conflict, and Consensus in Colonial Boston, 1745–1765," *Studies in Popular Culture* 15 (1993): 15–28.

5. On Macintosh, see Young, "Ebenezer Macintosh," 15–34. On Pope's Day and popular political culture, see Alfred Young, "English Plebeian Culture and Eighteenth-Century American Radicalism," in Margaret C. Jacob and James R. Jacob, eds., *The Origins of Anglo-American Radicalism* (London, 1984), 185–212; Simon P. Newman, *Parades and the Politics of the Street: Festive Culture in the Early American Republic* (Philadelphia, 1997), 11–43; Shaw, *American Patriots and the Ritual of Revolution*, 204–31; Gary B. Nash, *The Urban Crucible: Social Change, Political Consciousness, and the Origins of the American Revolution* (Cambridge, MA, 1979); Paul A. Gilje, *The Road to Mobocracy: Popular Disorder in New York City, 1763–1834* (Chapel Hill, 1987), 3–68.

6. James T. Kloppenberg, *Towards Democracy: The Struggle for Self-Rule in European and American Thought* (New York, 2016), 94–188; Maura Jane Farrelly, *Anti-Catholicism in America, 1620–1860* (New York, 2017), 1–35.

7. Christopher Hill, *The World Turned Upside Down: Radical Ideas During the English Revolution* (London, 1972); Marcus Rediker and Peter Linebaugh, *The Many-Headed Hydra: Sailors, Slaves, Commoners, and the Hidden History of the Revolutionary Atlantic* (Boston, 2000); John Rees, *The Leveller Revolution: Radical Political Organization in England, 1640–1650* (London, 2016).

8.   See Nash, *Urban Crucible*, 233–63; John J. McCusker and Russell R. Menard, *The Economy of British America, 1607–1789* (Chapel Hill, 1985), 211–94.

9.   Farrelly, *Anti-Catholicism in America*, 71–84. On corruption and republican thought, see Bernard Bailyn, *The Ideological Origins of the American Revolution* (Cambridge, MA, 1967), 55–159; Gordon S. Wood, *The Creation of the American Republic, 1776–1787* (Chapel Hill, 1969), 28–36.

10. Farrelly, *Anti-Catholicism in America*, 69–103; Gilje, *Road to Mobocracy*, 37–41.

11. Gilje, *Road to Mobocracy*, 37–41.

12. Brendan McConville, *The King's Three Faces: The Rise and Fall of Royal America, 1688–1776* (Chapel Hill, 2006), 62–76; Richard Bushman, *King and People in Provincial Massachusetts* (Chapel Hill, 1992). McConville's *King's Three Faces* is a particularly important reinterpretation.

13. Thomas Hobbes, *The Leviathan* (1651); John Locke, *The Second Treatise of Government* (1689); Lois G. Schwoerer, "Locke, Lockean Ideas, and the Glorious Revolution," *Journal of the History of Ideas* 51 (October-December 1990): 531–48; Eric Nelson, *The Royalist Revolution: Monarchy and the American Founding* (Cambridge, MA, 2014), 29–65.

14. Daniel Leonard and James Wilson, quoted in Nelson, *Royalist Revolution*, 32, 35.

15. Thomas Jefferson to John Jay, 23 August 1785, Avalon Project, Yale University Law School; Edmund Morgan, *Inventing the People: The Rise of Popular Sovereignty in England and America* (New York, 1988); Rhys Isaac, "Evangelical Revolt: The Nature of the Baptist Challenge to the Traditional Order in Virginia, 1765–1775," *William and Mary Quarterly* 31 (July 1974): 345–68; Aubrey C. Land, "Economic Base and Social Structure: The Northern Chesapeake in the Eighteenth Century," *Journal of Economic History* 25 (1965): 639–54.

16. McConville, *King's Three Faces*, 170–82. On "naïve monarchism," see Daniel Field, *Rebels in the Name of the Tsar* (Boston, 1976); James C. Scott, *Domination and the Arts of Resistance: Hidden Transcripts* (New Haven, 1990). On forms of slave "royalism" and their flight to the British during the Revolutionary War, see Gary B. Nash, *The Forgotten Fifth: African Americans in the Age of Revolution* (Cambridge, MA, 2006); Steven Hahn, *The Political Worlds of Slavery and Freedom* (Cambridge, MA, 2009), 55–114.

17. Petition to the King, 8 July 1775, Journals of the Continental Congress, Avalon Project, Yale University Law School; Nelson, *Royalist Revolution*, 63–65.

18. See, especially, Holger Hock, *Scars of Independence: America's Violent Birth* (New York, 2017).

19. Gilje, *Road to Mobocracy*, 67; David Waldstreicher, *In the Midst of Perpetual Fêtes: The Making of American Nationalism, 1776–1820* (Chapel Hill, 1997), 30–31.

20. "A Declaration and Remonstrance Of the distressed and bleeding Frontier Inhabitants Of the Province of Pennsylvania," 13 February 1764, in John R. Dunbar, ed., *The Paxton Papers* (The Hague, 1957), 101–10. The best treatment of this episode is Kevin Kenny, *Peaceable Kingdom Lost: The Paxton Boys and the Destruction of William Penn's Holy Experiment* (New York, 2009). On Pontiac's War, see Gregory Evans Dowd, *War under Heaven: Pontiac, the Indian Nations, and the British Empire* (Baltimore, 2002).

21. Dowd, *War under Heaven*, 191–212.
22. Alan Taylor, "Agrarian Independence: Northern Land Rioters after the Revolution," in Alfred F. Young, ed., *Beyond the American Revolution: Explorations in the History of American Radicalism* (Dekalb, IL, 1993), 221–45; Rachel Klein, "Ordering the Backcountry: The South Carolina Regulation," *William and Mary Quarterly* 38 (October 1981): 661–80; Brendan McConville, *These Daring Disturbers of the Public Peace: The Struggle for Property and Power in Early New Jersey* (Philadelphia, 2003); Edward Countryman, "'Out of the Bounds of the Law': Northern Land Rioters in the Eighteenth Century," in Alfred F. Young, ed., *The American Revolution: Essays in the History of American Radicalism* (Dekalb, IL, 1976), 39–61.
23. McConville, *These Daring Disturbers of the Peace*, 137–201; Taylor, "Agrarian Independence," 221–37; Marvin L. Michael Kay, "The North Carolina Regulation, 1766–1776," and Michael Merrill and Sean Wilentz, "The Key of Libberty: William Manning and Plebeian Democracy, 1747–1814," both in Young, ed., *The American Revolution*, 73–108, 247–71; Countryman, "'Out of the Bounds of the Law'," 39–61.
24. Benjamin Rush, "An Account of the Progress of Population, Agriculture, Manners, and Government, in Pennsylvania," *Essays Literary, Moral, and Philosophical* (Philadelphia, 1806), 226-47.
25. Klein, "Ordering the Backcountry," 661–72; Countryman, "'Out of the Bounds of the Law,'" 56; McConville, *These Daring Disturbers of the Peace*, 218.
26. Peter Silver, *Our Savage Neighbors: How Indian War Transformed Early America* (New York, 2008), 95–160; Dowd, *War under Heaven*, 203–12. For an alternative context, see Richard White, *The Middle Ground: Indians, Empires, and Republics in the Great Lakes Region, 1650–1815* (New York, 1991).
27. See, for example, Michael A. McDonnell, *The Politics of War: Race, Class, and Conflict in Revolutionary Virginia* (Chapel Hill, 2007); Woody Holton, *Forced Founders: Indians, Debtors, Slaves and the Making of the American Revolution in Virginia* (Chapel Hill, 1999).
28. McDonnell, *Politics of War*, 6; Robert Gross, *The Minutemen and Their World* (New York, 1976); Rachel Klein, *Unification of a Slave State: The Rise of the Planter Class in the South Carolina Backcountry, 1760–1808* (Chapel Hill, 1992); Alan Taylor, *Liberty Men and Great Proprietors: The Revolutionary Settlement on the Maine Frontier* (Chapel Hill, 1990); Kenny, *Peaceable Kingdom Lost*, 226–31.
29. Colin G. Calloway, *The American Revolution in Indian Country: Crisis and Diversity in Native American Communities* (New York, 1995); Woody Holton, *Liberty Is Sweet: The Hidden History of the American Revolution* (New York, 2021), 169–554; Patrick Griffin, *American Leviathan: Empire, Nation, and Revolutionary Frontier* (New York, 2007).
30. Constitution of Pennsylvania, 28 September 1776, Avalon Project, Yale University Law School; Wood, *Creation of the American Republic*, 127–255; Alan Taylor, *American Revolutions: A Continental History, 1750–1804* (New York, 2016), 358–63; Eric Foner, *Tom Paine and Revolutionary America* (New York, 1976), 107–44.
31. Although Vermont's Constitution of 1777 has long been regarded as having abolished slavery, its Declaration of Rights, after proclaiming that "all men are born equally free and independent," determined that "therefore, no male person . . . ought to be holden by law to serve any person as a slave, servant, or

apprentice *after he arrives at the age of twenty-one Years*, nor female in like manner, after she arrives to the age of eighteen years . . . unless they are bound by their own consent, after they arrive to such age, or bound by law, for the payment of debts, damages, fines, costs, etc." Constitution of Vermont, 8 July 1777, Chap. I; Constitution of Virginia, 29 June 1776, Sec. 1, both in Avalon Project. Vermont is usually credited with enacting the first emancipation provision in the United States and, indeed, it anticipated the contours of other emancipation statutes in the Northeast and Middle Atlantic: they all involved gradual emancipation, based on gender and age, and encased "freedom" with the prospects of further perpetual servitude.

32. Constitution of New Jersey, 1776, XIX; Virginia Constitution, Sec. 6, both in Avalon Project; Constitution of Massachusetts, 1780, Chap. VI, National Humanities Institute.

33. On the dimensions of this crisis, see Taylor, *American Revolutions*, 363–68; Michael Klarman, *The Framers' Coup: The Making of the United States Constitution* (New York, 2016), 73–125; Terry Bouton, *Taming Democracy: "The People," the Founders, and the Troubling End of the American Revolution* (New York, 2009), 88–104.

34. Woody Holton, *Unruly Americans and the Origins of the Constitution* (New York, 2007), 21–44.

35. Holton, *Unruly Americans,* 21–83; Bouton, *Taming Democracy*, 114–24; Taylor, *American Revolutions*, 363–67.

36. On state responses, see Klein, *Unification of a Slave State*, 109–237; George W. Van Cleeve, "The Anti-Federalists' Toughest Challenge: Paper Money, Debt Relief, and the Ratification of the Constitution," *Journal of the Early Republic* 34 (Winter 2014): 529–60.

37. On Shays's Rebellion, see Leonard L. Richards, *Shays's Rebellion: The American Revolution's Final Battle* (Philadelphia, 2002); David P. Szatmary, *Shays' Rebellion: The Making of an Agrarian Insurrection* (Amherst, 1984).

38. See Woody Holton's excellent treatment in *Unruly Americans*, 145–61. Also see Klarman, *Framers' Coup*, 73–125; Bouton, *Taming Democracy*, 197–215.

39. Holton, *Unruly Americans*, 179–80; Klarman, *Framers' Coup*, 73–125.

40. Thomas Jefferson to James Madison, 30 January 1787, Founders.Archives.Gov, National Archives; Klarman, *The Framers' Coup*, 11–125; Gerald Leonard and Saul Cornell, *The Partisan Republic: Democracy, Exclusion, and the Fall of the Founders' Constitution, 1780s–1830s* (New York, 2019), 8–15; Taylor, *American Revolutions*, 372–73.

41. See Nelson, *The Royalist Revolution*, 184–208; John L. Harper, *American Machiavelli: Alexander Hamilton and the Origins of U.S. Foreign Policy* (New York, 2004), 36–37. Early in the convention, many of the delegates hoped to devise a legislature that was based entirely on indirect representation. Connecticut's Roger Sherman, who had helped draft the Declaration of Independence, thought that no part of the legislature should be subject to popular election and that the people "should have as little to do as may be about the Government." See Gary Kornblith and John Murrin, "The Dilemmas of Ruling Elites in Revolutionary America," in Steve Fraser and Gary Gerstle, eds., *Ruling America: A History of Wealth and Power in a Democracy* (Cambridge, MA, 2005), 40–41.

42. David Waldstreicher, *Slavery's Constitution: Revolution to Ratification* (New York,

2009); Nelson, *The Royalist Revolution*, 199–203; Wood, *Creation of the American Republic*, 471–75. As Madison put it in a letter to Washington before the convention met: "A negative *in all cases whatsoever* on the legislative acts of the States, as heretofore exercised by the Kingly prerogative, appears to me to be absolutely necessary." What we know of the convention proceedings comes from Madison's notes, the private correspondence of delegates, and documents collected much later. There were slave rebellions in New York in 1712 and South Carolina in 1739, maroon wars in the Caribbean, and what is known as "Tacky's Revolt" in Jamaica in 1760. See, especially, Vincent Brown, *Tacky's Revolt: The Story of an Atlantic Slave War* (Cambridge, MA, 2020). "I tremble for my country," Jefferson wrote in his *Notes on the State of Virginia* in discussing the consequences of enslavement, "when I reflect that God is just; that his justice cannot sleep forever."

43. See, for example, John Jay, "Federalist 2–4," Alexander Hamilton, "Federalist 5–9, 12, 23, 28–30, 32, 68–70," James Madison, "Federalist 10, 37, 39, 45, 51," all in Cass Sunstein, ed., *The Federalist* (Cambridge, MA, 2009). The notes made by Madison have also been relied on for an important perspective on the convention's proceedings. For an in-depth account, see Mary Sarah Bilder, *Madison's Hand: Revising the Constitutional Convention* (Cambridge, MA, 2015).

44. On the ratification contest, see Pauline Maier, *Ratification: The People Debate the Constitution, 1787–1788* (New York, 2010); Klarman, *Framers' Coup*, 305–545; Saul Cornell, *The Other Founders: Anti-Federalism and the Dissenting Tradition in America, 1788–1828* (Chapel Hill, 1999), 19–143; Taylor, *American Revolutions*, 392.

45. Quoted in Taylor, "Agrarian Independence," 232. Also see Cornell, *The Other Founders*, 22–23; Maier, *Ratification*, 70–95.

46. See Federal Farmer, 9 October 1787, in Herbert Storing, ed., *The Anti-Federalist: Writings by Opponents of the Constitution* (Chicago, 1981), 42; Cornell, *The Other Founders*, 26–33. As was true of *The Federalist*, Anti-Federalists wrote under pseudonyms.

47. Baron de Montesquieu, *The Spirit of the Laws* (New York, 1949), Book IX, 120–21; Madison, "Federalist 10," in Sunstein, ed., *The Federalist*, 52–61.

48. See, for example, An Old Whig, October-November 1787, in Herbert Storing Jr., ed., *The Complete Anti-Federalist*, 7 vols. (Chicago, 1981), III, 32; Brutus, 18 October 1787, Centinel, October 1787, Address and Reasons of Dissent, 18 December 1787, all in Storing, ed., *Anti-Federalist*, 16, 18–91, 114–16, 209–13.

49. Isaac Kramnick, "The Great National Discussion: The Discourse of Politics in 1787," *William and Mary Quarterly* 45 (January 1988): 3–32; Taylor, "Agrarian Independence," 222–45; Saul Cornell, "Aristocracy Assailed: The Ideology of Backcountry Anti-Federalism," *Journal of American History* 76 (March 1990): 1148–72.

50. *Carlisle Gazette*, 2 January 1788, in Merrill Jensen et al., eds., *Ratification of the Constitution by the States* (Philadelphia, 1976), 670–73; Bouton, *Taming Democracy*, 216–43; Waldstreicher, *In the Midst of Perpetual Fêtes*, 92–97; Thomas P. Slaughter, *The Whiskey Rebellion: Frontier Epilogue to the American Revolution* (New York, 1986).

51. Thomas Jefferson, *Notes on the State of Virginia* (1785; New York, 1954), 137–43; Thomas Jefferson to Henry Lee, 8 May 1825, quoted in Gordon Wood, *Empire of Liberty: A History of the Early Republic, 1789–1815* (New York, 2009), 9; Helena

Rosenblatt, *The Lost History of Liberalism: From Ancient Rome to the Twenty-First Century* (Princeton, 2018).

52. Morgan, *Inventing the People*; Jefferson, *Notes on the State of Virginia*, 146–47; Wood, *Empire of Liberty*, 52–94.

53. Franklin, quoted in Wood, *Empire of Liberty*, 74.

54. Prince Hall et al. to the Honorable Council and House of [Represent]atives for the State of Massachusetts-Bay, 13 January 1777, *Collections of the Massachusetts Historical Society*, 5th Ser., III (Boston, 1877), 432–37. Previous petitions were sent in 1773 and 1774.

55. See, for example, C. S. Manegold, *Ten Hills Farm: The Forgotten History of Slavery in the North* (Princeton, 2010), 228–36. A similar case involving the enslaved woman Mumbet, also known as Elizabeth Freeman, was adjudicated at the time in Stockbridge, with a judge ruling in her favor. Also see Joanne Pope Melish, *Disowning Slavery: Gradual Emancipation and "Race" in New England, 1780–1860* (Ithaca, NY, 1998); Ira Berlin, *The Long Emancipation: The Demise of Slavery in the United States* (Cambridge, MA, 2015).

CHAPTER FOUR

TOCQUEVILLE, LINCOLN, AND THE
EXPULSIVE 1830s

1. See Alexis de Tocqueville, *Democracy in America*, J. P. Mayer, ed., trans. by George Lawrence (New York, 1969), 11–12.

2. Abraham Lincoln, "The Perpetuation of Our Political Institutions: Address Before the Young Men's Lyceum of Springfield, Illinois," 27 January 1838, in Roy P. Basler, ed., *Abraham Lincoln: His Speeches and Writings* (New York, 1946), 76–85.

3. Lincoln, "Perpetuation of Our Political Institutions," 78–80; Kelly Kennington, *In the Shadow of Dred Scott: St. Louis Freedom Suits and the Legal Culture of Slavery in Antebellum America* (Athens, GA, 2017), 182–83. Lincoln also noted the hanging of gamblers in Mississippi. The status of slavery and the enslaved remained complicated owing first to the ambiguities in the Northwest Ordinance. As Scott Heerman points out in his important book, there were slave sales and the transmissibility of chattel property in Illinois as late as the 1830s. See Heerman, *The Alchemy of Slavery: Human Bondage and Emancipation in the Illinois Country, 1730–1865* (Philadelphia, 2018), 135–68.

4. The literature on abolitionism is enormous, but for some especially valuable examples see Manisha Sinha, *The Slave's Cause: A History of Abolition* (New Haven, 2017); Gary Nash, *Forging Freedom: The Formation of Philadelphia's Free Black Community, 1720–1840* (Cambridge, MA, 1988); Richard Newman, *The Transformation of American Abolitionism: Fighting Slavery in the Early Republic* (Chapel Hill, 2002); Eddie S. Glaude Jr., *Exodus! Religion, Race, and Nation in Early Black America* (Chicago, 2000); David Brion Davis, *The Problem of Slavery in the Age of Emancipation* (New York, 2014).

5. Abolitionism had an anarchistic streak that is often underappreciated. See Lewis

Perry, *Radical Abolitionism: Anarchy and the Government of God in Antislavery Thought* (Ithaca, NY, 1983).

6. For an especially insightful argument, see David Brion Davis, "Immediatism in British and American Antislavery Thought," *Mississippi Valley Historical Review* 49 (September 1962): 209–30.

7. See, especially, the important work of Larry E. Tise, *Proslavery: A History of the Defense of Slavery in America, 1701–1840* (Athens, GA, 1987).

8. Here I part company with some recent scholarly assessments that look more favorably on colonization as a realistic approach to slave emancipation and one that was committed to the eradication of the evils of slavery and the uplift of Africans and African Americans. See, for example, Davis, *Problem of Slavery in the Age of Emancipation*, 83–165. On the expulsion of Native peoples from east of the Mississippi River during the 1830s, see Claudio Saunt, *Unworthy Republic: The Dispossession of Native Americans and the Road to Indian Territory* (New York, 2020). Removal or removalism is the term most often associated with policy toward free Blacks and Native Americans but "expulsionism" seems to me more appropriate as a historical phenomenon of the period. On the connected expulsionism directed against Blacks and Native peoples, see Samantha Seeley, *Race, Removal, and the Right to Remain: Migration and the Making of the United States* (Chapel Hill, 2021).

9. James Brewer Stewart, *Holy Warriors: The Abolitionists and American Slavery* (New York, 1996), 67–68; David Roediger, *The Wages of Whiteness: Race and the Making of the American Working Class* (London, 1991), 95–110; Leonard Richards, *"Gentlemen of Property and Standing": Anti-Abolition Mobs in Jacksonian America* (New York, 1970), 69–71.

10. Richards, *"Gentlemen of Property and Standing,"* 3–46; David Grimstead, *American Mobbing, 1828–1861: Toward Civil War* (New York, 1998), 33–82; Daniel Walker Howe, *What Hath God Wrought: The Transformation of America, 1815–1848* (New York, 2007), 411–45.

11. Richards, *"Gentlemen of Property and Standing,"* 62.

12. Steven Hahn, *The Political Worlds of Slavery and Freedom* (Cambridge, MA, 2009), 1–54; Ira Berlin, *The Long Emancipation: The Demise of Slavery in the United States* (Cambridge, MA, 2015).

13. Lydia Maria Child, *An Appeal in Favor of that Class of Americans Called Africans* (Boston, 1833), 6, 10.

14. See, for example, Leon Litwack, *North of Slavery: The Negro in the Free States, 1790–1860* (Chicago, 1961); Eugene Berwanger, *The Frontier Against Slavery: Western Anti-Negro Prejudice and the Slavery Extension Controversy* (Urbana, IL, 1967); Kevin Waite, *West of Slavery: The Southern Dream of a Transcontinental Empire* (Chapel Hill, 2021). Also see Nicholas Guyatt, *Bind Us Apart: How Enlightened Americans Invented Racial Segregation* (New York, 2016) on "separate but equal" as a founding principle of the American republic.

15. George M. Fredrickson, *The Black Image in the White Mind: The Debate on Afro-American Character and Destiny, 1817–1914* (New York, 1971), 1–96; Reginald Horsman, *Race and Manifest Destiny: The Origins of American Racial Anglo-Saxonism* (Cambridge, MA, 1981), 79–186; Tise, *Proslavery*, 286–346.

16. Kate Masur, *Until Justice Be Done: America's First Civil Rights Movement, from the Revolution to Reconstruction* (New York, 2021), 12 and passim.

17. On the convent destruction, see Jeanne Hamilton, "The Nunnery as Menace: The Burning of the Charlestown Convent, 1834," *U.S. Catholic Historian* 14 (Winter 1996): 35–65; Maura Jane Farrelly, *Anti-Catholicism in America, 1620–1860* (New York, 2018), 134–45; Ray Allen Billington, *The Protestant Crusade: A Study of the Origins of American Nativism* (1938; Chicago, 1964), 32–84. On the Philadelphia anti-Black riot, see John Runcie, "'Hunting the Nigs' in Philadelphia: The Race Riot of 1834," *Pennsylvania History* 39 (April 1972): 187–218.

18. Ray Allen Billington, "The Burning of the Charlestown Convent," *New England Quarterly* 10 (March 1937): 4–24; Paul A. Gilje, *Rioting in America* (Bloomington, IN, 1996), 64–66; Rebecca Theresa Reed, *Six Months in a Convent* (Boston, 1835). Also see Hidetaka Hirota, *Expelling the Poor: Atlantic Seaboard States and 19th Century Immigration Policy* (New York, 2017).

19. Paul E. Johnson and Sean Wilentz, *The Kingdom of Matthias: A Story of Sex and Salvation in 19th-Century America* (New York, 1994).

20. On Smith, see, especially, Richard L. Bushman, *Joseph Smith: Rough Stone Rolling* (New York, 2005).

21. Benjamin E. Park, *Kingdom of Nauvoo: The Rise and Fall of a Religious Empire on the American Frontier* (New York, 2020), 6–21; Leonard J. Arrington, *The Great Basin Kingdom: An Economic History of the Latter-Day Saints, 1830–1900* (Cambridge, MA, 1958), 3–22; Bushman, *Joseph Smith*, 294–373.

22. Sarah Barringer Gordon, *The Mormon Question: Polygamy and Constitutional Conflict in Nineteenth-Century America* (Chapel Hill, 2002); David L. Bigler and Will Bagley, *The Mormon Rebellion: America's First Civil War, 1857–1858* (Norman, OK, 2011).

23. See David Brion Davis, "Some Themes of Countersubversion: An Analysis of Anti-Mason, Anti-Catholic, and Anti-Mormon Literature," *Mississippi Valley Historical Review* 47 (September 1960): 205–24; T. Ward Frampton, "'Some Savage Tribe': Race, Legal Violence, and the Mormon War of 1838," *Journal of Mormon History* 40 (Winter 2014): 175–207; Richard Bushman, "Mormon Persecutions in Missouri, 1833," *Brigham Young University Studies* 3 (Autumn 1960): 11–20; J. Spencer Fluhman, *"A Peculiar People": Anti-Mormonism and the Making of Religion in Nineteenth-Century America* (Chapel Hill, 2012), 21–102.

24. Lilburn M. Boggs, 27 October 1838, Missouri Mormon War, Missouri State Archives, Jefferson City, MO; Park, *Kingdom of Nauvoo*, 30.

25. Park, *Kingdom of Nauvoo*, 222–67.

26. See, especially, Alexander Keyssar, *The Right to Vote: The Contested History of Democracy in the United States* (New York, 2000), 26–52. Recent research suggests that, for a variety of reasons, what changed was less voter turnout at the local level than much greater turnout for national elections. See, for example, the important articles in the *Journal of the Early Republic* 33 (Summer 2013).

27. On early national political culture, see David Waldstreicher, *In the Midst of Perpetual Fêtes: The Making of American Nationalism, 1776–1820* (Chapel Hill, 1997); Simon P. Newman, *Parades and the Politics of the Streets: Festive Culture in the Early American Republic* (Philadelphia, 1997).

28. See Grimsted, *American Mobbing*, 181–98. Also see Richard Franklin Bensel, *The American Ballot Box in the Mid-Nineteenth Century* (New York, 2004).

29. *Viva voce* voting prevailed in Virginia, Kentucky, Missouri, Arkansas, and Illinois during the 1830s. See Keyssar, *Right to Vote*, 28. Also see Bensel, *American Ballot in the Mid-Nineteenth Century*, 26–85, 138–86.

30. See, for example, John Mack Faragher, *Sugar Creek: Life on the Illinois Prairie* (New Haven, 1986), 140–70; Don H. Doyle, *The Social Order of a Frontier Community: Jacksonville, Illinois, 1825–1870* (Urbana, IL, 1978), 169–77.

31. On *herrenvolk* democracy in the antebellum South, see Fredrickson, *Black Image in the White Mind*, 43–70.

32. John Hope Franklin, *The Militant South, 1800–1861* (Cambridge, MA, 1956); Bertram Wyatt Brown, *Southern Honor: Ethics and Behavior in the Old South* (New York, 1982), 327–461; Sally Hadden, *Slave Patrols: Law and Violence in Virginia and the Carolinas* (Cambridge, MA, 2003); Christopher J. Olsen, *Political Culture and Secession in Mississippi: Masculinity, Honor, and the Antiparty Tradition, 1830–1860* (New York, 2000), 17–37; Harry S. Laver, "Rethinking the Social Role of the Militia," *Journal of Southern History* 68 (November 2002): 777–816; William Faulkner, *Requiem for a Nun* (New York, 1951), 5. Militia musters were common and served similar social and political purposes outside the slave states as well. Wherever they took place, they could also descend into chaos and drunkenness.

33. Galusha Grow, "The Last Days of the Duello in Congress," *Saturday Evening Post*, 23 June 1900, 1194; and especially Joanne B. Freeman, *The Field of Blood: Violence in Congress and the Road to Civil War* (New York, 2018).

34. See, especially, Paul Goodman, *Toward a Christian Republic: Antimasonry and the Great Transition in New England, 1826–1836* (New York, 1988); Howe, *What Hath God Wrought*, 167–70; Davis, "Some Themes of Counter-Subversion," 206–24.

35. Goodman, *Toward a Christian Republic*, 3–19; Howe, *What Hath God Wrought*, 268–70; Raymie E. McKerrow, "Antimasonic Rhetoric: The Strategy of Excommunication," *Communication Quarterly* 37 (Fall 1989): 276–90.

36. Goodman, *Toward a Christian Republic*, 3–53, 105–245; Howe, *What Hath God Wrought*, 269–70l; Ronald Formisano, *The Transformation of Political Culture: Massachusetts Parties, 1790s–1840s* (New York, 1983), 198–221; Kathleen Kutolowski, "Antimasonry Reexamined: The Social Bases of the Grassroots Party," *Journal of American History* 71 (September 1984): 269–93.

37. "Republican Party Platform of 1856," 18 June 1856, The American Presidency Project, UC Santa Barbara.

38. Kerry A. Trask, *Black Hawk: The Battle for the Heart of America* (New York, 2006).

39. David Donald, *Lincoln* (New York, 1995), 43–46; Saunt, *Unworthy Republic*, 53–170. On Lincoln's early experience with Native peoples, see Christopher W. Anderson, "Native Americans and the Origin of Abraham Lincoln's Views on Race," *Journal of the Abraham Lincoln Association* 37 (Winter 2016): 11–29.

40. Colin G. Calloway, *The American Revolution in Indian Country: Crisis and Diversity in Native American Communities* (New York 1995); Constitution of the United States, Art. I, Secs. 2 and 8.

41. Francis P. Prucha, *The Great Father: The United States Government and the Indians,* 2 vols. (Lincoln, NE, 1984), I, 35–178.
42. William G. McLoughlin, *Cherokee Renaissance in the New Republic* (Princeton, 1986); Theda Perdue, *Slavery and the Evolution of Cherokee Society, 1540–1866* (Knoxville, 1979).
43. Stephen Warren, *The Shawnees and Their Neighbors, 1795–1870* (Urbana, IL, 2008); Claudio Saunt, *A New Order of Things: Property, Power, and the Transformation of the Creek Indians, 1733–1816* (New York, 1999); Barbara Krauthamer, *Black Slaves, Indian Masters: Slavery, Emancipation, and Citizenship in the Native American South* (Chapel Hill, 2015). The Supreme Court issued mixed rulings in two Georgia cases—*Cherokee Nation* v. *Georgia* (1831) and *Worcester* v. *Georgia* (1832)—that still offered Native peoples some room. On the one side the Court determined that while the Cherokee did occupy a sovereign status of sorts ("domestic dependent nations") they had no standing as a foreign state and thus no right to sue Georgia. On the other side, the Court called the "Cherokee Nation" a "distinct community, occupying its own territory," over which Georgia law had no jurisdiction. President Jackson, however, regarded the decisions as just interpretations of the Constitution and refused to enforce them, allowing the Georgians to do what they liked.
44. Anthony F. C. Wallace, *The Long Bitter Trail: Andrew Jackson and the Indians* (New York, 1993); Michael P. Rogin, *Fathers and Children: Andrew Jackson and the Subjugation of the American Indian* (New York, 1975).
45. John K. Mahon, *History of the Second Seminole War, 1835–1842* (Gainesville, 2010); Trask, *Black Hawk.*
46. Saunt, *Unworthy Republic*; Theda Perdue and Michael D. Green, *The Cherokee Nation and the Trail of Tears* (New York, 2007).
47. See David A. Nichols, *Lincoln and the Indians: Civil War Policy and Politics* (Urbana, IL, 1978); Jeffrey Ostler, *The Plains Sioux and U.S. Colonialism from Lewis and Clark to Wounded Knee* (New York, 2004), 13–107; Alvin M. Josephy Jr., *The Civil War in the American West* (New York, 1991); Pekka Hamalainen, *Lakota America: A New History of Indigenous Power* (New Haven, 2019), 252–67. I have discussed this in "Slave Emancipation, Indian Peoples, and the Projects of a New American Nation-State," *Journal of the Civil War Era* 3 (September 2013): 307–30.
48. Nichols, *Lincoln and the Indians,* 94–127; Hahn, "Slave Emancipation and Indian Peoples," 307–30. Four of those who conspired with John Wilkes Booth to assassinate Lincoln, one of whom had been in Confederate service, and all of whom were Confederate sympathizers, were tried and executed by a military commission.
49. Clifford Krainik and Michele Krainik, "Photographs of Indian Delegates at the President's 'Summer House,'" *White House History* 25 (Spring 2009); Nichols, *Lincoln and the Indians,* 129–201.
50. "Address on Colonization to a Deputation of Negroes," 14 August 1862, in Roy P. Basler, ed., *The Collected Works of Abraham Lincoln,* 9 vols. (New Brunswick, NJ, 1953), V, 371–75; "Annual Message to Congress," 1 December 1862, in Basler, ed., *Lincoln: His Speeches and Writings,* 676.
51. Tocqueville, *Democracy in America,* 316–39.
52. Tocqueville, *Democracy in America,* 340–63; Cheryl Welch, "Creating *Concitoyens*:

Tocqueville on the Legacy of Slavery," in Raf Geenens and Annelien De Dijn, eds., *Reading Tocqueville: From Oracle to Actor* (Hampshire, 2007), 31–36.

53.   Tocqueville, *Democracy in America*, 358–87.

54.   Tocqueville, *Democracy in America*, 252. Among those who have emphasized the civic and communitarian features in Tocqueville are Robert Putnam and Michael Sandel.

55.   Tocqueville, *Democracy in America*, 44, 62–63, 96, 224–25, 252, 254–55, 375, 399, 692–93, 697.

56.   Sheldon Wolin, *Tocqueville Between Two Worlds: The Making of a Political and Theoretical Life* (Princeton, 2001), 229–40.

CHAPTER FIVE
THE MEASURES OF BONDAGE

1.   *New York Times*, 1 February 1865. An earlier version of this chapter, prepared as my presidential address to the Southern Historical Association, was published as, "Emancipation, Incarceration, and the Boundaries of Coercion." *Journal of Southern History*. v. 88, no. 1 February 2022: 5–38.

2.   Michael Vorenberg, *Final Freedom: The Civil War, the Abolition of Slavery, and the Thirteenth Amendment* (New York, 2001).

3.   Jefferson had first come up with the language in his draft of the Ordinance of 1784, but the prohibition on slavery was deleted in a narrow vote. Dane proposed the wording of Article VI of the Northwest Ordinance, which he appeared to take from his Massachusetts colleague Rufus King, who offered it, unsuccessfully, in connection to the Land Ordinance of 1785. To Dane's astonishment, Article VI was incorporated into the Northwest Ordinance; slaveholding interests put up little opposition. See Peter Onuf, *Statehood and Union: A History of the Northwest Ordinance* (Notre Dame, IN, 2019), 110–12; Eric Foner, *The Second Founding: How the Civil War and Reconstruction Remade the Constitution* (New York, 2019), 31–32. On the impact of British convicts as indentured servants, see Alan Atkinson, "The Free-Born Englishman Transported: Convict Rights as a Measure of Eighteenth-Century Empire," *Past and Present* 144 (August 1994): 88–115; A. Roger Ekirch, *Bound for America: The Transportation of British Convicts to the Colonies, 1718–1775* (Oxford, 1990); Rebecca McLennan, *The Crisis of Imprisonment: Protest, Politics, and the Making of the American Penal State, 1776–1941* (New York, 2008), 30–32. According to Virginia's Richard Henry Lee, the Northwest Ordinance "seemed necessary, for the security of property among uninformed, and perhaps licentious people, as the greater part of those who go there are, that a strong toned government exist, and the rights of property be clearly defined." See Richard Henry Lee to George Washington, 15 July 1787, Founders' Online, National Archives. On Jefferson's interest in penal reform and reform of the criminal code, see Paul Knepper, "Thomas Jefferson, Criminal Code Reform, and the Kentucky Penitentiary at Frankfort," *Register of the Kentucky Historical Society* 91 (Spring 1993): 129–49.

4.   William M. Carter Jr., "Race, Rights, and the Thirteenth Amendment," *U.C. Davis Law Review* 40 (April 2007): 1311–79; Michele Goodwin, "The Thirteenth Amendment: Modern Slavery, Capitalism, and Mass Incarceration," 104 *Cornell Law*

Review 899 (2019): 899–990; Ava Duvernay, "13th" (2016). On convict lease and other forms of legal repression, see Alex Lichtenstein, *Twice the Work of Free Labor: The Political Economy of Convict Labor in the New South* (London, 1996); David Oshinsky, *"Worse than Slavery": Parchman Farm and the Ordeal of Jim Crow Justice* (New York, 1996); William Cohen, *At Freedom's Edge: Black Mobility and the Southern White Quest for Racial Control, 1861–1915* (Baton Rouge, 1991); Douglas A. Blackmon, *Slavery by Another Name: The Re-Enslavement of Black Americans from the Civil War to World War II* (New York, 2008); Edward L. Ayers, *Vengeance and Justice: Crime and Punishment in the Nineteenth-Century South* (New York, 1985). On the Thirteenth Amendment and Black criminalization, see Khalil Gibran Muhammad, *The Condemnation of Blackness: Race, Crime, and the Making of Modern America* (Cambridge, MA, 2011).

5. The most powerfully conceived and brilliantly presented arguments about the "problems" of slavery and freedom are to be found in David Brion Davis, *The Problem of Slavery in Western Culture* (Ithaca, NY, 1966); Davis, *The Problem of Slavery in the Age of Revolution, 1770–1823* (Ithaca, NY, 1975); Thomas Holt, *The Problem of Freedom: Race, Labor, and Politics in Jamaica and Britain, 1832–1938* (Baltimore, 1991); Ira Berlin et al., *Freedom: A Documentary History of Slave Emancipation, 1861–1867,* 5 vols. (New York, 1982–2012); Eric Foner, *Reconstruction: America's Unfinished Revolution, 1863–1877* (New York, 1988).

6. Gustave de Beaumont and Alexis de Tocqueville, *On the Penitentiary System in the United States and Its Application in France* (Philadelphia, 1833), 32–59.

7. Benjamin Rush, *An Enquiry into the Effects of Public Punishments upon Criminals and upon Society* (Philadelphia, 1787). Also see Max Mishler, "The Atlantic Origins of Mass Incarceration: Punishment, Abolition, and Racial Inequality" (PhD diss., New York University, 2016), 55–56. On Rush and the development of the penitentiary system in Pennsylvania, see Michael Meranze's outstanding *Laboratories of Virtue: Punishment, Revolution, and Authority in Philadelphia, 1760–1835* (Chapel Hill, 1996). On developments in Britain, see Michael Ignatieff, *A Just Measure of Pain: The Penitentiary in the Industrial Revolution, 1750–1850* (New York, 1978).

8. McLennan, *Crisis of Imprisonment*, 14–52; Meranze, *Laboratories of Virtue*, 19–171.

9. Charles Dickens, *American Notes for General Circulation* (London, 1842), 81–94.

10. Jonathan A. Glickstein, *American Exceptionalism, American Anxiety: Wages, Competition, and Degraded Labor in the Antebellum United States* (Charlottesville, 2002), 163–82.

11. I am indebted to the insights of Max Mishler in his pathbreaking dissertation, "Atlantic Origins of Mass Incarceration." But also see Meranze, *Laboratories of Virtue*, 1–18, 131–216; Sally Gershman, "Alexis de Tocqueville and Slavery," *French Historical Studies* 9 (Spring 1976): 467–83. See also Alexis de Tocqueville, *Writings on Empire and Slavery*, Jennifer Pitts, ed., (Baltimore, 2001).

12. Mishler, "Atlantic Origins," 7–98; Meranze, *Laboratories of Virtue*, 131–72.

13. Mishler, "Atlantic Origins," 47–133.

14. On emancipation in the Northeast and Middle Atlantic, see Sarah Gronningsater, *The Arc of Abolition: The Children of Gradual Emancipation and the Origins of National Freedom* (Philadelphia, forthcoming); Steven Hahn, *The Political Worlds of Slavery and Freedom* (Cambridge, MA, 2009); Ira Berlin, *The Long Emancipation: The Demise of Slavery in the United States* (Cambridge, MA, 2015); Stephen Kantrowitz, *More than Freedom: Fighting for Black Citizenship in a White Republic, 1829–1889* (New York, 2013), 13–174.

15. Mishler, "Atlantic Origins," 99–181; Adam Hirsch, "From Pillory to Penitentiary: The Rise of Criminal Incarceration in Early Massachusetts," *Michigan Law Review* 80 (1982): 1179–269. Connecticut began to use an old copper mine as a prison, called the Old Newgate Prison, in 1773. Also see Leslie Harris, *In the Shadow of Slavery: African Americans in New York City, 1626–1863* (Chicago, 2003); Shane White, *Somewhat More Independent: The End of Slavery in New York City* (Athens, GA, 1991).

16. McLennan, *Crisis of Imprisonment*, 83–85. Also see Robert Perkinson, *Texas Tough: The Rise of America's Prison Empire* (New York, 2010), 79–81.

17. Mishler, "Atlantic Origins," 143–81.

18. Ira Berlin et al., *Freedom: A Documentary History of Emancipation, 1861–1867*, ser. 1, vol. 1, *The Destruction of Slavery* (New York, 1986). On Lincoln and the slavery question, see Eric Foner, *The Fiery Trial: Abraham Lincoln and Slavery* (New York, 2010).

19. There is a very large literature on wartime emancipation, but see Ira Berlin et al., *Freedom: A Documentary History of Emancipation, 1861–1867*, ser. 1, vol. 2, *The Black Military Experience* (New York, 1981); W. E. B. Du Bois, *Black Reconstruction in America, 1860–1880* (New York, 1935), 55–127; Steven Hahn, *A Nation under Our Feet: Black Political Struggles in the Rural South from Slavery to the Great Migration* (Cambridge, MA, 2003), 62–115: James Oakes, *Freedom National: The Destruction of Slavery in the United States, 1861–1865* (New York, 2013); and, most recently, Joseph P. Reidy, *Illusions of Emancipation: The Pursuit of Freedom and Equality in the Twilight of Slavery* (Chapel Hill, 2020).

20. Vorenberg, *Final Freedom,* 36–88; Foner, *Second Founding,* 23–56.

21. Foner, *Second Founding,* 23–56; Vorenberg, *Final Freedom,* 89–114.

22. Howard quoted in Lea S. VanderVelde, "The Labor Vision of the Thirteenth Amendment," *University of Pennsylvania Law Review* 138 (1989): 480; Holt, *The Problem of Freedom*; Diana Paton, *No Bond but the Law: Punishment, Race, and Gender in Jamaican State Formation, 1780–1870* (Durham, NC, 2004); Tocqueville, *Writings on Empire and Slavery.*

23. Thomas B. Wilson, *The Black Codes of the South* (University, AL, 1965); Declan M. Hahn, "The Georgia Black Code as American Law: Race, Law, and Labor in the Nineteenth Century American Republic" (Honors thesis, Emory University, 2016), 8–27.

24. Foner, *Reconstruction,* 228–280; Steven Hahn et al., eds., *Freedom: A Documentary History of Emancipation,* ser. 3, vol. 1, *Land and Labor in 1865* (Chapel Hill, 2007), 392–493.

25. Hahn, *A Nation under Our Feet,* 116–264. It is important to point out that, in the state constitutional conventions that made Republican rule possible, Black delegates were far more reluctant than white unionists to penalize former Confederates politically by disfranchising them.

26. Eric Foner, *Nothing but Freedom: Emancipation and Its Legacy* (Baton Rouge, 1982), 39–73; Steven Hahn, "Hunting, Fishing, and Foraging: Common Rights and Class Relations in the Postbellum South," *Radical History Review* 26 (1982): 37–64; Fitzhugh quoted in Cohen, *At Freedom's Edge,* 28. The Black Codes were nullified less because they coerced laborers than because they were racially discriminatory. Vagrancy laws thus remained on the books or were quickly revised,

and they were fortified by other "race neutral" labor laws after Reconstruction regimes were dismantled.

27. Cohen, *At Freedom's Edge,* 23–43; Blackmon, *Slavery by Another Name,* 13–83; Dennis Childs, *Slaves of the State: Black Incarceration from the Chain Gang to the Penitentiary* (Minneapolis, 2015); Sarah Haley, *No Mercy Here: Gender, Punishment, and the Making of Jim Crow Modernity* (Chapel Hill, 2016); Talitha L. Le Flouria, *Chained in Silence: Black Women and Convict Labor in the New South* (Chapel Hill, 2015). On the northern influence, see Hahn, "Georgia Black Code as American Law," 28–69.

28. Jeffrey A. Drobny, "Where Palm and Pine are Blowing: Convict Labor in the North Florida Turpentine Industry, 1877–1923," *Florida Historical Quarterly* 72 (April 1994): 411–34; Perkinson, *Texas Tough,* 83–94.

29. Lichtenstein, *Twice the Work of Free Labor;* Ayers, *Vengeance and Justice;* Oshinsky, *"Worse than Slavery";* Karin Shapiro, *A New South Rebellion: The Battle Against Convict Labor in the Tennessee Coal Fields, 1871–1896* (Chapel Hill, 1996); Blackmon, *Slavery by Another Name.*

30. Drobny, "Where Palm and Pine are Blowing," 428–29; Oshinsky, *"Worse than Slavery,"* 55–84; Mary Ellen Curtin, *Black Prisoners and Their World in Alabama, 1865–1900* (Charlottesville, 2000); Matthew J. Mancini, *One Dies Get Another: Convict Leasing in the American South, 1866–1928* (Columbia, SC, 1996).

31. Morgan and Donnelly quoted in James Gray Polk, "Mass Incarceration, Convict Leasing, and the Thirteenth Amendment: A Revisionist Account," *New York University Laws Review* 94 (December 2019): 1467, 1480. Although many historians now argue that the criminal exception clause of the Thirteenth Amendment enabled convict lease and other forms of convict involuntary servitude, Pope insists that the historical record suggests a view of the amendment far less compatible with these devices and potentially available to draw mass incarceration into legal question. The great likelihood is that convict lease and related forms of legal repression would have developed without the amendment's "exception clause," especially in view of the penal labor precedents in the northern states.

32. Pope, "Mass Incarceration, Convict Lease, and the Thirteenth Amendment," 1501–25.

33. On antebellum Republican ideals, see Eric Foner, *Free Soil, Free Labor, Free Men: The Ideology of the Republican Party before the Civil War* (New York, 1970). On the "able-bodied" as a crucial determination of citizenship and belonging, see Barbara Welke, *Law and Borders of Belonging in the Long Nineteenth-Century United States* (New York, 2010), esp. 21–93.

34. *Annual Report of the Board of Charities of Massachusetts* (October 1866), 40–41. Howe was also a member of the American Freedmen's Inquiry Commission, which recommended the establishment of the Freedmen's Bureau. Also see Amy Dru Stanley, *From Bondage to Contract: Wage Labor, Marriage, and the Market in the Age of Slave Emancipation* (New York, 1998), 98–137.

35. Stanley, *From Bondage to Contract,* 108–110; Alexander Keyssar, *Out of Work: The First Century of Unemployment in Massachusetts* (New York, 1986); Kenneth L. Kusmer, *Down and Out, On the Road: The Homeless in American History* (New York, 2002), 50–56.

36. For Lincoln's views, see "Annual Address before the State Agricultural Society," 30 September 1859, and "Annual Address to Congress," 3 December 1861, both in Roy P. Basler, ed., *Abraham Lincoln: His Speeches and Writings* (Cleveland,

1946), 500–503, 633–34. On the significance of immigrants and their American-born children to the composition of the working class, see Herbert G. Gutman, "Class Composition and the Development of the American Working Class, 1840–1890," in Gutman, *Power and Culture: Essays on the American Working Class,* ed. Ira Berlin (New York, 1987), 380–94.

37. David Montgomery, "The Shuttle and the Cross: Weavers and Artisans in the Kensington Riots of 1844," *Journal of Social History* 5 (Summer 1972): 411–46; Tyler Anbinder, *Nativism and Slavery: The Northern Know Nothings and the Politics of the 1850s* (New York, 1992); Peter Way, *Common Labor: Workers and the Digging of North American Canals, 1780–1860* (Baltimore, 1993); Peyton Hurt, "The Rise and Fall of the 'Know Nothings' in California," *California Historical Society Quarterly* 9 (March 1930): 16–49.

38. Parkinson and Adams quoted in Alexander Keyssar, *The Right to Vote: The Contested History of Democracy in the United States* (New York, 2000), 122–23; David Montgomery, *Beyond Equality: Labor and the Radical Republicans, 1862–1872* (New York, 1967). The issue of the eight-hour workday assumed growing importance among organized workers.

39. John G. Sproat, *The Best Men: Liberal Reformers in the Gilded Age* (New York, 1968); Keyssar, *Right to Vote,* 118–27.

40. On the California story of Civil War and Reconstruction, see Stacy L. Smith, *Freedom's Frontier: California and the Struggle over Unfree Labor, Emancipation, and Reconstruction* (Chapel Hill, 2013); and Kevin Waite, *West of Slavery: The Southern Dream of a Transcontinental Empire* (Chapel Hill, 2021).

41. Smith, *Freedom's Frontier,* 206–30; Beth Lew-Williams, *The Chinese Must Go: Violence, Exclusion, and the Making of the Alien in America* (Cambridge, MA, 2018); Joshua Paddison, *American Heathens: Religion, Race, and Reconstruction in California* (Berkeley, 2012). The Chinese Exclusion Act effectively marked an entire ethnic group as inassimilable and subject to exclusion.

42. LaWanda Cox, "The American Agricultural Wage Earner, 1865–1900: The Emergence of a Modern Labor Problem," *Agricultural History* 22 (April 1948): 106–10; Ahmed A. White, "A Different Kind of Labor Law: Vagrancy Law and the Regulation of Harvest Labor, 1913–1924," *University of Colorado Law Review* 75 (2004): 668–718; Gunther Peck, *Reinventing Free Labor: Padrones and Immigrant Workers in the North American West, 1880–1930* (New York, 2000); Howard Lamar, "From Bondage to Contract: Ethnic Labor in the American West, 1600–1890," in Steven Hahn and Jonathan Prude, eds., *The Countryside in the Age of Capitalist Transformation: Essays in the Social History of Rural America* (Chapel Hill, 1985), 293–326.

43. James D. Schmidt, *Free to Work: Labor Law, Emancipation, and Reconstruction, 1815–1880* (Athens, GA, 1999), 208–35; Frank Tobias Higbie, *Indispensable Outcasts: Hobo Workers and Community in the American Midwest, 1880–1930* (Urbana, IL, 2003), 1–65; Kelly Lytle Hernandez, "Hobos in Heaven: Race, Incarceration, and the Rise of Los Angeles, 180–1910," *Pacific Historical Review* 83 (August 2014): 410–47; White, "A Different Kind of Labor Law," 668–86.

44. See, especially, VanderVelde, "The Labor Vision of the Thirteenth Amendment," 437–505.

45. Karen Orren, *Belated Feudalism: Labor, Law, and Liberal Development in the United States* (New York, 1991).

46. See, especially, Robert Steinfeld, *Coercion, Contract, and Free Labor in the Nineteenth Century* (New York, 2001); Christopher L. Tomlins, *Law, Labor, and Ideology in the Early Republic* (New York, 1993), 259–92; Orren, *Belated Feudalism*, 68–134. By the time of the Civil War, only six states had rejected the common law tradition.

47. See Fred A. Shannon, *The Farmers' Last Frontier: Agriculture, 1860–1897* (1945; Armonk NY, 1973), 359–67; Harold D. Woodman, *New South–New Law: The Legal Foundations of Credit and Labor Relations in the Postbellum Agricultural South* (Baton Rouge, 1995).

48. David Montgomery, *The Fall of the House of Labor: The Workplace, the State, and American Labor Activism, 1865–1925* (New York, 1987), 112–70; Daniel Nelson, *Managers and Workers: The Origins of the New Factory System in the United States, 1880–1920* (Madison, WI, 1975).

49. Steinfeld, *Invention of Free Labor*, 147–72; Paul Finkleman, "Evading the Ordinance: The Persistence of Bondage in Indiana and Illinois," *Journal of the Early Republic* 9 (Spring 1989): 21–51.

50. Steinfeld, *Coercion, Contract, and Free Labor*, 253–303. On the peonage cases of the early twentieth century, see Pete Daniel, *The Shadow of Slavery: Peonage in the South, 1901–1969* (Urbana, IL, 1990). The flaw in the Anti-Peonage Act was that, although voluntary and involuntary servitude were both outlawed, the law only encompassed cases of peonage.

51. William E. Forbath, *Law and the Shaping of the American Labor Movement* (Cambridge, MA, 1991). On the antebellum period, see Morton Horwitz, *The Transformation of American Law, 1780–1860* (Cambridge, MA, 1977).

52. Orren, *Belated Feudalism*, 68–159; Forbath, *Law and the Shaping of the Labor Movement*, 37–58.

53. U.S. Strike Commission, *Report on the Chicago Strike of June–July 1894* (Washington, DC, 1895), 129–80; Forbath, *Law and the Shaping of the Labor Movement*, 59–97. On antebellum conspiracy and combination cases, see Tomlins, *Law, Labor, and Ideology*, 107–79.

CHAPTER SIX

MODERNIZING ILLIBERALISM

1. *Official Proceedings of the Second National Conference on Race Betterment*, 4–8 August 1915 (Battle Creek, 1915), 40–42, 63–64; *The Second International Congress of Eugenics*, 1921 (Baltimore, 1923).

2. *Proceedings of the First American Birth Control Conference*, 11–12 November 1921 (New York, 1921), 14–15, 207–9.

3. On Sanger, see, especially, David M. Kennedy, *Birth Control in America: The Career of Margaret Sanger* (New Haven, 1970), 1–36; Linda Gordon, *The Moral Property of Women: A History of Birth Control Politics in America* (Urbana, IL, 2002), 125–210.

4. Edwin Black, *The War Against the Weak: Eugenics and America's Campaign to Create a Master Race* (Washington, DC, 2012), 9–123.

5. Margaret Sanger, *The Pivot of Civilization* (New York, 1922), 22, 25, 80–81, 86; *Proceedings of First American Birth Control Conference*, 1–3.

6. See, for example, Mark Mazower, *Dark Continent: Europe's Twentieth Century* (New York, 1998), 76–103; Nancy Leys Stepan, *The Hour of Eugenics: Race, Gender, and Nation in Latin America* (Ithaca, NY, 1991), 1–62; Chloe Campbell, *Race and Empire: Eugenics in Colonial Kenya* (Manchester, 2007); Barbara Weinstein, *The Color of Modernity: São Paulo and the Making of Race and Nation in Brazil* (Durham, NC, 2015). There is, it should be said, growing interest in eugenics in the twenty-first-century United States. See Alexandra Minha Stern, *Eugenic Nation: Faults and Frontiers of Better Breeding in Modern America* (Berkeley, 2016); Paul A. Lombardo, ed., *A Century of Eugenics in America* (Bloomington, IN, 2011).

7. On movements of producers, organized chiefly around the ideology of "anti-monopoly," see Edward T. O'Donnell, *Henry George and the Crisis of Inequality: Progress and Poverty in the Gilded Age* (New York, 2015); Steven Hahn, *A Nation without Borders: The United States and Its World in an Age of Civil Wars, 1830–1910* (New York, 2016), 401–47; Alex Gourevitch, *From Slavery to the Cooperative Commonwealth: Labor and Republican Liberty in the Nineteenth Century* (New York, 2015). On elite anti-modernism, see, especially, T. J. Jackson Lears, *No Place of Grace: Antimodernism and the Transformation of American Culture, 1880–1920* (New York, 1983).

8. See, for example, Michael McGerr, *A Fierce Discontent: The Rise and Fall of the Progressive Movement in America, 1870–1920* (New York, 2003); Thomas C. Leonard, *Illiberal Reformers: Race, Eugenics, and American Economics in the Progressive Era* (Princeton, 2016), 3–16; Louis Menand, *The Metaphysical Club: A Story of Ideas in America* (New York, 2002); R. Jeffrey Lustig, *Corporate Liberalism: The Origins of Modern American Political Theory, 1890–1920* (Berkeley, 1982), 78–194.

9. Leonard, *Illiberal Reformers*, 3–74; James T. Kloppenberg, *Uncertain Victory: Social Democracy and Progressivism in European and American Thought, 1870–1920* (New York, 1988), 64–94, 199–394; McGerr, *Fierce Discontent*, 40–181.

10. Herbert Croly, *The Promise of American Life* (1909; Middleton, DE, 2021), 18, 96, and passim.

11. Croly, *Promise of American Life*, 141, 143, 238, 272. Also see Rogers Smith, *Civic Ideals: Conflicting Visions of Citizenship in U.S. History* (New Haven, 1997), 412–24, for an insightful treatment of Croly.

12. Croly, *Promise of American Life*, 18, 238, 244, 249–50.

13. See, especially, Martin J. Sklar, *The Corporate Reconstruction of American Capitalism, 1890–1916: The Market, the Law, and Politics* (New York, 1988). See also James Weinstein, *The Corporate Ideal in the Liberal State, 1900–1918* (Boston, 1968); David Noble, *America by Design: Science, Technology, and the Rise of Corporate Capitalism* (New York, 1977); Daniel Rodgers, *Atlantic Crossings: Social Politics in a Progressive Age* (Cambridge, MA, 1988); William G. Robbins, *Socializing Capital: The Rise of the Large Corporation in America* (Princeton, 1997).

14. On the relations and networks of the precorporate era, those of what has been called "proprietary capitalism," see Philip Scranton, *Proprietary Capitalism: The Textile Manufacture in Philadelphia, 1800–1885* (New York, 1984); Olivier Zunz, *Making America Corporate, 1870–1920* (Chicago, 1990), 11–36; Glenn Porter and Harold Livesay, *Merchants and Manufacturers: Studies in the Changing Structure of Nineteenth-Century Marketing* (Baltimore, 1971).

15. Robbins, *Socializing Capital*; Kenneth I. Lipartito and David Sicilia, eds., *Constructing Corporate America: History, Politics, Culture* (New York, 2004).

16. On the extension of "substantive due process" to corporations, see *Santa Clara County* v. *Southern Pacific Railroad Company*, 118 US 394 (1886). On the emerging "rule of reason" doctrine, see *United States* v. *E. C. Knight Company* 156 US 1 (1895); *United States* v. *American Tobacco Company* 221 US 106 (1911); *Standard Oil Company* v. *United States* 221 US 1 (1901). Also see Sklar, *Corporate Reconstruction of American Capitalism*, 44–57, 86–175; Naomi Lamoreaux, *The Great Merger Movement in American Business, 1895–1904* (Cambridge, MA, 1985).

17. David Montgomery, *The Fall of the House of Labor: The Workplace, the State, and American Labor Activism,1865–1925* (New York, 1987), 214–56; Daniel Nelson, *Frederick W. Taylor and the Rise of Scientific Management* (Madison, WI, 1980); Noble, *America by Design*, 257–95.

18. Croly, *Promise of American Life*, 262–67.

19. Weinstein, *Corporate Ideal in the Liberal State*, 3–39; Alan Dawley, *Struggles for Justice: Social Responsibility and the Liberal State* (Cambridge MA, 1995), 114–15; Lustig, *Corporate Liberalism*, 113–15.

20. Weinstein, *Corporate Ideal in the Liberal State*, 139–71.

21. Croly, *Promise of American Life*, 214–34.

22. Charles Francis Adams Jr., "The Protection of the Ballot in National Elections," *Journal of Social Science* 1 (June 1869): 91–111; Francis Parkman, "The Failure of Universal Suffrage," *North American Review* 127 (July-August 1978): 1–20; Alexander Keyssar, *The Right to Vote: The Contested History of Democracy in the United States* (New York, 2000), 118–71.

23. Leon Fink, *Workingmen's Democracy: The Knights of Labor and American Politics* (Urbana, IL, 1983); Steven Hahn, *A Nation under Our Feet: Black Political Struggles in the Rural South from Slavery to the Great Migration* (Cambridge MA, 2003), 317–464.

24. On the disfranchisement of Black and poor white voters in the South, see C. Vann Woodward, *Origins of the New South, 1877–1913* (Baton Rouge, 1951), 321–49; J. Morgan Kousser, *The Shaping of Southern Politic: Suffrage Restriction and the Establishment of the One-Party South, 1880–1910* (New Haven, 1974); Michael Perman, *The Struggle for Mastery: Disfranchisement in the South, 1888–1908* (Chapel Hill, 2001). Wilson quoted in Leonard, *Illiberal Reformers*, 49–50. *Williams* v. *Mississippi* originated in a lawsuit brought by a Black man, Henry Williams, indicted for murder by an all-white jury. Williams claimed that Mississippi's laws, which only permitted registered voters to serve on juries, violated his rights under the Fourteenth Amendment. The Court ruled 9–0 against him.

25. See McGerr, *A Fierce Discontent*, 118–46; McGerr, *The Decline of Popular Politics: The American North, 1865–1928* (New York, 1986); Nancy Cohen, *The Reconstruction of American Liberalism, 1865–1914* (Chapel Hill, 2002), 110–40, 217–56; Sven Beckert, *The Monied Metropolis: New York City and the Consolidation of the American Bourgeoisie, 1850–1896* (New York, 2001), 207–36.

26. On these political reforms, see Keyssar, *Right to Vote*, 127–71. Massachusetts passed the first state-wide Australian ballot law in 1888. The first registration occurred after Black men were enfranchised in the former rebellious South in 1867, but it was carried out by the U.S. Army intent on identifying newly eligible voters and making sure that ex-Confederates, disfranchised by the Reconstruc-

394 Notes to Pages 191–196

tion Acts and Fourteenth Amendment, were unable to vote. But this was the last
time registration was carried out by the federal government and with determination. Thereafter, voter registration was left to the states, and it has remained
voluntary rather than mandatory.

27. On the shifts in the turnout of eligible voters, see Walter Dean Burnham, *Critical Elections and the Mainsprings of American Politics* (New York, 1970); V. O. Key, *Southern Politics in State and Nation* (New York, 1949); McGerr, *Decline of Popular Politics*, 184–210; Keyssar, *Right to Vote*, 116–74. On the contradictory aspects of the woman suffrage campaign, see Ellen Dubois, *Feminism and Suffrage: The Emergence of an Independent Woman's Movement in America, 1848–1869* (Ithaca, NY, 1978); Dubois, *Woman Suffrage and Women's Rights* (New York, 1998); Marjorie Spruill Wheeler, *New Women of the New South: The Leaders of the Woman Suffrage Movement in the Southern States* (New York, 1993); Louise Newman, *White Women's Rights: The Racial Origins of Feminism in the United States* (New York, 1999). On "authoritarian enclaves," see Robert Mickey, *Paths Out of Dixie: The Democratization of Authoritarian Enclaves in the Deep South, 1944–1972* (Princeton, 2015).

28. Roosevelt quoted in Harold Howland, *Theodore Roosevelt and His Times: A Chronicle of the Progressive Movement* (New Haven, 1921), 99.

29. Roosevelt quoted in Sklar, *Corporate Reconstruction of American Capitalism*, 356–57; Lustig, *Corporate Liberalism*, 29–30; Gary Gerstle, *American Crucible: Race and Nation in the Twentieth Century* (Princeton, 2001), 65–80.

30. Sklar makes this point in *Corporate Reconstruction of American Capitalism*, 419–25; Dawley, *Struggles for Justice*, 141–50.

31. Grosvenor Clarkson quoted in Weinstein, *Corporate Ideal in the Liberal State*, 223, 220–33, and McGerr, *Fierce Discontent*, 285, 283–94.

32. Gerald E. Shenk, *Work or Fight!: Race, Gender, and the Draft in World War One* (New York, 2008); McGerr, *Fierce Discontent*, 286; John Carson, "Army Alpha, Army Brass, and the Search for Army Inteligence," *Isis* 84 (1993): 278–309.

33. Clarkson quoted in Weinstein, *Corporate Ideal in the Liberal State*, 233.

34. In a courageous piece of investigative journalism, Ida B. Wells demonstrated that lynching victims were more likely to be accused of murder, arson, assault, and theft than rape or other sexual transgressions, and that interracial sex was largely consensual. See Wells, *Southern Horrors: Lynch Law in All its Phases* (New York, 1892). For important historical treatments of lynching, see W. Fitzhugh Brundage, *Lynching in the New South: Georgia and Virginia, 1880–1930* (Urbana, IL, 1993); Crystal N. Feimster, *Southern Horrors: Women and the Politics of Rape and Lynching* (Cambridge, MA, 2009); Amy Louise Wood, *Lynching and Spectacle: Witnessing Racial Violence in America, 1890–1940* (Chapel Hill, 2009); Edward L. Ayers, *Vengeance and Justice: Crime and Punishment in the Nineteenth-Century South* (New York, 1984), 238–55; Stewart E. Tolnay and E. M. Beck, *A Festival of Violence: An Analysis of Southern Lynchings, 1880–1930* (Urbana, IL, 1993).

35. Iver Bernstein, *The New York City Draft Riots: Their Significance for American Society and Politics in the Age of the Civil War* (New York, 1990); Daniel R. Biddle and Murray Dubin, *Tasting Freedom: Octavius Catto and the Battle for Equality in Civil War America* (Philadelphia, 2010); Cameron McWhirter, *Red Summer: The Summer of 1919 and the Awakening of Black America* (New York, 2011); Tim Madi-

gan, *The Burning: Massacre, Destruction, and the Tulsa Race Riot of 1921* (New York, 2001).

36. Beth Lew-Williams, *The Chinese Must Go: Violence, Exclusion, and the Making of the Alien in America* (Cambridge, MA, 2018), 91–112, 247–53; Benjamin H. Johnson, *Revolution in Texas: How a Forgotten Rebellion and Its Bloody Suppression Turned Mexicans into Americans* (New Haven, 2003); John R. Wunder, *Gold Mountain Turned to Dust: Essays on the Legal History of the Chinese in the Nineteenth-Century American West* (Albuquerque, 2018), 3–34.

37. Croly, *Promise of American Life*, 235. Also see Peggy Pascoe, *What Comes Naturally: Miscegenation Law and the Making of Race in America* (New York, 2009); Diane M. Sommerville, *Rape and Race in the Nineteenth-Century South* (Chapel Hill, 2004); Martha Hodes, *Black Women, White Men: Illicit Sex in the Nineteenth-Century South* (New Haven, 1997); J. Douglas Smith, *Managing White Supremacy: Race, Politics, and Citizenship in Jim Crow Virginia* (Chapel Hill, 2002). Even the Nazis regarded the "one-drop" rule of racial classification as extreme.

38. See the essays of John T. Morgan, Nathan Southgate Shaler, Howard Odum, Philip Alexander Bruce, and Frank Clark in I. A. Newby, ed., *The Development of Segregationist Thought* (Homewood, IL, 1968), 22–28, 54–78, 91–97; Grace E. Hale, *Making Whiteness: The Culture of Segregation in the South, 1890–1940* (New York, 1999). Also see the important contribution of Gregory Downs, *Declarations of Dependence: The Long Reconstruction of Popular Politics in the South, 1861–1908* (Chapel Hill, 2011), 185–212.

39. On the trends in the South and South Africa, see John Cell, *The Highest Stage of White Supremacy: The Origins of Segregation in South Africa and the United States* (Cambridge, UK, 1982); George M. Fredrickson, *White Supremacy: A Comparative Study in American and South African History* (New York, 1981). On the dynamics in the South, see C. Vann Woodward, *The Strange Career of Jim Crow* (New York, 1955); Howard Rabinowitz, *Race Relations in the Urban South, 1865–1890* (Urbana, IL, 1980); Edward Ayers, *The Promise of the New South: Life after Reconstruction* (New York, 1993); Glenda Gilmore, *Gender and Jim Crow: Women and the Politics of White Supremacy in North Carolina, 1896–1920* (Chapel Hill, 1996).

40. Edgar Gardner Murphy, *The Problems of the Present South* (New York, 1904), 151–202; Walter Rauschenbusch, "The Problem of the Black Man," *American Missionary* 68 (1914): 732–33; McGerr, *Fierce Discontent*, 186–95; Joel Williamson, *The Crucible of Race: Black-White Relations in the American South since Emancipation* (New York, 1984), 331–32, 415–55.

41. On the nature of racial segregation in the Northeast and Midwest, and the violence that would be provoked when Black families defied it, see Thomas Sugrue, *Sweet Land of Liberty: The Forgotten Struggle for Civil Rights in the North* (New York, 2008), 3–84; Richard Rothstein, *The Color of Law: A Forgotten History of How Our Government Segregated America* (New York, 2017); Kevin Boyle, *Arc of Injustice: A Saga of Race, Civil Rights, and Murder in the Jazz Age* (New York, 2004). On the segregation of the federal bureaucracy, see Eric S. Yellin, *Racism in the Nation's Service: Government Workers and the Color Line in Woodrow Wilson's America* (Chapel Hill, 2013); Gerstle, *American Crucible*, 44–127.

42. For my perspective on the Panama Canal I am indebted to the remarkable schol-

arship of Julie Greene, *The Canal Builders: Making America's Empire at the Panama Canal* (New York, 2009).

43. Theodore Roosevelt, "Message to Congress Regarding Conditions in Panama," 17 December 1906, Miller Center, University of Virginia; Greene, *The Canal Builders*, 75–158.

44. Greene, *The Canal Builders*, 15–74.

45. On the insular cases, see Amy Kaplan, *The Anarchy of Empire in the Making of American Culture* (Cambridge, MA, 2002), 146–70; Juan R. Torruella, "The Insular Cases: The Establishment of a Regime of Political Apartheid," *University of Pennsylvania Journal of International Law* 29 (2007): 284–345; Bartholomew H. Sparrow, *The Insular Cases and the Emergence of American Empire* (Lawrence, KS, 2006).

46. Theodore Roosevelt, *Campaigns and Controversies* (New York, 1926), 371; Louise Barnet, *Atrocity and American Military Justice in Southeast Asia: Trial by Army* (London, 2010), 17–19; Walter L. Williams, "United States Indian Policy and the Debate over Philippine Annexation: Implications for the Origins of American Imperialism," *Journal of American History* 66 (March 1980): 810–31. On Cuban insurgency, see Ada Ferrer, *Insurgent Cuba: Race, Nation, and Revolution, 1868–1898* (Chapel Hill, 1999); Ferrer, *Cuba: An American History* (New York, 2021), 129–84. On the Philippines, see Paul A. Kramer, *The Blood of Government: Race, Empire, the United States, and the Philippines* (Chapel Hill, 2006); Reynaldo Clemena Ileto, *Pasyon and Revolution: Popular Movements in the Philippines, 1840–1910* (Manila, 1979).

47. Theodore Roosevelt, "Annual Message to Congress," 6 December 1904, Miller Center, University of Virginia.

48. Theodore Roosevelt, "The Strenuous Life," in *The Works of Theodore Roosevelt in Fourteen Volumes* (New York, 1912), 1–15. Also see Kristin L. Hoganson, *Fighting for American Manhood: How Gender Politics Provoked the Spanish-American and Philippine-American Wars* (New Haven, 1998); Gail Bederman, *Manliness and Civilization: A Cultural History of Gender and Race in the United States, 1880–1917* (Chicago, 1996).

49. Roosevelt, "The Strenuous Life," 13–15.

50. See, especially, Christopher Lasch, "The Moral and Intellectual Rehabilitation of the Ruling Class," in *The World of Nations: Reflections on American History, Politics, and Culture* (New York, 1974), 80–99; Lears, *No Place of Grace*, 3–58.

51. Lasch, "Anti-Imperialists, the Philippines, and the Inequality of Man," in *World of Nations*, 70–79.

52. Theodore Roosevelt, "Citizenship in a Republic," Address at the Sorbonne, Paris, 23 April 1910, Theodore Roosevelt Center, Dickinson State University, North Dakota; Gerstle, *American Crucible*, 53–59.

53. Natalie Ring, *The Problem South: Region, Empire, and the New Liberal State, 1880–1930* (Athens, GA, 2012), 135–74; Albert Bushnell Hart, *The Southern South* (New York, 1910).

54. I am indebted to the ideas and formulations in Ring's *The Problem South*.

55. See Peter A. Coclanis and David L. Carlton, eds., *Confronting Southern Poverty in the Great Depression: The Report on Economic Conditions of the South with Related Documents* (Boston, 1996); Bruce J. Schulman, *From Cotton Belt to Sunbelt: Federal Policy, Economic Development, and the Transformation of the South, 1938–1980* (New York, 1991), 3–38.

CHAPTER SEVEN
FASCIST PULSES

1. See, especially, Erez Manela, *The Wilsonian Moment: Self-Determination and the International Origins of Anti-Colonial Nationalism* (New York, 2007).
2. "An Address to the Senate," 10 July 1919, in Arthur S. Link, ed., *The Papers of Woodrow Wilson*, Vol. 61 (Princeton, 1989), 426–36; "The Pueblo Speech," 25 September 1919, *Voices of Democracy: The U.S. Oratory Project*, UMd.edu.
3. On Mexico, see Friedrich Katz, *The Secret War in Mexico: Europe, the United States, and the Mexican Revolution* (Chicago, 1981), 156–202, 298–326. On Russia, see Christopher Lasch, *The American Liberals and the Russian Revolution* (New York, 1962).
4. David Kennedy, *Over Here: The First World War and American Society* (New York, 1980), 231–95; Julie Greene, *Pure and Simple Politics: The American Federation of Labor and Political Activism, 1881–1917* (New York, 1998), 242–73; David Montgomery, *The Fall of the House of Labor: The Workplace, the State, and American Labor Activism, 1865–1925* (New York, 1987), 356–58.
5. Montgomery, *Fall of the House of Labor*, 370–410; Cal Winslow, *Radical Seattle: The General Strike of 1919* (New York, 2020); John Higham, *Strangers in the Land: Patterns of American Nativism, 1860–1925* (New Brunswick, NJ, 1955), 194–233.
6. William Preston Jr., *Aliens and Dissenters: Federal Suppression of Radicals, 1903–1933* (Urbana, IL, 1963), 208–37, but see, especially, Adam Hochschild, *American Midnight: The Great War, a Violent Peace, and Democracy's Forgotten Crisis* (New York, 2022), a penetrating view of the repression imposed during this period.
7. On the connections between colonial rule in the Philippines and the creation of what he calls a Wilsonian "security state," see Alfred McCoy, *Policing America's Empire: The United States, the Philippines, and the Rise of the Surveillance State* (Madison, WI, 2009), 15–174, 293–348. Also see Adam Goodman, *The Deportation Machine: America's Long History of Expelling Immigrants* (Princeton, 2020), 1–36; Preston, *Aliens and Dissenters*, 11–87, 208–72.
8. Ralph E. Weber and Ralph H. Van Deman, eds., *The Final Memoranda: Major General Ralph H. Van Deman, Father of U.S. Military Intelligence* (Wilmington, 1988), 30–31; Emerson Hough, *The Web* (1919; Sterling Ford, UK, 2019), 12–13. Van Deman was in charge of military intelligence in Manila during the U.S.-Philippine War and continued to develop the range of military intelligence long thereafter, focusing especially on political dissidents. Hough is best known as a western novelist.
9. Hough, *The Web*, 28, 122, 133–34, 139; McCoy, *Policing America's Empire*, 300–12.
10. Quoted in Hough, *The Web*, 59–60, 79–80; McCoy, *Policing America's Empire*, 304–5, 309–10.
11. Hough, *The Web*, 66–67; Weber and Van Deman, eds., *The Final Memoranda*, 33–34; Ann Hagedorn, *Savage Peace: Hope and Fear in America, 1919* (New York, 2007), 31; Peter Baker, "The Tragic, Forgotten History of Black Military Veterans," *New Yorker*, 27 November 2016.
12. Nan Elizabeth Woodruff, *American Congo: The Black Freedom Struggle in the Delta* (Cambridge, MA, 2003), 74–109; Cameron McWhirter, *Red Summer: The Summer of 1919 and the Awakening of Black America* (New York, 2012).
13. Barbara Foley, *Spectres of 1919: Class and Nation in the Making of the New Negro*

(Urbana, IL, 2003), 1–69; Thomas Sugrue, *Sweet Land of Liberty: The Forgotten Struggle for Civil Rights in the North* (New York, 2009), 3–85.

14. Higham, *Strangers in the Land*, 224.

15. *American Legion Weekly*, 4 July 1919; Stephen R. Ortiz, *Beyond the Bonus March and GI Bill: How Veteran Politics Shaped the New Deal* (New York, 2009), 16–31.

16. Ortiz, *Beyond the Bonus March*, 19–21. The Veterans of Foreign Wars (VFW) was organized earlier, by veterans returning from Cuba and the Philippines in 1899, and its social composition was more lower middle class, with small businessmen and skilled workers predominating.

17. *American Legion Weekly*, 1 August 1919, 5 December 1919, 26 December 1919, 4 June 1920.

18. *American Legion Weekly*, 26 December 1919; *American Legion Monthly*, October 1926.

19. *American Legion Weekly*, 5 January 1923; Owsley quoted in John P. Diggins, *Mussolini and Fascism: The View from America* (Princeton, 1972), 205–207.

20. Higham, *Strangers in the* Land, 224. On Italian fascists, see Robert O. Paxton, *The Anatomy of Fascism* (New York, 2004), 58–62, 87–91; R. J. B. Bosworth, *Mussolini's Italy: Life under the Fascist Dictatorship, 1915–1945* (New York, 2005), 93–149. For an outstanding case study, see Anthony Cardozo, *Agrarian Elites and Italian Fascism: The Province of Bologna, 1901–1926* (Princeton, 1983).

21. Journalist Stanley Frost quoted in Kenneth T. Jackson, *The Ku Klux Klan in the City, 1915–1930* (New York, 1967), xii. There is a large, and growing, literature on the "second" Ku Klux Klan. The most recent and helpful synthesis is Linda Gordon, *The Second Coming of the Ku Klux Klan: The Ku Klux Klan of the 1920s and the American Political Tradition* (New York, 2017). But also see David M. Chalmers, *Hooded Americanism: The History of the Ku Klux Klan* (Durham, NC, 1987); Thomas R. Pegram, *One Hundred Percent Americanism: The Rebirth and Decline of the Ku Klux Klan in the 1920s* (Chicago, 2011); Wyn Craig Wade, *The Fiery Cross: The Ku Klux Klan in America* (New York, 1998); and a host of state and local studies.

22. Gordon, *Second Coming of the Ku Klux Klan*, 63–79; Jackson, *Ku Klux Klan in the City*, 14–15, 233–49; David Chalmers, "The Ku Klux Klan in Politics in the 1920s," *Mississippi Quarterly* 18 (Fall 1965): 234–35.

23. There is dispute over the Klan's peak membership, with some suggesting four to six million, but two to four million is more likely. For an excellent account of Klan membership and recruiting techniques, see Nancy MacLean, *Behind the Mask of Chivalry: The Making of the Second Ku Klux Klan* (New York, 1994), 3–22, 52–74.

24. Tony Montalbano, "Temperance, Traditionalism, and the Ku Klux Klan in Syosset-Woodbury," Oysterbayhistorical.org; Gordon, *Second Coming of the KKK*, 93–107.

25. Hiram W. Evans, "The Klan's Fight for Americanism," *North American Review* 223 (March 1926): 38–39. On the rise of Protestant fundamentalism, see, especially, George M. Marsden, *Fundamentalism and American Culture* (New York, 2006).

26. Kathleen M. Blee, "Women in the 1920s Ku Klux Klan Movement," *Feminist Studies* 17 (Spring 1991): 57–77.

27. See Kathleen M. Blee, *Women of the Klan: Racism and Gender in the 1920s* (Berkeley, 2008), 33 and 1–3, 11–69, 105–6; MacLean, *Behind the Mask of Chivalry*, 98–124; Gordon, *Second Coming of the KKK*, 109–37.

28. Chalmers, "Ku Klux Klan in Politics," 234–47; Gordon, *Second Coming of the KKK*, 163–71.

29. Chalmers, *Hooded Americanism,* 39–197; Chalmers, "Ku Klux Klan in Politics,"239–40; Gordon, *Second Coming of the KKK*, 164–79.

30. Gordon, *Second Coming of the KKK*, 2–3, 139–61; Chalmers, "Ku Klux Klan in Politics," 234–47.

31. MacLean, *Behind the Mask of Chivalry*, 179–80. MacLean offers especially acute insights about the Klan and fascism, and a broad international context.

32. Sarah Churchwell, *Behold America: The Entangled History of "America First" and the "American Dream"* (New York, 2018), 117–21; MacLean, *Behind the Mask of Chivalry*, 177–88; Diggins, *Mussolini and Fascism*, 206–7.

33. Gordon, *Second Coming of the Ku Klux Klan*, 95. There is a large literature on Prohibition, but for an especially fine analysis, see Lisa McGirr, *The War on Alcohol: Prohibition and the Rise of the American State* (New York, 2015). Also see Daniel Okrent, *Last Call: The Rise and Fall of Prohibition* (New York, 2010).

34. Willard quoted in McGirr, *War on Alcohol*, 17.

35. Recent studies, however, remind us of the ways in which states and localities could set controls on admission, bolstered during the first half of the nineteenth century by how the issue of slavery left much of this power in the hands of the states. The major federal intervention before the late nineteenth century was in outlawing the international slave trade in 1808. See Aristide Zolberg, *A Nation by Design: Immigration Policy in the Fashioning of America* (Cambridge, MA, 2008); Kunal Parker, *Making Foreigners: Immigration and Citizen Law in America, 1600–2000* (New York, 2015); and especially Kevin Kenny, *The Problem of Immigration in a Slaveholding Republic: Policing Mobility in the Nineteenth-Century United States* (New York, 2023).

36. An act in amendment to the various acts relative to immigration and the importation of aliens under contract or agreement to perform labor, 26 Stat. 1084, 3 March 1891. Also see Mae Ngai, *Impossible Subjects: Illegal Aliens and the Making of Modern America* (Princeton, 2004), 1–55; Beth Lew-Williams, *The Chinese Must Go: Violence, Exclusion, and the Making of the Alien in America* (Cambridge, MA, 2018); Daniel Okrent, *The Guarded Gate: Bigotry, Eugenics, and the Law that Kept Two Generations of Jews, Italians, and Other European Immigrants Out of America* (New York, 2019), 33–68.

37. Lodge quoted in Okrent, *The Guarded Gate*, 52. The Immigration Restriction League (IRL) was organized in 1894 by Lodge's fellow Boston Brahmins and helped spearhead the restriction drive motivated by the same racial perspectives that Lodge enunciated.

38. Okrent, *The Guarded Gate*, 259–312.

39. Reece Jones, *White Borders: The History of Race and Immigration in the United States from Chinese Exclusion to the Border Wall* (Boston, 2021), 69–81; Okrent, *The Guarded Gate*, 259–327; Higham, *Strangers in the Land*, 300–30; 21–55.

40. *New York Times*, 27 April 1924; Ngai, *Impossible Subjects*, 20–55; Jones, *White*

Borders, 75–82; Okrent, *The Guarded Gate*, 313–71. Also see Gary Gerstle, *American Crucible: Race and Nation in the Twentieth Century* (Princeton, 2001), 95–122.

41. For a particularly helpful account of the American response to Italian fascism, see Diggins, *Mussolini and Fascism*. Also see Katy Hull, *The Machine Has a Soul: American Sympathy with Italian Fascism* (Princeton, 2021).

42. Diggins, *Mussolini and Fascism*, 24–28, 146–47, 160.

43. Croly quoted in Diggins, *Mussolini and Fascism*, 204. Also see Martin Sklar, *The Corporate Reconstruction of American Capitalism, 1890–1916: The Market, the Law, and Politics* (New York, 1988); Jonathan Levy, *Ages of American Capitalism: A History of the United States* (New York, 2021), 325–54.

44. *Kansas City Star*, 9 August 1922; Diggins, *Mussolini and Fascism*, 59–61; Churchwell, *Behold America*, 120–27.

45. *American Federationist* 30 (November 1923).

46. Diggins, *Mussolini and Fascism*, 220–23.

47. On Hitler's and Nazi views of the United States and its racial policies, see James Q. Whitman, *Hitler's American Model: The United States and the Making of Nazi Race Law* (Princeton, 2017), 11–13, 27, 46–47, 54, 78–79. Also see Timothy Snyder, *Bloodlands: Europe between Hitler and Stalin* (New York, 2010); Carroll P. Kakel, *The American West and the Nazi East: A Comparative and Interpretive Perspective* (London, 2011). As Nazi Herbert Krier wrote, "American immigration legislation shows that in the USA a clear understanding has been achieved that a unified North American *Volk* body can only emerge from the 'Melting pot' if wholly foreign racial population masses are not tossed in with the core population. . . ."

48. Whitman, *Hitler's American Model*, 27, 60–65.

49. Edwin Black, *The War Against the Weak: Eugenics and America's Campaign to Create a Master Race* (Washington, DC, 2012), 261–318; David Turner, "Foundations of Holocaust: American Eugenics and the Nazi Connection," *Jerusalem Post*, 30 December 2012.

50. For an excellent collection of essays, see Steve Fraser and Gary Gerstle, eds., *The Rise and Fall of the New Deal Order, 1930–1980* (Princeton, 1989).

51. Churchwell, *Behold America*, 174–77; Philip Jenkins, "'It Can't Happen Here': Fascism and Right-Wing Extremism in Pennsylvania, 1933–1942," *Pennsylvania History* 62 (Winter 1995): 31–52.

52. Churchwell, *Behold America*, 174–78; Steven Ross, *Hitler in Los Angeles: How Jews Foiled Nazi Plots Against Hollywood and America* (New York, 2017); Bradley W. Hart, *Hitler's American Friends: The Third Reich's Support in the United States* (New York, 2018); Salaina Catalano, "When It Happened Here: Michigan and the Transnational Development of American Fascism, 1920–1945," *Michigan Historical Review* 46 (Spring 2020): 29–67; Leo Ribuffo, *The Old Christian Right: The Protestant Right from the Great Depression to the Cold War* (Philadelphia, 1983), 63–79.

53. Jenkins, "It Can't Happen Here," 31–52.

54. On Huey Long, see, especially, Alan Brinkley, *Voices of Protest: Huey Long, Father Coughlin, and the Great Depression* (New York, 1982), 8–81. Also see William Ivy Hair, *The Kingfish and His Realm: The Life and Times of Huey P. Long* (Baton Rouge, 1991); T. Harry Williams, *Huey Long* (New York, 1981).

55. Brinkley, *Voices of Protest*, 82–193; Charles Gallagher, *Nazis of Copley Square: The Forgotten Story of the Christian Front* (Cambridge, MA, 2021).

56. First Inaugural Address of Franklin D. Roosevelt, 4 March 1933, Avalon Project, Yale University Law School.

57. I'm indebted here to the brilliant study of Ira Katznelson, *Fear Itself: The New Deal and the Origins of Our Time* (New York, 2013).

58. Katznelson, *Fear Itself*, 96–129, 234–36; *Volkisher Beobacter*, 11 May 1933, quoted in Wolfgang Schivelbusch, *Three New Deals: Reflections on Roosevelt's America, Mussolini's Italy, and Hitler's Germany, 1933–1939* (New York, 2006), 17–18.

59. Thomas Ferguson, "Industrial Conflict and the Coming of the New Deal: The Triumph of Multinational Liberalism in America," in Fraser and Gerstle, eds., *The Rise and Fall of the New Deal Order*, 3–31; Schivelbusch, *Three New Deals*, 17–48; Katznelson, *Fear Itself*, 227–34.

60. Pete Daniel, *Breaking the Land: The Transformation of Cotton, Tobacco, and Rice Cultures since 1880* (Urbana, IL, 1985), 153–289; Robert Mickey, *Paths Out of Dixie: The Democratization of Authoritarian Enclaves in America's Deep South, 1944–1972* (Princeton, 2015), 33–91.

61. H. Arthur Steiner, "Fascism in America?" *American Political Science Review* 29 (October 1935): 821.

62. Frank, Shaw, and Hallgren quoted in Schivelbusch, *Three New Deals*, 27–28, 36–37; Sinclair Lewis, *It Can't Happen Here* (1935; New York, 1970), 77.

63. See, especially, Kim Phillips-Fein, *Invisible Hands: The Businessman's Crusade Against the New Deal* (New York, 2009), 3–25.

CHAPTER EIGHT
THE "OTHER" NINETEEN-SIXTIES

1. The best treatments of Wallace's 1963–64 college lecture tour and his 1964 Democratic primary campaign are Dan T. Carter, *The Politics of Rage: The Origins of the New Conservatism, and the Transformation of American Politics* (New York, 1995), 194–223; Ben Hubing, *George Wallace in Wisconsin: The Divisive Campaigns that Shaped a Civil Rights Legacy* (Charleston, 2022), 17–46. Also see Stephan Lesher, *George C. Wallace: American Populist* (Cambridge, MA, 1994), 267–310; Jody Carlson, *George C. Wallace and the Politics of Powerlessness: The Wallace Campaigns for the Presidency, 1964–1976* (New York, 1981), 26–66.

2. Carter, *Politics of Rage*, 226–35. For a very insightful local history, see Jefferson Cowie, *Freedom's Dominion: A Saga of White Resistance to Federal Power* (New York, 2022).

3. Richard Hofstadter, "The Long View: Goldwater in History," *New York Review of Books*, 8 October 1964.

4. U.S. Department of Commerce, Bureau of the Census, *Negro Population by County, 1960 and 1950* (Washington, DC, 1966).

5. There is a growing literature on the development and politics of these neighborhoods, but the starting point should be Thomas Sugrue, *The Origins of the Urban Crisis: Race and Inequality in Postwar Detroit* (Princeton, 1996), a brilliant study of race and class. Also see Timothy J. Lombardo: *Blue Collar Conservatism:*

Frank Rizzo's Philadelphia and Populist Politics (Philadelphia, 2018); Jonathan Rieder, *Canarsie: The Jews and Italians of Brooklyn Against Liberalism* (Cambridge, MA, 1985); Kenneth Durr, *Behind the Backlash: White Working-Class Politics in Baltimore, 1940–1980* (Chapel Hill, 2003).

6. Sugrue, *Origins of the Urban Crisis*, 209–30; Kevin Boyle, *The Shattering: America in the 1960s* (New York, 2021), 1–43.

7. Sugrue, *Origins of the Urban Crisis*, 231–58; *Los Angeles Times*, 18 January 2016.

8. Thomas Sugrue, *Sweet Land of Liberty: The Forgotten Struggle for Civil Rights in the North* (New York, 2008), 87–252; Richard Rothstein, *The Color of Law: A Forgotten History of How Our Government Segregated America* (New York, 2017), 139–51, and especially 145–46; Arnold Hirsch, "Massive Resistance in the Urban North: Trumbull Park, Chicago, 1953–1966," *Journal of American History* 82 (September 1995): 522–50.

9. See, especially, Sugrue, *Origins of the Urban Crisis*, 218–29. But also see Lombardo, *Blue Collar Conservatism*, 21–48; Becky M. Nicolaides, *My Blue Heaven: Life and Politics in the Working-Class Suburbs of Los Angeles, 1920–1965* (Chicago, 2002), 272–326.

10. Sugrue, *Origins of the Urban Crisis*, 250–51; Lombardo, *Blue-Collar Conservatism*, 10, 146–47; Nicolaides, *My Blue Heaven*, 294–95. On the defense of segregation among white women of the South, see Elizabeth Gillespie McRae's excellent *Mothers of Massive Resistance: White Women and the Politics of White Supremacy* (New York, 2018).

11. Sugrue, *Sweet Land of Liberty*, 207–13; Rothstein, *Color of the Law*, 195–200.

12. Sugrue, *Sweet Land of Liberty*, 228–30; Paige Glotzer, *How the Suburbs Were Segregated: Developers and the Business of Exclusionary Housing, 1890–1960* (New York, 2020); Kenneth Jackson, *Crabgrass Frontier: The Suburbanization of the United States* (New York, 1987).

13. Nicolaides, *My Blue Heaven*, 306–15; California Proposition 14, Ballotpedia.com.

14. Richard Kluger, *Simple Justice: The History of Brown v. Board of Education and Black America's Struggle for Equality* (New York, 2004); Sugrue, *Sweet Land of Liberty*, 162–99.

15. Numan V. Bartley, *The Rise of Massive Resistance: Race and Politics in the South during the 1950s* (Baton Rouge, 1969); McRae, *Mothers of Massive Resistance*, 109–84; Sugrue, *Sweet Land of Liberty*, 454–56.

16. See, for example, Zebulon Vance Miletsky, *Before Busing: A History of Boston's Long Black Freedom Struggle* (Chapel Hill, 2022).

17. On the Boston episode, see J. Anthony Lukas, *Common Ground: A Turbulent Decade in the Lives of Three American Families* (New York, 1986), and especially the more analytical Ronald Formisano, *Boston Against Busing: Race, Class, and Ethnicity in the 1960s and 1970s* (Chapel Hill, 1991). Also see Jennifer Hochschild, *The New American Dilemma: Liberal Democracy and School Desegregation* (New Haven, 1984).

18. Formisano, *Boston Against Busing*, 44–171; McRae, *Mothers of Massive Resistance*, 220–25.

19. See, for example, Mallory Lutz, "The Hidden Cost of Brown: African American Educators' Resistance to Desegregating Schools," *Online Journal of Rural Research and Policy* 12 (2017); Brett Gadsden, *Between North and South: Delaware, Desegrega-*

tion, and the Myth of Southern Exceptionalism (Philadelphia, 2012); Adam Fairclough, *A Class of Their Own: Black Teachers in the Segregated South* (Cambridge, MA, 2007).

20. See Sugrue, *Sweet Land of Liberty*, 475–77; Jerald Podair, *The Strike that Changed New York: Blacks, Whites, and the Ocean Hill-Brownsville Crisis* (New Haven, 2004); Charles S. Isaacs, *Inside Ocean-Hill Brownsville: A Teacher's Education, 1968–1969* (Albany, 2014).

21. Formisano, *Boston Against Busing*, 147; Marilyn Morgan, "Roaring for Rights: Women and Boston's Anti-Busing Movement," 17 March 2017, Archivespublichistory.org.

22. For an important perspective, see Robert O. Self, *All in the Family: The Realignment of American Democracy Since the 1960s* (New York, 2012).

23. An Equal Rights Amendment with somewhat different language was first introduced by Alice Paul of the National Women's Party in 1921 and it came before Congress nearly every year thereafter only to meet defeat until a half century later. On the history of the ERA, see Rebecca DeWolf, *Gendered Citizenship: The Original Conflict Over the Equal Rights Amendment, 1921–1963* (Lincoln, NE, 2021).

24. Donald T. Crichlow, *Phyllis Schlafly and Grassroots Conservatism* (Princeton, 2005), 214–27.

25. Critchlow, *Phyllis Schlafly*, 62–136.

26. Critchlow, *Phyllis Schlafly*, 183–217.

27. See Marjorie Spruill, *Divided We Stand: The Battle Over Women's Rights and Family Values that Polarized American Politics* (New York, 2017), 71–113; Critchlow, *Phyllis Schlafly*, 218–22; John S. Huntington, *Far Right Vanguard: The Radical Roots of Modern Conservatism* (Philadelphia, 2021), 111–42.

28. Scott Filpse, "Below-the-Belt Politics: Protestant Evangelicals, Abortion, and the Foundation of the New Religious Right, 1960–75," in David Farber and Jeff Roche, eds., *The Conservative Sixties* (New York, 2003), 127–41; Kristen Luker, *Abortion and the Politics of Motherhood* (Berkeley, 1984), 126–57; Stacie Taranto, *Kitchen Table Politics: Conservative Women and Family Values in New York* (Philadelphia, 2017), 59–125.

29. Phyllis Schlafly, "What's Wrong with Women's Rights?" *Phyllis Schlafly Report* 5 (February 1972).

30. On the "New Deal Order," see Gary Gerstle and Steve Fraser, eds., *The Rise and Fall of the New Deal Order, 1930–1980* (Princeton, 1990); Gary Gerstle, *The Rise and Fall of the Neoliberal Order* (Princeton, 2022).

31. See, for example, Lisa McGirr, *Suburban Warriors: The Origins of the New American Right* (Princeton, 2002); Bruce J. Schulman, *From Cotton Belt to Sunbelt: Federal Policy, Economic Development, and the Transformation of the South, 1938–1980* (New York, 1994); Kirkpatrick Sale, *Power Shift: The Rise of the Southern Rim and Its Challenge to the Eastern Establishment* (New York, 1975); Bethany Moreton, *To Serve God and Wal-Mart: The Making of Christian Free Enterprise* (Cambridge, MA, 2010); Lizbeth Cohen, *A Consumer's Republic: The Politics of Mass Consumption in Postwar America* (New York, 2003).

32. McGirr, *Suburban Warriors*, 54–110.

33. See McGirr, *Suburban Warriors*, 75–81; Huntington, *Far-Right Vanguard*, 111–78; Jonathan M. Schoenwald, "We Are an Action Group: The John Birch Society

and the Conservative Movement in the 1960s," in Farber and Roche, eds., *The Conservative Sixties*, 20–36. Also see Edward H. Miller, *A Conspiratorial Life: Robert Welch, the John Birch Society, and the Revolution of Modern Conservatism* (Chicago, 2022); D. J. Mulloy, *The World of the John Birch Society: Conspiracy, Conservatism, and the Cold War* (Nashville, 2014); and, most recently, Matthew Dallek, *Birchers: How the John Birch Society Radicalized the American Right* (New York, 2023).

34. Schoenwald, "We Are an Action Group," 31; Huntington, *Far-Right Vanguard*, 157–60.
35. Schoenwald, "We are an Action Group," 28–29; Donald T. Critchlow, *The Conservative Ascendancy: How the Republican Right Rose to Power in Modern America* (Lawrence, KS, 2011), 56–59; Dallek, *Birchers*, 135–206.
36. See, especially, John A. Andrew III, *The Other Side of the Sixties: The Young Americans for Freedom and the Rise of Conservative Politics* (New Brunswick, NJ, 1997).
37. Andrew, *Other Side of the Sixties*, 53–63; Critchlow, *Conservative Ascendancy*, 59–60, 128–30.
38. Andrew, *Other Side of the Sixties*, 75–101, 205–20; Critchlow, *Conservative Ascendancy*, 128–31.
39. Andrew, *Other Side of the Sixties*, 102–4.
40. Betty E. Chmaj, "Paranoid Patriotism: The Radical Right and the South," *Atlantic*, November 1962; Jeff Roche, "Cowboy Conservatism," in Farber and Roche, eds., *Conservative Sixties*, 79–92.
41. See Evelyn A. Schlatter, "'Extremism in the Defense of Liberty': The Minutemen and the Radical Right," in Farber and Roche, eds., *Conservative Sixties*, 37–50.
42. Carter, *Politics of Rage*, 295–98; Huntington, *Far-Right Vanguard*, 191–93.
43. Darren Dochuk, *From Bible Belt to Sunbelt: Plain Folk Religion, Grassroots Politics, and the Rise of Evangelical Conservatism* (New York, 2012); Nicole Hemmer, *Messengers of the Right: Conservative Media and the Transformation of American Politics* (Philadelphia, 2016); Carter, *Politics of Rage*, 298–300; Huntington, *Far-Right Vanguard*, 181–91.
44. Carter, *Politics of Rage*, 307–17. On the assortment of ballot requirements and the challenges of a federal system of politics, see Alexander Keyssar, *The Right to Vote: The Contested History of Democracy in the United States* (New York, 2000).
45. Elizabeth Hinton, *America on Fire: The Untold History of Police Violence and Black Rebellion Since the 1960s* (New York, 2021); Malcolm McLaughlin, *The Long Hot Summer of 1967: Urban Rebellion in America* (New York, 2014); Michael A. Cohen, *American Maelstrom: The Election of 1968 and the Politics of Division* (New York, 2018). On the Kerner Commission report, see Stephen Gillon, *Separate and Unequal: The Kerner Commission and the Unraveling of American Liberalism* (New York, 2018); Jelani Cobb, ed., *The Essential Kerner Commission Report* (New York, 2021).
46. See Rick Perlstein, *Nixonland: The Rise of a President and the Fracturing of America* (New York, 2008), 227–356; Angie Maxwell and Todd Shields, *The Long Southern Strategy: How Chasing White Voters in the South Changed American Politics* (New York, 2019), 1–132.
47. Carter, *Politics of Rage*, 338–42.
48. *Washington Post*, 12 April 1968; Carter, *Politics of Rage*, 326–31.
49. Lesher, *George C. Wallace*, 421–23; Carlson, *Wallace and the Politics of Powerlessness*, 85–125.
50. "Crowd at the Wallace Rally on Boston Common," 9 October 1968, Peter Simon

Collection, Special Collections and University Archives, University of Massachusetts, Amherst; "Lyndon B. Johnson and Hubert Humphrey on 30 September 1968," Presidential Recordings Digital Division, Miller Center, University of Virginia; Carter, *Politics of Rage*, 356–67.

51. Carter, *Politics of Rage*, 367–70; Lesher, *George C. Wallace*, 423–31.

52. Carter, *Politics of Rage*, 367–68, 400–414; Lesher, *George C. Wallace*, 460–62. Lesher argues that there was no deal.

53. Theodore H. White, *The Making of a President, 1972* (New York, 1973), 48–95; Carter, *Politics of Rage*, 417–18.

54. Carter, *Politics of Rage*, 426–38; Lesher, *George C. Wallace*, 470–83; Carlson, *Wallace and The Politics of Powerlessness*, 133–62.

55. *Washington Post*, 17 March 1995; Carter, *Politics of Rage*, 445–68.

56. *New York Times*, 25 October 1968; "TRB from Washington," *New Republic*, 9 November 1968, 4; Carter, *Politics of Rage*, 364–67; Lesher, *George C. Wallace*, 421–23.

CHAPTER NINE
NEOLIBERALS AND ILLIBERALISM

1. "Remarks on Signing the Violent Crime Control and Law Enforcement Act of 1994," 13 September 1994, www.govinfo.gov, 1539–41; Lauren-Brooke Eisen, "The 1994 Crime Bill and Beyond: How Federal Funding Shapes the Criminal Justice System," *Brennan Center for Justice*, 9 September 2019; David Johnston and Tim Weiner, "Seizing the Crime Issue Blurs Party Lines," *New York Times*, 1 August 1996; Udi Ofer, "How the 1994 Crime Bill Fed the Mass Incarceration Crisis," www.aclu.org, 4 June 2019.

2. *New York Times*, 24 July 1992; Andrew Glass, "Clinton Signs 'Welfare to Work' Bill, 22 August 1996," *Politico*, 22 August 2018.

3. See Gary Gerstle's important *The Rise and Fall of the Neoliberal Order: America and the World in the Free Market Era* (New York, 2022), 141–88. Also see Nicholas Lemann, *Transaction Man: The Rise of the Deal and the Decline of the American Dream* (New York, 2019), 143–78; Michael Katz, *The Price of Citizenship: Redefining the American Welfare State* (New York, 2001).

4. On the emergence of neoliberalism and the establishment of the Mont Pelerin Society, see Quinn Slobodian, *Globalists: The End of Empire and the Birth of Neoliberalism* (Cambridge, MA, 2018); Angus Burgin, *The Great Persuasion: Reinventing Free Markets Since the Depression* (Cambridge, MA, 2012); Jamie Peck, *Constructions of Neoliberal Reason* (New York, 2010).

5. Gerstle, *Rise and Fall of the Neoliberal Order*, 73–140; Lemann, *Transaction Man*, 100–135; Holly Sklar, ed., *Trilateralism: The Trilateral Commission and Elite Planning for World Management* (Boston, 1980).

6. Jay Peterzell, "The Trilateral Commission and the Carter Administration," *Economic and Political Weekly* 51 (17 December 1977): 2097–2104; Andrew Downer Crain, "Ford, Carter, and Deregulation in the 1970s," *Journal on Telecommunication and High Technology Law* 5 (2007): 413–45; Kim Phillips-Fein, *Fear City: New York's Fiscal Crisis and the Rise of Austerity Politics* (New York, 2018); Michel Fou-

cault, *The Birth of Biopolitics: Lectures at the Collége de France, 1978–79* (New York, 2004); and, especially, Wendy Brown's *Undoing the Demos: Neoliberalism's Stealth Revolution* (New York, 2015), 47–78. Among the members of the Carter Administration who were also members of the Trilateral Commission were Vice President Walter Mondale, National Security Advisor Zbigniew Brzezinski, Secretary of State Cyrus Vance, Secretary of Defense Harold Brown, Treasury Secretary W. Michael Blumenthal, Paul Warnke of the U.S. Arms Control Agency, and U.N. Representative Andrew Young.

7. Gerstle, *Rise and Fall of the Neoliberal Order*, 107–140; also see Sean Wilentz, *The Age of Reagan: A History, 1974–2008* (New York, 2008), 139–50, 194–200; Kevin M. Kruse and Julian E. Zelizer, *Fault Lines: A History of the United States since 1974* (New York, 2020), 26–112; David Harvey, *A Brief History of Neoliberalism* (New York, 2005).

8. Gerstle, *Rise and Fall of the Neoliberal Order*, 141–88. Gerstle stresses the significance of the Cold War and its ending in accounting for the triumph of a neoliberal "order" in the United States during the 1990s.

9. There is a vast literature demonstrating the ways in which the government and the courts, especially at the state and local levels, were crucial to the economic growth and development of the United States during the nineteenth century. On the neoliberal recognition of the role that states must play in advancing their projects, see Harvey, *Brief History of Neoliberalism*, 64–86; Burgin, *The Great Persuasion*, 87–122; Slobodian, *Globalists*, 91–120; Nancy MacLean, *Democracy in Chains: The Deep History of the Radical Right's Stealth Plan for America* (New York, 2018). Gerstle makes a special point of emphasizing the ways in which neoliberal perspectives, especially regarding the state, are rooted in nineteenth-century liberalism. See Gerstle, *Rise and Fall of the Neoliberal Order*, 5–7.

10. See, especially, Elizabeth Hinton, *From the War on Poverty to the War on Crime: The Making of Mass Incarceration in America* (Cambridge, MA, 2016), 27–133. Also see Khalil Gibran Muhammad, *The Condemnation of Blackness: Race, Crime, and the Making of Modern Urban America* (Cambridge, MA, 2010). The best-known and, at the time, influential argument about Black pathologies is Daniel Patrick Moynihan's 1965 report, *The Negro Family: A Case for National Action*, which he prepared while serving as assistant secretary of labor in the Johnson administration.

11. See Nikhil Pal Singh, *Race and America's Long War* (Oakland, 2017), 35–73.

12. Hinton, *From the War on Poverty to the War on Crime*, 124–29; Elizabeth Hinton, *America on Fire: The Untold Story of Police Violence and Black Rebellion since the 1960s* (New York, 2021); Otto Kerner et al., ed. *Report of the National Advisory Commission on Civil Disorders* (New York, 1968). The concept of a "carceral state," which owes its origins in part to Michel Foucault, who wrote of the "carceral Archipelago" in his *Discipline and Punish: The Birth of the Prison* (1975; New York, 1978), in general refers to the state apparatus, at local and federal levels, increasingly devoted to the surveillance, policing, arrest, indictment, conviction, plea bargaining, incarceration, and paroling of alleged criminal offenders and the communities in which they reside. But it could also refer to the state as a whole as surveillance in the service of warding off crime and terror becomes more and more important to the state's expected mission.

13. See Marie Gottschalk, *The Prison and the Gallows: The Politics of Mass Incarceration in America* (Cambridge, MA, 2006); Heather Ann Thompson, *Blood in the Water: The Attica Rebellion of 1971 and Its Legacy* (New York, 2017); Hinton, *From the War on Poverty to the War on Crime*, 134–79.

14. *Los Angeles Times*, 6 September 1990; Hinton, *From the War on Poverty to the War on Crime*, 134–217; James Forman Jr., *Locking Up Our Own: Crime and Punishment in Black America* (New York, 2018).

15. James Austin and Garry Coventry, *Emerging Issues on Privatized Prisons,* National Council on Crime and Delinquency, Bureau of Justice Assistance (February 2001); The Sentencing Project, *Capitalizing on Mass Incarceration: U.S. Growth in Private Prisons* (August 2018); Robert Perkinson, *Texas Tough: The Rise of America's Prison Empire* (New York, 2010).

16. See, especially, the analysis of Ruth Wilson Gilmore, *Golden Gulag: Prisons, Surplus, Crisis, and Opposition in Globalizing California* (Berkeley, 2007).

17. On the early history of policing, see Eric H. Monkkonen, *Police in Urban America, 1860–1920* (New York, 1981). On slave patrols and the impact of the Fugitive Slave Laws, see Sally Hadden, *Slave Patrols: Law and Violence in Virginia and the Carolinas* (Cambridge, MA, 2003); R. J. M. Blackett, *The Captive's Quest, Fugitive Slaves, the 1850 Fugitive Slave Law, and the Politics of Slavery* (New York, 2018).

18. Federal troops were deployed in an Army of Occupation in the former Confederate states until 1877, when some were sent to put down the Great Railroad Strike of 1877, one of a number of episodes in which they would be ordered into action—especially if the handling of the U.S. mail was involved. The National Guard built on the structure of state militias and was formally authorized by the National Defense Act of 1916. See Eric Foner, *Reconstruction: America's Unfinished Revolution, 1863–1877* (New York, 1988); Michael Doubler, *Civilian in Peace, Soldier in War: The Army National Guard, 1636–2000* (Lawrence, KS, 2003).

19. Byron Engle quoted in Stuart Schrader, *Badges without Borders: How Global Counterinsurgency Transformed American Policing* (Berkeley, 2019), 5; Hinton, *America on Fire*, 11. Schrader's book is an important effort to put American policing into international perspective. For the ways in which imperial policing, as in the Philippines, could be deployed within the United States, see Chapter Seven, "Fascist Pulses."

20. Radley Balko, *Rise of the Warrior Cop: The Militarization of America's Police Forces* (New York, 2014), xi–xii, 54–68, 145–46, 157–58; Christian Parenti, *Lockdown America: Police and Prisons in the Age of Crisis* (London, 2008). During the First World War and the subsequent Red Scare, radicals of foreign birth were deported as punishment for their activities, but during the 1980s proposed exile for drug offenders involved those born in the United States, as was the case with the colonization movement.

21. Balko, *Rise of the Warrior Cop*, 177–93, 209–10.

22. Balko, *Rise of the Warrior Cop*, 194–95, 218–20. The eviction policy was part of the Housing Opportunity Extension Act of March 1996. See *New York Times*, 29 March 1996. As the *Los Angeles Times* put it, "Conceivably a family could be left homeless by the actions of one of its members." *Los Angeles Times*, 29 March 1996.

23. See Tony Messenger's remarkable study, *Profit and Punishment: How America Criminalizes the Poor in the Name of Justice* (New York, 2021). Most of the states have enacted such fee structures, and while "board" and "pay-to-stay" charges are

often waived by courts in large cities, this is not the case outside of them, especially where they are needed to fund local expenditures. Also see Phil A. Neel, *Hinterland: America's New Landscape of Class and Conflict* (London, 2018), 133–35.

24. The Sentencing Project, *Voting Rights in an Era of Mass Incarceration: A Primer* (July 2021); National Council of State Legislatures, "Felon Voting Rights," 28 June 2021. Only in Maine, Vermont, and the District of Columbia can felons vote while incarcerated.

25. See Steve J. Stern, *Battling for Hearts and Minds: Memory Struggles in Pinochet's Chile, 1973–1988* (Durham, NC, 2006), 57–58.

26. Milton Friedman to General Augusto Pinochet, 21 April 1975, www.docs.Google .com.

27. Isabella Cuervo-Lorens, "An 'Implacable Enemy': Milton Friedman and the 'Chilean Miracle,'" *Foreign Affairs Review* (November 2019); Daniel Matamala, "The Complicated Legacy of the 'Chicago Boys' in Chile," *Promarket* (21 September 2021).

28. Michel Crozier, Samuel P. Huntington, and Joji Watanuki, *The Crisis of Democracy: Report on the Governability of Democracies to the Trilateral Commission* (New York, 1975), 2–3. The report was the work of the Trilateral Commission's Task Force on the Governability of Democracies, organized under the directorship of Zbigniew Brzezinski (later President Jimmy Carter's National Security Advisor) and discussed by Commission members at a meeting in Kyoto, Japan, in the spring of 1975.

29. Crozier, Huntington, and Watanuki, *Crisis of Democracy*, 64–65, 102–3, 174–75, 188. At the discussion of the report in Kyoto, members of the Trilateral Commission agreed on the importance of "reasonable rates of economic growth and relatively stable prices," and that the "governability of democracy seems dependent on the sustained expansion of the economy."

30. Crozier, Huntington, and Watanuki, *Crisis of Democracy*, 102–15. Huntington took his idea of an "excess of democracy" from the historian David Donald, who had blamed it, especially its Jacksonian version, for the explosion of the Civil War.

31. See Nancy MacLean's powerful *Democracy in Chains*, which focuses on Buchanan.

32. MacLean, *Democracy in Chains*, 154–68; Amy Offner, *Sorting Out the Mixed Economy: The Rise and Fall of Welfare and Developmental States in the Americas* (Princeton, 2019); Ada Ferrer, *Cuba: An American History* (New York, 2021). On the making of Chile's constitution, see Stern, *Battling for Hearts and Minds*, 170–74.

33. MacLean, *Democracy in Chains*, 169–89.

34. See, especially, Katherine Stewart, *The Power Worshippers: Inside the Dangerous Rise of Religious Nationalism* (New York, 2019); Michelle Goldberg, *Kingdom Coming: The Rise of Christian Nationalism* (New York, 2007). Also see Eric L. McDaniel, Irfan Nooruddin, and Allyson F. Shortle, *The Everyday Crusade: Christian Nationalism in American Politics* (New York, 2022).

35. Stewart, *Power Worshippers*, 102–68; "I hope to see the day," Jerry Falwell proclaimed, "when, as in the early days of our country, we don't have public schools. The churches will have taken them over again and Christians will be running

them. . . . The public school system is damned." See Falwell, *America Can Be Saved!* (Murfreesboro, TN, 1979).

36. Stewart, *Power Worshippers*, 8–9, 40–53.
37. See Margaret O'Mara, *The Code: Silicon Valley and the Remaking of America* (New York, 2019), 184–87.
38. On the role of the federal government in the development and modernization of the South and West, see Bruce J. Schulman, *From Cotton Belt to Sunbelt: Federal Policy, Economic Development, and the Transformation of the South, 1938–1980* (New York, 1994); Michelle Nickerson and Darren Dochuk, eds., *Sunbelt Rising: The Politics of Space, Place, and Region* (Philadelphia, 2011). Also see O'Mara, *The Code*, 1–66.
39. See, especially, O'Mara, *The Code*, 285–301.
40. Esther Dyson, "Friend or Foe," *Wired*, 1 August 1995; Tim Murphy, "Your Daily Newt: A $40 Billion Entitlement for Laptops," *Mother Jones*, 20 December 2011; Gary C. Jacobsen, "The 1994 Elections in Perspective," *Political Science Quarterly* 111 (Summer 1996): 203–23; O'Mara, *The Code*, 326–27; Gerstle, *Rise and Fall of the Neoliberal Order*, 163–65. Gingrich was a great fan of Alvin Toffler's *Future Shock* (1970) and *The Third Wave* (1980), both of which imagined a much smaller state and a decentralized distribution of power.
41. There is a growing volume of evidence and investigation testifying to the tech-driven forms of exploitation at workplaces. See, for example, Emily Guendelsberger, "I Worked at an Amazon Fulfillment Center; They Treated Workers Like Robots," *Time* Magazine, 18 July 2019; Chase Thiel et al., "Monitoring Employees Makes Them More Likely to Break Rules," *Harvard Business Review*, 27 June 2022; and, especially, Jodi Cantor et al., "The Amazon That Customers Don't See," *New York Times*, 15 June 2021.
42. See Alex Rosenblat, *Uberland: How Algorithms are Rewriting the Rules of Work* (Berkeley, 2018); "Battle Over Rideshare Worker Classification Continues," *National Law Review* 12 (9 September 2022).
43. Karen Levy, *Data Driven: Truckers, Technology, and the New Workplace Surveillance* (Princeton, 2022); "ELDs for Trucks: What are the Benefits of Installing ELD's in Your Fleet," *Samsara*, 20 September 2021.
44. My understanding and thinking about this phenomenon owes much to Shoshana Zuboff's brilliant *The Age of Surveillance Capitalism: The Fight for a Human Future at the New Frontier of Power* (New York, 2019).
45. Zuboff, *Age of Surveillance Capitalism*, 27–174.
46. Zuboff, *Age of Surveillance Capitalism*, 98–127. The "right to be forgotten" or the General Data Protection Regulation (GDPR) evolved from an EU Court of Justice ruling in 2014. The GDPR provides that "the data subject shall have the right to obtain from the controller the erasure of personal data concerning him or her without undue delay and the controller shall have the obligation to erase personal data without undue delay." Although the GDPR includes a number of conditions, it is supplemented by a right to access personal information. Search-engine companies have vigorously and, so far successfully, fought against such legislation in the United States despite the support it has from a very large share of the American public. See "Everything You Need to Know About the 'Right to be Forgotten,'" GDPR.eu.

47. *Los Angeles Times*, 25 August 1997; Ashley Craddock, "Gore, California Tech Pals to Talk Education," *Wired*, 13 March 1997.

48. See, for example, Al Gore, "Information Superhighways Speech," 21 March 1994, International Telecommunications Union, vlib.iue.it; "Remarks by Vice President Al Gore," Digital Divide Event, 28 April 1998, clintonwhitehouse3 .archives.gov. Gore has also been accused of claiming to have "invented" the internet, but in truth he only took a fair amount of credit for the political support it came to receive.

CHAPTER TEN
SPECTERS OF RACE WAR AND REPLACEMENT

1. *Chicago Tribune*, 4 November 2008; *New York Times*, 4 November 2008.

2. Daniel Schorr, "A New, 'Post-Racial' Political Era in America," *All Things Considered*, National Public Radio, 28 January 2009. Also see *Washington Post*, 21 January 2009; *Le Monde*, 6 November 2008; *Der Spiegel*, 5 November 2008; *The Times* [London], 5 November 2008; *The Guardian,* 5 November 2008.

3. See, especially, Theda Skocpol and Vanessa Williamson, *The Tea Party and the Remaking of Republican Conservatism* (New York, 2012), 3–18; Sam Jackson, *Oath Keepers: Patriotism and the Edge of Violence in a Right-Wing Antigovernment Group* (New York, 2020), 29–37.

4. On the battles during Obama's transition that led to the marginalization of his grassroots supporters, see Micah L. Sifry, "Obama's Lost Army," *New Republic*, 9 February 2017.

5. Kathleen Belew, *Bring the War Home: The White Power Movement and Paramilitary America* (Cambridge, MA, 2018).

6. Easily the best treatment of Duke is to be found in Lawrence Powell, *Troubled Memory: Anne Levy, the Holocaust, and David Duke's Louisiana* (Chapel Hill, 2000), 404–99; and Lawrence Powell, "Slouching Toward Baton Rouge: The 1989 Legislative Election of David Duke," in Douglas D. Rose, *The Emergence of David Duke and the Politics of Race* (Chapel Hill, 1992), 12–40. Also see William V. Moore, "David Duke: The White Knight," in Rose, *The Emergence of David Duke*, 41–58; Brett Barrouquere, "White Shadow: David Duke's Lasting Influence on White Supremacy," *Southern Poverty Law Center*, 17 May 2019, 1–16; Tyler Bridges, *The Rise and Fall of David Duke* (Create Space Publishing, 2018).

7. Powell, *Troubled Memory*, 442–45; Lawrence Powell, "Read My Liposuction: The Makeover of David Duke," *New Republic*, 15 October 1990.

8. Powell, *Troubled Memory*, 446–49.

9. Powell, *Troubled Memory*, 450–51; Barrouquere, "White Shadow," 1–5; *Washington Post*, 1 July 1990.

10. *Los Angeles Times*, 7 October 1990. Visiting an exhibit on the Holocaust at the Louisiana State Capitol, survivor Anne Levy confronted David Duke when she saw him looking at the photographs, demanding to know why, as a Holocaust denier, he was there. She soon was playing an important public role in reminding voters that Duke was aligned with the Nazis. See Powell, *Troubled Memory*, 483–99.

11. Powell, *Troubled Memory*, 477–79.
12. On the election returns, see Micheal W. Giles and Melanie A. Buckner, "David Duke and the Black Threat: An Old Hypothesis Revisited," *Journal of Politics* 55 (August 1993), 702–13.
13. Percy quoted in Powell, *Troubled Memory*, 9.
14. Patrick Buchanan, "A Crossroads in Our Country's History," 10 December 1991, Democracy in Action, *Field Guide to the 1992 Presidential Campaign*; Nicole Hemmer, "The Man Who Won the Republican Party Before Trump Did," *New York Times*, 8 September 2022; Nicole Hemmer, *Partisans: The Conservative Revolutionaries Who Remade American Politics in the 1990s* (New York, 2022), 67–92.
15. Patrick Joseph Buchanan, "Culture War Speech: Address to the Republican National Convention, 17 August 1992," *Voices of Democracy: The U.S. Oratory Project*; John Dillin, "Buchanan Looks Toward 1996," *Christian Science Monitor*, 15 April 1992; Jerome Jamin, "Pat Buchanan, Far-Right Thinking, Ethnic Loyalty, and Liberal Democracy," in A. James McAdams and Alejandro Castillon, eds., *Contemporary Far-Right Thinkers and the Future of Liberal Democracy* (London, 2022), 45–65.
16. *New York Times*, 18 October 1977; *Los Angeles Times*, 9 November 1994; Hemmer, *Partisans*, 83–87; Greg Grandin, *The End of the Myth: From the Frontier to the Border Wall in the Mind of America* (New York, 2019), 223–24. Proposition 187 also enabled the Republicans to win both houses of the California state legislature, but opponents quickly brought suit and Proposition 187 was ruled unconstitutional by a federal district court in 1999. Buchanan in fact complained as early as 1991 that David Duke was "stealing" from him and threatened to "sue that dude for intellectual property theft." See Lawrence Powell, *Troubled Memory: Anne Levy, the Holocaust, and David Duke's Louisiana* (Chapel Hill, 2019), 2nd ed., xvii.
17. Erika Lee, "The Chinese Exclusion Example: Race, Immigration, and American Gatekeeping, 1882–1924," *Journal of American Ethnic History* 21 (April 2002): 36–62; Mae Ngai, *Impossible Subjects: Illegal Aliens and the Making of Modern America* (Princeton, 2004); Grandin, *The End of the Myth*, 159–67.
18. David Turner, "Foundations of the Holocaust," *Jerusalem Post*, 25 January 2013; Jerry Krammer, "The Hart-Celler Immigration Act of 1965," *Center for Immigration Studies*, 30 September 2015; Ngai, *Impossible Subjects*, 227–64; Jones, *White Borders*, 83–104; Alexandra Minna Stern, "From 'Race Suicide' to 'White Extinction': White Nationalism, Nativism, and Eugenics Over the Past Century," *Journal of American History* 109 (September 2022): 353–55. The Hart-Celler Act didn't eliminate quotas. Numerical quotas were placed on immigration by hemisphere, and there was a 20,000-person cap per country. But the quotas were not, as before, tied to what historian Mae Ngai calls a "hierarchy of racial desirability."
19. Adam Goodman, *The Deportation Machine: America's Long History of Expelling Immigrants* (Princeton, 2020), 110–13; Jones, *White Borders*, 96–99.
20. "John Tanton's Private Papers Expose More than Twenty Years of Hate," *Intelligence Report: The Tanton Files*, Southern Poverty Law Center, 30 November 2008; Goodman, *The Deportation Machine*, 109–18; Jones, *White Borders*, 129–36. The Pioneer Fund was established in 1937 by textile magnate and eugenics devotee Wickcliffe Draper and tasked with promoting "race betterment" by privileging the genetic stock of those deemed "descended predominately from white persons who

settled the original thirteen states prior to the adoption of the Constitution." See "Pioneer Fund," Southern Poverty Law Center.

21. Ana Raquel Minian, *Undocumented Lives: The Untold Story of Mexican Migration* (Cambridge, MA, 2018), 14–46; Neil Foley, *Mexicans in the Making of America* (Cambridge, MA, 2014), 123–47; Irvin Ibarguen, "Coveted Across the Continuum: The Politics of Mexican Migration in Transnational Perspective, 1942–1965" (PhD diss., Harvard University, 2018); Jorge Durand, Douglas S. Massey, and Emilio Parrado, "The New Era of Mexican Migration to the United States," *Journal of American History* 86 (September 1999): 518–36. The centerpiece of the Reagan policies came in the form of the 1986 Immigration Reform and Control Act (IRCA), which, with bipartisan support, also cracked down on employers who knowingly hired undocumented workers and increased appropriations for the Border Patrol.

22. Grandin, *End of the Myth*, 249–53.

23. State of the Union, 1995 (delivered version), 24 January 1995; Goodman, *Deportation Machine*, 174–76. In his lengthy address, Clinton highlighted the recently passed "very tough crime bill—longer sentences, three strikes and you're out almost 60 new capital punishment offenses, more prisons, more prevention, 100,000 more police." All of this was part of a "New Covenant" he was proposing.

24. Laura Smith, "The Man Responsible for the Modern NRA Killed a Hispanic Teenager Before Becoming a Border Agent," *Timeline*, 6 July 2017; Kelly Lytle Hernandez, *Migra! A History of the U.S. Border Patrol* (Berkeley, 2010), 68–69.

25. Adam Winkler, *Gunfight: The Battle Over the Right to Bear Arms in America* (New York, 2013); Matthew J. Lacombe, *Firepower: How the NRA Turned Gun Owners into a Political Force* (Princeton, 2021); Joel Achenbach et al., "How the NRA's True Believers Converted a Marksmanship Group into a Mighty Gun Lobby," *Washington Post*, 12 January 2013. The NRA's first president was General Ambrose Burnside, who was well positioned to observe the poor shooting skills of many Union soldiers.

26. Lacombe, *Firepower*, 136–48; Achenbach et al., "NRA's True Believers."

27. Achenbach et al., "NRA's True Believers."

28. Rukmani Bhatia, "Guns, Lies, and Fear: Exposing the NRA's Messaging Playbook," Center for American Progress, 24 April 2019; Lacombe, *Firepower*, 18–43. As Lacombe argues, the NRA was long a political and ideological organization. What changed in 1980 was that it entered *partisan* politics.

29. LaPierre quoted in Lacombe, *Firepower*, 123–24.

30. Jonathan M. Metzl, *Dying of Whiteness: How the Politics of Racial Resentment is Killing America's Heartland* (New York, 2019), 68–69; Pew Research Center, "America's Complex Relationship with Guns," 22 June 2017. Most gun owners overall support the Republican Party, but that support is a bit softer than is true among NRA members: about 60 percent are Republicans or lean Republican. The NRA claims to have had about five million members in 2019, though that figure has not been confirmed, and in recent years membership does seem to be dipping.

31. Kim Parker, "Among Gun Owners NRA Members Have a Unique Set of Views and Experiences," Pew Research Center, 5 July 2017; Metzl, *Dying of Whiteness*, 68–75.

32. Miller quoted in Belew, *Bring the War Home*, 146.

33. Arie Perliger, *American Zealots: Inside Right-Wing Domestic Terrorism* (New York, 2020), 9–69.
34. Catrina Doxsee, "Examining Extremism: The Militia Movement," *Center for Strategic and International Studies*, 21 August 2021; "The Militia Movement," *Southern Poverty Law Center*; Belew, *Bring the War Home*, 187–209; Perliger, *American Zealots*, 53–69.
35. Jennifer Steinhauer, "Veterans Fortify the Ranks of Militias Aligned with Trump's Views," *New York Times*, 10 June 2021; "Michigan's Active Right-Wing Extremist Groups" (March 2022), progressmichigan.org.
36. On the press and Democratic reaction to the bombing, see *Washington Post*, 8 May 1995, 3 September 1995; *Los Angeles Times*, 8 May 1995, 9 May 1995; *Buffalo News*, 27 April 1995; *Ethical Spectacle*, June 1995. As a spokesman for the Militia of Montana put it, "We've got a bimbo like Newt Gingrich. He's part of the problem."
37. See Cynthia Miller-Idriss, *Hate in the Homeland: The New Global Far Right* (Princeton, 2020), 4–28; Sarah Shurts, "Intellectuals and the Illiberal Discourses of Identity," in McAdams and Castillon, eds., *Contemporary Far-Right Thinkers*, 27–44.
38. Linda Gordon, *The Moral Property of Women: A History of Birth Control Politics in America* (Urbana, IL, 2002); Thomas C. Leonard, *Illiberal Reformers: Race, Eugenics, and American Economics in the Progressive Era* (Princeton, 2016); Paul A. Lombardo, ed., *A Century of Eugenics in America* (Bloomington, IN, 2011); Alexandra Minna Stern, *Eugenic Nation: Faults and Frontiers of Better Breeding in Modern America* (Oakland, 2016).
39. Miller-Idriss, *Hate in the Homeland*, 11; Phillip Bump, "Tucker Carlson Plays Dumb on Replacement Theory, then Espouses It," *Washington Post*, 18 May 2022; Domenico Montanaro, "How 'Replacement Theory' Went Mainstream on the Political Right," National Public Radio, 17 May 2022.
40. For important perspectives on what was unfolding, see Jefferson Cowie, *Freedom's Dominion: A Saga of White Resistance to Federal Power* (New York, 2022).
41. Skocpol and Williamson, *Tea Party and Remaking of Republican Conservatism*, 45–82; Skocpol, "Elite and Popular Roots," 3–23; Arlie Russell Hochschild, *Strangers in Their Own Land: Anger and Mourning on the American Right* (New York, 2018), 135–51; Alan I. Abramowitz, "Partisan Polarization and the Rise of the Tea Party Movement," paper presented to the Annual Meeting of the Political Science Association, September 2011.
42. See Justin Gest, *The New Minority: White Working Class Politics in an Age of Immigration and Inequality* (New York, 2016); Daniel Oesch, "Explaining Workers' Support for Right-Wing Populist Parties in Western Europe," *International Political Science Review* 29 (June 2008): 349–73.
43. Brian Montopoli, "Tea Party Supporters: Who They Are and What They Believe," CBS News, 14 December 2012; Kate Zernike and Megan Thee-Brenan, "Poll Finds Tea Party Backers Wealthier and More Educated," *New York Times*, 14 April 2010; Skocpol and Williamson, *Tea Party and Remaking of Republican Conservatism*, 19–44.
44. See, for example, Dylan Riley and Robert Brenner, "Seven Theses on American Politics," *New Left Review* 138 (November-December 2022): 5–27; Lauren Lumpkin, "In a City Full of Adjunct Faculty Members Many Struggle to Get

By," *Washington Post*, 26 April 2022; Caroline Frederickson, "There is No Excuse for How Universities Treat Adjuncts," *The Atlantic*, 15 September 2015.

45. Important too in 2016 was the refusal of middle- and upper-middle-class Republicans, many influenced by the Tea Party and the conservative networks sustaining it, to stay at home or switch their votes after revelations of Trump's egregiously predatory behavior surfaced.

46. Gest, *The New Minority*, 188–200; *New York Times*, 9 December 2008, 8 November 2016; James Surowiecki, "Economic Populism at the Primaries," *New Yorker*, 14 February 2016; Jennifer M. Silva, "Don't Discount the Support for Bernie in Trump Country," *Market Watch*, 10 March 2020.

47. Pippa Norris and Ronald Inglehart, *Cultural Backlash: Trump, Brexit, and Authoritarian Populism* (New York, 2019), 294–363; April Gordon, "Reflections on Ukraine, Georgia, and Armenia," *A New Eurasian Far Right Rising* (Freedom House, 2020); "Europe and Right-Wing Nationalism: A Country-by-Country Guide," BBC News, 13 November 2019.

48. John Chrobak, "The International Embrace of Parler by Right-Wing and Populist Parties," *Illiberalism Studies Program*, 25 January 2021; Grant A. Silverman, "Social Media and Paramilitary Movement Politics of the Far Right," *Illiberalism Studies Program*, 10 February 2022.

49. Cas Mudde, "Surprised to See U.S. Republicans Cozying Up to the European Far Right? Don't Be," *The Guardian*, 15 October 2021; "Former Vice President Mike Pence Praises Government's Vision on Family Policy," *Budapest Times*, 24 September 2021; "Why Is Tucker Carlson in Budapest?" *Newsweek*, 3 August 2021; Philip Bump, "Hungary Turned Authoritarian. So Tucker Carlson Went to Hungary," *Washington Post*, 3 August 2021; David Folkenflik, "Hungary's Autocratic Leader Tells U.S. Conservatives to Join His Culture War, NPR, 4 August 2022.

50. Andrew Marantz, "Does Hungary Offer a Glimpse of Our Authoritarian Future?" *New Yorker*, 4 July 2022.

51. Zach Schonfeld, "GOP Lawmakers Celebrate Right-Wing Candidates's Win in Italy," *The Hill*, 26 September 2022; Camille Gijs, "Europe's Right Wing Cheers Meloni's Win," *Politico*, 26 September 2022;

52. Eleonora Vallin, "From the KKK to an Italian Village," *La Stampa*, 11 December 2013; "Italy to Expel ex-Klansman David Duke," *Haaretz*, 8 December 2013; "Former Klan Leader Duke Expelled from Italy," *Intelligence Report*, Southern Poverty Law Center, 25 February 2014.

CONCLUSION

1. Isabella Murray, "Marjorie Taylor Greene Refuses to Back Down from 'National Divorce' Proposal," abcnews.go.com, 22 February 2023; Elaine Godfrey, "Never Mind Marjorie Taylor Greene's 'National Divorce,'" *The Atlantic*, 23 February 2023.

2. Katelyn Caralle, "A Third of Americans Agree with Marjorie Taylor Greene," DailyMail.com, 2 March 2023; Margaret Talev, "The American Index," Axios com, 16 March 2023; Alexandra Minna Stern, *Proud Boys and the White Ethnostate: How the Alt-Right is Warping the American Imagination* (Boston, 2019).

3. For an especially interesting treatment, see Andrew Sartori, *Liberalism in Empire: An Alternative History* (Berkeley, 2014). Although we generally imagine liberal ideas and values flowing down from thinkers like John Locke, this should remind us that they flow perhaps as significantly up from ordinary folk in struggle for their own rights and destinies.

4. See, especially, James Weinstein, *The Decline of Socialism in America, 1912–1925* (New York, 1967); James R. Green, *Grass-Roots Socialism: Radical Movements in the Southwest, 1895–1943* (Baton Rouge, 1978); Alan Brinkley, *Voices of Protest: Huey Long, Father Coughlin, and the Great Depression* (New York, 1983).

5. For some of the changing interpretations, see John D. Hicks, *The Populist Revolt: A History of the Farmers' Alliance and the People's Party* (Minneapolis, 1931); C. Vann Woodward, *Tom Watson: Agrarian Rebel* (New York, 1938); Richard Hofstadter, *The Age of Reform* (New York, 1955); Lawrence C. Goodwyn, *Democratic Promise: The Populist Moment in America* (New York, 1976). More recently, and with an international perspective, see Jan-Werner Muller, *What Is Populism?* (Philadelphia, 2016); Pippa Norris and Ronald Inglehart, *Cultural Backlash: Trump, Brexit, and Authoritarian Populism* (New York, 2019); Ernesto Laclau, *On Populist Reason* (London, 2005); Samuel Issacharoff, *Democracy Unmoored: Populism and the Corruption of Popular Sovereignty* (New York, 2023).

6. For a discussion of the Grimes County episode, see Steven Hahn, *A Nation under Our Feet: Black Political Struggles in the Rural South from Slavery to the Great Migration* (Cambridge, MA, 2003), 393–400, 437–40; and, especially, Lawrence C. Goodwyn's remarkable "Populist Dreams and Negro Rights: East Texas as a Case Study," *American Historical Review* 76 (December 1971): 1435–56.

INDEX

abolitionist movement, 108–13
   anarchist streak in, 381–82n5
   anti-Catholicism and, 162
   colonization and, 109, 111–12, 114,
      136, 148, 151, 381n8, 407n19
   emancipation and, 153
   free labor ideal and, 159
   Freemasonry and, 129
   Native removal and, 133
   nativism and, 231
   penal reform and, 148–50, 388n15
   post-emancipation coerced labor and,
      153, 154, 172–73
   post-emancipation era, 154
   radical alternatives and, 351, 352
   vagrancy laws and, 161
abortion, 264–65, 302
Adams, Charles Francis, 163
Adams, Charles Francis, Jr., 185
Adams, John, 78, 86, 91, 94
Adams, Samuel, 72–73
Addams, Jane, 206
Affordable Care Act, 340
AFL-CIO, 277
Agnew, Spiro T., 277
Agricultural Adjustment Act (AAA)
   (1933), 243–44
Aguinaldo, Emilio, 204
Allen, Richard, 271
Allende, Salvador, 298
Alliance for Border Control, 326
Alternative for Germany (AfD), 343

Amazon, 308
American Birth Control League, 174–75
American Conservative Political Action
   Committee (CPAC), 345
American Dilemma, An: The Negro Problem
   and Modern Democracy (Myrdal), 343
American Enterprise Institute, 262
American exceptionalism
   American studies movement and,
      23, 25
   Cold War-era explication of, 22
   1830s solidification of, 107
   liberal tradition view as basis of, 1, 13,
      366n4
   Lincoln ideal and, 106
   See also liberal tradition view
American Federation of Labor (AFL),
   212, 232, 236
American historiography
   on colonial backcountry rebellions, 81
   "cultural turn," 31–32
   early orientation of, 17–18
   feminist history, 29
   microhistorical approaches, 31
   origin stories in, 12, 36–37, 96, 101,
      370n38
   progressive school, 18–19
   social history, 29, 31
   See also liberal tradition view
American imperialism
   interwar protofascism and, 213
   liberal tradition view on, 27

American imperialism (*continued*)
  1960s critiques of liberal tradition
    view and, 30
  Panama Canal Zone and, 202–3, 207
  Progressivism and, 207
  racism and, 204–6
  Woodrow Wilson and, 211
American Independent Party, 273,
    274–75
American Legion, 218–21, 223, 239–40
American Liberty League, 246
American Opinion, 267, 268
*American Political Tradition and the Men
    Who Made It, The* (Hofstadter),
    16–17
American Protective League (APL),
    214–16, 223
American Railway Union, 171
American Revolution
  American origin stories and, 36
  backcountry settlers and, 84–85, 131
  Constitutional Congress and, 93
  emancipation and, 77, 87, 149
  enslavement and, 77, 95
  Freemasonry and, 127, 128
  monarchism and, 77–79, 85–86
  Native peoples and, 85, 131
  radical alternatives and, 351
  republicanism and, 86
  See also American Revolution
    approach
American Revolution approach
  anti-Catholicism and, 69–70, 72–74
  monarchism and, 75–77
  Stamp Act protests, 67–69, 72, 73
Americans for Democratic Action, 21
American studies movement, 23–24, 25
Andrew Jackson: Symbol for an Age (Ward),
    24
anti-abortion movement, 264–65
anti-Catholicism, 69–73
  abolitionist movement and, 162
  American Protective League and, 215
  American Revolution approach and,
    69–70, 72–74
  anti-corruption and, 72–73
  Anti-Federalists and, 97

British North America, 69–70, 72–73
  Cold War-era political right and, 23
  1830s, 116–17
  English Civil War and, 71
  Freemasonry and, 129
  Ku Klux Klan and, 222, 226, 227, 228
  nativism and, 161, 162–63
  1960s tempering of, 264
  post-Revolutionary state constitutions
    and, 87
anti-communism
  John Birch Society, 263, 267–69,
    271–72, 273
  McCarthyism, 22, 23, 263
  1960s, 262, 263, 264, 266, 267 70
  George Wallace and, 250
  Young Americans for Freedom,
    269–72
  See also Cold War
anti-democratic perspectives
  Constitution and, 93, 102
  immigration and, 187–88
  liberal tradition view and, 16
  neoliberalism and, 287, 299–301, 313,
    408nn28–30
  North American colonization and, 45
  post-emancipation era, 187–88
  post-Revolutionary period, 92, 93,
    102
  Progressivism and, 189–91, 193
  republicanism and, 71
  Tocqueville on, 138, 139
  twenty-first-century political right
    and, 33, 323, 330
anti-federal government perspectives
  Anti-Federalists and, 96–98
  militias and, 317, 333, 334
  neoliberalism and, 301–2, 303, 304
  1960s political right and, 270
  racism and, 315, 330
  Tea Party movement and, 338
  twenty-first-century political right
    and, 35, 315, 317, 322, 330, 332,
    333, 334, 337
  George Wallace and, 247–48, 250
  See also deregulation
Anti-Federalists, 96–97, 99–100, 138

anti-nuclear movement, 352
Anti-Peonage Act (1867), 159, 170,
    391n50
antiradicalism
    expulsionism and, 407n19
    immigration policy and, 233
    interwar protofascism and, 220, 222,
        223
    policing history and, 292
    See also interwar protofascism
Anti-Saloon League, 229
anti-Semitism
    American Protective League and, 215
    David Duke and, 318, 320, 330
    immigration policy and, 325
    interwar protofascism and, 241
    Ku Klux Klan and, 222
    Populism and, 23
    twenty-first-century political right
        and, 317, 330, 332, 335
antislavery movement. *See* abolitionist
    movement
Arminianism, 109, 110
Articles of Confederation, 74, 87–88, 93
    See also post-Revolutionary period
Aryan Nations, 332, 350
Asiatic Exclusion League, 214

backcountry settlers, 79–85, 130–31
    American Revolution and, 84–85, 131
    aspirations to feudalism and enslaver
        status, 48, 62, 81, 83
    colonial disfranchisement of, 47
    colonial rebellions of, 47, 62, 79–81
    expulsionism and, 82–84, 103
    Andrew Jackson and, 132
    liberal tradition view and, 79, 80–81
    local authority and boundaries and,
        84–85, 99, 103
    migration of, 48–49, 81
    Native expulsion and, 83–84, 130–31
    post-Revolutionary rebellions, 89, 90,
        91–92, 93
    See also Native-colonist conflicts
Bacon's Rebellion (1676), 47, 62
Balko, Radley, 295
Bannon, Steve, 335, 345

Baruch, Bernard, 194
Basche, Julius A., 234
Battle of Bad Axe, 130
Battle of Horseshoe Bend (1814), 132
Beard, Charles A., 18
Beaumont, Gustave de, 105, 144–45
Beccaria, Cesare, 145
Becker, Carl, 18
Beecher, Lyman, 117
behavioral revolution, 27–28
Belcher, Jonathan, 74
Bell, Daniel, 28
Bellamy, Francis, 14
Bellow, Saul, 325
Belmont, August, 185
Bergen, Brooke, 296–97
Berkeley, William, 44–45, 47, 61–62
Bernard, Francis, 68
Bettelheim, Bruno, 25
Biden, Joe, 294
Bill of Rights, 12, 50, 96, 99–100
birth control, 174–75, 176, 264
Birth of a Nation, 222
Black, Hugo, 226
Black Codes, 114–15, 154–55, 159, 160,
    388n26
Black freedom struggles
    abolitionist movement and, 108–9,
        110–11, 113, 149
    Great Migration and, 217
    interwar protofascism and, 217–18
    local authority and boundaries and,
        259–60
    Long Hot Summer (1967), 275
    Native peoples and, 133
    1960s uprisings, 275, 289, 317, 328
    Nixon and, 277
    radical alternatives and, 352, 353
    Reconstruction and, 155–56, 188, 356
    school desegregation, 256–57, 279
    self-defense and, 328
    slavery to freedom narrative, 13,
        143–44
    See also civil rights movement;
        emancipation
Black Great Migrations, 217, 223,
    250–54

Black Hawk, 129–30, 133
Black Hawk War, 129–30
Black Lives Matter, 13, 353
Black Panthers, 13, 328
Blackstone, William, 49, 72
Blumenthal, W. Michael, 406n6
Body of Liberties (Massachusetts), 50, 51, 53
Boebert, Lauren, 346
Bolshevik Revolution (1917), 211, 213
Bolsonaro, Jair, 12
Book of Mormon (Smith), 118–19
Boorstin, Daniel, 16, 22
Boston busing crisis, 257–59
Boston Tea Party, 70
Bracero program, 326
Bradley, Bill, 286
Bradley Foundation, 303
Branch Davidians, 333, 334
Brazil, 12
Bream, Louis, 319
Brewer, Holly, 372n14
Brexit, 11, 344
British National Party, 344
British North America
    anti-Catholicism, 69–70, 72–73
    coerced labor, 49, 52–53, 64
    coercion, 52, 53, 56–57, 374n27
    enslavement in, 49
    expulsionism, 53–54, 63, 374n28
    feudalism and, 48, 49, 50–51, 61–62, 64, 81
    indentured servitude in, 46–47, 48, 64
    local authority and boundaries, 53, 56, 65, 81
    monarchism in, 73–77
    Native expulsion, 130–31
    rebellion in, 47, 62, 79, 80–81
    Salem witchcraft trials, 56–57
    social/economic stratification, 72, 80, 81, 82
    See also American Revolution approach; backcountry settlers; Native-colonist conflicts; North American colonization
Brooks, Preston, 126–27
Brotherhood of Elks, 218

Brothers of Italy, 12, 343
Brown, Edmund G. (Pat), 255
Brown, Harold, 406n6
Brown, H. Rap, 277
Brown, John, 160
Brown v. Board of Education, 14, 256, 257, 259, 268
Bryan, William Jennings, 193, 206
Brzezinski, Zbigniew, 406n6, 408n28
Buchanan, James M., 300–301
Buchanan, Pat, 271, 322–23, 326, 330, 411n16
Buckley, William, 263, 267, 269
Buffett, Warren, 325
Burke, Edmund, 111
Burnham, James, 22
Burnside, Ambrose, 412n24
Bush, George H. W., 320, 322
Bush, George W., 33, 330
Business Roundtable, 284
Butler, Nicholas Murray, 185, 245

Calhoun, John C., 301
Calloway, Colin, 85
Camp of the Saints, The (Raspail), 335
Camus, Renaud, 335
Canny, Nicholas, 40
capitalism
    American origin stories and, 36
    Christian nationalism and, 303
    corporate, 193–94
    corporations and, 182
    end of Cold War and, 32
    enslavement and, 33, 36, 370n35
    global financial crisis (2007–2008) and, 33
    left movements on, 34
    migrant labor and, 165–66
    1960s critiques of liberal tradition view and, 28, 30
    North American colonization and, 38–39
    Populism on, 354
    Progressivism and, 169, 179–80
    wage labor and, 162
Capitalism and Freedom (Friedman), 298
carceral state, 289, 330, 406n12

Carlson, Tucker, 345
Carmichael, Stokely, 277
Carnegie, Andrew, 185
Carrington, Morris, 357
Carter, Harlon, 327–29
Carter, Jimmy, 285, 286, 406n6
Carto, William, 320
Carville, James, 318
Catholicism, 264, 302
    See also anti-Catholicism
Cato Institute, 284
Chaffee, Adna, 204
Charles I (king of England), 70
checks and balances, 12
Cherokee Nation v. Georgia (1831), 385n43
Cherokees, 131–32, 385n43
Chesapeake colonies, 43, 44–45, 47,
    58–59, 61–62
Chickasaws, 132
Child, Lydia Maria, 114
Chile, 297–98, 301
Chinese Exclusion Act (1882), 165,
    390n41
Chinese immigrants, 162, 163, 165, 197,
    231, 323, 390n41
Christian Anti-Communist Crusade,
    267, 273
Christian Crusade, 268, 273
Christian Front, 241
Christian Identity movement, 332
Christianity. *See* Catholicism; Protestant
    Christianity
Christian nationalism, 35, 302–4,
    408–9n35
Churchill, Winston, 176
Cilley, Jonathan, 126
Citizens Councils, 268, 273
Civil Rights Act (1866), 170
Civil Rights Act (1875), 170
civil rights movement
    Black pathology theories and, 288
    Confederate flag as response to, 14
    critiques of liberal tradition view and,
        28
    enslavement studies and, 24
    1960s political right and, 263, 270
    school desegregation and, 257

    successes of, 316
    George Wallace and, 247, 248, 249
    See also school desegregation
Civil War
    coerced labor and, 150–51
    Confederate disenfranchisement,
        393–94n26
    corporations and, 183
    draft riots during, 196
    emancipation and, 151–53
    enslaved people's service in, 152
    executions and, 385n48
    liberal tradition view and, 16
    National Rifle Association and, 328,
        412n25
    Native peoples and, 134–35
    1960s critiques of liberal tradition
        view and, 28–29
    penal reform and, 150–51
    political systems and, 408n30
    radical alternatives and, 352
    Thanksgiving and, 14
    wage labor and, 163
Clarkson, Grosvenor, 195
class
    feminism and, 261
    imperialism and, 205, 206
    industrialization and, 151
    Ku Klux Klan and, 223
    1960s critiques of liberal tradition
        view and, 29–30
    penal reform and, 151
    social engineering and, 177
    See also working class
Clayton Anti-Trust Act (1914), 186, 194,
    211–12
Cleveland, Grover, 185, 232
Clinton, Bill
    Pat Buchanan and, 323
    criminal justice system and, 282–83,
        287, 290–91, 331, 412n23
    drug war and, 294–95, 407n22
    immigration policy and, 326–27
    liberal tradition view of American
        history and, 32–33
    neoliberalism and, 282–83, 286
    tech industry and, 305–6, 307, 313

Clinton, Hillary, 341
coerced labor
    British North America, 49, 52–53, 64
    Civil War and, 150–51
    convict lease system, 157–59, 172,
        389n31
    courts on, 169–72, 391n50
    migrant laborers and, 166
    North American colonization and,
        42–45, 49, 59, 64, 371n8
    penal reform and, 146–47, 150, 160
    as spectrum, 49
    See also enslavement; post-emancipation
        coerced labor
coercion
    British North America, 52, 53, 56–57,
        374n27
    characteristics of illiberalism and, 4
    data mining and, 310–11
    1830s political system and, 384n32
    enslavement and, 125
    mass incarceration and, 142
    neoliberalism and, 287
    post-emancipation era, 114–15, 143–
        44, 149
    Puritanism and, 53, 55–56
    rebelliousness against, 56–57
    Reconstruction and, 154–55, 156,
        388–89n26
    slavery to freedom narrative and, 144
    workplace surveillance, 308–10
    See also coerced labor
Cold War
    end of, 12, 31–32, 286, 344, 406n8
    labor movement and, 251
    left movements and, 20, 21–22,
        368n15
    liberal tradition view establishment
        and, 19–22, 31
    McCarthyism and, 22, 23, 263
    neoliberalism and, 284
    policing and, 293, 295
    political right and, 22–23
    radical alternatives and, 352
    Sunbelt suburbs and, 266
    tech industry and, 305
    See also anti-communism

colonial era. *See* British North America
colonial New England, 51–57
    coerced labor, 52–53
    expulsionism, 53–54, 374n28
    feudalism, 50–51
    migrant population, 51–53
    monarchism in, 74
    Native-colonist conflicts, 61, 62–63
    Native peoples, 58, 61
    Puritan theology and, 54–55
    Salem witchcraft trials, 56–57
    social/economic stratification, 52–53
    See also Puritanism
colonization movement, 109, 111–12,
        114, 136, 148, 151, 381n8, 407n19
Commentaries (Blackstone), 49
Committee for Cultural Freedom, 21
common law, 167–69, 170, 391n46
Commons, John R., 189
Common Sense (Paine), 78, 84
communism
    Bolshevik Revolution, 213
    Chinese revolution, 22
    1930s, 19, 21
    See also anti-communism; Cold War
communitarianism, 138
community defense. *See* expulsionism;
        local authority and boundaries
Community Oriented Police Services
        (COPS), 295
Comprehensive Crime Control Bill
        (1984), 290
Confederate flag, 14
Congress for Cultural Freedom, 21
Congress of Industrial Organizations
        (CIO), 239, 244, 251
Conrad, Alfred H., 25
conservatism, 9
    See also political right
Conservative Caucus, 271
Conservative Mind, The (Kirk), 270
Conservative Society of America (CSA),
        268
conspiracy theories, 23, 127–28
Constitution
    American origin stories and, 12, 36,
        101

anti-monarchism in, 74
commerce clause, 285
Native peoples and, 131
popular sovereignty and, 101, 102
See also Bill of Rights; *specific
amendments*
Constitutional Convention, 93–101
Anti-Federalists and, 96–97, 99–100
areas of agreement within, 93–94
fears of slave rebellions and, 95,
380n42
on federal government power, 94–96
indirect representation and, 379n41
monarchism and, 94
radical alternatives and, 351
Contract with America, 306
convict lease system, 157–59, 172,
389n31
Coolidge, Calvin, 232, 233324
cooperative commonwealth, 354
corporations
Gilded Age creation of, 181–84
labor movement and, 184
legal support for, 171–72
New Deal and, 243
Progressivism and, 177, 181–82, 185–
86, 192–93
tech industry and, 312
Woodrow Wilson and, 193–94
See also corporatism
corporatism
Italian fascism and, 234
labor movement and, 184, 185, 186,
212
political systems and, 187, 191–92,
193–94, 195–96, 234–35
Cotton, Tom, 346
Coughlin, Charles E., 241, 355
courts
coerced labor and, 169–72, 391n50
common law, 167–69, 170, 391n46
corporations and, 182, 183
labor movement and, 184
Creeks, 132
criminal justice system
carceral state, 289, 330, 406n12
court fees, 295–96, 407–8n23

drug war, 290, 293, 294–95, 296,
407nn20,22
felon disfranchisement, 297
gun ownership and, 331
Lyndon Johnson and, 288
"law and order" messaging, 282–83
policing, 292–95, 407n18
See also courts; law-and-order campaigns; mass incarceration
Croly, Herbert
corporations and, 181–82
democracy and, 186–87, 189, 190
eugenics and, 176, 197–98, 208
European fascism and, 235
labor movement and, 184–85
on nationalism, 180, 181, 192, 193,
207
socialism and, 180–81
Cromwell, Oliver, 71
Cronkite, Walter, 325
Cruz, Ted, 344–45, 346
cultural homogeneity
British North America, 54
characteristics of illiberalism and, 3, 4
interwar protofascism and, 214
See also expulsionism
"cultural turn," 31–32
culture war, 322–23, 327

Daley, Richard, 275
Dane, Nathaniel, 142, 386n3
D'Annunzio, Gabriele, 221
data mining, 310–11, 409n46
Davis, J. W. H., 357
Debs, Eugene V., 171
Declaration of Independence
abolitionist movement and, 109
American origin stories and, 12, 36,
101
monarchism and, 77–78
universalism and, 102, 103
Delany, Martin, 13
democracy
backcountry settlers and, 82, 103
Black Reconstruction politicians and,
156
characteristics of illiberalism and, 5

democracy (*continued*)
  1830s franchise expansion and, 122, 124
  enslavement and, 125
  frontier thesis and, 18
  illiberal, 2, 140, 191
  Jacksonian, 24, 107, 408n30
  Jeffersonian, 16, 76, 111, 180, 187
  Lincoln ideal and, 106
  Progressivism and, 180, 181, 186–87
  Tocqueville on, 105
  triumphalism of liberal tradition view and, 32, 33
  urban political machines and, 164
  See also liberal tradition view; political systems
Democracy in America (Tocqueville), 22, 105–6, 136–38
Democratic Leadership Council (DLC), 286
Democratic Party
  convict lease system and, 157
  emancipation and, 153
  Equal Rights Amendment and, 261
  immigration and, 161–62, 187
  imperialism and, 206
  Jim Crow regime and, 198, 246, 276
  "law and order" messaging and, 282
  Mormonism and, 121
  National Convention (1968), 275
  neoliberalism and, 286
  New Deal and, 242
  1960s Black uprisings and, 275
  Obama and, 316
  origins of, 162
  postwar segregation and, 256
  Progressivism and, 193–94
  tech industry and, 286, 305–6, 307, 313
  Vietnam War and, 278
  working class and, 188, 251
Deng Xiaoping, 286
DePugh, Robert, 273
deregulation, 283, 285, 286, 300, 302, 306, 307
DeVos, Betsy, 304
DeVos/Prince family, 303

Dewey, George, 205
Díaz, Porfirio, 211
Dickens, Charles, 147
Diggers, 71, 351
digital technology. *See* tech industry
Discipline and Punish: The Birth of the Prison (Foucault), 406n12
disfranchisement
  backcountry settlers, 47
  ex-Confederates, 393–94n26
  felons, 297
  immigrants, 161–63, 164, 187, 190, 231
  Jim Crow regime and, 164, 189, 191, 195, 393n24
  political right and, 301
  Progressivism and, 187–89, 190–91, 393–94n26
  voter registration and, 190–91, 393–94n26
Dodik, Milorad, 345
Doerr, John, 312
Dolan, Terry, 271
dominion theory, 75
Donald, David, 408n30
Donnelly, Ignatius, 159
dotcom bubble, 310
Douglas, Stephen, 121
Draper, Wickcliffe, 325, 411–12n20
Dred Scott v. Sandford (1857), 152, 155
Dreiser, Theodore, 176
Drennan, John, 124
Dr. Strangelove or: How I Learned to Stop Worrying and Love the Bomb (Kubrick), 278
drug war, 290, 293, 294–95, 296, 407nn20,22
Du Bois, W. E. B., 218
dueling, 126
Dukakis, Michael, 286
Duke, David
  background of, 318–19
  Pat Buchanan and, 323411n16
  European right and, 346–47
  immigration policy and, 326, 332
  "national divorce" proposal and, 350
  National Rifle Association and, 330

as neo-Nazi, 318, 319, 320, 410n10
political career of, 319–22
Unite the Right rally and, 335
Durant, Will, 176
Dyson, Esther, 304, 307

Eastern State Penitentiary, 145, 147
economic inequality. *See* social/
economic stratification
Edwards, Edwin, 321, 322
Ehrlich, Anne, 324–25
Ehrlich, Paul, 324–25
1830s
abolitionist movement, 108–12
anti-abolitionist violence, 112–13
anti-Catholicism, 116–17
franchise expansion, 122, 162
Freemasonry, 127–29
individualism, 107
Lincoln on illiberalism during, 106–7,
381n3
lynchings, 108
Mormonism, 118–22, 129
Native removal, 132–34
political system, 122–27, 128–29,
383nn26,29,32
proslavery ideology, 115
status of enslavement during, 113–14,
381n3
Tocqueville on, 105–6, 137–40
Eighteenth Amendment. *See* Prohibition
Eisenhower, Dwight, 262, 263, 284
Elaine race massacre (1919), 217
Eliot, Charles W., 185
Elizabeth I (queen of England), 41
Elkins, Stanley, 25, 369n24
Ellis, Havelock, 175, 176
emancipation
American Revolution and, 77, 87,
149
Civil War and, 151–53
Northwest Ordinance on, 141–43,
153, 381n3, 386n3
penal reform and, 149–50
post-Revolutionary state constitutions
and, 149, 378–79n31
radical alternatives and, 352

Thirteenth Amendment and, 141–42,
152, 153–54
universalism and, 103–4, 381n55
See also post-emancipation era
Emancipation Proclamation, 134, 135, 152
Emergency Quota Act (1921), 232
"end of history," 32–33
End of Ideology, The (Bell), 28
Engel v. Vitale (1962), 274
Engle, Byron, 293
English Civil War, 47, 70–71, 74–75, 76,
81, 351
Enlightenment, 32, 115, 127, 145, 149,
178
Enquiry into the Effects of Public Punish-
ments upon Criminals and upon Society,
An (Rush), 145
enslaved people
Civil War service, 152
emancipation and, 152
rebellions of, 95, 317, 380n42
enslavement
American origin stories and, 36–37
American Revolution and, 77, 95
backcountry settlers and, 48, 81, 83
British North America, 49
capitalism and, 33, 36, 370n35
Cherokees and, 131
class and, 29
coerced labor as spectrum and, 49
Constitutional Convention and, 95
1830s political system and, 125
1830s status of, 113–14, 381n3
Jim Crow regime and, 195
liberal tradition view and, 15–16,
24–26, 143, 369n24
Locke and, 46, 372n14
Mormonism and, 120
of Native peoples, 50, 63, 75, 372n9
1960s critiques of liberal tradition
view and, 28–29
North American colonization and,
42, 44, 46–48, 50, 64, 372nn10,14
policing history and, 292
political right on, 36
proslavery ideology, 112–13, 115,
117–18

enslavement (*continued*)
  1619 Project on, 36–37, 370n38
  slave codes and, 46, 374n27
  Tocqueville on, 137–38
  See also abolitionist movement; eman-
    cipation; enslavers
enslavers
  Anti-Federalists and, 97, 99, 100
  backcountry settler aspirations, 48,
    81, 83
  feudalism and, 62
  local authority and boundaries and,
    99, 100
  Second Great Awakening and, 117
environmentalism, 324–25
Equal Rights Amendment (ERA), 260–
    62, 264–65, 403n23
Espionage Act (1917), 212, 232
eugenics
  contemporary interest in, 392n6
  immigration policy and, 208, 232
  Ku Klux Klan and, 227
  Nazi Germany and, 237–38
  origins of, 175–76
  Progressivism and, 176–77, 197–98,
    207–8, 336
  Margaret Sanger and, 174–75
Eurabia (Ye'or), 335
European fascism, 220–21, 227–28,
    233–38, 239, 241
European Union, 311, 409n46
Evans, Hiram, 224
Evans, M. Stanton, 270
expulsionism
  backcountry settlers and, 82–84, 103
  British North America, 53–54, 63,
    374n28
  characteristics of illiberalism and, 4
  colonization movement as, 109, 111–
    12, 114, 136, 148, 382n8, 407n19
  drug war and, 294, 407n20
  1830s political system and, 127
  First World War and, 407n19
  Freemasonry and, 128
  immigration policy and, 165, 390n41
  mass incarceration and, 287
  McCarthyism and, 22

monarchism and, 103
Mormonism and, 119–22
neoliberalism and, 287, 295, 407n22
post-emancipation era, 114–15, 197
See also disfranchisement; Native
    expulsion

Fairness Doctrine, 285
Falwell, Jerry, 271, 273, 302, 408–9n35
family authority, 264–65
Farmer-Labor Party, 355
Farmers' Alliance, 158, 355
Faulkner, William, 125
Federal Bureau of Investigation (FBI),
    213–14
federal government power
  Constitutional Convention on, 94–96
  emancipation and, 152, 153
  immigration policy and, 231, 232
  neoliberalism on, 301–2
  New Deal and, 242–43, 244
  "problem South" and, 209
  Progressivism and, 192–93, 194
  Prohibition and, 230
  Reconstruction and, 155
  regulation, 192–93, 194, 309
  Sunbelt and, 266, 305
  tech industry and, 304–5, 311
  Tocqueville on, 138
  Whiskey Rebellion and, 100–101
  See also anti-federal government
    perspectives
Federal Housing Administration (FHA),
    254
Federalist Papers, 95–96, 99
Federalists, 95–96, 99, 112, 113
Federal Reserve System, 186, 194
Federal Trade Commission Act (1914),
    186, 194
Federation for American Immigration
    Reform (FAIR), 325
feminism
  birth control and, 175
  criminal justice system and, 289
  Equal Rights Amendment, 260–62,
    264–65, 403n23
  historiography and, 29

Ku Klux Klan and, 225–26
radical alternatives and, 352
feminist history, 29
feudalism
    British North America and, 48, 49,
        50–51, 61–62, 64, 81
    liberal tradition view and, 15, 367n9
    North American colonization and,
        39, 40, 44–45, 52, 64–65, 66
    origins of illiberalism and, 4
    Tocqueville on, 105
    unraveling of, 39–40
    wage labor and, 167, 171
Fidesz Party (Hungary), 343, 345–46
Fiedler, Leslie, 22
Fifteenth Amendment, 152, 163–64,
    165, 188, 231, 261
Fifth Amendment, 183
Filmer, Robert, 45–46
First Amendment, 274, 311
First Great Awakening, 97
First World War
    American Legion and, 218–19, 221
    American Protective League and,
        214–16
    expulsionism and, 407n19
    immigration policy and, 232
    intelligence testing and, 176, 194–95
    labor movement and, 212
    Prohibition and, 230
    racial violence after, 196, 216–17
    repression after, 213, 407n19
    Versailles Treaty, 210–11
Fisher, Irving, 174, 176
Fitzhugh, George, 156
Fordism, 235
foreign policy
    Ku Klux Klan and, 227
    liberal tradition view and, 27
    neoliberalism and, 297–98, 301
    post-Revolutionary period, 88
    Woodrow Wilson and, 210–11
    See also American imperialism
Foucault, Michel, 285, 370n33, 406n12
Fourteenth Amendment
    Christian nationalists on, 303
    corporations and, 171–72, 183

ex-Confederate disfranchisement and,
    393–94n26
importance of, 152, 188
Jim Crow regime and, 393n24
miscegenation and marriage laws and,
    197
Native peoples and, 165
segregation and, 200
Supreme Court on, 170
Fox News, 335, 336
France, 343
franchise. *See* disfranchisement; voting
    rights
Frank, Waldo, 245
Franklin, Benjamin, 65, 79, 103, 127
Freedmen's Bureau, 155, 389n34
free labor ideal
    feudalism and, 167
    post-emancipation coerced labor and,
        147, 150–51, 159, 166–67
    Reconstruction and, 142
    slavery/freedom binary and, 160, 161,
        166–67
    Thirteenth Amendment and, 169
    wage labor and, 155, 159
    See also wage labor
Freeman, Elizabeth (Mumbet), 381n55
Freemasonry, 127–29, 223
French and Indian (Seven Years') War,
    68, 79, 85
French Revolution, 3, 12, 101, 141
Friedman, Milton, 174, 284, 297–98,
    301, 302–3
frontier thesis, 18
Fuentes, Nick, 350
Fugitive Slave Acts, 292
Fukuyama, Francis, 32
Fundamental Constitutions of Carolina
    (1669), 45
fundamentalism
    1920s, 214, 224–25
    1960s, 273–74, 302

Galton, Francis, 175
game theory, 28
Garrison, William Lloyd, 109, 112
Garrity, W. Arthur, Jr., 258–59

Garvey, Marcus, 13, 217, 218
Gary, Elbert, 234
Gates, Bill, 340
Gates, Daryl, 290, 293
gay rights movement, 352
gender. *See* patriarchy; women
General Data Protection Regulation
    (GDPR), 409n46
George, Henry, 192
George III (king of England), 73, 74,
    77–79
German American Bund, 239, 241
Gerstle, Gary, 283, 406nn8–9
gig economy, 308
Gilbert, Humphrey, 41
Gilded Age
    corporations during, 181–84
    critiques of liberalism during, 178–79
    See also Progressivism
Gingrich, Newt, 304, 306–7, 334,
    413n36
Glass-Steagall Banking Act (1933), 243,
    283
global financial crisis (2007–2008), 33
Glorious Revolution (England) (1688),
    71, 74, 75
Goethals, George Washington, 202
Goethe, C. M., 238
Goldwater, Barry
    John Birch Society and, 268, 269, 272
    1964 electoral defeat, 249–50, 256,
        266, 284
    Phyllis Schlafly and, 262–63
    George Wallace and, 277
    Young Americans for Freedom and,
        271
Gompers, Samuel, 185, 212, 235–36
Gorbachev, Mikhail, 31, 286
Gordon, Linda, 225, 227
Gore, Al
    criminal justice system and, 282
    neoliberalism and, 286, 307, 313
    political right and, 323
    tech industry and, 305, 306, 307, 312–
        13, 410n48
Gorham, Nathan, 92
Grady, Henry, 208

Gramm-Leach Bill (1999), 283
Graves, William, 126
Great Depression, 239, 240, 355
great migration (New England), 51–52
Great Migrations of African Americans,
    217, 223, 250–54
Great Recession (2007–2008), 296, 340
great replacement theory, 335–37, 346
Great Society, 3, 249, 284
Green, William, 236
Greenback Labor Party, 158, 188, 192,
    355, 356
Greene, Marjorie Taylor, 346, 349
Greer, Allan, 52
Grimes County interracial coalition,
    356–57, 358
Grow, Galusha A., 126
Gun Control Act (1968), 328
gun rights movement. *See* National Rifle
    Association

Haiti, 211, 317
Hakluyt, Richard the Elder, 38, 40
Hakluyt, Richard the Younger, 38, 40
Hamilton, Alexander, 92, 94, 95–96, 181
Handlin, Oscar, 26–27
Hanna, Mark, 185, 186
Hannah-Jones, Nikole, 36
Harberger, Arnold, 297–98
Harding, Warren G., 226, 232
Hargis, Billy, 268, 273, 274
Harlem Renaissance, 352
Harrington, James, 71
Hart, Gary, 286
Hart-Celler Act (1965), 324, 411n16
Hartz, Louis, 15–16, 26, 28, 34, 367n9,
    370n36
Harvey, John, 83
Hayden, Tom, 270–71
Hayek, Friedrich, 284, 298
Haynes, Jack, 357
headright system, 44, 45
Heerman, Scott, 381n3
Henry, Patrick, 68
Henry VIII (king of England), 70
Heritage Foundation, 284
Hicks, Granville, 22

Hicks, John, 18
Hicks, Louise Day, 258–59
hierarchy
  abolitionist movement on, 110
  Black Codes and, 116
  Catholicism and, 54, 71
  characteristics of illiberalism and,
    3, 4
  colonization of Ireland and, 40
  Native peoples and, 59
  1960s political right and, 270
  Panama Canal Zone and, 201–2, 207
  Puritanism and, 50–51
  racism and, 15
  Second Great Awakening and, 117
  tech industry and, 311
  See also social/economic
    stratification
Higham, John, 26, 27, 221
Hitler, Adolf, 236–37, 324
Hobbes, Thomas, 2, 74–75, 110
Hobsbawn, Eric, 14
Hofstadter, Richard, 16–17, 23, 249,
    266, 365–66n8
Hook, Sidney, 22
Hoover, J. Edgar, 213
Hough, Emerson, 214, 215, 216
House Un-American Activities Commit-
    tee (HUAC), 22
Housing Opportunity Extension Act
    (1996), 407n22
housing segregation
  postwar Black northern migration
    and, 251–54
  postwar suburbs and, 254–56
  restrictive covenants, 200, 254–55
Howard, Jacob, 153–54
Howard, John, 145
Howe, Samuel Gridley, 160, 389n34
Hulliung, Mark, 34
Humphrey, Hubert H., 21, 275, 276,
    277, 278, 280
Hungary, 343, 345–46
Huntington, Samuel P., 299–300, 313,
    408n30
Hutchinson, Anne, 54
Hutchinson, Thomas, 67, 68, 69, 72, 73

Illegal Immigration Reform and Immi-
    grant Responsibility Act (1996),
    326–27
"illiberal democracy," 2, 140, 191
Illiberalism
  Alexis de Tocqueville and, 136–40
  American Revolution and, 70–85
  Anti-Catholicism and, 55–56, 67–75,
    97, 116–18, 134–36, 161–63,
    221–33
  Anti-Federalism and, 97–101
  Anti-Mormonism and, 118–22, 162
  Bill Clinton and, 282–83, 294–95,
    305–8, 312–13
  characteristics of, 3, 4
  Chicago School and, 297–304
  coherence of, 4
  current views of, 1–2
  emancipation and, 141–51, 159–73
  hi-tech and, 304–13
  historical roots of, 4, 365–66n8
  immigration and, 161–65, 228–33,
    323–37
  Jacksonian democracy and, 105–29
  liberal intentions and, 10
  MAGA movement and, 35
  mass incarceration and, 287–97
  Native peoples and, 57–63, 79–81,
    129–37, 166
  Neoliberalism and, 282–313
  1960s and, 247–81
  Penitentiary and, 144–51
  Progressivism and, 17–18
  political systems and, 5–6
  Puritans and, 49–57
  reinvention of, 35
  settler colonialism and, 42–66, 79–85
  variations in, 4–5
immigration
  anti-democratic perspectives and,
    187–88
  disfranchisement and, 161–63, 164,
    187, 190, 231
  liberal tradition view and, 26–27
  1960s critiques of liberal tradition
    view and, 29
  Prohibition and, 230

immigration (*continued*)
  race war fears and, 317
  social engineering and, 177
  twenty-first-century political right
    and, 315, 317, 322
  wage labor and, 161
  See also immigration policy; nativism
Immigration Act (1891), 231, 399n36
Immigration Act (Johnson-Reed Act)
  (1924), 232–33, 324
immigration policy
  Chinese Exclusion Act, 165, 390n41
  environmentalism and, 324–25
  eugenics and, 208, 232
  First World War and, 232
  great replacement theory and, 336
  interwar protofascism and, 231–32,
    324–25, 399nn36–37
  Johnson-Reed Act, 232–33
  Ku Klux Klan and, 232
  nativism and, 230–31, 399n35
  Nazi Germany and, 237, 324, 400n47
  racism and, 233, 323–24, 325, 332,
    336, 411n18
  Reagan administration and, 326, 412n21
  Tea Party movement and, 338
  twenty-first-century political right
    and, 323–27, 411n16
Immigration Reform and Control Act
  (IRCA) (1986), 412n21
Immigration Restriction League (IRL),
  214, 324, 399n37
incarceration. *See* mass incarceration;
  penal reform
indentured servitude
  disfranchisement and, 46–47
  enslavement and, 48
  legal ambiguity on, 169
  North American colonization and,
    42, 43–44, 52–53, 64
  Thirteenth Amendment and, 142–43
Indian removal. *See* Native expulsion
Indian Removal Act (1830), 133
Indigenous peoples. *See* Native peoples
individualism
  Gilded Age critiques of liberalism
    and, 178

liberalism and, 15, 36, 107
  neoliberalism and, 284, 287
  1960s political right and, 271
  Progressivism and, 180
  twenty-first-century political right
    and, 35
Industrial America in the World War (Clarkson), 195
industrialization
  Civil War and, 150, 163
  class and, 151
  coerced labor and, 49, 158
  immigration and, 231
  Jim Crow regime and, 198–99
  migrant labor and, 165–66
  Progressivism and, 178
  social engineering and, 177
  wage labor and, 163
Industrial Workers of the World (IWW),
  212, 215, 216, 220
intelligence testing, 176, 194–95
internet, 305–6, 312–13, 344, 410n48
  See also tech industry
Interstate Commerce Act (1887), 192
interwar protofascism
  American Legion and, 218–21, 223
  American Protective League and,
    214–16, 223
  Black freedom struggles and, 217–18
  corporatism and, 234–35
  European fascism and, 220–21, 227–
    28, 233–38, 239, 241
  FBI creation and, 213–14
  immigration policy and, 231–32, 324–
    25, 399nn36–37
  Ku Klux Klan and, 214, 221–28
  nativism and, 214
  New Deal and, 241–45
  1930s, 239–41
  100 percent Americanism and, 214,
    218, 219
  racial violence, 196–97, 216–17
  Red Scare and, 213
  vigilantism and, 215–16, 220, 224,
    227, 229
Intolerable Acts (1774), 73–74
invented traditions, 14

Ireland, English colonization of, 40–41
Islamophobia, 335
Italy
    fascism, 220–21, 227, 233–35
    twenty-first-century political right,
        346–47
It Can't Happen Here (Lewis), 245

Jackson, Andrew, 130, 132–33, 385n43
Jacksonian democracy, 24, 107, 408n30
James, William, 236
James I (king of England), 59
Jay, John, 92, 95
Jefferson, Thomas
    backcountry rebellions and, 84, 93
    emancipation and, 142, 153
    enslavement and, 137
    on "Negro problem," 198
    political systems and, 101–2
    racism of, 102, 114
    slave rebellions and, 380n42
    See also Jeffersonian democracy
Jeffersonian democracy, 16, 76, 111,
    180, 187
Jim Crow regime
    Black community institutions and, 259
    Confederate flag and, 14
    and enslavement, 195
    Democratic Party and, 198, 246, 276
    disfranchisement, 164, 189, 191, 195,
        393n24
    interracial coalitions during, 356–57
    Ku Klux Klan and, 222
    labor movement, 170
    lynchings and, 108, 195–96, 394n34
    Nazi Germany and, 237
    New Deal and, 246
    1960s political right and, 268
    northern precursors of, 115
    one-drop rule and, 197, 395n37
    Republican Southern Strategy and, 276
    resistance to, 217–18
    school desegregation and, 256
    segregation, 198–200, 207, 218, 219
    Thirteenth Amendment and, 143
    George Wallace and, 249, 250, 273,
        337

    See also post-emancipation coerced
        labor
Jobs, Steve, 304, 305
John Birch Society (JBS), 263, 267–69,
    271–72, 273, 274–75, 276, 300
Johnson, Albert, 232
Johnson, Andrew, 154
Johnson, James Weldon, 216–17
Johnson, J. Bennett, 321
Johnson, Lyndon
    Goldwater defeat and, 249, 256
    Great Society and, 284
    immigration policy and, 324
    Kerner Commission and, 275, 289
    mass incarceration and, 288, 289
    Vietnam War and, 275, 278
Johnson-Reed Act (1924), 232–33, 324
Jordan, David Starr, 176
Journal (Winthrop), 53, 374n28

Kean, Thomas, 100
Keefe, Daniel, 185
Kennard, Jim, 356, 357
Kennedy, John F., 272, 288
Kennedy, Robert F., 275
Kerner Commission, 275, 289, 293
Keynesianism, 284, 285, 286
King, Martin Luther, Jr., 13, 247, 253,
    275, 277, 280
King, Rufus, 386n3
King Philip's War (1675–78), 62–63
Kirk, Russell, 270
Kloppenberg, James, 370n36
Knight, Frank, 284
Knights of Labor, 158, 355
Knights of the Ku Klux Klan, 318–19,
    323
Knott, Walter, 267
Know Nothing Party, 129, 161–62,
    187
Knox, Clifford, 328–29
Knox, Henry, 131
Koch brothers, 300–301
Koch Foundation, 284
Krier, Herbert, 400n47
Kristol, Irving, 22
Kubrick, Stanley, 278

Ku Klux Klan, 214, 221–29
  David Duke and, 318–19, 322
  European fascism and, 239
  immigration policy and, 232
  membership of, 222–23, 398n23
  twenty-first-century political right
    and, 316
  Unite the Right rally and, 335
  George Wallace and, 273

labor movement
  American Protective League vigilan-
    tism and, 215–16
  Black freedom struggles and, 218
  Cold War and, 251
  convict lease system and, 158
  corporatism and, 184, 185, 186, 212
  disfranchisement and, 189
  eight-hour workday and, 171, 390n38
  European fascism and, 235–36
  First World War and, 212
  Gilded Age, 178
  immigration policy and, 232
  interwar protofascism and, 213, 214
  interwar radicalism of, 212–13
  Jim Crow regime and, 170
  legal constraints on, 171–72
  neoliberalism and, 285, 308
  New Deal and, 243
  1960s political right and, 277, 280
  penal reform and, 147
  Populism and, 354–55
  post-Civil War legislative reforms,
    171
  Progressivism and, 184–86
  racism and, 339
  radical alternatives and, 351, 352
  school desegregation and, 260
  twenty-first-century political right
    and, 341
  voting rights and, 164
  weakening of, 308, 316
  Woodrow Wilson and, 210, 211–12
Lacombe, Matthew J., 412n28
Lake, Kari, 346
Lamarck, Jean-Baptiste, 178
Lamont, Thomas, 234

Landon, Alf, 246
Land Ordinance (1785), 386n3
land ownership
  colonial backcountry settlers and,
    81, 83
  colonial New England, 52
  English Civil War and, 71
  Native-colonist conflicts and, 59–61
  Reconstruction and, 155
  republicanism and, 76, 110
LaPierre, Wayne, 330, 331, 332
Laud, William, 70
Laughlin, Harry, 232, 238
Law and Justice Party (Poland), 344
law-and-order campaigns, 215, 276–77,
    282–83
"law and order" messaging, 282–83
League of Nations, 210, 211, 227
Lee, Richard Henry, 386n3
left movements
  Cold War and, 20, 21–22, 368n15
  criticisms of liberalism, 33–34
  Great Depression and, 240
  inclusion and, 9–10
  1930s, 19
  1960s critiques of liberal tradition
    view and, 28, 30
  Second World War and, 19
Lehman, Herbert, 272
LeMay, Curtis, 277–78
Le Pen, Jean-Marie, 343
Le Pen, Marine, 346
Levellers, 56, 71, 82, 351, 374n31
Levitt, William, 254–55
Levy, Anne, 410n10
Levy, Barry, 53
Lewis, Sinclair, 245
liberalism
  characteristics of, 2–3
  Gilded Age critiques of, 178–79, 206
  grassroots invocations of, 353–54,
    415n3
  hegemony of, 31
  individualism and, 15, 36, 107
  left criticisms of, 33–34
  New England colonial plantations as
    seed beds of, 51–52

1960s critiques of, 274
political systems and, 5
post-Cold War triumphalism of, 32–33
self-ownership and, 46, 110, 142
See also republicanism
liberal self, 46, 110, 114
Liberal Tradition in America, The (Hartz),
15–16, 26, 28, 34, 367n9, 370n36
liberal tradition view, 12–13, 15–37
American studies movement and,
23–24, 25, 29
as basis of American exceptionalism
and, 1, 13, 366n4
as break from earlier historiography,
17–19
Cold War-era establishment of,
19–22, 31
colonial backcountry rebellions and,
79, 80–81
contemporary emergence of illiberalism and, 12
criticisms as intrinsic to, 33–34
current invocations of, 3–4, 11–13,
33, 366n2
1830s political system and, 122
1830s solidification of, 107
emancipation and, 142
enslavement and, 15–16, 24–26, 143,
369n24
on foreign policy, 27
Hartz on, 15–16, 367n9
Hofstadter on, 16–17, 23, 365–66n8
immigration and, 26–27
invented elements of, 14
invention of, 6, 11–37
Lincoln ideal, 106
Native peoples and, 58
New Deal and, 16, 19, 20, 31, 238
1960s and, 249–50, 266
1960s critiques of, 28–30, 370n31
origin story of, 36
persistent invocation of, 30–31
political right and, 16, 22–23
postmodern "cultural turn" and,
31–32
quantitative/functional methods and,
27–28, 32, 369n27

racial capitalism and, 33, 370n35
reinvention of, 34–35
1619 Project and, 36–37
Tocqueville and, 105–6
triumphalism of, 32–33
twenty-first-century political right
and, 3, 11–13, 33, 342, 350, 366n2
US embrace of, 13–14
Liberator, The, 109
Liberty Lobby, 320
Lieber, Francis, 145
Lincoln, Abraham
assassination of, 385n48
emancipation and, 142, 151–52
free labor ideal and, 161, 162
on illiberalism, 106–7, 381n3
Mormonism and, 121
Native peoples and, 129–30, 134–35
Progressivism and, 193
racism and, 135–36
Thanksgiving and, 14
Lincoln ideal, 106
Lindsay, John, 325
Lippman, Walter, 242, 245
Little, Earl, 224
Little Crow, 134
local authority and boundaries
American Protective League and, 215
Anti-Federalists and, 97, 99–100, 138
Articles of Confederation and, 88
backcountry settlers and, 84–85, 99, 103
Bill of Rights and, 100
Black freedom struggles and, 259–60
Black northern migration and, 251–
52, 253–54
British North America, 53, 56, 65, 81
characteristics of illiberalism and, 3, 4
cultural homogeneity and, 54
1830s political system and, 122–23
Huey Long and, 240–41
lynchings and, 195–96
monarchism and, 103
Native-colonist conflicts and, 85
1960s political right and, 250, 264–65,
274, 280
patriarchy and, 264–65
postwar federal benefits and, 251

local authority and boundaries
(*continued*)
Puritanism and, 54
school desegregation and, 256–57,
259
Tocqueville on, 138–39
twenty-first-century political right
and, 35
Locke, John
American origin stories and, 101
anti-Catholicism and, 71
Constitutional Convention and, 98
enslavement and, 46, 372n14
individualism and, 15
monarchism and, 75
on Native peoples, 58
North American colonization and,
45–46, 372n14
on self-ownership, 46, 110
on social/political contract, 2
Lodge, Henry Cabot, 206, 231–32, 233,
399n37
Long, Huey, 240–41, 245, 249, 355
Long Hot Summer (1967), 275
Louisiana Coalition Against Racism and
Nazism, 320
Lovejoy, Elijah, 108, 121
Luce, Henry, 27
Lustig, Jeffrey, 193
Lyft, 308–9
Lynch, Charles, 78
lynchings, 108, 195–96, 216, 394n34

Machiavelli, Niccolò, 41, 110
Mackintosh, Ebenezer, 69, 70
Madison, James, 92, 93, 94–96, 98, 99,
380n42
MAGA movement, 35
Magna Carta, 102
majoritarianism
characteristics of illiberalism and, 3
Manhattan Institute, 284
Manhattan Project, 305
Marxism, 29–30
Masons, 127–29, 223
Massachusetts, 53, 104
See also colonial New England

mass incarceration
carceral state and, 289, 330, 406n12
coercion and, 142
National Rifle Association and, 330
neoliberalism and, 287–92
penal reform and, 389n31
racism and, 287–88, 289, 290
Thirteenth Amendment and, 159
twenty-first-century political right
and, 316
masterless men, 39–40, 156–57
Masur, Kate, 116
Matthias, Robert, 117, 118
May, Cordelia Scaife, 325
Mayflower Compact, 51
McAdoo, William G., 226
McCarthy, Eugene, 275, 325
McCarthyism, 22, 23, 263
McCormick, Cyrus, 185
McDonnell, Michael, 84
McGirr, Lisa, 230
McGovern, George, 279–80
McIntosh, Francis, 108
McLennan, Rebecca, 147, 150
McVeigh, Timothy, 333–34
Mein Kampf (Hitler), 236, 318
Meloni, Giorgia, 346
Mendel, Gregor, 178
Mengele, Josef, 237–38
Mercer Family Foundation, 303
Meredith, James, 263
Metacom (Wampanoag sachem), 62,
63
Metzger, Tom, 319
Mexican immigrants, 325–26, 327
Mexican Revolution (1910–1920), 197,
211
Meyer, John R., 25
microhistorical approaches, 31
Mid-Atlantic colonies, 63–66, 79
migrant labor, 165–66
Military Cooperation and Enforcement
Act (1981), 294
militias, 272–73, 315, 317, 333–34,
413n36
Miller, Glenn, 332
Miller, Perry, 23–24, 55, 368n21

Miller, Stephen, 335
Milton, John, 71
Minutemen, 272–73
miscegenation and marriage laws, 197–
    98, 227, 237
Mises, Ludwig von, 284
Mitchell, John, 185
"Modell of Christian Charitie, A" (Win-
    throp), 50–51, 373n23
monarchism
    American Revolution and, 77–79,
        85–86
    American Revolution approach and,
        75–77
    British North America, 73–77
    colonial backcountry rebellions and,
        93
    Constitutional Convention and, 94
    post-Revolutionary period, 102–3
    Shays's Rebellion and, 92
Mondale, Walter, 406n6
Monroe Doctrine, 204, 205
Montesquieu, 98–99, 145
Mont Pelerin Society, 284, 300
Moore, Michael, 330
Moral Majority, 271, 273, 302
Morawiecki, Mateusz, 346
Morgan, Edmund S., 53, 102
Morgan, John T., 158–59
Morgan, J. P., 185
Mormonism, 118–22, 129
Morris, William, 358–59
Moynihan, Daniel Patrick, 406n10
Murphy, Edgar Gardner, 199–200
Muskie, Edmund, 280
Mussolini, Benito, 220–21, 227, 233–34,
    235, 236
Myrdal, Gunnar, 343

NAACP (National Association for the
    Advancement of Colored People),
    217, 218, 256, 258
National Association for the Advance-
    ment of White People (NAAWP),
    319
National Association of Manufacturers,
    186, 239, 245–46

National Civic Federation, 185–86, 193,
    194, 236
National Defense Authorization Secu-
    rity Act (1997), 295
National Guard, 293, 294, 407n18
National Industrial Recovery Act
    (NIRA), 243
National Rally/National Front (France),
    343
National Recovery Administration
    (NRA), 245
National Review, 263, 267, 269, 271–72
National Rifle Association (NRA), 328–
    32, 334, 412nn25,28,30
National Science Foundation, 305
National Union for Social Justice, 241
Native-colonist conflicts
    American Revolution and, 85
    Anti-Federalists and, 97
    backcountry rebellions and, 62, 79–80
    enslavement and, 49
    land ownership and, 59–61
    Native expulsion and, 83–84
    Restoration and, 61–62
    witchcraft trials and, 57
    See also Native expulsion
Native expulsion
    backcountry settlers and, 83–84,
        130–31
    colonial New England, 63
    colonization movement and, 112
    Indian Territory and, 133–34
    Andrew Jackson and, 132–33
    Lincoln and, 134–35
    Theodore Roosevelt on, 204
    Supreme Court on, 385n43
    terminology for, 382n8
    Tocqueville on, 137
Native peoples
    American Revolution and, 85, 131
    Civil War and, 134–35
    coerced labor and, 164–65
    cultural accommodation and,
        131–32
    disease and, 57, 375nn33,39
    enslavement of, 50, 63, 75, 372n9
    feudalism and, 40

Native peoples (*continued*)
hierarchy and, 59
Mormonism and, 118, 120, 121
North American colonization and,
40, 42, 57, 58–63, 372n9
radical alternatives and, 353
Tocqueville on, 137
See also Native-colonist conflicts;
Native expulsion
nativism
abolitionist movement and, 231
anti-Catholicism and, 161, 162–63
disenfranchisement and, 161–62,
187–88
Freemasonry and, 129
immigration policy and, 230–31,
399n35
interwar protofascism and, 214
Ku Klux Klan and, 222
liberal tradition view on, 26
Populism and, 23
social engineering and, 177
Nazi Germany, 236–38, 241, 242, 243,
324, 395n37, 400n47
*Negro Family, The: A Case for National
Action* (Moynihan), 406n10
Nelson, Eric, 75
neo-Confederates, 335
neoliberalism, 282–92
anti-democratic perspectives and,
287, 299–301, 313, 408nn28–30
broad appeal of, 286–87
Chile and, 297–98
Christian nationalism and, 302–4
Bill Clinton and, 282–83, 286
court fees and, 295–96, 407–8n23
definitions of liberalism and, 3
deregulation and, 283, 285, 286, 300,
302, 306, 307
end of Cold War and, 286, 406n8
foreign policy and, 297–98, 301
gig economy and, 308–9
immigration policy and, 326
mass incarceration and, 287–92
1970s economic crises and, 284–85
origins of, 283–84, 406n9

political right and, 300–304
radical alternatives and, 352
Reagan and, 285–86
social/economic stratification and,
313
tech industry and, 286, 304–8, 311
Trilateral Commission and, 284, 285,
406n6
workplace power dynamics and,
307–8
neo-Nazis
David Duke and, 318, 319, 320,
410n10
European right and, 344
"national divorce" proposal and, 350
Unite the Right rally and, 317, 334
white power movement and, 316
New Deal
American exceptionalism and,
366n4
characteristics of liberalism and, 3
conservative backlash against, 22,
245–46, 267, 270
federal government power and, 242–
43, 244
interwar protofascism and, 241–45
Italian fascism and, 234
liberal tradition view and, 16, 19, 20,
31, 238
Huey Long and, 241
neoliberalism and, 284
Populism and, 355
Progressivism and, 29
radical alternatives and, 352
southern landowners and, 243–44
Sunbelt suburbs and, 266
working class and, 251
New England Anti-Slavery Society,
109
New England Mind (Miller), 23–24
New Guard, The, 270
"New Negro," 217
New Republic, The, 180
New Right party (Denmark), 343–44
Ngai, Mae, 411n18
Nichols, Terry, 334

Niebuhr, Reinhold, 21
1920s. *See* interwar protofascism
1960s
Black uprisings, 275, 289, 317, 328
environmentalism, 324–25
liberal tradition view and, 249–50, 266
National Rifle Association, 328
radical alternatives during, 352
See also 1960s political right
1960s political right
anti-abortion movement, 264–65
anti-communism and, 262, 263, 264,
266, 267–70
anti-ERA campaign, 262, 263–64
Jim Crow regime and, 268
militias, 272–73
Nixon campaign (1968), 275–77,
278
Protestant evangelicalism and, 264, 266
Sunbelt suburbs and, 266–67
See also Goldwater, Barry; Wallace,
George C.
Nineteenth Amendment, 191
Nixon, Richard, 261, 263, 271, 275–77,
278, 279, 322
Non-Partisan League, 355
Norse explorers, 375n33
North American colonization
capitalism and, 38–39
coerced labor and, 42–45, 49, 59, 64,
371n8
enslavement and, 42, 44, 46–48, 50,
64, 372nn10,14
European masterless men and, 40
feudalism and, 39, 40, 44–45, 52,
64–65, 66
indentured servitude and, 42, 43–44,
52–53, 64
Locke and, 45–46, 372n14
Mid-Atlantic colonies, 63–66
migrant population, 51–53, 65
Native peoples and, 40, 42, 57, 58–63,
372n9
radical alternatives and, 351
slave trade and, 42, 46, 47
See also British North America

North American Free Trade Agreement
(NAFTA), 283, 326
Northwest Ordinance (1787), 134, 141–
43, 153, 169, 381n3, 386n3

Oath Keepers, 315
Obama, Barack
American exceptionalism and, 13
election of, 314–15
liberal triumphalism and, 33
policing and, 295
progressive coalition of, 315–16
reelection of, 341
right-wing backlash and, 315, 317,
334, 337–39
Tea Party movement and, 337–39, 340
Office of Public Safety (OPS), 293
Oklahoma City bombing (1995),
333–34
Olin Foundation, 303
Oliver, Andrew, 67, 68–69, 72, 73
100 percent Americanism
American Legion and, 219
immigration policy and, 233
interwar protofascism and, 214, 218,
219
Ku Klux Klan and, 222, 223–24
Nazi Germany and, 239
Prohibition and, 229
social engineering and, 177
one-drop rule, 197, 395n37
Operation Gatekeeper, 326
Orbán, Viktor, 345–46
Owsley, Alvin, 221, 228

Packard, David, 305
Paine, Thomas, 78, 84, 86
Paley, William Dudley, 239
Palladino, Elvira "Pixie," 260–61
Palmer, A. Mitchell, 213, 218
Palmer Raids, 213
Panama Canal Zone, 201–3
Panic of 1873, 160–61
Parkman, Francis, 163
Parrington, Vernon, 18
Parsons, Talcott, 27

Partisan Review, 20
patriarchy
    anti-feminism and, 264–65
    1830s political system and, 127
    Second Great Awakening and, 117
    twenty-first-century political right
        and, 35
Patriotic Party, 273
patronage, 123, 124–25
Paul, Alice, 403n23
Paxton Boys, 79–80, 84
Peculiar Institution, The: Slavery in the Ante-
    bellum South (Stampp), 24–25
penal reform, 144–51
    abolitionist movement and, 148–50,
        388n15
    coerced labor and, 146–47, 150, 160
    mass incarceration and, 389n31
    Rush and, 145–46
    Tocqueville on, 144–45
Pence, Mike, 345
penitentiary system. *See* penal reform
Penn, John, 79
Penn, William, 64
Pennsylvania, 64, 79, 86
Pequot War (1636–38), 61
Percy, Walker, 321–22
Pershing, John, 211
Phillips, Howard, 271
Phillips, Ulrich B., 24–25
Pinchot, Gifford, 176
Pinkertons, 214
Pinochet, Augusto, 298, 301
Pioneer Fund, 325, 411–12n20
Pledge of Allegiance, 14
Plessy v. Ferguson (1896), 199, 203
policing, 292–95, 407n18
political right, 9
    Christian nationalism, 302–4,
        408–9n35
    Cold War era, 22–23
    criticisms of liberalism, 33
    enslavement studies and, 36
    liberal tradition view and, 16, 22–23
    militias, 272–73, 315, 317, 333–34,
        413n36
    neoliberalism and, 300–304

New Deal and, 246
    See also 1960s political right; twenty-
        first-century political right
political systems
    Articles of Confederation and, 87–88
    characteristics of illiberalism and, 5–6
    characteristics of liberalism and, 5
    Civil War and, 408n30
    colonial New England, 51
    Constitution on, 93–97
    corporatism, 187, 191–92, 193–94,
        195–96, 234–35
    1830s, 122–27, 128–29,
        383nn26,29,32
    Ku Klux Klan and, 226–27
    liberal tradition view and, 12–13,
        366n4
    Lincoln ideal and, 106
    political right and, 301
    Populism on, 355
    post-Revolutionary state constitutions
        and, 86–87, 89–90
    Progressivism and, 178, 187, 189–91,
        193, 299
    radical alternatives and, 351, 352,
        355
    urban political machines and, 164, 188
    See also anti-democratic perspectives;
        Constitution; Constitutional Con-
        vention; democracy; monarchism;
        republicanism; voting rights
Pompeo, Mike, 346
Pontiac's War (1763–66), 79–80
Pope, John, 134–35
Pope's Day, 69–70, 72, 73, 74
Popper, Karl, 284
Popular Front, 21
popular sovereignty, 81, 101, 102, 138
    See also democracy
Population Bomb, The (Ehrlich and
    Ehrlich), 324–25
Populism
    Cold War-era political right and, 23
    convict lease system and, 158
    government regulation and, 192
    Grimes County coalition and, 356–
        57, 358

Hofstadter on, 17, 23
1960s critiques of liberal tradition
  view and, 29
radical alternatives and, 354–57, 358
twenty-first-century political right
  and, 354
voting rights and, 189
Populist (People's) Party (1890s), 354
Populist Party (1988), 319–20
Port Huron Statement (SDS), 269, 271
post-emancipation coerced labor,
  172–73
  abolitionist movement and, 153, 154,
    172–73
  Black Codes and, 154–55
  as continuation of enslavement, 172
  convict lease system, 157–59, 172,
    389n31
  free labor ideal and, 147, 150–51, 159,
    166–67
  sharecroppers, 168
  Supreme Court and, 170
  vagrancy laws and, 156–57, 160–61,
    164–66, 388–89n26
post-emancipation era
  anti-democratic perspectives, 187–88
  Black Codes, 154–55, 159, 160,
    388n26
  Black political empowerment, 155–
    56, 188
  coercion and, 114–15, 143–44, 149
  expulsionism, 114–15, 197
  Freedmen's Bureau, 155, 389n34
  liberal tradition view and, 16
  miscegenation and marriage laws,
    197–98
  northern racial violence, 196–97
  northern segregation, 200
  penal reform and, 148–49
  Thirteenth Amendment and, 153–54,
    158–59
  See also Jim Crow regime; post-eman-
    cipation coerced labor
postmodernism, 32, 370n33
post-Revolutionary period, 85–92
  Articles of Confederation, 74, 87–88,
    93

backcountry rebellions, 89, 90, 91 -92,
  93
debt crisis, 88–91, 92, 100
monarchism, 102–3
Native peoples, 131
state constitutions, 86–87, 89–90,
  104, 149, 167, 378–79n31
Whiskey Rebellion, 100–101
postwar era
  American studies movement, 23–24, 25
  Black northern migration, 250–54
  federal benefits, 251
  quantitative/functional methods, 27–28
  See also Cold War
Powhatans, 58, 59
Prager, Dennis, 345
privatization, 291, 296, 298, 302
Progressive (Bull Moose) Party, 193
progressive school in American historiography, 18–19
Progressivism, 177–81
  capitalism and, 169, 179–80
  corporations and, 177, 181–82, 185–
    86, 192–93
  corporatism and, 235
  disfranchisement and, 187–89, 190–
    91, 393–94n26
  eugenics and, 176–77, 197–98, 207–8,
    336
  government regulation and, 192–93,
    194
  Hofstadter on, 17
  immigration policy and, 233
  imperialism and, 207
  Jim Crow regime and, 209
  labor movement and, 184–86
  liberal tradition view and, 16
  nationalism and, 180, 181, 192, 193
  1960s critiques of liberal tradition
    view and, 29
  political systems and, 187, 189–91,
    193, 299
  "problem South" and, 208–9
  segregation and, 199–200, 207
  social engineering and, 177
  socialism and, 179–81
  social theories of, 179–80

Progressivism (*continued*)
   temperance movement and, 230
   wage labor and, 178, 185–86
Prohibition
   Ku Klux Klan and, 228–29
   social engineering and, 177, 229
   temperance movement and, 229–30
Promise of American Life, The (Croly), 180,
   193
Proposition 14 (California), 255–56
Proposition 187 (California), 323, 326,
   411n16
proslavery ideology, 112–13, 115,
   117–18
Protestant Christianity
   abolitionist movement and, 109
   anti-ERA campaign and, 264
   characteristics of illiberalism and, 3
   enslavement and, 46
   First Great Awakening, 97
   Freemasonry and, 127, 128–29
   Ku Klux Klan and, 223, 224–25
   Native peoples and, 61, 131
   1920s fundamentalism, 214, 224–25
   1960s fundamentalism, 273–74, 302
   post-Revolutionary state constitutions
     and, 87
   proslavery ideology and, 115
   Protestant evangelicalism, 264, 266,
     340
   Second Great Awakening, 109, 115,
     117–18, 128–29
   Tea Party movement and, 338
   See also Puritanism
Protestant Reformation, 39, 41, 70, 71
Proud Boys, 317, 350
Pullman strike (1894), 171
Puritanism
   American studies movement on,
     23–24, 368n21
   anti-Catholicism and, 70, 71
   coercion and, 53, 55–56
   English Civil War and, 70
   hierarchy and, 50–51
   local authority and boundaries and,
     54
   monarchism and, 74

   Native peoples and, 61, 131
   theology of, 54–55
   See also colonial New England
Putnam, Carleton, 318
Putney Debates (1647), 71, 374n31

Quakerism
   abolitionist movement and, 109, 148
   anti-Catholicism and, 71
   colonial Pennsylvania and, 64, 79
   enslavement and, 48
   penal reform and, 145, 148
   postwar northern segregation and,
     255
   radical alternatives and, 351
quantitative methods, 27–28, 32, 369n27
Quebec Act (1774), 73
Quock Walker case (1781), 104, 142

Race and Reason: A Yankee View (Putnam), 318
racial capitalism, 33, 370n35
racial violence
   Great Migration and, 217
racism
   American imperialism and, 204–6
   Black Codes, 114–15, 154–55, 160,
     388n26
   Black pathology theories, 288, 406n10
   culture war and, 323
   David Duke and, 318–19, 320, 330,
     332
   European condemnation of, 343
   experiments in, 203–4
   former enslavers and, 154
   great replacement theory, 335–37,
     346
   immigration policy and, 233, 323–24,
     325, 332, 336, 411n18
   incarceration and, 151
   Jefferson, 102, 114
   Lincoln and, 135–36
   mass incarceration and, 287–88, 289,
     290
   "national divorce" proposal and, 350
   National Rifle Association and, 330
   Obama election and, 315, 316

Pioneer Fund and, 325, 411–12n20
Populism and, 355–56
race war fears and, 317–18
Reconstruction and, 339
Tea Party movement and, 338, 339
Tocqueville on, 137
twenty-first-century demographic
 drift and, 316, 336
twenty-first-century political right
 and, 315, 316–17, 323, 334–36, 350
Unite the Right rally, 317, 334–35,
 350
white power movement, 316–17, 332,
 340
See also Black freedom struggles;
 enslavement; Jim Crow regime;
 Ku Klux Klan; post-emancipation
 coerced labor
radical alternatives, 351–59
Populism and, 354–57, 358
struggles for, 358–59
twenty-first-century political right
 and, 352–53
Rainsborough, Thomas, 374n31
Ranters, 71, 351
Raspail, Jean, 335
rational choice theory, 28, 32, 369n27
Rauh, Joseph, 21
Rauschenbusch, Walter, 200
Rawls, John, 369n27
Reagan, Ronald, and administration
Pat Buchanan and, 322
Clinton administration and, 283
criminal justice system and, 290,
 293–94
David Duke and, 320
immigration policy and, 326, 412n21
National Rifle Association and, 328,
 329, 332
neoliberalism and, 285–86, 302
racism and, 339
tech industry and, 305
Young Americans for Freedom and,
 271
Reconstruction, 154–56
Black political empowerment and,
 156, 188

coercion and, 154–55, 156,
 388–89n26
Populism and, 355
Progressivism and, 179
racist responses to, 339
Thirteenth Amendment and, 142
See also post-emancipation era
Red Scare, 213, 407n19
Red Summer (1919), 216–17
Reed, David A., 233
Regulators, 82–83, 84
Reno, Janet, 294–95
republicanism
American origin stories and, 101
anti-Catholicism and, 72–73
backcountry rebellions and, 82, 92, 93
colonial New England and, 51
Constitutional Convention and, 98
English Civil War and, 71
land ownership and, 76, 110
monarchism and, 74–75
post-Revolutionary state constitutions
 and, 86–87
radical alternatives and, 351
social/economic stratification and, 76
Tocqueville on, 105–6
See also American Revolution
Republican Party
Pat Buchanan and, 322
Christian nationalism and, 303–4
convict lease system and, 157
corporations and, 192–93
David Duke and, 319, 320
election of 1964 and, 249–50
emancipation and, 151, 153
Equal Rights Amendment and, 261
free labor ideal and, 159, 166–67
Freemasonry and, 129
great replacement theory and, 336
imperialism and, 206
John Birch Society and, 271
National Rifle Association and, 329,
 331, 412n30
nativism and, 162
neoliberalism and, 302
post-Civil War Supreme Court and,
 170

Republican Party (*continued*)
Reconstruction and, 155
Phyllis Schlafly and, 262
Southern Strategy, 276
tech industry and, 305, 306–7
Thirteenth Amendment and, 141, 159
twenty-first-century political right
and, 317–18, 323, 331, 411n16
voting rights and, 188
See also Goldwater, Barry
Restoration (England), 61–62
restrictive covenants, 200, 254–55
Reuther, Walter, 21
Rhode Island, 48
Richards, Leonard, 113
rideshare industry, 308–9
right to privacy, 311, 409n46
Rising Tide of Color Against White World
Supremacy, The (Stoddard), 174, 232
Rizzo, Frank, 275
Robinson, Cedric, 370n35
Rockefeller, David, 284
Rockefeller, Nelson, 271, 289–90
Rockefeller Foundation, 237–38
Rodgers, Daniel T., 373n23
Roemer, Buddy, 321
Roe v. Wade, 264, 302
Rohrabacher, Dana, 271
Roosevelt, Eleanor, 21
Roosevelt, Franklin D., 14, 209, 241–43,
246
See also New Deal
Roosevelt, Theodore
anti-democratic perspectives and, 189
Herbert Croly and, 180, 181
eugenics and, 176, 207–8
FBI and, 213–14
federal government power and,
192–93
imperialism and, 204, 205, 207, 211
labor movement and, 186
Panama Canal Zone and, 201–2
segregation and, 200
Root, Elihu, 203
Rosewood race massacre (1923), 217
Ross, Edward A., 189
Rousselot, John, 271

Royal African Company, 46, 47
Ruby Ridge incident (1992), 333
Rumford, William Byron, 255
Rush, Benjamin, 82–83, 102, 145
Rusher, William, 271–72

Safe Streets Act (1968), 293
Salem witchcraft trials, 56–57
Sanborn, Franklin B., 160
Sanders, Bernie, 341
Sanger, Margaret, 174–75, 176, 208
Santa Clara v. Southern Pacific Railroad
(1886), 183
Sauk, 129–30, 133
Scaife, Richard, 303
Schlafly, Phyllis, 262, 265
Schlesinger, Arthur, Jr., 19, 20, 21, 22,
368n15
Schlesinger, Arthur, Sr., 18
school desegregation
Brown v. Board of Education, 14, 256,
257, 259, 268
busing issue, 257–59, 279
Christian nationalism and, 302–3
civil rights movement and, 257
local authority and boundaries and,
256–57, 259
working class and, 257–58, 279
school prayer, 274
Schools of Anti-Communism, 267, 268
Schorr, Daniel, 315
Schuchman, Robert, 270
Schumpeter, Joseph, 174
Schwarz, Fred, 267, 268, 273
scientific management, 177, 184, 235
Scott, Garrett, 356, 357
Second Amendment, 328, 329, 331
Second Continental Congress, 77–78,
87
Second Great Awakening, 109, 115,
117–18, 128–29
Second Seminole War (1835–42), 133
Second Treatise of Government (Locke), 2,
58, 372n14
Second World War
liberal tradition view and, 12, 19, 31
New Deal and, 246

Sunbelt suburbs and, 266
tech industry and, 304–5, 311
segregation, 198–200, 202, 207, 218,
219
See also housing segregation; Jim Crow
regime; school desegregation
Selective Service Administration, 194
self-ownership, 46, 110, 142
Seminoles, 133
Sessions, Jeff, 345
Seven Years' (French and Indian) War,
68, 79, 85
sharecroppers, 168
Sharon Statement (YAF), 269–70
Shaw, Roger, 245
Shawnees, 132
Shays, Daniel, 91
Shays's Rebellion (1786–87), 91–92
Sherman, Roger, 379n41
Sherman, William T., 155
Sherman Anti-Trust Act (1890), 183,
192, 212
Sidney, Algernon, 71
Sierra Club, 324
Silver, Peter, 65
Silver Legion, 239
Sinclair, Upton, 240, 241
Sioux, 134–35
1619 Project, 36–37, 370n38
*Slavery: A Problem in American Institutional
and Intellectual Life* (Elkins), 25
slavery. *See* enslavement
slavery/freedom binary
abolitionist movement and, 110
enslavement institutionalization and,
49
free labor ideal and, 160, 161, 166–67
liberal tradition view and, 13
Thirteenth Amendment and, 143–44,
153–54, 166
slave trade, 42, 46, 47, 95
Smith, Al, 226
Smith, Henry Nash, 23
Smith, John, 51, 59
Smith, Joseph, 118–19, 120–21
Smith, Rogers, 370n31
social Darwinism, 170

social/economic stratification
British North America, 72, 80, 81, 82
Cherokees and, 132
colonial backcountry rebellions and,
80, 81, 82
1830s political system and, 123–24,
384n29
left movements on, 34
neoliberalism and, 313
1960s critiques of liberal tradition
view and, 30
Populism on, 354
Progressive critiques of, 178, 180
republicanism and, 76, 82
See also feudalism; hierarchy
social engineering
immigration policy and, 233
imperialism and, 205
interwar protofascism and, 214
Panama Canal Zone and, 201–2
political systems and, 191–92
Prohibition and, 177, 229
segregation and, 199
See also eugenics
Social Gospel, 179, 200, 224
social history, 29, 31
socialism
labor movement and, 212
political right perceptions of, 301–2,
340
Progressivism and, 179–81
radical alternatives and, 352
Socialist Party, 355
Société pour l'Abolition de l'Esclavage, 148
Soros, George, 330
South Africa, 198
South Carolina, 45–46
Spain, 343, 344–45, 346
Spirit of the Laws, The (Montesquieu),
98–99
Stamp Act (1765), 67–69, 72, 73, 75
Stampp, Kenneth, 24–25, 26
Stigler, George, 284
Stoddard, Lothrop, 174, 176, 232
Stolberg, Benjamin, 240
STOP ERA, 262, 263–64
Strangers in the Land (Higham), 26, 27

Strout, Richard, 281
structural functionalism, 27
Students for a Democratic Society
    (SDS), 269, 271
suffrage. *See* voting rights
Summers, Lawrence, 286
Sumner, Charles, 126, 143
Sumner, William Graham, 174
Sunbelt, 266–67, 305, 340
Sunstein, Cass, 13
Supreme Court
    on abortion, 264
    corporations and, 183
    criminal justice system and, 289
    election of 2000 and, 33
    immigration policy and, 323
    imperialism and, 203
    Jim Crow regime and, 199, 222
    on Native expulsion, 385n43
    Native peoples and, 132
    1960s political right and, 268
    post-emancipation era, 170
    school desegregation and, 14, 256
    on school prayer, 274
    See also specific cases
Susquehannocks, 62
SWAT (Special Weapons and Tactics),
    293–94, 295
Sweden, 12

Taft, William Howard, 185
Tannenbaum, Frank, 369n24
Tanton, John, 325
Tarbell, Ida, 234
Taylor, Frederick Winslow, 184
Taylorism, 184, 235
Teague, J. H., 357
Tea Party movement, 315–16, 337–40,
    414n45
tech industry, 304–12
    data mining and, 310–11, 409n46
    Democratic Leadership Council and,
    286
    federal government power and, 304–
    5, 311
    wage labor and, 307–10, 409n41
Telecommunications Act (1996), 283

temperance movement, 225, 229–30
    See also Prohibition
Texas, 197
Thanksgiving, 14
Thatcher, Margaret, 285–86
Theory of Justice, A (Rawls), 369n27
Third International (Comintern), 213
Thirteenth Amendment
    coerced labor and, 150–51, 158–59,
    389n31
    coercion and, 143–44
    emancipation and, 141–42, 152,
    153–54
    exception clause, 142–43, 150,
    158–59
    Northwest Ordinance and, 141–42,
    153, 169
    passage of, 141
    slavery/freedom binary and, 143–44,
    153–54, 166
    Supreme Court on, 170
Three-Fifths Clause, 95
Thurmond, Strom, 261, 276, 277
Tobin, James, 174
Tocqueville, Alexis de, 16, 22, 105–6,
    136–40, 144–45, 148
totalitarianism, 20–21
Tower, John, 272
Townshend, Francis, 240, 241
Trail of Tears, 133
Trilateral Commission, 284, 285, 299–
    300, 313, 406n6, 408nn28–29
Trilling, Lionel, 16, 20
Truman, Harry, 226
Trump, Donald
    Christian nationalism and, 304
    election of, 341, 414n45
    MAGA movement and, 35
    precursors of, 342
    twenty-first-century political right
    and, 11, 12, 35, 317–18, 338, 339
    Unite the Right rally and, 317, 335,
    350
Truth, Sojourner, 117
Tsongas, Paul, 286
Tubman, Harriet, 13
Tucker, St. George, 89

Tulsa race massacre (1921), 196, 217
Turner, Frederick Jackson, 18
Turner Diaries, The, 332, 334
twenty-first-century political right
 anti-democratic perspectives and, 33,
  323, 330
 anti-federal government perspectives
  and, 35, 315, 317, 322, 330, 332,
  333, 334, 337
 Pat Buchanan and, 322–23, 326, 330,
  411n16
 culture war and, 322–23, 327
 European right and, 343–47
 great replacement theory and, 335–
  37, 346
 immigration and, 315, 317, 322
 immigration policy and, 323–27,
  411n16
 liberal tradition view, 3, 11–13, 33,
  342, 350, 366n2
 militias, 315, 317, 333–34, 413n36
 "national divorce" proposal, 349–50
 National Rifle Association and, 328–
  32, 412nn28,30
 Obama election and, 315, 317, 334,
  337–39
 Viktor Orbán and, 345–46
 precursors of, 342–43
 racism and, 33, 315, 316–17, 323,
  334–36, 350
 radical alternatives and, 352–53
 Tea Party movement, 315–16, 337–40
 transnational networks and, 344
 white working class and, 339, 340–41
 See also Duke, David
Two Treatises of Government (Locke), 45

Uber, 308–9
Union League, 188
unions. *See* labor movement
United Kingdom Independence Party,
 344
United Mine Workers strike (1902), 186
Unite the Right rally (Charlottesville,
 2017), 317, 334–35, 350
U.S.-Spanish-Cuban-Filipino War
 (1898), 203, 204, 205–6

universalism
 American origin stories and, 37
 Declaration of Independence and,
  102, 103
 emancipation and, 103–4, 381n55
 English Civil War and, 71
 Levellers and, 56, 374n31
Universal Negro Improvement Associa-
 tion (UNIA), 217, 218
University of Chicago, 284, 297–98
Uprooted, The (Handlin), 26–27
urban political machines, 164, 188

vagrancy laws, 156–57, 160–61, 164–66,
 388–89n26
Vance, Cyrus, 406n6
Van Deman, Ralph H., 214, 216,
 397n8
Vardaman, James K., 216
Vaux, Roberts, 145, 148
Vermont, 378–79n31
Versailles Treaty, 210–11
Veterans of Foreign Wars (VFW),
 398n16
Vidal, Gore, 325
Vietnam War
 anti-federal government perspectives
  and, 304
 criminal justice system and, 288
 1960s critiques of liberal tradition
  view and, 28, 30
 1960s political right and, 250, 275
 George Wallace and, 278
 white power movement and, 316, 340
vigilantism, 215–16, 220, 224, 227, 229,
 239, 326
Viguerie, Richard, 271
Villa, Pancho, 211
Vinland, 375n33
violence
 Black northern migration and,
  252–53
 characteristics of illiberalism and, 6
 1830s political system and, 123,
  126–27
 Jim Crow regime and, 155, 357, 358
 lynchings, 108, 195–96, 216, 394n34

violence (*continued*)
  1960s anti-communist militias and,
    273
  postwar northern segregation and,
    255
  segregation and, 200
  See also vigilantism
Virginia. *See* Chesapeake colonies
*Virgin Land: The American West as Symbol
  and Myth* (Smith), 23
Vital Center, The (Schlesinger), 22
voter registration, 190–91, 393–94n26
voting rights
  African Americans, 155
  1830s franchise expansion, 122, 162
  Fifteenth Amendment, 152, 163–64
  Nineteenth Amendment, 191
  See also disfranchisement
Vox Party (Spain), 343, 344–45, 346

Waco siege (1993), 333, 334
wage labor
  coercion and, 160
  common law and, 167–69, 170,
    391n46
  disfranchisement and, 161–63
  feudalism and, 167, 171
  "foreman's empire" and, 168–69
  free labor ideal and, 155, 159
  gig economy and, 308–9
  immigration and, 161
  Progressivism and, 178, 185–86
  radical alternatives and, 354
  scientific management and, 184
  slavery/freedom binary and, 160, 161
  tech industry and, 307–10, 409n41
  See also working class
Wahunsonacock (Powhatan leader), 58,
  59
Wald, Lillian, 176
Walker, Quok, 104, 142
Wallace, George C., 247–49, 250, 261,
  273, 274–75, 276, 277–81, 337
Wallace, Henry, 19, 21, 368n15
Walnut Street Penitentiary, 146
Wampanoags, 62–63
Ward, John William, 24

War Industries Board, 194, 195, 243
Warnke, Paul, 406n6
War on Poverty, 288, 289
Warren, Earl, 268
Washington, Booker T., 199, 200, 218
Washington, George, 85, 92, 100, 102,
  127, 131
Washington, John, 62
Watergate scandal, 30, 304
Watts riots (1965), 289
Weaver, Randy, 333
Wechsler, James, 22
Welch, Robert, 263, 267, 269, 272
welfare reform, 283, 327
Wells, Ida B., 394n34
western expansion, 18, 23, 58, 237
Weyrich, Paul, 271
Whig Party, 16, 121, 122, 129, 162, 187
Whipple, Henry B., 135
Whiskey Rebellion (1794), 100–101
White, Edward Douglass, 226
White, Theodore H., 279
White Aryan Resistance (WAR), 319
White Man's Union (Texas), 357, 358
white nationalism, 33, 334, 350
White Patriot Party, 332
white power movement, 316–17, 332,
  340
white supremacy, 35, 316–18, 324, 335
  See also racism
Willard, Frances, 230
Williams, Roger, 54, 60, 63, 70
Williams, William Appleman, 27
Williams v. Mississippi (1898), 189,
  393n24
Wilmot Proviso (1846), 142
Wilson, Charles, 312
Wilson, Henry, 166–67
Wilson, James, 75, 100
Wilson, Pete, 323
Wilson, Woodrow
  corporations and, 193–94
  eugenics and, 176
  First World War and, 194, 195
  foreign policy and, 210–11
  immigration policy and, 232
  labor movement and, 210, 211–12

racism of, 189, 216
segregation and, 200
Winthrop, Henry, 50
Winthrop, John
anti-Catholicism and, 70
coercion and, 53, 55–56
expulsionism and, 374n28
feudalism and, 52
hierarchy and, 50–51
"A Modell of Christian Charitie,"
50–51, 373n23
on Native peoples, 59–60
Winthrop, Samuel, 50
Wolin, Sheldon, 139
Woman Rebel, 175
woman suffrage, 127
women
abolitionist movement and, 109,
153
anti-Catholicism and, 118
feminist history on, 29
Jim Crow regime and, 254
John Birch Society and, 269
Ku Klux Klan and, 225–26
postwar segregation and, 253–54
STOP ERA and, 262, 263–64
temperance movement and, 225, 229
voting rights, 191, 225, 226
See also feminism
Women for Constitutional Government,
263
Women's Christian Temperance Union
(WCTU), 225, 229
Woodhull, Victoria, 176

Woodward, C. Vann, 18
Worcester v. Georgia (1832), 385n43
working class
federal postwar benefits and, 251
feminism and, 261
interwar protofascism and, 214
radicalism of, 163
school desegregation and, 257–58,
279
temperance movement and, 230
twenty-first-century political right
and, 339, 340–41
urban political machines and, 188
Woodrow Wilson on, 211
See also labor movement; wage labor
World War I. *See* First World War
world war II. *See* Second World War
Wyatt, Francis, 44

X, Malcolm, 13
xenophobia. *See* nativism

Yannopolous, Milo, 345
Ye'or, Bat, 335
Young, Andrew, 406n6
Young, Brigham, 121–22
Young Americans for Freedom (YAF),
269–72
Youth Offenses Control Act (1961), 288

Zakaria, Fareed, 11
Zemmour, Eric, 345, 346
Zero Population Growth (ZPG), 325
Zuboff, Shoshana, 310